W9-DBD-764

2004 02 10

COPYRIGHT LAW

COPYRIGHT
LAW

160201

DAVID VAVER

Reuters Professor of Intellectual Property &
Information Technology Law, University of Oxford

Director, Oxford Intellectual Property Research Centre

Fellow, St. Peter's College, Oxford

IRWIN
LAW

A Quicklaw Company

Published in 2000 by
Irwin Law Inc.
Suite 930, Box 235
One First Canadian Place
Toronto, Ontario
M5X 1C8

ISBN: 1-55221-034-0

Canadian Cataloguing in Publication Data

Vaver, D.
   Copyright law

(Essentials of Canadian law)
Includes bibliographical references and index.
ISBN 1-55221-034-0

1. Copyright – Canada.   I. Title.   II. Series.

KE2799.V38 1999   346.7104'82   C99-931881-0
KF2994.V38 1999

Printed and bound in Canada.

1   2   3   4   5   04   03   02   01   00

SUMMARY
TABLE OF CONTENTS

DETAILED
TABLE OF CONTENTS

CHAPTER 9:
ENFORCEMENT   252

To my mother and my late father
and
to the students whom I have taught
and who have taught me

FOREWORD

The twentieth century has witnessed a revolution in communications. At the dawn of the century, people communicated largely by word of mouth and the marks their hands could make on paper. At the end of the century people still communicate in the time-honoured ways. But they also communicate by telephone, radio, the electronic images of film and television, and the Internet. Moreover, it is not only the devices of communication that have changed; the nature of communication itself has been transformed. As Marshall McLuhan documented, the medium has now become the message.

These changes in the way people communicate and the significance of communication in their lives and commerce are reflected in the law. Canada's copyright law has undergone a succession of amendments, most recently in 1997 with the passage of Bill C-32. Canada has also assumed new copyright obligations under the *North American Free Trade Agreement* of 1992, and with its ratification of the *Rome* and *Berne Conventions* on new and emerging modes of communication. The law of copyright, once simple, is now technical and complex.

Canadians, more than ever before, need a comprehensive guide to copyright law. David Vaver's *Intellectual Property Law* in 1997 went a great way to filling this need with respect not only to copyright but to patents and trade-marks. It quickly became clear, however, that more was required. The changes in communications law required a book devoted exclusively to copyright that would permit more detailed treatment of various aspects of this burgeoning area of the law. The result is this volume. It will, I predict, be of great assistance to communicators everywhere, as well as to the lawyers, academics, and jurists who seek to give legal shape to the complex, important, and fascinating world of communication.

The Right Honourable Beverley McLachlin
Chief Justice of Canada

PREFACE

No sooner had the manuscript of my book on intellectual property law in this series been completed in 1996 than it became clear that a more detailed book on copyright law alone was needed. Not only could the abbreviated treatment in the earlier book of some important topics be expanded, but the new work could also detail and comment on the major amendments to the *Copyright Act* that were passed after *Intellectual Property Law* was first published in early 1997. That book mentioned the amendments as they had appeared in early versions of Bill C-32, but the Act that was passed on 25 April 1997 differed in a number of key respects.

The 1997 amendments culminated an active decade of copyright reform that is still far from over. During its course, Canada acceded to new copyright obligations found in the *North American Free Trade Agreement* of 1992 and the *World Trade Organization Agreement* of 1994. It also ratified the *Rome Convention* of 1961, dealing with the rights of performers, broadcasters, and sound-recording manufacturers, and the most recent (1971) version of the *Berne Convention*. Accession to further treaties on copyright, neighbouring rights, and perhaps databases is also on the horizon as policy makers grapple with the implications of digital technologies and the growing traffic on the Internet.

In writing this book, I have retained or adapted much material that appeared in *Intellectual Property Law*. The introductory and concluding chapters are similar in substance, although the emphasis is now more on copyright. The treatment of some topics that were previously covered only lightly is now more expansive. Thus, questions dealing with the duration of copyright, authorship and ownership, owner rights and remedies are considered in more detail. The changes introduced in the 1997 amendments are also examined in depth. In particular, the new rights of performers and of sound-recording makers and broadcasters; the copyright exceptions relating to libraries, museums, archives, educational institutions, and the perceptually disabled; the new infringement remedies; and the many technical changes are all discussed, and areas where improvement is still needed are highlighted. The discussion is more complex than in *Intellectual Property Law* because the law itself has become more complex. The aim has nevertheless been to write in a way that makes the law accessible to the widest range of people affected by it: not just lawyers and law students, but also the creative community and the general public.

The writing started in 1997 during my tenure at Osgoode Hall Law School at York University, Toronto. I completed the work after assuming the new Reuters Chair in Intellectual Property and Information Technology Law at the University of Oxford, and the directorship of the Oxford Intellectual Property Research Centre at St. Peter's College in July 1998. My friend and Osgoode colleague Professor Reuben Hasson kept me, as always, *au courant* with newspaper and magazine clippings dealing with intellectual property issues. I acknowledge with gratitude the debt the final text owes to William L. Hayhurst, QC, and to Jeffrey Richstone, who read the draft manuscript meticulously and provided many helpful criticisms, suggestions, and comments. Any remaining errors and infelicities are mine.

Thanks are due to Chief Justice Beverley McLachlin for providing a Foreword, to my researcher Stephen Palethorpe for working on the Index, to Rosemary Shipton for editing the manuscript, to Maraya Raduha for editing the proofs, to my publisher Jeffrey Miller for guiding the work through its various phases, and to William Kaplan for his encouragement of the project.

COPYRIGHT: AN OVERVIEW

A. INTRODUCTION

The central object of copyright law is to grant authors rights of exploitation in their original literary, artistic, dramatic, and musical works, and also to grant them rights to ensure that their work is properly credited and is not changed in a way that harms the author's reputation (so-called "moral rights"). This object was supplemented in 1997 in Canada, following international trends, by the grant of similar rights of exploitation to performers and of enhanced rights to distributors of works and performances, mainly record companies and broadcasters. The rationale for the reform was that, without authors and works, there would be nothing for performers to perform or for distributors to distribute, while, without performers or distributors, authors and their works would languish. Copyright law is seen as establishing incentives and rewards for all players on the cultural field — from originator to distributor — to fulfil their respective roles for the benefit of themselves and of society generally.

Copyright law is part of the law of intellectual property, and its history, operation, and justifications may be conveniently considered within that wider context. Apart from copyright, intellectual property laws establish various schemes through patents, through the registration of other rights, and through the common and civil law to protect inventions and original designs, trade-marks and trade-names, integrated circuit topographies, plant and seed varieties, trade secrets and

1

business confidences, goodwill and other business interests. Intellectual property is a paradoxical body of law. It starts from the premise that ideas are free as the air — a common resource for all to use as they can and wish. It then proceeds systematically to undermine that notion.

Some commentators try to trace the origins of intellectual property or copyright law to time immemorial. Glossing an institution with the patina of antiquity makes it seem natural, inevitable, indisputable. In the case of copyright, the attempt is, however, wholly implausible. We do find instances of the Ancients attacking or criticizing unauthorized or unattributed copying of their work, but not everyone found this conduct immoral, let alone illegal. At the time that Martial railed in the first century A.D. against plagiarists of his verse, the legal codes of Rome did not mention copyright law once. Monks furiously copied any worthwhile manuscript they could lay their hands on through to medieval times. The ethos was one of sharing knowledge, not enclosing it. In the sixth century, we do find the aphorism "To every cow her calf, and so to every book its copy" uttered by the Irish King Diarmid as his judgment in the case of Abbot Finnian against Saint Columba. Columba had secretly copied a psalter while a guest of the abbot, his old mentor, and the king ordered Columba to give up his copy. Interestingly, not only did Columba refuse to abide by the king's judgment but he also effectively overturned it by stirring up a war that ousted the monarch.[1] When the supreme tribunals in Scotland and England were asked in the late eighteenth century to affirm that copyright was part of the unwritten law of the land, a majority of their judges firmly repulsed the idea. They laid down that anybody could copy a published work as much as he liked without needing the consent of the author or the initial publisher. Copying was forbidden only so long as the work was kept private to the author or his intimates.[2]

Only legislatures could change that position — which they did, but initially only to a very limited extent. In 1710 the English Parliament enacted the first copyright law during the reign of Queen Anne. The

---

1   In any event, St. Columba may have been guilty less of a breach of copyright than of a breach of faith. We do not know how much of the psalter he copied was the abbot's own work and how much was copied by the abbot from others: compare G. McFarlane, *Copyright: The Development and Exercise of the Performing Right* (Eastbourne: John Offord Publications, 1980) at 15–16; H. Streibich, "The Moral Right of Ownership to Intellectual Property: Part I — From the Beginning to the Age of Printing" (1975) 6 Memphis State U. L. Rev. 1 at 10–11.

2   *Donaldson v. Beckett* (1774), 2 Bro. Parl. Cas. 129 (H.L.), rejecting a common law copyright for published works and allowing protection only under the *Copyright Act, 1710* (U.K.), 8 Anne, c. 19.

Statute of Anne was really a response to the protectionist bent of the London book trade, then reeling from the demise of its role as the Crown's censor of books. But its idea caught on. France repackaged this protectionism more attractively as a basic human right after the French Revolution of 1789. In that guise, copyright expanded internationally to cover the whole gamut of the creative arts and beyond, into the murky world of tax tables, lottery numbers, computer programs, and now Internet traffic.

Other intellectual property laws also started appearing. Industrial design protection (then also called "copyright") came out of late eighteenth-century England to give the textile trade lead time against foreign competition. Trade-marks — first used by ancient merchants to identify their goods, and later by guild craftsmen as guarantees of quality — began being protected by judges during the Industrial Revolution, and eventually gave rise to national trade-mark registries in the second half of the nineteenth century. More recently, semiconductor chip makers and seed companies have persuaded the relevant authorities that integrated circuit topographies and new plant varieties need and deserve protection as well.

The argument has always been that, without protection, people would not let the public have the benefit of the good ideas they had, through fear of competition from imitators. Those who sowed had to be protected from those who wanted to reap without sowing. The Bible could be used to support that sentiment.

Even before Confederation, Canada's settlers took the need to protect intellectual property as a self-evident truth. Today's intellectual property laws are direct descendants of laws tracing back before 1867. Upper Canada passed a trade-mark law in 1860, anticipating Britain's by fifteen years, but Canadian statutes were mostly modelled on earlier British and, occasionally, U.S. laws. Thus, the first Canadian copyright statute was passed by Lower Canada in 1832 and was eventually replaced by a more elaborate law in 1868 after Confederation. Although more recent Canadian revisions have moved away from their foreign forebears in form, they are typical of those established by other major nations in substance.

This outcome is no accident. The late nineteenth century saw the creation of two major international multilateral treaties on intellectual property. The *Paris Convention for the Protection of Industrial Property* of 1883 [*Paris Convention*] covered patents, trade-marks, designs, and unfair competition. The *Berne Convention for the Protection of Literary and Artistic Works* of 1886 [*Berne Convention*] covered authors' rights. Britain, as an initial signatory, brought itself and its empire into these folds. So, early in its history, Canada came to protect foreign authors and enterprises alongside its native born — at least those native born descended from settlers. Both the *Paris* and the *Berne Conventions* were highly Eurocentric treaties that ignored the culture of indigenous peoples. Native culture was thought to be free for the taking, the product of many and so the preserve of none — except when it was transformed by the mediation of Europeans, whereupon it magically gained cultural legitimacy.

The pattern of reciprocal and intensifying international protection continued after Canada attained full control over its foreign policy in the early twentieth century. Canada actively participated in the periodic revisions of the *Paris* and *Berne Conventions* that took place during the century. But, until recently, Canada had adhered only to the 1934 revision of *Paris* and to the 1928 revision of *Berne*. The latest 1967 revision of the *Paris Convention* was not ratified until 1996, and the latest 1971 revision of the *Berne Convention* was ratified on 26 June 1998. At the same time, Canada joined the *Rome Convention for the Protection of Performers, Producers of Phonograms and Broadcasting Organisations* of 1961 [*Rome Convention*] as of 4 June 1998.

The most recent major international developments have been the *North American Free Trade Agreement* of 1992 [*NAFTA*], the *Agreement on Trade-Related Aspects of Intellectual Property Rights* [*TRIPs*] appended to the *World Trade Organization Agreement* of 1994 [*WTO Agreement*], and the *WIPO Copyright Treaty* of 1996 and the *WIPO Performances and Phonograms Treaty* of 1996 [*WIPO Treaties*].[3] The former two agreements mandated the entrenchment of national treatment and high standards of protection for intellectual property, including copyright, first in North America and then worldwide.[4] Non-observance can lead to trade sanctions against offenders. The process continues under the aegis of the World Intellectual Property Organization [WIPO], an arm of the United Nations, with the *WIPO Treaties*. The latter intensify and expand copyrights further, especially to regulate digital technologies. In 1998 the United States enacted legislation (the *Digital Millennium Copyright Act*) to implement the *WIPO Treaties*, and Canada may

---

3   The *WIPO Treaties* may be found at <http://clea.wipo.int/lpbin/lpext.dll> at links "Intellectual Property," and "Texts of WIPO-Administered Treaties."

4   Ratification by Canada of the latest version of the *Berne Convention for the Protection of Literary and Artistic Works* (Paris, 1971), 9 September 1886, 828 U.N.T.S. 221 [*Berne*] was little more than a formality, since the *North American Free Trade Agreement*, 17 December 1992, Can. T.S. 1994 No. 2 [*NAFTA*], and the *Agreement on Trade-Related Aspects of Intellectual Property Rights, Including Trade in Counterfeit Goods* (1994), 25 I.I.C. 209 [*TRIPs*], obliged Canada to bring all its intellectual property laws substantively in line with what *Berne* (1971) required.

follow suit shortly. International law, driven largely by transnational corporate power, often shielded behind co-opted author and performer organizations, has effectively curbed national sovereignty in the field of copyright and intellectual property policy generally.

1) Why "Intellectual"? Why "Property"?

Why were these rights thought necessary? Why do they even deserve the labels "intellectual" or "property"? It was not always so. The talk once was more of "privilege" than "property," as grants of monopoly depended on the favour of the monarch and the royal entourage. This favouritism changed in the West during the eighteenth century as the forces of the Enlightenment and the Industrial Revolution consciously worked to switch discourse from privilege to property. Capitalists want to "own" whatever their enterprise produces and to exclude everyone else from its enjoyment except on their terms. Ownership includes control of not merely *tangible* items of commerce exchangeable for profit but also the *intangible*: ideas, schemes, designs, writings, product and business imagery, and even relationships with the public, or "goodwill." Everything can be turned into cash. Those who imitate or appropriate such assets can then be called thieves and pirates, whether the activity took place on land or at sea. Judges can rule that taking intellectual property is not actually theft, since it is not technically "property" – its owner is still left in possession after the taking[5] – but such decisions can be treated as pettifoggery.

Lawyers and lawmakers have sometimes joined in the rhetoric that treats property as a transcendental notion. A 1985 parliamentary sub-committee report on copyright reform took as its lodestar the assertion "that 'ownership is ownership is ownership': the copyright owner owns the intellectual works in the same sense as a landowner owns land."[6] As a prescription for policy making, this notion is fatuous at best and question-begging at worst: unsurprisingly, the committee did not recommend that copyright should embrace 999-year leases, zoning, and a registry that guarantees title. As description, the statement is a half-truth. The half that is not true is as important as the half that is. Copyright and intellectual property are peculiarly Western conceits. They

---

5   *R. v. Stewart*, [1988] 1 S.C.R. 963 [*Stewart*].

6   House of Commons, Standing Committee on Communications and Culture, *Report of the Sub-Committee on the Revision of Copyright: A Charter of Rights for Creators: Minutes of Proceedings & Evidence of the Sub-Committee on Communications and Culture on the Revision of Copyright* (Ottawa: Supply & Services, 1985) at 9.

are founded on a modern emphasis on the individual and on individual rights, and on encouraging and celebrating creativity and innovation as paths to both self-fulfilment and social advance. By contrast, Eastern and traditional cultures that emphasize social obligation, submersion of the self, respect for tradition, and the replication of traditional forms and themes provide inhospitable soil for Western conceptions of intellectual property. They do, however, create fertile sources for serious misunderstanding and conflict between peoples and nations.

What is indisputable is that intellectual property has become the new wealth of the late twentieth century, and wealth must be measurable and hence commoditized. The law in Canada and most Western nations has come to accept this capitalist imperative. For many purposes, intellectual property is classed as personal property (a *chose in action* or incorporeal moveable,[7] for those who like legal mystique). It can be bought and sold, licensed, and used to obtain credit. It may be part of the matrimonial assets available to spouses on marriage breakdown; on death, it may form part of an estate. It can be charged, taxed, subjected to a trust, and often taken in satisfaction of a judgment debt.[8] On insolvency, it can pass to the official assignee in bankruptcy or to a corporate receiver to be sold off for the benefit of creditors.[9] It cannot — any more than any other asset — be expropriated without compensation. Its deliberate infringement may, if a criminal conviction results, brand an offender as "undesirable" under immigration law and may make him internationally immobile.[10]

Yet not all intellectual property rights can technically be called property.[11] Even those that can may not everywhere have all the usual attributes of property. The right to stop one's name or image from being used in advertising may, according to some provincial privacy laws, die with the person and cannot be assigned, although at common law the right may pass to the estate and may also be licensed.[12] Authors'

---

7   *De Montigny v. Cousineau*, [1950] S.C.R. 297 at 306 (copyrights).

8   D. Vaver, "Can Intellectual Property Be Taken to Satisfy a Judgment Debt?" (1991) 6 Banking & Finance L. Rev. 225 [Vaver, "Seizure"].

9   But a landlord cannot distrain intellectual property for unpaid rent, since the property, being intangible, is not located on the rented premises: *Modatech Systems Inc. v. Bastion Development Corp.* (1998), 161 D.L.R. (4th) 449 (B.C.C.A.). However, if legislation specifically allows the seizure of intangibles such as intellectual property, a fictional location will be found for the property: see Vaver, "Seizure," *ibid.* at 263–64.

10   *Bun v. Canada (Minister of Citizenship & Immigration)* (1998), 148 F.T.R. 73 (T.D.).

11   Compare *Compo Co. v. Blue Crest Music Inc.* (1979), [1980] 1 S.C.R. 357 at 372–73 [*Compo*].

12   *Gould Estate v. Stoddart Publishing Co.* (1996), 30 O.R. (3d) 520 (Gen. Div.), aff'd (1998), 80 C.P.R. (3d) 161 (Ont. C.A.) [*Gould*].

"moral rights" — rights to attribution and to prevent distortion and unfavourable association of an author's work — also cannot be assigned, but do pass to the estate on the author's death.[13] Trade secrets are in even more of a twilight zone: they are a mishmash of contract, equity, and property law,[14] and are probably capable of being passed on in bankruptcy, but are otherwise of uncertain assignability. Most trade-marks are assignable to others, but some may not be. The trade-mark a famous artist puts on her works to indicate authorship may fall into this latter class because nobody else may be able to use it without deceiving the public.

In short, we can talk about intellectual property as we talk about military intelligence: as useful shorthand for a phenomenon, but with no implication that its components — intellectual or property — do or should exist. In particular, to call copyright "property," as one may sometimes properly do, should not close off debate about what rights attach or should attach to a particular activity. There is, after all, property and property. To compare the rights someone has in a manuscript or a Web site with those he has in an automobile or a piece of land is an exercise in contrast more than anything else.

What intellectual property law needs, whenever a policy or a concrete dispute is being debated or resolved, is a careful weighing and balancing of interests. How the appropriate balance may be struck is discussed in the chapters that follow (particularly chapters 5 and 7) and is reconsidered structurally in the conclusion (chapter 10). At this point it is necessary to say only that throwing property onto the scales contributes nothing to this balancing exercise.[15] At worst, it unfairly tends to bias the process in favour of protection, at the expense of other values. Against copyright or intellectual property as absolute ideals are ranged values of at least equal importance: the right of people to imitate others; to work, compete, talk, and write freely; and to nurture common cultures. The way intellectual property should be reconciled with these values — or vice versa — has changed much over time and continues to vary among countries and among legal systems. The adjustments occur for social and economic reasons; they are not preordained by natural law. Where a particular line should be drawn can

---

13   *Copyright Act*, R.S.C. 1985, c. C-42 [*C Act*; unless otherwise indicated, references to the Act are as amended], s. 14.1(2); see chapter 6, "Authors' Moral Rights."

14   *LAC Minerals Ltd. v. International Corona Resources Ltd.*, [1989] 2 S.C.R. 574, 61 D.L.R. (4th) 14 at 74.

15   A similar point in relation to the breach of confidence action was made in *Cadbury Schweppes Inc. v. FBI Foods Ltd.* (1999), 167 D.L.R. (4th) 577 (S.C.C.).

certainly not be answered by circularities such as "intellectual property is property" or "ownership is ownership is ownership." For example, at one time newspapers freely borrowed news items from one another. Western writers and dramatists used to recycle stories and plots that had come down from old Greco-Roman times — and some still do. Popular works used to be translated without any thought of seeking the author's consent; indeed, the original author would as likely thank the translator for causing the author's thoughts to be brought before a wider audience. Practices like these may now be frowned on in many Western countries as inconsistent with the cult of originality and individualism. Will the denizens of cyberspace be as censorious tomorrow? Are many even as censorious today?

2) Justifying Intellectual Property

How is legal protection for intellectual property commonly justified?[16] Morally, a person may be said to have a "natural right" to the product of her brain; a variant is to say that society should reward persons to the extent that they have produced something useful for society: as one sows, so should one reap. However plausible as prescriptions, these arguments have never been accepted to the full — or even the half full. We know that ideas are not protected once they leave their producer's brain and, when society does protect ideas after they have taken some concrete shape, the protection is always limited in time and in space: nobody anywhere has ever argued for worldwide protection of every new idea in perpetuity. Nor, if social reward is the criterion, can we say exactly what services deserve what reward. Does a pulp novelist read by millions merit as much as the inventor of insulin, even if readers are shown to need the pulp for their sustenance as much as a diabetic needs insulin to survive? And why should an intellectual property right be the appropriate reward? Isaac Newton could get no patent for the principle of gravity, yet his idea has proved more scientifically and socially useful over time than the finest Stephen King thriller, for which society thinks fit to award King or his assignee a copyright for the author's life plus fifty years. The decision on who gets the monopoly right where two or more persons invent something independently, without knowing of the other's work, is often more a matter of luck than anything else: the history of science and invention suggests that

---

16   Based on D. Vaver, "Some Agnostic Observations on Intellectual Property" (1991) 6 I.P.J. 125 at 126–28.

the phenomenon of simultaneous discovery is the rule, not the exception.[17] The sower who first turns up at a patent office will reap; the other sower will rue.

On the economic plane, patents and copyrights are supposed to encourage work to be disclosed to the public and to increase society's pool of ideas and knowledge. Yet much inventiveness and research are kept secret, and the law rigorously protects that decision, whether or not disclosure would be more socially useful than secrecy. Whoever finds the cure for AIDS or cancer can lock the recipe in a drawer forever. Copyright law, too, allows an author not to publish his work and shades off into a tool of censorship. The Australian government stopped the publication of embarrassing official documents about its duplicitous policy towards East Timor by asserting copyright in its literary creativity.[18] J.D. Salinger also used copyright to stop an unofficial biography that quoted from the author's correspondence. The biographer could paraphrase the ideas found in the publicly archived correspondence, but could not use Salinger's expression without the author's permission.[19] The law of confidential information can sometimes stop even paraphrase, as historian William D. Le Sueur found out at the beginning of the twentieth century. His biography of William Lyon Mackenzie was suppressed because Mackenzie's heirs had given him access to their forebear's papers so he could depict Mackenzie as one of the "Makers of Canada," not the "puller down" that Le Sueur ultimately suggested he was. Le Sueur owned the copyright in his manuscript, but Mackenzie's heirs were able to enjoin its publication as a breach of confidence.[20]

At a more basic level, intellectual property regimes are said to encourage the initial creative act. Yet, in the centuries before copyright and patent laws were established or were rigorously enforced, inventive and creative work flourished throughout the world. And if the *Statute of Monopolies* of 1624 really did encourage greater inventiveness, why did the Industrial Revolution take more than a century to arrive in England?

---

17   R.K. Merton, *The Sociology of Science: Theoretical and Empirical Investigations* (Chicago: Chicago University Press, 1973) at 356. Compare *Kewanee Oil Co.* v. *Bicron Corp.*, 416 U.S. 470 (1974) at 490–91: "If something is to be discovered at all very likely it will be discovered by more than one person. . . . Even were an inventor to keep his discovery completely to himself, . . . there is a high probability that it will be soon independently developed."

18   *Australia* v. *John Fairfax & Sons Ltd.* (1980), 147 C.L.R. 39 (Austl. H.C.).

19   *Salinger* v. *Random House Inc.*, 811 F.2d 90 (2d Cir. 1987).

20   *Lindsey* v. *Le Sueur* (1913), 29 O.L.R. 648 (C.A.); C. Harvey & L. Vincent, "Mackenzie and Le Sueur: Historians' Rights" (1980) 10 Man. L.J. 281.

Such a time lag suggests a lack of, or at least a serious discrepancy between, cause and effect in the law. In any event, much creative and inventive work today is carried out by employees who work for reasons other than intellectual property. The system celebrates quite trivial advents compared with the body of public knowledge on which they have built. The pygmy standing on the giant's shoulders may well see further than the giant, but the giant usually represents the contributions of many communities and individuals over centuries. In focusing on the present and the individual, intellectual property laws tend to discount the accumulated social wisdom of the past.

The strongest economic argument for intellectual property is utilitarian: without such rights, much research and creativity would not be carried on or would not be financed by capitalists. But this argument is only partly true. No doubt, less activity would occur – but how much less, and in what areas? It seems impossible to argue that the current laws encourage just the right amount of research, creativity, and financing, and in just the right areas. In any event, the rationale fails to make the case for intellectual property. If the allocation of these property rights is simply a means to an end — to make the fruits of creativity and research available to users — one must ask if the means is the most effective way to that end. If the rights restrict availability and usage more than they increase them, they are unjustifiable; if the converse, one must ask if there are better means of increasing availability and use, either by modifying the rights or by finding alternative means.

3) Intellectual Property versus Other Means

Questions about how intellectual property is justifiable tend to be ignored. They sit uncomfortably with capitalist societies driven by notions of property, fences, privatization, and markets. Alternatives to intellectual property are often denounced as government subsidies or as other "interferences" in the free play of market forces. This designation conveniently ignores the fact that establishing a property right is in itself a form of subsidy. True, the state may pay no money from general revenue, but it sheds this responsibility by dictating that one person or one class of people should pay another person or another class a fee — that is, subsidize them — ostensibly for the benefit of the community as a whole. It is a subsidy with a difference. Questions of who can benefit directly and who must pay directly or indirectly are constrained by the classification of intellectual property.

One example will suffice. Assume for argument's sake that it is a good idea to compensate musicians for the unauthorized taping of their records, as the *Act to Amend the Copyright Act* of 1997[21] [the *1997 Act*] affirms. There are many ways to achieve this end. Direct grants may be made from central funds, as is the case with Canadian authors, who are compensated annually for public library lending of their books. Or the Canada Council or the provincial arts councils may be funded to subsidize struggling musicians. Or tax write-offs may be allowed for private contributions to societies representing such musicians. Or buyers of blank tapes may be given vouchers, redeemable on later record purchases.[22] The money could come from general revenue or from direct taxes imposed on blank tapes. The beneficiaries could be precisely targeted: struggling performers could be preferred over the well-heeled; or Canadian performers, or certain record companies, could be favoured over others.

The *1997 Act,* however, enacts a private tax, though it is not called that. The euphemism employed is a "right to remuneration."[23] Makers and importers of blank audio tapes must pay sums to the holders of this right: composers, lyricists, performers, and record companies. The cost will be passed on to all buyers of tapes. Whether they use the tapes to record their friends' records or their own performances, or to transfer a compact disk they own onto a tape for the car, does not matter. Packaged as a copyright, this tax cannot discriminate between the wealthy and the struggling musician, the Canadian-owned record company and the branch plant of a major foreign company. It must conform to Canada's international treaty obligations, such as the *Berne Convention* requirement of equal treatment for all foreign composers and lyricists. It also has a political consequence. Other governments will undoubtedly pressure Canada, under threat of trade reprisals, to give their performers and record companies equal treatment, too. Canada is willing to

---

21   S.C. 1997, c. 24 [*1997 Act*]. See further section B(14)(c), "Blank Audio Recording Media Levy," in chapter 7.

22   See, for example, the voucher scheme proposed by the Federal Cultural Policy Review Committee, *Report* (Ottawa: Information Services Department of Communications, 1982) (Co-chairs: L. Applebaum & J. Hébert) at 224.

23   The Australian High Court ruled the comparable Australian blank tape levy to be a tax and invalidated it, since the Australian Constitution forbids tax measures from being mixed up in a bill with other non-tax matters such as copyright: *Australian Tape Manufacturers Assn. Ltd.* v. *Australia* (1993), 176 C.L.R. 480 (Austl. H.C.). If classified as a "tax" in Canada, the levy must conform to ss. 53 and 54 of the *Constitution Act, 1867*; for example, Parliament cannot improperly delegate too much of its power to set the rate of levy to the Copyright Board: compare *Eurig Estate* v. *Ontario Court (General Division), Registrar* (1998), 165 D.L.R. (4th) 1 (S.C.C.). The Copyright Board has, however, held that the levy is not, constitutionally, a tax: *Private Copying*, Decision of 17 December 1999, at <www.cb-cda.gc.ca/decisions/tocopy-e.html> [*Private Copying*].

extend the benefits of this tax at least to countries that provide Canadians with like benefits. This coverage means either that the local tax will go up or that the amount each performer receives will go down. If the tax goes up, demand for tapes may decline as people search for cheaper substitutes, and the returns to beneficiaries will also further decline.

This approach is different from the way intellectual property is usually discussed today. The discourse is of intellectual property as opposed to subsidy, whereas it could equally be framed around intellectual property as itself subsidy. Thomas Macaulay could in 1841 speak frankly in the British House of Commons of copyright as "a tax on readers for the purpose of giving a bounty to writers"; but talk today of taxes and subsidies is even more emotionally charged than in nineteenth-century Britain. The result is to prevent the fullest range of policy options for a given objective from being openly aired and debated. Instead, entrepreneurs — who have no difficulty co-opting authors and performers with the lure of untold riches — press for rights. Direct subsidies or taxes mean more government involvement, an outcome inimical to the political agenda of most entrepreneurs. Worse still, subsidies and taxes can come and go with governments. Rights, in contrast, once granted, can rarely be taken away, at least for long. Record companies in 1971 lost the right to charge for the play-time their records got on radio and television. Twenty-six years later, the *1997 Act* gave the right back to them. The difference is that, this time, the right is fully entrenched by international law, since Canada has adhered to the international treaty (*Rome Convention*) guaranteeing the right.

4) Traditional Perspective: Balancing Owner and User Interests

A more traditional way of viewing copyright traces back to the Western Enlightenment. It rejects the idea that copyright or other intellectual property rights are somehow "natural." It recognizes these rights as limited by other values. On this view, copyright is seen as the product of competing interests and values. Lord Mansfield expressed copyright's dilemma in this way: "[W]e must take care to guard against two extremes equally prejudicial; the one, that men of ability, who have employed their time for the service of the community, may not be deprived of their just merits, and the reward of their ingenuity and labour; the other, that the world may not be deprived of improvements, nor the progress of the arts be retarded."[24] In practice, this policy produces two poles in constant ten-

---

24   *Sayre v. Moore* (1785), 1 East. 361n, 102 E.R. 139n.

sion. One, driven by the "rough practical test that what is worth copying is prima facie worth protecting," pulls towards protection.[25] The second pole pulls towards broad rights of use. It holds that culture and the economy need a dynamically functioning public domain, so "care must always be taken not to allow . . . [patent and copyright laws] to be made instruments of oppression and extortion."[26]

Even within a liberal democratic framework, modern courts — often composed of judges who, as lawyers, acted for entrepreneurs and so easily empathize with their viewpoint — often favour protection for most products that result from intellectual endeavour or for which a demand exists, just as they extend property rights to the tangible creations of manual labour. If they deny property status to an intellectual creation or other valuable intangible, they decide in effect that everyone is free to use it; the originator can benefit from her creation only in competition with others who did not share its cost of creation and development. There is, of course, a tendency to gloss over the fact that the person claiming protection is often not the originator, but the firm to which the originator is bound in contract. But this slippage also occurs when property rights in the products of manual labour are allocated, and is treated as inevitable under capitalist modes of production.

Despite the tendency of some judges to let their natural rights instincts roam free, no intellectual property law says that every tangible product or idea deserves protection. Indeed, the opposite is true. The way intellectual property laws are carefully circumscribed shows that copying or independently producing an identical item is acceptable, even to be encouraged, unless it is clearly prohibited. Keeping a broad public domain itself encourages experimentation, innovation, and competition — and ultimately the expectation of lower prices, better service, and broader public choice.

Further, the decision to protect, once taken, must be matched by an equally careful decision on how far to protect. Overprotection imposes social costs by stopping or discouraging others from pursuing otherwise

---

25   *University of London Press Ltd.* v. *University Tutorial Press Ltd.,* [1916] 2 Ch. 601 at 610. The aphorism conveniently begs all questions of initial eligibility, protectability, and even infringement.

26   *Hanfstaengl* v. *Empire Palace*, [1894] 3 Ch. 109 at 128 (C.A.), approved 100 years later in *Canadian Assn. of Broadcasters* v. *Society of Composers, Authors & Music Publishers of Canada* (1994), 58 C.P.R. (3d) 190 at 196 (Fed. C.A.); similarly for trade-marks, *United Artists Corp.* v. *Pink Panther Beauty Corp.* (1998), 80 C.P.R. (3d) 247 (Fed. C.A.).

desirable activities. Before the public is excluded, clear harm should first be found to the particular right-holder or the intellectual property system as a whole. The restrictive treatment of parody by copyright law — penalizing humorous comments on products or business activity — is an example of business interests being overly protected to the disadvantage of an effectively operating public domain. Copyright law as written does not mandate these results. They come from knee-jerk tendencies to interpret the law to prefer business investment over critical comment, and not to ignore some grievances as *de minimis*. Intellectual property's legitimacy suffers with each such decision. Protection should be confined to intellectual property's "just" merits. The "progress of the arts" of which Mansfield spoke two centuries ago must, overall, not be retarded. The contribution of a later actor to this progress must be assessed as carefully as that of the first on the scene.

B. SOME GENERAL FEATURES OF COPYRIGHT LAW

The specifics of copyright law are examined in the chapters that follow. In this introduction, some general features of copyright law and its relationship with other intellectual property rights are noted.

1) Territoriality

Copyright, like other intellectual property, is both territorial and international. It is territorial in that a Canadian copyright is effective in Canada only. It cannot be infringed by acts occurring entirely in France. Nor can a French copyright be infringed by acts done in Canada. An infringement in France must be pursued there according to French law; a French owner whose copyright is infringed in Canada must pursue the infringer according to Canadian law in a Canadian court. At the same time, intellectual property rights are international in that their existence does not depend on where the activity creating them took place. A book written by a French author in France automatically has a Canadian copyright; a computer program written in Canada automatically has a French copyright. These rights are protected by a web of interlinking international treaties by which almost every country in the world is bound. These treaties ensure that national laws do not discriminate against foreign producers and owners. Canadian laws implement these treaties, which are therefore essential background material for understanding and even interpreting

Canadian law.[27] But harmonization as a goal, one that is striven for in the European Union [EU], is still far off the world agenda. Significant differences in approach and detail exist between national laws. So an infringement in country **A** may not necessarily infringe in country **B**; a right valid in country **A** may without incongruity be denied or found invalid in country **B**.

The dual national and international face of intellectual property rights has its controversial aspect. The rights are often used to create non-tariff barriers to trade by preventing parallel imports. Since a Canadian copyright is in law a separate and different right from a French copyright, a protected product lawfully made in France but exported to Canada may infringe a Canadian copyright. This phenomenon allows intellectual property rights to be manipulated to prevent parallel imports where the same entity owns or controls both protected products. Far from disapproving, the international treaties reinforce this right, and free-market unions such as the EU often recognize it. The result is to reinforce the policies of multinational corporations, which can set the price and quality of items differently in one country from another.

These traditional constructs are coming under both legal and technological stress. For example, the territoriality principle is breached in the EU, which allows one state's copyright law to be enforced in another state. A Dutch copyright owner may therefore sue a British firm in a British court for infringing a Dutch copyright. U.S. federal courts may also adjudicate on infringements occurring outside the United States if the United States is considered a natural and convenient jurisdiction for the litigation. Canadian courts may eventually go this route too.[28] Meanwhile, partly influenced by *NAFTA*, they are embarking on their own program of harmonizing Canadian copyright law with U.S. law. Authoritative U.S. appellate decisions on what subject matter qualifies for copyright, what constitutes "originality," and what acts infringe may be

---

27 *National Corn Growers Assn. v. Canada (Import Tribunal)*, [1990] 2 S.C.R. 1324, 74 D.L.R. (4th) 449 at 482–83 (S.C.C.) (*GATT*); *Milliken & Co. v. Interface Flooring Systems (Canada) Inc.* (1993), 52 C.P.R. (3d) 92 (Fed. T.D.), aff'd (1994), 58 C.P.R. (3d) 157 (Fed. C.A.); *Norowzian v. Arks Ltd. (No. 2)*, [1999] F.S.R. 79 (Ch.), aff'd *The [London] Times*, 11 November 1999 (C.A.) (copyright and *Berne*).

28 *Canada (Human Rights Commission) v. Canadian Liberty Net*, [1998] 1 S.C.R. 626, affirming the Federal Court's jurisdiction to issue an injunction against an offshore telephone service that let Canadian callers access racist messages. See also *Pearce (Gareth) v. Ove Arup Partnership Ltd.*, [1999] 1 All E.R. 769 (C.A.); *L.A. News Service v. Reuters Television International Ltd.*, 149 F.3d 987 (9th Cir. 1998).

particularly influential.[29] The traffic is still largely one way: U.S. courts and lawyers seem as ignorant of the decisions of Canadian courts as Americans are of much else that emanates from Canada.

The most serious challenge to these structures and tendencies may come as much from instantaneous communication technologies as from law. A Canadian may upload her writings or artwork electronically onto an Internet server located in Germany. From there, the material may be downloaded by another user located in Canada, Uganda, or Thailand. What law applies to the uploading: Canadian, German, or both? What law applies to the downloading: German, Canadian, Ugandan, Thai, or some combination?[30] The rules governing conflicts of laws work even more arbitrarily in cyberspace. Critical events like uploading, accessing, downloading, and redistribution of material may occur anywhere. Concepts of territoriality may simply create chance applications of one or another country's laws. In the extreme, those laws may become practically unenforceable.

2) Cumulative Rights

Copyright is distinct from any property rights in the tangible item to which it relates. Selling a book does not transfer any interest in the copyright, but the copyright owner cannot prevent the buyer from using the article, at least in its expected way. For example, a book owner should be able, without objection, to photocopy and insert a page to replace one that was accidentally torn. But this power may not extend to photocopying all or most of a book to replace one that was lost or substantially destroyed. Such a reconstruction would infringe the copyright owner's exclusive right to reproduce the work.[31] And those with thoughts of livening up some dreary artwork will find that distortions or other prejudicial changes may infringe the moral rights of the artist.[32]

Intellectual property rights are also distinct from one another. So, for example, a copyright owner cannot rely on its copyright to insulate it

---

29   *Tele-Direct (Publications) Inc.* v. *American Business Information Inc.* (1997), 76 C.P.R. (3d) 296 (Fed. C.A.).

30   The Copyright Board dealt with some of these issues in connection with the provision of music on the Internet: see *Statement of Royalties to Be Collected for the Performance or the Communication by Telecommunication, in Canada, of Musical or Dramatico-Musical Works (Tariff 22), Phase I: Legal Issues,* Copyright Board Decision of 27 October 1999. See section A(5), "Telecommunication," in chapter 5.

31   See section B(8), "Repairs and Modifications," in chapter 7.

32   Moral rights live on for fifty years after the author dies and may be exercised by the estate. See chapter 6.

from other wrongs it may commit in relation to the work. For example, the material in the work may have been obtained in breach of confidence. The work's title may be objectionable as a tortious passing-off if it suggests that the work is a sequel of another well-known work. The contents may also violate an author's moral right of attribution or integrity.

Intellectual property rights may also be held cumulatively. A firm's logo may be registered as a trade-mark, a textile pattern may be registered as an industrial design, a computer program can be protected by a patent, yet copyright protection for all three is often cumulatively claimed and accepted.[33] This theory treats intellectual property rights like products in a supermarket: a shopper with enough money and information can acquire as many varieties as she wishes. Cumulative protection is nevertheless controversial, especially as intellectual property has come to occupy more terrain and to have a greater impact on everyday affairs. The question, whether a rule of "only one per customer" should replace "take as many as you can carry," has become more insistent.

Copyright is central to this debate because it arises automatically once a work is created. Copyrights are therefore ubiquitous. They last a long time: up to fifty years after the author's death. Producers may also apply for a twenty-year patent or a ten-year design registration. These monopolies, though shorter term, provide more intense protection than copyright against independent creators as well as imitators. The question arises of whether the right-holder may fall back on copyright when the other monopoly expires. Grants of patents and design rights are supposed to encourage and reward the production and disclosure of work that might not otherwise be produced or disclosed. Once the reward is exhausted on expiry of the monopoly, why should additional copyright protection automatically continue for decades longer?

The legislation itself partly discourages dual protection. Copyright and moral rights are not infringed by the use of any method or principle of manufacture or construction, by the application of purely utilitarian features to articles, or generally by the application of design features to any mass-produced useful article.[34] The occasional court has even claimed that it is "not the intention of Parliament (nor is it desirable) to interpret the *Patent Act* and the *Copyright Act* to give overlapping

---

33 For example, *Apple Computer Inc.* v. *Mackintosh Computers Ltd.* (1986), 10 C.P.R. (3d) 1 (Fed. T.D.), aff'd (1987), [1988] 1 F.C. 673 (C.A.), aff'd [1990] 2 S.C.R. 209.

34 *C Act*, above note 13, ss. 64.1(1)(a) & (d); ss. 64(1) & (2).

protection."[35] This proposition, if true, would apply equally to the *Copyright Act* in its relation to other intellectual property laws, and to intellectual property laws in their relation to one another. The object is to match the new product or technology to the protective system that fits it best, and to minimize overlap except where the law explicitly authorizes it for good reason.[36]

Instances where multiple protection is being denied are on the increase. Thus, no additional duty of confidentiality was placed on a firm that received for evaluation a sample that was already adequately protected by a copyright that the firm was bound to observe. The submitter could use copyright to prevent the firm from bypassing him and placing orders with someone else. The court thought that imposing a duty of confidentiality was warranted only if valuable data, such as manufacturing instructions, were also passed on. Otherwise such a duty merely added another unnecessary layer of uncertainty and complexity.[37]

3) Marking and Registration Optional

Copyright and dealings in copyright may be registered at the Copyright Office in Hull, Quebec. Registration is optional. A copyright or the grant of an interest in copyright is fully effective, whether registered or not. Registration is a simple exercise, which gives the registrant useful procedural and evidentiary advantages. Only a relatively small minority of copyrights or deals are ever registered — unsurprisingly, given the enormous amount of protected material that is produced daily worldwide.[38]

It is, however, quite common to see references to copyright on goods or on their advertising or packaging. Books, films, computer programs, and advertisements often carry a legend such as "© Jane Bloggs 1999" or "Copyright Jane Bloggs 1999." This marking is not mandatory in Canada, but it is legally useful.[39] It notifies the existence

---

35   *Matrox Electronic Systems Ltd.* v. *Gaudreau*, [1993] R.J.Q. 2449 at 2457 (S.C.). Similarly, *Tennessee Eastman Co.* v. *Canada (Commissioner of Patents)*, [1974] S.C.R. 111; *Cuisenaire* v. *South West Imports Ltd.*, [1968] 1 Ex. C.R. 493, aff'd on other grounds [1969] S.C.R. 208.

36   For example, *Integrated Circuit Topography Act*, S.C. 1990, c. 37, s. 26; *C Act*, above note 13, s. 64(3).

37   *Carflow Products (UK) Ltd* v. *Linwood Securities (Birmingham) Ltd.* (1996), 36 I.P.R. 205 at 209–10 (Pat. Ct.).

38   See section C, "Registration and Expungement," in chapter 8.

39   A false marking can be disadvantageous, particularly if the lie is deliberate. If persisted in, the practice may cause the refusal of discretionary relief (injunctions, accounts of profits, etc.) for lack of "clean hands."

of a right or a claim and reduces the ranks of potential "innocent" infringers who might win a judge's sympathy. It can also clarify a right-holder's intentions where users are uncertain of their rights. Thus, on the Internet, right-holder notices often spell out what users may and may not do with material that can easily be accessed, downloaded, manipulated, reproduced, and redistributed electronically or in hard copy. The notices may technically be licences,[40] so disobedience may mean infringing the owner's copyright. Since the difficulties of detecting and enforcing such infringements are well known, the notices often operate on another level: as appeals to users' sense of honesty and fair play. In cyberspace, a version of the golden rule — Do unto your neighbour as you would have your neighbour do unto you — may gain in moral force what it lacks in legal sanction.

Because marking is not mandatory, the onus is squarely on all users to ensure that an activity does not infringe some copyright or other intellectual property right of which they may be totally unaware. Even courts sympathetic to the innocent usually do not hesitate to grant injunctions and issue orders to withdraw offending goods.

4) Relationship of Copyright with Provincial Laws

Despite amendments over the years, the *Copyright Act* is based structurally and conceptually on the United Kingdom *Copyright Act* of 1911. The Canadian Act is partly a code. It says how copyright and moral rights arise, their nature, who gets them, how the rights may be transferred or exercised, and what recourse is available against infringers. No province can pass a copyright law in competition with the Act, nor may provincial law recognize or enforce an equivalent or similar right.[41]

Such features have caused the Supreme Court to declare that "copyright law is neither tort law nor property law in classification, but is statutory law . . . Copyright legislation simply creates rights and obligations upon the terms and circumstances set out in the statute."[42] This clarification forestalls arguments that common or civil law principles automatically solve a copyright dispute, or that the *Copyright Act* is merely a backdrop for such principles. Instead, courts must resolve disputes first by reading and construing the Act, without presupposing what result the common or civil law would have reached.[43]

---

40   See section B(3), "Licences," in chapter 8.
41   *C Act*, above note 13, s. 89.
42   *Compo*, above note 11 at 372–73.
43   *Bishop v. Stevens*, [1990] 2 S.C.R. 467.

The situation is nevertheless more complex than the Supreme Court's statement implies, for the Act is only a partial code. It leaves much unsaid about copyright: for example, whether copyright can be inherited, co-owned, seized by unpaid creditors, or used as security to raise money. These questions are answered partly by interpreting the Act and partly by referring to provincial law. Despite the Supreme Court's dictum, courts have characterized copyright as property — an incorporeal moveable or *chose in action* — precisely to handle issues such as inheritability, co-ownership, exigibility, and the suitability of copyright as collateral. Similarly, while the Act requires assignments and exclusive licences to be in writing, it leaves the question of their interpretation — for example, whether the language of a document reveals an intention to assign or license — to provincial law. Moreover, when one assesses damages for infringement of copyright, the Act specifies that infringement attracts "all remedies by way of injunction, damages, accounts and otherwise that are or may be conferred by law for the infringement of a right." Common law and equitable rules and principles must be applied to fashion these remedies.

Characterization of copyright is, indeed, often indispensable. Suppose the issue arises whether a contract, will, or statute that refers to "property" includes a copyright. To dismiss the question by saying that copyright is not "property law in classification, but is statutory law" would be wrong. One must ask, first, whether the contours the *Copyright Act* creates for copyright are capable of rendering it property in law. To that, the answer is, yes.[44] Second, one must ask whether this form of property was intended to be encompassed by the language of this particular contract, will, or statute. The first question involves construing the *Copyright Act*. The second involves construing the particular contract, will, or statute. It is perfectly possible to conclude that copyright is property within the meaning of one instrument, but is not property within the meaning of another.[45]

---

44   For example, *Planet Earth Productions Inc. v. Rowlands* (1990), 73 O.R. (2d) 505 (H.C.J.) [*Planet Earth*].

45   Compare *Stewart*, above note 5, with *Planet Earth, ibid.*

5) Constitutional Problems

The *Copyright Act* comes under Parliament's exclusive power to legislate in respect of "Copyrights,"[46] as does the *Industrial Design Act*; indeed, design rights in the nineteenth century were commonly called "copyrights." The *Integrated Circuit Topography Act*, with its design-like ICTs, probably also falls under "Copyrights," although it may equally be upheld under Parliament's power to regulate "Trade and Commerce."[47] Of course, the fact that these laws may have been enacted to fulfil international treaty obligations does not by itself bring them within federal power. Other rights that prop up copyrights, such as actions for passing-off or breach of confidence, fall under provincial jurisdiction as "Property and Civil Rights in the Province" or "Matters of a merely local or private Nature in the Province."[48]

A law may be constitutional as a whole, yet individual provisions may not be. For example, performers' rights over their live performances, found in the *Copyright Act*, are categorically different from copyrights historically, and so might not qualify constitutionally as "Copyrights"; but, if enacted as a *WTO Agreement* or *Rome Convention* obligation, such rights can be supported by reference to the "Trade and Commerce" power. Alternatively, they may validly "round out" intellectual property schemes if, for instance, a "rational functional connection" between the provision and a valid-as-a-whole scheme can be shown. Otherwise, they enter provincial territory and become invalid exercises of the federal legislative power. The blank audio recording media levy enacted in the *1997 Act* is, indeed, being challenged on such constitutional grounds. Included in the claimed infirmities are allegations that the levy is an improper form of taxation and is not legislation on "Copyrights" because it covers media that record both copyright and non-copyright material. The challenge has, so far, been rejected.[49]

---

46 *Constitution Act, 1867* (U.K.), 30 & 31 Vict., c. 3 [*1867 Act*], s. 91(23). The setting up and disbanding of compulsory licence schemes and rate-fixing tribunals may fall within this power: *Society of Composers, Authors & Music Publishers of Canada v. Landmark Cinemas of Canada Ltd.* (1992), 45 C.P.R. (3d) 346 (Fed. T.D.). Similarly with patents: *Smith, Kline & French Laboratories Ltd. v. Canada (A.G.),* [1986] 1 F.C. 274 (T.D.), aff'd [1987] 2 F.C. 359 (C.A.); *Apotex v. Tanabe Seiyaku & Nordic* (1994), 59 C.P.R. (3d) 38 (Ont. Gen. Div.).

47 *1867 Act, ibid.*, s. 91(2).

48 *1867 Act, ibid.*, ss. 92(13) & 92(16).

49 *Evangelical Fellowship of Canada v. Canadian Musical Reproduction Rights Agency,* [1999] F.C.J. 1391 (C.A.), denying judicial review and remitting the point for decision to the Copyright Board, which dismissed all constitutional objections: *Private Copying*, above note 23.

Further constitutional questions may involve the relationship between copyright and the *Canadian Charter of Rights and Freedoms*. For example, may guarantees of freedom of the media and expression permit comparative advertising or parodies that include copyright material? If the *Charter* protects commercial speech (as the Supreme Court has held), should it not also protect speech in furtherance of a labour dispute?[50] Will the Internet be recognized as a new form of communication that may require all present intellectual property constraints to be reshaped in the light of the imperatives of free expression?[51]

Canadian courts have, however, not been much impressed so far by *Charter* arguments in copyright cases. Thus, *Charter* claims of free speech and press did not move a Quebec court to allow a law publisher the right to copy the judgments of the province's courts for free. Along similar lines, the Federal Court has declined to consider *Charter* claims raised by a law society to justify the provision of a photocopy service for its members, although the court indicated that it might have listened to such claims where, for example, an individual litigant had been prejudiced in his access to legal resources because of an inability to take advantage of the law society's service.[52] The Copyright Board has also dismissed *Charter* challenges to the blank audio recording media levy.[53]

---

50   Current first instance decisions have so far been unsympathetic: *Rôtisseries St-Hubert Ltée* v. *Syndicat des Travailleur(euses) de la Rôtisserie St-Hubert de Drummondville (CSN)* (1986), 17 C.P.R. (3d) 461 (Que. S.C.); *Cie générale des établissements Michelin/Michelin & Cie* v. *CAW Canada* (1996), 71 C.P.R. (3d) 348 (Fed. T.D.); compare *International Association of Machinists & Aerospace Workers, AFL-CIO* v. *Winship Green Nursing Center,* 914 F. Supp. 651 (D. Me. 1996), aff'd on other grounds, 103 F.3d 196 (1st Cir. 1996).

51   Compare *Reno* v. *American Civil Liberties Union,* 117 S.Ct. 2329 (1997), invalidating the part of the *Communications Decency Act 1996* that criminalized "patently offensive" material that was not obscene or child pornography.

52   See the parody cases, above note 50; *Wilson & Lafleur Ltée* v. *Société québécoise d'information juridique,* [1998] A.Q. 2762 (S.C.); *CCH Canadian Ltd.* v. *Law Society of Upper Canada* (9 November 1999), (Fed T.D.) [unreported].

53   *Private Copying,* above note 23.

FURTHER READINGS

Canadian

ECONOMIC COUNCIL OF CANADA, *Report on Intellectual and Industrial Property* (Ottawa: Information Canada, 1971)

HARRIS, L.E., *Canadian Copyright Law*, 2d ed. (Toronto: McGraw-Hill Ryerson, 1995)

HARRIS, L.E., *Digital Property: Currency of the 21st Century* (Toronto: McGraw-Hill Ryerson, 1998)

HAYHURST, W.L., "Intellectual Property Laws in Canada: The British Tradition, the American Influence and the French Factor" (1996) 10 I.P.J. 265

HENDERSON, G.F., ed., *Copyright and Confidential Information Law of Canada* (Toronto: Carswell, 1994)

HOWELL, R.G., L. VINCENT, & M.D. MANSON, *Intellectual Property Law: Cases and Materials* (Toronto: Emond Montgomery, 1999), Part I (Copyright Law)

HUGHES, R.T., *Hughes on Copyright and Industrial Design* (Toronto: Butterworths, 1984) (regularly updated)

MIKUS, J.-P., *Droit de l'édition et du commerce du livre* (Montreal: Editions Thémis, 1996)

RICHARD, H., & L. CARRIÈRE, eds., *Canadian Copyright Act – Annotated*, 3 vols. (Toronto: Carswell, 1993) (updated periodically)

SOOKMAN, B.B., *Computer Law: Acquiring and Protecting Information Technology* (Toronto: Carswell, 1989) (updated periodically) c. 3

TAMARO, N., *The 1998 Annotated Copyright Act* (Toronto: Carswell, 1997)

TAWFIK, M.J., *The Secret of Transforming Art into Gold: Intellectual Property Issues in Canada-U.S. Relations.* Canadian-American Public Policy Paper No. 20 (Orono, Me.: Canadian-American Center, 1994)

TREBILCOCK, M.J., & R. HOWSE, *The Regulation of International Trade*, 2d ed. (New York: Routledge, 1999) c. 10

VAVER, D., "Canada," in P.E. Geller & M.B. Nimmer, eds., *International Copyright Law & Practice*, 10th update (New York: Matthew Bender, 1998)

VAVER, D., "The Copyright Amendments of 1997: An Overview"
(1997) 12 I.P.J. 53

Other

ALFORD, W.P., *To Steal a Book Is an Elegant Offense: Intellectual
Property Law in Chinese Civilization* (Stanford, Cal.: Stanford
University Press, 1995)

AMERICAN ASSOCIATION OF LAW SCHOOLS INTELLECTUAL PROPERTY
SECTION, "Symposium on Compliance with the TRIPs Agreement"
(1996) 29 Vand. J. Transnat'l L. 1

BRANSCOMB, A.W., *Who Owns Information? From Privacy to Public
Access* (New York: Basic Books, 1994)

BRUSH, S.B., & D. STABINSKY, eds., *Valuing Local Knowledge: Indigenous
People and Intellectual Property Rights* (Washington, DC: Island
Press, 1996)

CORNISH, W., *Intellectual Property: Patents, Copyright, Trade Marks and
Allied Rights*, 4th ed. (London: Sweet & Maxwell, 1999)

D'AMATO, A., & D.E. LONG, eds., *International Intellectual Property Law*
(London: Kluwer, 1997) cc. 1, 2, and 11

DRAHOS, P., *A Philosophy of Intellectual Property* (Aldershot, UK:
Dartmouth Pub., 1996)

GARNETT, K., et al., *Copinger & Skone James on Copyright*, 14th ed.
(London: Sweet & Maxwell, 1999)

GOLDSTEIN, P., *Copyright: Principles, Law & Practice* (Boston: Little
Brown, 1989)

GOLDSTEIN, P., *Copyright's Highway: From Gutenberg to the Celestial
Jukebox* (New York: Hill & Wang, 1994)

GORDON, W.J., & K.L. PORT, eds., "Symposium on Intellectual
Property Law Theory" (1993) 68 Chi.-Kent L. Rev. 1

HARRIS, J.W., *Property and Justice* (Oxford: Clarendon Press, 1996)

KAPLAN, B., *An Unhurried View of Copyright* (New York: Columbia
University Press, 1967)

KERNAN, A., *The Death of Literature* (New Haven, Conn.: Yale
University Press, 1990), especially cc. 4 and 5

LADAS, S.P., *Patents, Trademarks and Related Rights: National and International Protection* (Cambridge, Mass.: Harvard University Press, 1975)

LADDIE, H., P. PRESCOTT, & M. VITORIA, *The Modern Law of Copyright*, 3d ed. (London: Butterworths, 1999)

LAHORE, J., *Intellectual Property in Australia: Copyright Law* (Sydney: Butterworths, 1988) (updated regularly)

MCKEOUGH, J., & A. STEWART, *Intellectual Property in Australia*, 2d ed. (Sydney: Butterworths, 1997)

MOORE, A.D., *Intellectual Property: Moral, Legal, and International Dilemmas* (Lanham, Md.: Rowman & Littlefield, 1997)

NIMMER, M.B., & D. NIMMER, *Nimmer on Copyright* (New York: Matthew Bender, 1983) (updated annually)

PHILLIPS, J., & A. FIRTH, *Introduction to Intellectual Property Law*, 3d ed. (London: Butterworths, 1995)

PHILLIPS, J.J., R. DURIE, & I. KARET, *Whale on Copyright*, 5th ed. (London: Sweet & Maxwell, 1997)

REICHMAN, J.H., "Charting the Collapse of the Patent-Copyright Dichotomy: Premises for a Restructured International Intellectual Property System" (1995) 13 Cardozo Arts & Ent. L.J. 475

RICKETSON, S., *The Berne Convention for the Protection of Literary and Artistic Works: 1886–1986* (London: Centre for Commercial Law Studies, Queen Mary College, 1987)

RICKETSON, S., *Intellectual Property: Cases, Material & Commentary*, 2d ed. (Sydney: Butterworths, 1997)

RICKETSON, S., *The Law of Intellectual Property*, 2d ed. (Melbourne, Victoria: Law Book Co., 1999)

ROTHNIE, W.A., *Parallel Imports* (London: Sweet & Maxwell, 1993)

SHERMAN, B., & A. STROWEL, eds., *Of Authors and Origins: Essays on Copyright Law* (Oxford: Clarendon Press, 1994)

SAMUELSON, P., "Implications of the Agreement on Trade Related Aspects of Intellectual Property Rights for Cultural Dimensions of National Copyright Laws" (1999) 23 Journal of Cultural Economics No. 12

WALLERSTEIN, M.B., M.E. MOGEE, & R.A. SCHOEN, eds., *Global Dimensions of Intellectual Property Rights in Science and Technology* (Washington, DC: National Academy Press, 1993)

Historical

FEATHER, J., *Publishing, Piracy and Politics: An Historical Study of Copyright in Britain* (New York: Mansell, 1994)

FOX, H.G., *The Canadian Law of Copyright and Industrial Designs*, 2d ed. (Toronto: Carswell, 1967)

JOHNS, A., *The Nature of the Book: Print and Knowledge in the Making* (Chicago & London: University of Chicago Press, 1998)

KEWES, P., *Authorship and Appropriation: Writing for the Stage in England 1660–1710* (Oxford: Clarendon Press, 1998)

PARKER, G.L., *The Beginnings of the Book Trade in Canada* (Toronto: University of Toronto Press, 1985)

PATTERSON, L.R., *Copyright in Historical Perspective* (Nashville: Vanderbilt University Press, 1968)

ROSE, M., *Authors and Owners: The Invention of Copyright* (Cambridge: Harvard University Press, 1993)

SEVILLE, C., *Literary Copyright Reform in Early Victorian England: The Framing of the 1842 Copyright Act* (Cambridge: Cambridge University Press, 1999)

SHERMAN, B., & L. BENTLY, *The Making of Modern Intellectual Property Law* (Cambridge: Cambridge University Press, 1999)

WHAT IS PROTECTED

A. INTRODUCTION

Copyright is solely protected under the *Copyright Act*.[1] The Act was largely rewritten in 1997 by *An Act to Amend the Copyright Act*[2] [*1997 Act*], although large portions of the statute continue to reflect the original Act of 1921 and the various amendments made to it over the years until 1997. The 1921 Act granted rights of exploitation mainly to authors of original literary, artistic, dramatic, and musical works. The *1997 Act* granted new or additional rights to performers and to distributors of traditional works. The latter rights are historically and conceptually different from the traditional rights granted to authors. We shall therefore deal with the rights granted to traditional and non-traditional subject matter separately.

1) Contours of Protection of Traditional Subject Matter

Copyright has long protected the work of authors. The work may be created through old or new technology. An artist using a paintbrush computer program today should be as fully protected as one with a real

---

1 *Copyright Act*, R.S.C. 1985, c. C-42 [*C Act*; unless otherwise indicated, references to the Act are as amended].
2 S.C. 1997, c. 24 [*1997 Act*].

brush and real canvas was in the nineteenth century. An electronic multimedia work or database should also be as fully protected as the traditional encyclopedia or card index. Protection is automatic and usually lasts for the author's life plus fifty years.

Up to the end of the nineteenth century, courts occasionally denied protection to material that was not "of enduring benefit to mankind." The written meanderings of a drunkard were rejected on this ground.[3] But twentieth-century courts retreated from tests that judged a work's quality, morality, or even legality. Trash and the sublime were found equal under copyright. Thus, ordinary letters and photographs, even the scrawl of a medium claiming to decipher voices from beyond, are protected as fully as the novels of Carol Shields or the paintings of the Group of Seven. Similarly, the possession of racist, pornographic, or other offensive material for distribution may be a crime, but their author can still, through copyright, prevent others from distributing unauthorized copies and so cutting into his illegal market.[4] Even works that infringe another's copyright may be protected: the unauthorized arranger of a musical work and the unauthorized translator of a play can stop others from copying their arrangement or translation.[5]

British courts nevertheless continue to assert an old practice of refusing to enforce copyright in material that is grossly immoral or deceptive or that has been obtained in breach of confidence.[6] The better view, however, is that unlawful content should not affect the existence of copyright, but may affect its ultimate ownership or what remedy is available for infringement.[7]

The original purpose of copyright may have been to encourage culture by providing incentives — to authors and artists to produce worthy work, and to entrepreneurs to invest in the financing, production, and distribution of the works. Whether copyright, as presently config-

---

3   *Fournet v. Pearson Ltd.* (1897), 14 T.L.R. 82 at 83 (Q.B.), aff'd on other grounds, *ibid.* (C.A.).

4   *Aldrich v. One Stop Video Ltd.* (1987), 39 D.L.R.(4th) 362 (B.C.S.C.) [*Aldrich*] (pornography), with the occasional shocked court dissenting: *Devils Films Inc. v. Nectar Video*, 49 U.S.P.Q.2d 1059 (S.D.N.Y. 1998); *Cummins v. Bond*, [1927] 1 Ch. 167 (medium's scrawl) [*Cummins*]; *Wall Pictures* (1997), 28 I.I.C. 282 (German Fed. Sup. Ct., 1995) (graffiti illegally painted on the Berlin wall) [*Wall Pictures*].

5   *Redwood Music Ltd. v. Chappell & Co. Ltd.* (1980), [1982] R.P.C. 109 (Q.B.); D. Vaver, "Translation and Copyright: A Canadian Focus" (1994) 16 E.I.P.R. 159 at 161.

6   *A.-G. v. Guardian Newspapers Ltd.* (*No. 2*), [1990] 1 A.C. 109 at 294 (H.L.) (equitable jurisdiction).

7   *Aldrich*, above note 4, at 395; see section F(1), "Copyright Created in Breach of Obligation," in chapter 9.

ured, achieves those ends is an interesting question. Many works, as we shall see, have little to do with culture and are simply industrial products. Protection for these products, as well as for fine art, runs for the author's life plus fifty years. The work may be produced by an employee, who never sees the copyright because it belongs to the employer; yet protection lasts as long, even though the original purpose of benefiting an author's surviving family is no longer there. No rational employer, financier, or entrepreneur needs protection that can run for well over a century.

By contrast, industrial designs for mass-produced items like automobiles or dishwashers are typically excluded from copyright protection. They, however, may be protected for ten years on registration under the *Industrial Design Act*.[8] Protection of this kind might seem more apt for the many purely industrial items that presently fall automatically under copyright. For many other items, such as business letters, outmoded trade-mark designs and advertisements, and most computer programs, long-term protection seems equally unnecessary: Has not the cost of producing now obsolete WordPerfect 4.0 been amortized many times over? Needless to say, producers of such items would violently disagree. Nobody wants to give up a benefit that one day may possibly have some value, even though the item was originally produced without any thought of such opportunism.

2) Details of Protection

The key features of copyright protection are as follows:

- Only original work is protected. This stipulation does not mean new work, but simply that the work must originate from the author, cannot be copied, and must involve some minimal intellectual effort. The level required can be judged from the fact that most private and commercial correspondence, however banal and cryptic, qualifies.[9]
- Copyright law prevents copying only. Nobody infringes unless they somehow copied a protected work. This requirement is what supposedly makes the long term of copyright tolerable and makes copyrights different from patents, industrial designs, or trade-marks, where the right may be infringed despite a defendant's independent creation.

---

8   See section B(7), "Industrial Design," in this chapter.
9   See section A(1), "Originality," in chapter 3.

- Copyright protects expression only, not ideas, schemes, systems, artistic style, or "any method or principle of manufacture or construction."[10] Anyone was (and is) free to paint funny-looking people holding guitars: what they cannot do is imitate Picasso's expression of these subjects.

3) Non-traditional Subject Matter: 1997 Amendments

Copyright has traditionally been the preserve of authors and artists, but performers, record producers, and broadcasters have internationally been accorded rights akin to copyright (sometimes called *droits voisins*: "neighbouring" or "allied" rights) by the *Rome Convention*. Theoretically, none of these persons is an author, none does anything "original," none produces a "work." Performers interpret or execute works, record producers record them, broadcasters transmit them, so none is entitled to a traditional copyright.

Nonetheless, since 1924, Canada has protected sound recordings by copyright for a flat fifty-year period, and in 1996 similar protection was extended to performers. The *1997 Act*[11] radically extended these protections and also granted copyright coverage for the first time to broadcasters for their communication signals, all for fifty years. Even though performers are often like authors, and indeed, when spontaneously improvising, can be authors, the protection is for the performance itself, not for any originality that went into it. Thus one hundred identical performances, whether recorded or not, of the same tune each have separate copyrights. Broadcasters do nothing original in transmitting or carrying a signal: it is their investment in distribution that is being protected.

Most traditional copyright principles nonetheless carry over to these non-traditional subject matters. In applying them, however, one should recall that performances, sound recordings, and broadcasts differ in justification and practice as much from one another as they do from traditional copyright works.

---

10   *C Act*, above note 1, s. 64.1(1)(d); see also *Agreement on Trade-Related Aspects of Intellectual Property Rights, Including Trade in Counterfeit Goods* (1994), 25 I.I.C. 209 [*TRIPs*], art. 9(2) (copyright protects "expressions and not . . . ideas, procedures, methods of operation or mathematical concepts as such").

11   Above note 2.

4) Registration

Registration of copyrights and dealings concerning copyright with the Copyright Office at Hull, Quebec, is optional, since copyright is fully protected automatically on creation of the work. Registration, however, creates a presumption of validity in litigation and some priority for registered grants of the copyright. Registration is particularly useful where the plaintiff's claim to title in the copyright is obscure or results from a chain of events, or where the item in question was produced far away in time or in place, for the person disputing what the register reveals bears the onus of proof.

Registration is a simple process. It involves filling out an application form and sending it at any time with the prescribed fee to the Copyright Office, which registers the details and issues a certificate, without even looking at a copy of the item in question.[12] About 10,000 registrations are issued annually. This figure may increase because of the extension of copyright to new subject matter since 1997.

B. WHAT IS PROTECTED?

First we shall examine the traditional subject matter that is protected, and then less traditional matter — sound recordings, performances, and broadcasts.

1) Literary, Dramatic, Musical, and Artistic Works

Every original literary, dramatic, musical, and artistic work is protected "whatever may be the mode or form of its expression."[13] The categories are further defined and illustrated in the Act, an approach that often seems like categorization for categorization's sake, but there seems to be enough flexibility to include evolving technologies. For example, the Act does not refer to multimedia works on CD-ROM, but this material can be protected as a "compilation":[14] the "mode or form" in which works are expressed is irrelevant, and a mixture of different forms — literary, musical, and so on — melded into a composite whole is

---

12   *C Act*, above note 1, ss. 36–58; see section C, "Registration and Expungement," in chapter 8.

13   *C Act, ibid.*, ss. 5(1) & 2, def. "every original literary, dramatic, musical and artistic work"; compare *Berne Convention for the Protection of Literary and Artistic Works* (Paris, 1971), 9 September 1886, 828 U.N.T.S. 221 [*Berne*], art. 2(1).

14   See section B(9), "Compilation," in this chapter.

expressly mentioned as being protectable as a compilation.[15] Still, there are difficulties where works cross formal boundaries. Classification is sometimes practically unavoidable because not every item is protected by the Act for the same duration or in the same way.[16]

Copyright protection extends to almost anything written, composed, drawn, or shaped. It therefore recognizes the diversity of cultural activity. In practice, however, copyright has sprawled into the realm of purely industrial products. Lottery tickets, advertisements, jingles, product instructions, company logos, computer programs, and internal company memoranda all jostle for protection under the law with the work of Margaret Atwood, Roch Carrier, Gordon Lightfoot, Carol Shields, and Michael Snow — not to mention Danielle Steele, Irving Berlin, and Roland Barthes. Since it does not matter whether a work is good or bad art, almost anything has come to be protected — both works whose creation was induced by the prospect of life-plus-fifty year protection and those that were not.

This comprehensiveness may or may not be a good thing. Its defenders claim it is the only practicable way to run the system, unless judges are to become arbiters of aesthetics. But easy entrance to copyright entails a corresponding need to monitor and delineate the scope of protection very carefully. For example, a lottery ticket can be reproduced in many different ways: by an artist who enlarges and frames a reproduction as a form of social commentary; by a magazine that illustrates an article on chaos theory by reproducing a stylized photograph of the ticket; by an employee who scans the ticket into her computer and uses elements from it to decorate her employer's Web site and letterhead; or by a lottery operator who takes the ticket for his own competing enterprise. Granted the ticket has copyright and granted all these acts may, on the face of it, be infringements: the question is, which should and which should not be treated legally as infringements? In other words, how far ought a copyright owner be able to control what others do with its work? Questions like these may ultimately be more crucial than the threshold question of whether a work is capable of having copyright protection. True, gatecrashers should be kept out, but courts should be at least as concerned to police what entrants do on copyright's expansive terrain — and what others may do with or to them.

---

15   *C Act*, above note 1, s. 2.1(1).

16   Some photographs, for example, are protected for a flat fifty years, while other artworks are usually protected for the artist's life plus fifty years. See section B, "Duration," in chapter 4.

That said, one must be aware of the enormous range of material that may be protected.

2) Literary Work: Books and Other Writings

Literary work covers everything expressed in print or writing: the form in which this occurs (paper, diskette, and the like) is irrelevant.[17] The Act mentions tables, computer programs,[18] books, pamphlets, and other writings, lectures (including addresses, speeches, and sermons), and translations as examples.[19] Also obviously included are novels, poems, biographies, histories, academic theses, newspaper articles, instruction manuals, preliminary drafts and working notes, and private diaries. Less obvious items have also been protected: *billets doux*, routine business letters,[20] examination papers, medical records, legal contracts and forms, instruction cards and product warranty forms, telegraph codes, even a list of computer-generated winning lottery numbers![21] But short combinations of words (e.g., trade-marks such as EXXON and slogans lacking any literary composition) or simple product instructions are not protected, since the effort to produce them is often trivial and granting protection risks monopolizing the ideas behind the expression.[22]

---

17 *Apple Computer Inc. v. Mackintosh Computers Ltd.* (1987), [1988] 1 F.C. 673 (C.A.), aff'd [1990] 2 S.C.R. 209 [*Apple*].

18 See section B(3), "Literary Work: Computer Programs," in this chapter.

19 *C Act*, above note 1, s. 2, defs. "literary work" and "every original literary, . . . [etc.] work."

20 Thus, in *Tett Brothers Ltd. v. Drake & Gorham Ltd.* (1934), [1928–1935] MacG. Cop. Cas. 492 (Ch.), the following letter (omitting "Dear Sir" and "Yours etc.") was protected as an "original literary work":

> Further to the writer's conversation with you of to-day's date, we shall be obliged if you will let us have full particulars and characteristics of "Chrystalite" or "Barex." Also we shall be obliged if you will let us have your lower prices for 1, 2, 3, 4 and 5 ton lots and your annual contract rates.
>
> We have been using a certain type of mineral for some time past and have not found it completely satisfactory, and as we shall be placing an order in the very near future we shall be obliged if you will let us have this information at your earliest convenience.

21 *Express Newspapers v. Liverpool Daily Post and Echo*, [1985] 1 All E.R. 680 (Ch.); *Wing v. Golden Gold Enterprises Co.* (1996), 66 C.P.R. (3d) 62 (Fed. T.D.) [*Wing*]; D. Vaver, "Copyright in Legal Documents" (1993) 31 Osgoode Hall L.J. 661 ["*Copyright*"].

22 *Exxon Corp. v. Exxon Insurance Consultants International Ltd.*, [1982] Ch. 119 (C.A.) [*Exxon*]; *Promotions Atlantiques Inc. v. Hardcraft Industries Ltd.* (1987), 17 C.P.R. (3d) 552 (Fed. T.D.); *Noah v. Shuba*, [1991] F.S.R. 14 at 33 (Ch.).

Since spontaneous speech and signing are unprotected, the audio recording of a speech is not a literary work. The maker of the recording will have copyright in the tape; the speaker may have a copyright as a performer, but not as the author of a literary work.[23]

E-mail is in a volatile position. Some missives may qualify as literary work, just as traditional letters do. But much activity on the Internet resembles conversation: person-to-person messages, "forums," and "discussion boards," where users instantly communicate with one another using a computer keyboard and screen instead of a telephone. This use could be analogized to instant versifying and a medium's automatic writing, which are considered protectable,[24] though these forms lack the interactivity that distinguishes speech, signing, and Internet exchanges from ordinary literary compositions. The Internet may have spawned a new hybrid: a communication literary in form, but oral in substance. Unlike most other laws, copyright usually celebrates form over substance. Whether this practice will continue with communication flows on the Internet remains to be seen.

3) Literary Work: Computer Programs

A computer program is defined as "a set of instructions or statements, expressed, fixed, embodied or stored in any manner, that is to be used directly or indirectly in a computer in order to bring about a specific result."[25] It includes source and object codes for operating and application programs, and may also include the screen display generated by the program. Component routines, such as a table of numbers operating as a program lock, may also find protection as a substantial part of the program if an original algorithm or logical structure is used. Attempts to protect the language in which the source code is written or a program's data structure have so far been repulsed. The language, its component words or symbols, and the program's overall structure are not themselves a "set of instructions" but rather enable the production of a set of instructions.[26] Most complex programs, such as a word-

---

23 *Gormley v. EMI Records (Ireland) Ltd.*, [1998] 1 I.L.R.M. 124 (Ire. H.C.), aff'd [1999] 1 I.L.R.M. 178 (Ire. S.C.). See section B(11)(b), "Performances," in this chapter.

24 *University of London Press Ltd. v. University Tutorial Press Ltd.*, [1916] 2 Ch. 601 at 609 [*University of London*]; *Cummins*, above note 4.

25 *C Act*, above note 1, s. 2, def. "computer program."

26 *Data Access Corp. v. Powerflex Services Pty. Ltd.* (1999), 45 I.P.R. 353 (Austl. H.C.), distinguishing *Autodesk Inc. v. Dyason* (1992), 173 C.L.R. 330 (Austl. H.C.); *Delrina Corp. v. Triolet Systems Inc.* (1993), 47 C.P.R. (3d) 1 at 28 (Ont. Gen. Div.) [*Delrina*].

processing program, include many smaller linked programs and so are also a compilation[27] of literary works. But a literary work produced using a word-processing program is obviously not part of the program: the work's copyright belongs to the writer, not the programmer.

Copyright protection for programs is awkward and causes many practical problems. Programmers may enjoy being called "binary bards," and the codes they produce may look like telegraph code books (long considered literary works). But the purpose of the program is to embody the code in electronic circuitry, where it functions like, and often replaces, machine parts. Infringement trials resemble patent trials in scope and expense, except that they are more amorphous. A patent has written claims that stake out what parts of the program are protected: a program that falls outside the claim does not infringe the patent. No such formality attends copyright. Courts have to figure out, case by case, what constitutes the program's "expression" — as distinct from its "idea" — that copyright alone protects. Most such cases involve major arguments over what exactly may or may not be taken from a program or its output. A U.S. judge recently wrote:

> [T]o assume that computer programs are just one more new means of expression, like a filmed play, may be quite wrong. The "form" — the written source code or the menu structure depicted on the screen — look hauntingly like the familiar stuff of copyright; but the "substance" probably has more to do with the problems presented in patent law or . . . in those rare cases where copyright law has confronted industrially useful expression. Applying copyright law to computer programs is like assembling a jigsaw puzzle whose pieces do not quite fit.[28]

4) A Digression: Integrated Circuit Topographies[29]

In the late 1970s semiconductor chip makers operating out of Silicon Valley in the United States became worried that their output might not be fully protected worldwide under copyright and patent laws. They therefore persuaded the U.S. Congress to pass the *Semiconductor Chip*

---

27 See section B(9), "Compilation," in this chapter.

28 *Lotus Development Corp.* v. *Borland International Inc.*, 49 F.3d 807 at 820 (1st Cir. 1995), aff'd 116 S.Ct. 804 (1996) [*Lotus*].

29 Integrated circuit topographies are not really literary works, but are so closely connected with computer programs that it was found convenient to deal with them here.

Protection Act of 1984. Shortly afterwards, the World Intellectual Property Organization convened an international meeting for the same purpose. It resulted in the *Washington Treaty on Intellectual Property in Respect of Integrated Circuits* of 1989, which almost nobody has ratified.

Canada nonetheless passed the *Integrated Circuit Topography Act* of 1990 to mirror the main aspects of the treaty. The Act excludes integrated circuit topographies — essentially layout designs embedded in computer semiconductor chips or circuit boards — from copyright protection, except for any computer program contained in a topography.[30] Integrated circuit topographies (ICTs) registered under the Act are protected for ten years against copying or independent creation. Time runs from the earlier of the date when the application was first filed or the topography was first commercially exploited. The work must be "original," which in this context means it must (a) not be copied, (b) be the result of an "intellectual effort," and (c) not be "commonplace" among ICT designers or manufacturers.[31]

The Act is open to members of the World Trade Organization, but, compared with the United States, traffic to date has been light. Between 1 January 1993 and 1 May 1999, thirty-eight registrations were issued, half nominally to Canadians. Whether the Act benefits Canada much is unclear. Elsewhere the main effect of comparable legislation has been to stop the parallel import of videogames, an enterprise already adequately protected in Canada by the copyright and patent laws. Advances in chip technology have gone beyond what the Act envisaged, and the fashion in Silicon Valley now is to patent wherever possible, instead of relying on the U.S. equivalent of the *ICT Act*.

5) Dramatic Work: Plays, Films, Choreography

Dramatic works such as plays, operas, and operettas traditionally involve a thread of related events that are narrated or presented by dialogue or by action. Protection extends to the structure: the characters' "relationships with and integration into the sequence of incidents, scenes, locale, moti-

---

30   *C Act*, above note 1, s. 64.2(1). How far *Anacon Corp. Ltd.* v. *Environmental Research Technology Ltd.*, [1994] F.S.R. 659 (Ch.), extending U.K. copyright protection to a circuit board diagram, may apply in Canada is unclear. In the United Kingdom, such a diagram may now be protected only under design, not copyright, legislation: *Mackie Designs Inc.* v. *Behringer Specialised Studio Equipment (UK) Ltd.*, [1999] R.P.C. 717 (Ch.).

31   *Integrated Circuit Topography Act*, S.C. 1990, c. 37 [*ICT Act*], ss. 2(2), 5, 4(1), & 4(2). The ten-year period runs to the end of the calendar year.

vation, and dramatic expression" through which the story evolves.[32] Historical characters or events, however, cannot be monopolized; incidents and characterizations ("ideas") may be taken from earlier non-fiction if the treatment and development ("form") are different.[33]

Choreography, mime, and recitation pieces are also protected if their "scenic arrangement or acting form" is "fixed in writing or otherwise."[34] This definition should cover abstract dance and mime if it has been previously recorded (e.g., by Labanotation) or if it is recorded as it occurs (e.g., by videotape). Choreographed marching bands and parades, ice-figure skating performances, sales promotions, and circus productions may also be included.[35] Two separate dramatic copyrights may arise where choreography or mime is filmed: one in the choreography or mime, the other in the film itself. The choreographic copyright protects the form of the dance; the film copyright protects the form of the finished film resulting from the skill of the camera work and editing.[36]

Oddly, only choreography is mentioned as requiring no story line for the work to be protected.[37] One trusts that this example intends to clarify, not amend, the law: otherwise, mime and other work within the dramatic arts would be unprotected if they lacked a story line.

A scene prepared to be photographed for the cover of a record album has not qualified as a dramatic work because it was "inherently static, having no movement, story or action."[38] Adding movement or action, however, does not change matters: spectacles like football, hockey, or roller derbies, however thrilling, have also not qualified. One reason given was their unpredictability: "no one bets on the outcome of a performance of *Swan Lake*," as one court put it.[39] Someone might very well bet on the outcome of an amateur or postmodernist

---

32   K.A. Raskin, "Copyright Protection for Fictional Characters" (1971) 2 Performing Arts Rev. 587 at 590.

33   *Harman Pictures NV* v. *Osborne,* [1967] 2 All E.R. 324 (Ch.) [*Harman Pictures*].

34   *C Act,* above note 1, s. 2, def. "dramatic work."

35   M.M. Traylor, "Choreography, Pantomime and the Copyright Revision Act of 1976" (1981) 16 New Eng. L. Rev. 227 at 229.

36   Compare *Norowzian* v. *Arks Ltd. (No. 2),* [1999] F.S.R. 79 (Ch.), aff'd on other grounds *The [London] Times,* 11 November 1999 (C.A.). See further section B(5)(a), "Film, Video, and Formats," in this chapter. The dancer or mime may also have a separate copyright in his or her performance: see section B(11)(b), "Performances," in this chapter.

37   *C Act,* above note 1, s. 2, def. "choreographic work."

38   *Creation Records Ltd.* v. *News Group Newspapers Ltd.* (1997), 39 I.P.R. 1 (Ch.) [*Creation*].

39   *FWS Joint Sports Claimants* v. *Canada (Copyright Board)* (1991), [1992] 1 F.C. 487 at 495 (C.A.) [*FWS*].

version of the ballet, but, that apart, this test unwittingly excludes much improvisational theatre and performance art. Perhaps it is getting harder to distinguish between sport and theatre, but it is not hard to see why dramatists and performers might, more than sports participants and coaches, need copyright to protect their livelihoods. A test that relies more on sociology than on essentialism may work better here. The myth that sports competitors may have copyright in their "moves" would then have easily been dispelled, as it was by a U.S. appeals court on the ground that competitors are not "authors" creating "works."[40]

a) Film, Video, and Formats

The Act protects "any cinematographic work." This term includes "any work expressed by any process analogous to cinematography," such as movies and material recorded electronically on any medium (e.g., video or computer disk), including any accompanying soundtrack.[41] A work may qualify even though it is not a "cinematographic production where the arrangement or acting form or the combination of incidents represented give the work a dramatic character."[42] Before 1994 only such productions with an "original character" were classed as "dramatic"; films without this characteristic — telecasts of live events like football or of hosted rock video programs like Terry David Mulligan's *Good Rockin' Tonight* — were simply protected as a series of photographs.[43] Today, both classes of production are considered to be dramatic works.

Radio and television formats are problematic. In 1933 the format for a children's radio sketch was protected because the structure of the show was clearly worked out,[44] but, more recently, a British television

---

40   *National Basketball Association v. Motorola Inc.*, 105 F.3d 841 (2d Cir. 1997).

41   *C Act*, above note 1, s. 2, defs. "dramatic work" and "cinematograph." Compare W.L. Hayhurst, "Audiovisual Productions: Some Copyright Aspects" (1994) 8 I.P.J. 319 at 326–28. The new definition of "sound recording" in the *C Act*, s. 2, inserted by the *1997 Act,* removes the uncertainty involving soundtracks by providing that a film soundtrack has no separate copyright as a sound recording.

42   This "original" (formerly "dramatic") character criterion is still relevant to the length of protection. See section B, "Duration," in chapter 4.

43   *Canadian Admiral Corp. v. Rediffusion Inc.*, [1954] Ex. C.R. 382 at 401 [*Canadian Admiral*]; *Australian Olympic Committee Inc. v. The Big Fights Inc.*, [1999] F.C.A. 1042, paras. 26–43 (Austl. Fed. Ct.) (edited and unedited films of Melbourne Olympic Games and events were not "dramatic works" and qualified only as photographs).

44   *Kantel v. Grant*, [1933] Ex. C.R. 84 [*Kantel*].

game-show format was denied copyright because it lacked certainty or unity: each show was different and did not "perform" the format.[45] The format for Mulligan's *Good Rockin' Tonight* was also thought to be unprotected because it had no story line or dramatic incident; but a format structured around the concept of a place where information on the "Top of the Pops" was gathered with high-tech equipment "lent enough dramatic incident and seminal story line" to qualify as a "dramatic work."[46] The distinction seems arbitrary.

6) Artistic Work

The following artistic works are specified in the Act: "paintings, drawings, maps, charts, plans, photographs, engravings, sculptures, works of artistic craftsmanship, . . . [and] architectural works," and "illustrations, sketches and plastic works relative to geography, topography, architecture or science."[47] For a non-specified work to qualify as artistic, one court has insisted that it "to some degree at least, be a work that is intended to have an appeal to the aesthetic senses not just an incidental appeal, . . . but as an important or one of the important objects for which the work is brought into being."[48] Coloured rods for teaching arithmetic to youngsters were found to fall outside this definition. More recently, however, coloured labels for file folders were thought to be artistic works. The court said that "artistic work" was simply "a general description of works which find expression in a visual medium as opposed to works of literary, musical or dramatic expression."[49]

---

45   *Green v. Broadcasting Corp. of New Zealand*, [1989] 3 N.Z.L.R. 18 (C.A.), aff'd [1989] 2 All E.R. 1066 (P.C.).

46   *Hutton v. Canadian Broadcasting Corp.* (1989), 102 A.R. 6 at 39 (Q.B.), aff'd (1992), 120 A.R. 291 (C.A.). Formats may be alternatively protected on breach of confidence or unjust enrichment principles: *Promotivate International Inc. v. Toronto Star Newspapers Ltd.* (1985), 53 O.R. (2d) 9 (H.C.J.) [*Promotivate*]; R. Casswell, "A Comparison and Critique of Idea Protection in California, New York, and Great Britain" (1992) 14 Loyola L.A. Int'l & Comp. L.J. 717.

47   *C Act*, above note 1, s. 2, defs. "artistic work" and "every original . . . artistic work."

48   *Cuisenaire v. South West Imports Ltd.*, [1968] 1 Ex. C.R. 493 at 514, aff'd on other grounds [1969] S.C.R. 208.

49   *DRG Inc. v. Datafile Ltd.* (1987), [1988] 2 F.C. 243 at 253 (T.D.), aff'd (1991), 35 C.P.R. (3d) 243 (Fed. C.A.) [*DRG*]. The design, however, lacked copyright protection because it should have been registered as an industrial design. See section B(7), "Industrial Design," in this chapter.

The latter approach, though preferable, does not remove all argument. The question "What is art?" has proved one of the more baffling of the twentieth century and shows every sign of continuing so into the twenty-first. For example, will a pile of bricks sitting on soil in the middle of a gallery qualify as an artistic work?[50] Were such a question to arise, the views of both the general public and art experts should be taken into account. If enough thinking people treat an object or activity as art, why should courts differ? Art is by its nature unpredictable, so categorical pronouncements about what can or cannot be admitted into the pantheon should be avoided. For instance, one might be tempted to disqualify ephemeral work that disappears after a few hours, except that sand and ice sculptures would irrationally be denied protection.[51] Somewhat oddly, in the light of copyright's cultural pretensions, it seems easier to extend legal recognition to those who do art for commerce than to those who do art for art's sake. Avant-gardism carries legal as well as social perils. Thus, the postmodernist artist who appropriates images for his work is labelled a copyright infringer, while the designer of commonplace logos or magazine covers is accepted as a genuine artist.[52]

a) Drawings, Plans, Cartoons, and Paintings
A drawing is simply lines drawn on paper or any other medium; included are sketches, illustrations, silhouettes, and pattern sheets cut from drawings.[53] The subject is irrelevant: landscapes, engineering and architectural drawings and plans, ideograms depicting items in a food store, even graffiti art, are all included.[54] Cartoon strips are protected; so too are the characters that appear in them. Thus, watches featuring characters from the Popeye cartoon strip — Popeye, Wimpy, Olive

---

50   The description roughly fits Carl Andre's *Equivalent VIII* installation in the Tate Gallery (1989), about which a whole book has been written: I. Ground, *Art or Bunk?* (New York: St. Martin's Press, 1989).

51   *Metix (U.K.) Ltd. v. G.H. Maughan (Plastics) Ltd.,* [1997] F.S.R. 718 at 721 (Pat. Ct.) [*Metix*]; compare *Creation*, above note 38 at 5.

52   Compare *Rogers v. Koons*, 960 F.2d 301 (2d Cir. 1992) (appropriation art enjoined), with *Allen v. Toronto Star Newspapers Ltd.* (1997), 152 D.L.R. (4th) 518 (Ont. Div. Ct.), and *IPC Magazines Ltd. v. MGN Ltd.,* [1998] F.S.R. 431 at 447–49 (Ch.) (magazine covers protected as art). See generally D. Vaver, "Rejuvenating Copyright" (1996) 75 C.B.R. 69 at 73–76.

53   *Lerose Ltd. v. Hawick Jersey International Ltd.* (1972), [1974] R.P.C. 42 at 47 (Ch.).

54   *Spiro-Flex Industries Ltd. v. Progressive Sealing Inc.* (1986), 13 C.P.R. (3d) 311 (B.C.S.C.); *2426-7536 Quebec Inc. v. Provigo Distribution Inc.* (1992), 50 C.P.R. (3d) 539 at 543 (Que. S.C.) [*2426-7536*]; *Wall Pictures*, above note 4.

Oyl, and Sweetpea — were found to infringe copyright in the cartoon and were banned from being imported into Canada. Earlier litigation in the United Kingdom resulted in a similar ban on unauthorized Popeye cartoon dolls, toys, and brooches. In both countries, the characters were said to constitute a substantial part of the artistic work — the cartoon strips — in which they appeared.[55]

The current minimalist view that drawings are simply lines drawn in any medium has not always prevailed. In the early 1900s a Christmas card maker tried to prevent competing card makers from imitating the various letters of the alphabet he drew for his cards, as well as short slogans such as "For Old Times Sake" and "Friends Ever" that he composed. All this material was produced in simple calligraphy, sometimes enclosed in a more or less fancy border. A Scottish court said that none of this work qualified even as a "drawing," let alone an "original" one. It was all just plain writing. To rise to the status of drawing, the work must have "some claim to a place — be it even a humble one — in the sphere of the fine arts" or must "possess some degree of artistic merit, as a product of artistic faculty."[56]

The decline in handwriting standards has encouraged modern courts to accept that any advance on chickenscrawl — even a person's signature — may amount to an original drawing, whether it is produced by hand or now, more commonly, by computer. One might sympathize if the goal were to protect the livelihood of minimalist artists. But the works that attract attention in practice are usually simple commercial art: logos and other business symbols. Thus, trade-marks as modest as a single stylized letter of the alphabet have been protected.[57]

The occasional anomaly still appears. Thus, a U.K. decision from the early 1980s asserts that "painting" does not include facial make-up and, moreover, that "[t]wo straight lines drawn with grease-paint with another line in between them drawn with some other colouring matter . . . by itself could not possibly attract copyright."[58] Neither comment is particularly persuasive. Most paintings are intended for hanging, but not all: body painting and tattooing are among the oldest known arts.

---

55   *King Features Syndicate Inc.* v. *Lechter*, [1950] Ex. C.R. 297 [*Lechter*]; *King Features Syndicate Inc.* v. *O. & M. Kleeman Ltd.*, [1941] A.C. 417 (H.L.) [*Kleeman*].

56   *Miller & Lang Ltd.* v. *Macniven & Cameron Ltd.* (1908), 16 S.L.T. 56 at 58 (Scot. O.H.).

57   *Roland Corp.* v. *Lorenzo & Sons Pty. Ltd.* (1991), 22 I.P.R. 245 at 248, aff'd (1992), 23 I.P.R. 376 (Austl. Fed. Ct.). Accord: *Visa International Service Assn.* v. *Auto Visa Inc.* (1991), 41 C.P.R. (3d) 77 at 87 (Que. S.C.); *Wing*, above note 21.

58   *Merchandising Corp. of America Inc.* v. *Harpbond* (1981), [1983] F.S.R. 32 at 47 (C.A.). The case involved pop singer Adam Ant's three coloured lines of greasepaint, supposedly mimicking Native Indian warpaint.

Copyright law cannot discriminate among different schools of art. Constable's expressionism and Barnett Newman's vertical stripe on a plain coloured field should be equal candidates for copyright.

b) Photographs[59]

This category includes photolithographs and "any work expressed by any process analogous to photography."[60] Both amateur and professional photographs are protected. No negative or other plate is required, so images produced by electronic cameras or xerography, photographs stored on computer disks, and holograms should all be protectable.[61] The fleeting images seen on a television screen or a computer monitor should, however, not qualify.[62] A single frame of a movie — perhaps enlarged for use as a poster — was formerly considered a photograph, since very often the whole film was classed in this way; but today the frame is probably protected as part of the dramatic work (the cinematographic work) in which it appears.[63]

What of a photograph that is scanned into a computer and then electronically manipulated, so that some or all of its features no longer resemble the original? At some stage, the photograph presumably loses its identity as such and dissolves into a generic artistic work or perhaps an original electronic "painting."[64] This classification presumably will depend on the degree of artistry used and the extent to which the result differs from the original scanned work.

c) Engraving and Sculpture

Engravings include "etchings, lithographs, woodcuts, prints and other similar works, not being photographs"; sculpture includes "casts and models," presumably for the purpose of sculpture.[65] Both the original

---

59   See generally Y. Gendreau, "Canada," in Y. Gendreau, A. Nordemann, & R. Oesch, eds., *Copyright and Photographs: An International Survey* (London, The Hague, Boston: Kluwer International, 1999) at 99.

60   *C Act*, above note 1, s. 2, def. "photograph."

61   *C Act*, ibid., ss. 10(1)(b) & 10(2)(b); *Bridgeman Art Library Ltd. v. Corel Corp.*, 25 F. Supp. 2d 421 (S.D.N.Y. 1998), aff'd on reargument 36 F. Supp. 2d 191 (S.D.N.Y. 1999).

62   See *Canadian Admiral*, above note 43, although the conservative approach there taken on what constitutes photography and its analogues no longer holds.

63   *Spelling Goldberg Productions Inc. v. BPC Publishing Ltd.*, [1981] R.P.C. 283 (C.A.).

64   Categorization may be important because some photographs are protected for a flat fifty years, while generic art works and paintings are protected for fifty years past the author's death. See section B, "Duration," in chapter 4.

65   *C Act*, above note 1, s. 2, defs. "engraving" and "sculpture."

engraved plate and the prints made from it are included, as are moulds and graphic labels produced by a non-photographic process from a photographic plate.[66]

Work outside traditional art, such as Hogarth or Rodin, has sometimes qualified. In New Zealand a wooden model of a frisbee was classed as a sculpture — the expression in three-dimensional form of a sculptor's idea — but not the frisbees themselves, which were produced through injection-moulding.[67] But the enthusiasm to treat machine parts and the moulds used to stamp them as sculptures is waning. Courts may now demand that these items pass the more rigorous criteria of industrial design laws and may deny them a sidewind copyright. Thus in Australia, machine parts and moulds have not qualified as engravings. Engraving "has to do with marking, cutting or working the surface — typically, a flat surface — of an object," not (as the New Zealand case had claimed) shaping an object by cutting. Nor were the items sculptures. While "some modern sculptures consist of or include parts of machines, . . . that does not warrant the conclusion that all machines and parts thereof are properly called sculptures."[68] Similarly, a British court has said that the common meaning of sculpture excludes functional moulds. Neither the public nor mould makers would consider such moulds to be art, nor would they consider such mould makers to be artists.[69]

d) Artistic Craftsmanship

A work of artistic craftsmanship is usually the product — typically durable and handmade — of an artist-craftsperson. The work need have no artistic merit, nor need be bought for its aesthetic appeal. Whether a work qualifies is judged objectively, aided by the expert evidence of designers and artisans. What the producer intended, how she proceeded, and what resulted are key issues. Chippendale chairs, Cellini candelabra, Coventry Cathedral tapestry, mass-produced fabric, stained-glass windows, hand-painted tiles, and wrought-iron gate work have been instanced as works of artistic craftsmanship. Clothing,

---

66 *DRG*, above note 49 at 546.

67 *Wham-O Manufacturing Co. v. Lincoln Industries Ltd.*, [1984] 1 N.Z.L.R. 641 (C.A.).

68 *Greenfield Products Pty. Ltd. v. Rover-Scott Bonnar Ltd.* (1990), 95 A.L.R. 275 at 284–85 (Austl. Fed. Ct.). See section B(7), "Industrial Design," in this chapter.

69 *Metix*, above note 51 at 722.

coloured rods for teaching children mathematics, and mass-produced toys have not qualified.[70]

e) Architecture

An "architectural work" means "any building or structure or any model of a building or structure."[71] This description, like some modern architecture itself, has shed its rococo elements over the years. Between 1924 and 1988 the definition referred to an architectural work of art, demanded an artistic character or design of the building or structure, and confined protection to that character or design. Judges progressively elevated this requirement virtually into one of novelty, over and above the requirement of originality.[72] Prefabricated cottage kits were found to lack copyright since they had no "panache," "flair," "individualism," "distinctiveness," or "uniqueness": "Are the homes novel in an artistic sense? Are they set apart in some way from what one *generally* sees?" asked one judge, sounding like a real estate broker's questionnaire.[73] Finding "panache" or its synonyms should no longer be needed. Designs for any sort of building (even mass-produced low-cost housing) and for the products of landscape architecture, such as garden or golf course layouts, are protectable.[74] In Australia, even the design of a swimming pool has been protected by copyright: the pool was called a structure, and the plug or mould from which the pool was made was called a model of it.[75]

---

70   *George Hensher Ltd.* v. *Restawile Upholstery (Lancaster) Ltd.* (1974), [1976] A.C. 64 (H.L.); *Merlet* v. *Mothercare* (1984), [1986] R.P.C. 115 (Ch.), appeal dismissed (1985), [1986] R.P.C. 129 (C.A.), leave to appeal refused [1986] R.P.C. 135 (H.L.); *Eldon Industries Inc.* v. *Reliable Toy Co.* (1965), [1966] 1 O.R. 409 (C.A.); *Coogi Australia Pty. Ltd.* v. *Hysport International Inc.* (1998), 41 I.P.R. 593 (Austl. Fed. Ct.).

71   *C Act*, above note 1, s. 2, def. "architectural work."

72   *C Act, ibid.*, s. 5(1).

73   *Viceroy Homes Ltd.* v. *Ventury Homes Inc.* (1991), 34 C.P.R. (3d) 385 at 389–91 (Ont. Gen. Div.), appeal settled and dismissed (1996) 69 C.P.R. (3d) 459 (Ont. C.A.) [emphasis in original].

74   *Hay* v. *Sloan*, [1957] O.W.N. 445 (H.C.J.); *Half Court Tennis Pty. Ltd.* v. *Seymour* (1980), 53 F.L.R. 240 (Qld. S.C.). Naval architecture may also possibly be protected: *Bayliner Marine Corp.* v. *Doral Boats Ltd.* (1985), [1986] 3 F.C. 346 (T.D.), rev'd on other grounds, [1986] 3 F.C. 421 (C.A.), to the contrary, on the pre-1988 definition, may not apply today.

75   *Darwin Fibreglass Pty. Ltd.* v. *Kruhse Enterprises Pty. Ltd.* (1998), 41 I.P.R. 649 (Austl. Fed. Ct.).

Architecture may also be protected through the copyright in underlying drawings and plans. To copy the interior or exterior design of a house or store, or distinctive features that make up a substantial part of the design, may be to copy indirectly the two-dimensional plans from which the house was built; the copier may infringe without having ever seen the plans.[76]

7) Industrial Design

Much artistic work is devoted to making products attractive to buyers and users. The *Copyright Act* removes full copyright protection from some of this "applied" artwork, applied as a design to a finished "useful article" such as a vase, kettle, or boat, but not an ornamental sculpture, if more than fifty copies of the article are made.[77] This provision means that a Chanel "original" may be fully protected by copyright; so may any other original dress design, until the fifty-first dress is made anywhere with the copyright owner's consent. Then anybody can copy the dress (a useful article) without infringing any copyright in it or any preliminary sketches and patterns. They cannot, however, copy or photograph the sketches or patterns themselves; these are merely "carrier[s] for artistic or literary matter," and so are not useful articles.[78]

The only protection that designs for mass-produced useful articles may receive comes from the *Industrial Design Act*.[79] The design must first be registered on the industrial design register after an application for it is examined and accepted by the Industrial Design Branch of the Canadian Intellectual Property Office. All World Trade Organization members may apply for this protection, which runs for ten years from registration against copiers and independent creators alike.[80] The design must be "original," in that it must not be copied, result from some "spark of inspiration," and either differ from earlier designs or be

---

76 *New Brunswick Telephone Co.* v. *John Maryon International Ltd.* (1981), 33 N.B.R. (2d) 543 (C.A.) [*John Maryon*]; 2426-7536, above note 54 at 543–44.

77 *C Act*, above note 1, s. 64.

78 *C Act, ibid.*; *Industrial Design Act*, R.S.C. 1985, c. I-9 [*ID Act*], s. 2, defs. "useful article" and "utilitarian."

79 Common law protection may occasionally be had for product shapes that function like trade-marks, where the market recognizes them as coming from a particular producer (whose identity need not be known): *Reckitt & Colman Products Ltd.* v. *Borden Inc.*, [1990] 1 All E.R. 873 (H.L.) (the yellow, lemon-shaped JIF lemon-juice container could not be imitated).

80 *C Act*, above note 1, s. 10(1).

applied to a different article.[81] About 2000 design registrations are issued annually.

Such design artwork has been treated differently from regular fine artwork at least since the nineteenth century. The originals that Turner produced from his atelier were thought to deserve long-term copyright protection more than the long runs of pottery that the Wedgwood factory turned out. Today, this differential treatment may perhaps be justified because designers are more likely to be on a payroll than are artisans, who (together with their heirs) may depend more on copyright for their subsistence; industrial designs change frequently and firms can usually amortize their costs and reap a profit within a decade; and imitation is more desirable in the commercial sphere than in the fine arts. This distinction is, of course, highly debatable, and some of it applies equally to the utilitarian articles that copyright does protect. Copyright continues to benefit from the image of the starving author in the garret, whereas the designer sitting in front of a computer monitor in an air-conditioned high-rise office tower rarely excites much parliamentary sympathy.[82]

The attempt to draw a bright line between fine art and industrial design is unfortunately undermined by the list of bric-à-brac that is specifically allowed to retain full copyright: trade-mark designs, labels, architectural works, textile designs, character merchandising items, pictures on mugs, articles sold in a set (unless more than fifty sets are made), and anything else the government feels like adding by regulation.[83] These items may also qualify for cumulative protection under the *Industrial Design Act*. Moreover, designers of mass-produced cloth receive full copyright protection, but designers of mass-produced clothing do not, revealing the arbitrariness of the policy separating industrial designs from copyright. Design policy in many other jurisdictions is equally incoherent.

---

81   *ID Act*, above note 78, s. 7(2); *Bata Industries Ltd.* v. *Warrington Inc.* (1985), 5 C.I.P.R. 223 at 231–32 (Fed. T.D.). This description is a stiffer test than originality for copyright; see section A(1), "Originality," in chapter 3.

82   In fact, both employees and freelancers under contract have no design rights; these rights vest automatically in their employer: *ID Act*, above note 78, s. 12(1).

83   *C Act*, above note 1, s. 64(3); D. Vaver, "The Canadian Copyright Amendments of 1988" (1988) 4 I.P.J. 121 at 132–38; W.L. Hayhurst, "Intellectual Property Protection in Canada for Designs of Useful Articles" (1989) 4 I.P.J. 381.

8) Musical Work

A musical work is defined as "any work of music or musical composition, with or without words." This definition replaces one in effect until 1993 which covered only "any combination of melody and harmony, or either of them, printed, reduced to writing or otherwise graphically produced or reproduced.[84] Experimental and aleatory music that had difficulty complying with the pre-1993 definition should now qualify more easily.

Problems with avant-garde music were not, however, the main reasons for the 1993 amendments. They were prompted by some odd interpretations of the Act that exonerated microwave and cable transmitters of music from any obligation to pay royalties to right-holders. These operators argued that copyright extended to communication of "the work"; their transmissions were not of "the work" because they did not transmit any "graphically produced" version; all they communicated was an acoustic presentation of the work. This, they claimed, fell outside the copyright owner's control. The courts agreed.[85] These decisions meant that virtually the only communications a copyright owner could control were those that featured a picture of the sheet music! Protests from the musical performing rights societies caused Parliament to drop the "graphic reproduction" requirement. At the same time, the "melody and harmony" requirement was also removed, presumably to avoid arguments that such works as drum solos were not protected.

Rearrangements, such as different piano versions of an opera score, have also long been protected as musical works. Each different arrangement can have its own separate copyright.[86] In practice, much early classical and jazz music remains in copyright, though its composer is long dead and buried, because the arranger who rejigs Beethoven's "Moonlight" Sonata for beginners by simplifying the source and including fingering, dynamic marks, tempo indications, slurs, and phrasing has copyright in her original arrangement.[87] Beethoven's heirs are entitled only to bathe in their forebear's reflected glory.

---

84   *Copyright Act*, R.S.C. 1985, c. C-42, as am. by S.C. 1993, c. 23, s. 1.
85   *C Act*, above note 1, s. 3(1)(f); *C.A.P.A.C.* v. *CTV Television Network*, [1968] S.C.R. 676; *Canadian Cable Television Assn.* v. *Canada (Copyright Board)*, [1993] 2 F.C. 138 (C.A.) [*Canadian Cable*].
86   *Wood v. Boosey* (1867), L.R. 2 Q.B. 340.
87   *Consolidated Music Publishers Inc.* v. *Ashley Publications Inc.*, 197 F. Supp. 17 at 18 (D.N.Y. 1961).

A performer also has a copyright in his or her performance, distinct from any copyright in the work performed.[88]

9) Compilation

Compilation is defined as a work resulting "from the selection or arrangement of literary, dramatic, musical or artistic works or of parts thereof" or of data.[89] A compilation of literary works is itself a literary work, a compilation of artistic works is an artistic work, and so on. A compilation of data — such as an electronic database — is classified according to the type of data: for example, literary material becomes a compilation of literary works. A mixed compilation — such as literary and artistic work — is classed according to whether the literary or artistic work makes up its "most substantial part."[90] This formula may prove troublesome. Is a catalogue of paintings that intersperses text "literary" or "artistic" in its "most substantial part"?

Just gathering data and sorting them in an obvious way may not involve "selection or arrangement," and so may not result in a protectable compilation.[91] In the United States this restriction has meant there is no protection for "white pages" telephone directories: either they lack any selection or arrangement at all or the purely alphabetic selection or arrangement is too commonplace or mechanical to be original.[92] Items like encyclopedias, dictionaries, anthologies, radio and television guides, betting coupons, and advertising brochures that select and arrange material from various sources, collections of "one-write" business forms, and

---

88   See section B(11)(b), "Performances," in this chapter.

89   C Act, above note 1, s. 2, def. "compilation," overturning the previous view that only compilations of literary works are protected: Re Royalties for Retransmission Rights of Distant Radio and Television Signals (1990), 32 C.P.R. (3d) 97 (Copyright Bd.), aff'd (sub nom. Canadian Cable Television Assn./Assn. Canadienne de Télévision par Cable v. American College Sports Collective of Canada Inc.) [1991] 3 F.C. 626 (C.A.) [Royalties]. The "broadcast day," denied protection by this decision, has since been protected as a compilation of dramatic works: Re Royalties for Retransmission Rights of Distant Television Signals 1995–1997 (28 June 1996), (Copyright Bd.) [Royalties 1995–97].

90   C Act, above note 1, s. 2.1(1).

91   R. v. Laurier Office Mart Inc. (1994), 58 C.P.R. (3d) 403 at 415–16 (Ont. Prov. Div.), aff'd (1995), 63 C.P.R. (3d) 229 (Ont. Gen. Div.).

92   Feist Publications Inc. v. Rural Telephone Service Co., 499 U.S. 340 (1991) [Feist]. See section A(1), "Originality," in chapter 3.

trade catalogues, all protected before 1994,[93] may still qualify under the more rigorous test because they involve more than industrious collection. Items like book or customer lists, sports programs or fixtures, "yellow pages" business directories, and driver training manuals collecting mainly government material may involve little more than industrious collection and so may now attract closer scrutiny.[94]

The U.S. approach has now been followed in Canada by the Federal Court of Appeal in the case of a yellow pages directory. The overall arrangement and look of the directory was conceded to be an original compilation. On the other hand, the organization of data comprising names, addresses, fax and phone numbers, and other information concerning subscribers was called "obvious and commonplace" and "so mechanical as to be devoid of a creative element." The compiler of another business directory could therefore freely take this information for its own purposes.[95]

10) Title of a Work

Titles have no copyright. This has been true of the Commonwealth and the United States since the late nineteenth century. It was also true of Canada up to the 1930s. Thus, in 1915, an Ontario court, relying on British precedent, refused to find any copyright in the title *The New Canadian Bird Book*.[96] In 1931, however, Parliament amended the *Copyright Act* to define "work" to include "the title thereof when such title is original and distinctive."[97] Presumably, the requirement of originality

---

93   *Bulman Group Ltd.* v. *"One Write" Accounting Systems Ltd.*, [1982] 2 F.C. 327 (T.D.); *Slumber-Magic Adjustable Bed Co.* v. *Sleep-King Adjustable Bed Co.* (1985), 3 C.P.R. (3d) 81 (B.C.S.C.).

94   See, for example, *École de Conduite Tecnic Aube Inc.* v. *1509 8858 Québec Inc.* (1986), 12 C.I.P.R. 284 at 298ff (Que. S.C.); *Index Téléphonique (N.L.) de Notre Localité* v. *Imprimerie Garceau Ltée* (1987), 18 C.I.P.R. 133 at 140–41 (Que. S.C.).

95   *Tele-Direct (Publications) Inc.* v. *American Business Information Inc.* (1997), 76 C.P.R. (3d) 296 at 309 (Fed. C.A.), aff'ing (1996), 113 F.T.R. 123 (T.D.) [*Tele-Direct*]. *British Columbia Jockey Club* v. *Standen* (1985), 66 B.C.L.R. 245 (C.A.), may need reconsideration in the light of *Tele-Direct*. See further section A(1), "Originality," in chapter 3.

96   *McIndoo* v. *Musson Book Co.* (1915), 35 O.L.R. 42 (H.C.), aff'd (1916) 35 O.L.R. 342 (C.A.) [*McIndoo*].

97   *C Act*, above note 1, s. 2, def. "work"; R. Stone, "Copyright Protection for Titles, Character Names and Catch-Phrases in the Film and Television Industry" [1996] 5 Ent. L. Rev. 178. The provision, being limited to a "work," does not therefore apply to the title of any sound recording, broadcast, or performance, although it may apply to the "works" contained in the record, broadcast, or performance.

and distinctiveness means that the title must result from some intellectual effort, not be copied, and when created, be striking enough to distinguish the work from others.

Whatever the amendment means, hardly any title the courts have considered since 1931 has fallen within its language. "The Man Who Broke the Bank at Monte Carlo," "Fleurs d'amour et Fleurs d'amitié," and "There Goes My Everything" for songs, the *Guinness Book of Olympic Records* for a book, and *Médecine d'aujourd'hui* for a television program and spin-off book have all been denied copyright protection.[98] In the leading case, the Privy Council refused to believe that Parliament in 1931 meant to change the law: maybe it just wanted to "settle doubts."[99] The court decided that the copyright owner of the song "The Man Who Broke the Bank at Monte Carlo" could not stop the use of that title for a movie that did not track the theme of the song or play its music. Titles continued to have no separate copyright. Instead, they fell under the copyright of the work to which they referred. Even then, a title was vulnerable unless it involved substantial literary composition and so amounted to a substantial part of the whole work, for example, the long book title of yore, which epitomized the book's subject on the title page.

Nobody will ever likely acquire a share in a copyright simply by suggesting a title.[100] The circumstances may sometimes call for reasonable payment, if, for example, the recipient of the suggestion led its supplier to believe the title was not being given gratis. Sometimes, too, for a work done in collaboration, the supply of an original and distinctive title by a collaborator may form part of her contribution and so help to determine her share in the overall copyright. But the mere supply of a title will hardly ever justify a claim of joint authorship.

a) Policy for Lack of Copyright Protection

Various reasons underlie the reluctance to protect titles by copyright. The smaller the blocks that copyright protects, the more the public domain shrinks and the higher the social costs incurred as people have

---

98   *Francis, Day & Hunter Ltd.* v. *Twentieth Century Fox Corp. Ltd.* (1939), [1940] A.C. 112 (P.C.) [*Fox*]; *Rochat* v. *La Société Radio-Canada*, [1974] C.S. 638; *Blue Crest Music Inc.* v. *Canusa Records Ltd.* (1974), 17 C.P.R. (2d) 149 at 155 (Fed. T.D.), aff'd (*sub. nom. Blue Crest Music Inc.* v. *Compo Co. Ltd.*) (1977), 30 C.P.R. (2d) 14 (Fed. C.A.), rev'd on other grounds (*sub nom. Compo Co.* v. *Blue Crest Music Inc.*) (1979), [1980] 1 S.C.R. 357; *Canadian Olympic Assn.* v. *Konica Canada Inc.* (1991), [1992] 1 F.C. 797 (C.A.); *Flamand* v. *Société Radio-Canada* (1967), 53 C.P.R. 217 (Que. S.C.) [*Flamand*].

99   *Fox, ibid.* at 125.

100 *Jacob* v. *Boisseau* (16 April 1996), A.Q. 911 (S.C.).

to avoid or pay for the use of everyday language and symbols. Titles typically involve little creativity, especially when compared with the work to which they refer. Nor are they in short supply; granting copyrights will not improve quality or quantity.

Literary and artistic practice also tolerate similar or even identical titles. No one mistook Ralph Ellison's *Invisible Man* for H.G. Wells's earlier *The Invisible Man*: the author's name distinguished the book as much as the title did. Had copyright protected titles and had Ellison or Wells long before seen but forgotten another similarly titled work circulating locally in some distant place, or even a drawing or a musical work, the earlier author could have required them to change their title; for copyright applies regardless of locality, competition, or subconscious recollection. Protection of this degree is unnecessary and, indeed, counter-productive.

b) Other Available Protection

Other protection for titles is often available. A title that is written in a fancy design may be protected as an artistic work. Reproducing the design may then infringe this artistic copyright. The unauthorized marketing of T-shirts carrying the *Crocodile Dundee* movie logo was stopped this way.[101] A very low level of graphic artistry may admit titles into the pantheon. Thus, in England, the magazine title *Woman*, in sloping lower-case sans-serif lettering, was protected.[102] Canadian protection may be more difficult. Even if *Woman* in commonplace lettering for a women's magazine may pass as "original" — and this is debatable — is it striking enough to be "distinctive"?

Since 1954, titles for printed publications have been registrable as trade-marks under the *Trade-marks Act* if the title is inherently distinctive or has become distinctive through use.[103] Periodicals or series, including titles like *Essentials of Canadian Law*, may qualify for this protection. So, too, do film or cartoon titles that are used to generate spin-off merchandise licensed through a single source. *Charlie Brown*, *Beauty and the Beast*, *Toy Story*, and even *Crocodile Dundee* are among recent examples. Book titles like the *Guinness Book of Olympic Records* may also qualify if associated with a single trade source, such as the Guinness brewing firm.

Titles are also protected against passing-off. The owner of the goodwill associated with a well-known title may prevent others from

---

101 *Paramount Pictures Corp* v. *Howley* (1991), 5 O.R. (3d) 573 (Gen. Div.).

102 *IPC Magazines Ltd.* v. *MGN Ltd.*, [1998] F.S.R. 431 at 438–39 (Ch.).

103 R.S.C. 1985, c. T-13, s. 2, def. "wares."

damaging that goodwill by using a later confusingly similar title to mislead the public into believing the second title is, or is connected with, the first. Nobody may issue a rival *Globe and Mail* newspaper or database, except perhaps as an isolated non-misleading spoof. Nor may a firm "spike the guns" of a rival, who has advertised the launch of a new title, by itself launching a similar work with a confusingly similar title.[104] By contrast, the publisher of *The New Canadian Bird Book* (or of *Copyright Law*, for that matter) cannot stop later books from bearing the same or a similar descriptive name, so long as their get-up or marketing do not misrepresent the one as being somehow connected with the other.[105]

c) Exceptional Copyright Protection

Although copyright for titles that lack any artistic element is regularly denied, there are anomalies. Both *Access to Canadian Income Tax* and *The Access Letter* were said to be original and distinctive titles for taxation services that provided information from Revenue Canada.[106] *This Hour Has Seven Days*, the title of a former weekly CBC television current affairs program, was also thought to be original and distinctive enough for it to be independently protectable.[107] The suggestions in those cases were, however, made in passing and are inconsistent with prior jurisprudence.[108]

Only one Canadian decision has banned a non-artistic title because it infringed copyright. The case involved *Popeye* used in conjunction with a drawing of the eponymous character on the dials of watches. The court found, with little discussion, that *Popeye* was an original and distinctive title. By itself, this finding seems implausible. The initial drawing of the pop-eyed sailor character was no doubt original, but the choice of *Popeye* as the title of the cartoon strip seems obvious: it is

---

104   *TV Guide Inc./Tv Hebdo Inc.* v. *Publications La Semaine Inc.* (1984), 6 C.I.P.R. 110 (Que. S.C.): the television guide *La Semaine* stopped *Télé Semaine* from starting up as a temporary "fighting brand."

105   *McIndoo*, above note 96; *International Press Ltd.* v. *Tunnell*, [1938] 1 D.L.R. 393 (Ont. C.A.) (*Who's Who in Canada* and *The Canadian Who's Who* may both circulate, where the second entrant makes sure buyers do not confuse the two).

106   *CCH Canadian Ltd.* v. *Butterworths Canada Ltd.* (1991), 36 C.P.R. (3d) 417 at 431 (Fed. T.D.).

107   *Flamand*, above note 98 at 225.

108   The *Access* titles are less distinctive than "The Man Who Broke the Bank at Monte Carlo," which was denied protection in *Fox*, above note 98. *This Hour Has Seven Days* may qualify as original and distinctive, but it cannot have a copyright independent of the work to which it refers: *Fox, ibid.*

simply the name of the leading character. The case was, however, unusual because the defendant actually admitted that its use of the Popeye drawing reproduced a substantial part of the copyright. The court therefore concluded, fairly enough, that both drawing and title should be enjoined, since the title was just incidental to the drawing and part of the substance that was taken.[109] No general principle about the copyrightability of titles emerges from this special case.

11) Sound Recordings, Performances, and Broadcasts

Sound recordings, performances, and broadcasts are non-traditional items that do not qualify as "works" and that lack an "author" in the traditional sense. In some countries, particularly in Europe, protection is extended to them through a system of "neighbouring" rights, but in Canada they are protected by copyright.

a) Sound Recordings

A sound recording is defined as "a recording, fixed in any material form, consisting of sounds, whether or not of a performance of a work." This definition modernizes the pre-1997 one that referred to "perforated rolls and other contrivances by means of which sounds may be mechanically reproduced."[110] A sound recording has its own separate copyright distinct from the copyright in the music, lyrics, or performance recorded. The recording may be protected even though what it records is not. For example, the sounds may comprise bird calls, crashing waves, spontaneous conversation, or music that may have fallen into the public domain.[111] Film soundtracks are excluded from the definition: they come under the film's copyright.[112]

As from 1997, qualifying makers of sound recordings, typically record companies, may collect money from public performances and broadcasts of their records, and also blank audio media royalties.[113]

---

109 *Lechter*, above note 55. *Popeye* alone was unprotected in similar U.K. litigation, although the United Kingdom lacks any equivalent to the Canadian definition of "work": *Kleeman*, above note 55.

110 *C Act*, above note 1, s. 2, def. "sound recording"; *1997 Act*, above note 2, ss. 55(1) & (2).

111 *C Act, ibid.*, s. 2, def. "sound recording," & 18(1); *Bouliane v. Service de Musique Bonanza Inc.* (1986), 18 C.I.P.R. 14 (Que. C.A.).

112 *C Act, ibid.* s. 2, defs. "sound recording" and "cinematographic work."

113 *C Act, ibid.*, ss. 18(1), 19–20, & 81. See section B(14)(c), "Blank Audio Recording Media Levy," in chapter 7.

b) Performances

Since 1996, performers from *WTO Agreement* states have been able to prevent the unauthorized recording and broadcasts of their performances. This coverage includes improvisations, whether the work performed is in copyright or in the public domain.[114] Protection applies retrospectively to unauthorized recordings made up to fifty years before — for example, of live Beatles or Elvis Presley concerts.

In 1997 coverage for performers was expanded to allow performers appropriately connected with *Rome Convention* states to collect money from the rental, public performance, or broadcast of records containing their performances. Performers from Canada, and from other states on a reciprocal basis, may also collect blank audio media royalties.[115]

The new provisions may have surprising consequences. Suppose a teacher tapes a child singing in class. The child is a performer, who consequently has a copyright in her performance. The teacher may therefore need the child's consent to make the tape. To avoid administrative burdens and issues such as whether the child is old enough to give an informed consent, the school may need to obtain consents signed in advance each year from its pupils' parents or guardians, for what may be ordinary classroom activities.

Such tapes may sometimes eventually have commercial potential, although nobody may have thought so at the time of making. Optimally, the copyright position should be clarified in advance in the annual consent form signed by parents or guardians. The pupil's copyright in her performance might be confirmed in that document, while co-ownership of the copyright in the sound recording could be conferred on the school and the teacher.[116] Such an allocation would be consistent with copyright policy. It would reflect the typical contributions of those involved and would also provide appropriate incentives for worthy work to be produced and commercialized. Other negotiated outcomes are, however, quite possible and permissible. Agreements reached early on, when enthusiasm is high, everyone is available, and events are still fresh in mind, are preferable to attempts to negotiate arrangements years later when circumstances may have changed.

---

114   *C Act, ibid.*, ss. 26 & 2, def. "performer's performance."

115   *C Act, ibid.*, ss. 15–17, 19–20, & 81. See section A(3), "Non-traditional Subject Matter: 1997 Amendments," in this chapter, and section A(4), "Sound Recordings, Performances, and Broadcasts," in chapter 4.

116   See section A(1)(c), "Joint Authors," in chapter 4.

c) Broadcasts

A broadcaster who televises or broadcasts a live event may acquire a traditional copyright in it as a cinematographic work if the event is simultaneously recorded. There is no traditional protection for a broadcast that is not recorded in some way, but the selection of programs transmitted during a twenty-four-hour or other longer period ("the broadcast day") may be protectable as an original compilation of dramatic works.[117]

Since 1997, broadcasters located in a *WTO Agreement* or *Rome Convention* state also have a copyright over unauthorized recording and reproduction of their transmissions. This right extends over any substantial part of their pre-recorded or live programming. A television broadcaster also has a limited public performance right where the public is charged an entrance fee to view a transmission. Cable retransmitters are excluded from these rights.[118]

FURTHER READINGS

CHOKSI, J., "The Integrated Circuit Topography Act: Approaching Ministerial Review" (1996) 12 Can. Intell. Prop. Rev. 379

FELDMAN, D.B., "Finding a Home for Fictional Characters: A Proposal for Change in Copyright Protection" 78 Cal. L. Rev. 687 (1990)

GENDREAU, Y., A. NORDEMANN, & R. OESCH, eds., *Copyright and Photographs: An International Survey* (London, The Hague, Boston: Kluwer International, 1999)

GINSBURG, J.C., "Copyright, Common Law, and *Sui Generis* Protection of Databases in the United States and Abroad" 66 Cincinnati L. Rev. 151 (1997)

GOLDBERG, R., *Performance Art: From Futurism to the Present* (London: Thames and Hudson, 1988)

---

117   *Royalties 1995–97*, above note 89. See section B(5)(a), "Film, Video, and Formats," in this chapter.

118   *C Act*, above note 1, ss. 21 & 2 (def. "broadcaster"). See section A(4), "Sound Recordings, Performances, and Broadcasts," and section A(9) "Substantial Infringement" in chapter 5.

HAYES, M.S., "Copyright Infringement on the Internet," in M. Racicot et al., *The Cyberspace Is Not a "No Law Land": A Study of the Issues of Liability for Content Circulating on the Internet* (February 1997), available at <http://strategis.ic.gc.ca>

HAYHURST, W.L., "Intellectual Property Protection in Canada for Designs of Useful Articles: sections 46 and 46.1 of the Copyright Act" (1989) 4 I.P.J. 381

HOWELL, R., "Database Protection and Canadian Laws" (October 1998), prepared for Industry Canada and Canadian Heritage, available at <http.//strategis.ic.gc.ca>

KEARNS, P., *The Legal Concept of Art* (Oxford: Hart Publishing, 1998) c. 3

KRAUSS, R.E., *Originality of the Avant-Garde and Other Modernist Myths* (Cambridge, Mass., & London: MIT Press, 1985)

NABHAN, V., *Droit d'auteur et banques d'information dans l'administration* (Québec: Gouvernement du Québec, 1992)

PILA, J., & A. CHRISTIE, "The Literary Work within Copyright Law: An Analysis of Its Present and Future State" (1999) 13 I.P.J. 133

TAKACH, G.F., *Computer Law* (Concord, Ont.: Irwin Law, 1998)

VAVER, D., "The Canadian Copyright Amendments of 1988" (1988) 4 I.P.J. 121

CHAPTER 3

CRITERIA FOR COPYRIGHTABILITY

A. LITERARY, DRAMATIC, MUSICAL, AND ARTISTIC WORKS

To be protected by copyright, a work must be (1) original, (2) fixed, and (3) appropriately connected to Canada, or to a *WTO Agreement*, *Berne Convention*, or *Universal Copyright Convention* member state.

1) Originality

Copyright protects only original work. The product must originate from its author, not be copied, and involve some intellectual effort.[1] The work need not be novel or non-obvious, criteria that must be met when a patent is sought for an invention. Little would qualify for copyright if patenting criteria were employed. So A and B, working independently, can each produce a similar or even identical "original" work and each will have his own copyright. This duplication can happen if they are both working to a similar plan or idea and using common sources. In such a case, A's work will not infringe B's copyright even if

---

1 *Copyright Act*, R.S.C. 1985, c. C-42 [*C Act*; unless otherwise indicated, references to the Act are as amended], s. 5(1) & s. 2, def. "every original literary, dramatic, musical and artistic work"; *Ladbroke (Football) Ltd. v. William Hill (Football) Ltd.,* [1964] 1 All E.R. 465 (H.L.).

B's was made first. Someone copying B's work will infringe only B's copyright, not A's.

In aesthetics, originality is very much a contested idea. The notion of the Author as Romantic Genius, who, like the original Creator, makes something out of nothing, has been under siege at least since Marcel Duchamp exhibited an up-ended urinal signed with a concocted name ("R. Mutt"). Was this "original" "art"? What made it so? The additions? The putting of a familiar object in a different context? The fact that an artist purported to sign it? What of Roy Lichtenstein's large-scale reproductions of frames from popular cartoons or of sketches from art history manuals? Would George Brecht's text, *Two Signs*, which reads in its entirety

TWO SIGNS
• SILENCE
• NO VACANCY

qualify as original?

The disintegration of Romanticism, at least outside Europe, has had its effect. Originality has been found in the most unlikely places. A poster of an out-of-copyright painting was called "original" because, inadvertently, it was not an exact copy. With an apparently straight face, the judge said that "[a] copyist's bad eyesight or defective musculature, or a shock caused by a clap of thunder" was enough to make the result original if the author "adopt[ed] it as his."[2] This decision meant that the more exact the copy, the less likely it was to have a copyright! Veering away from that conclusion, another court relocated originality in the preliminary work involved in converting a two-dimensional work into a three-dimensional engraving before running off multiple prints.[3]

In practice, originality may serve several public policy functions. First and foremost, it signals that enough has been done to create a

---

2   *Alfred Bell & Co. v. Catalda Fine Arts Inc.*, 191 F.2d 99 at 105 (2d Cir. 1951); *Bridgeman Art Library Ltd. v. Corel Corp.*, 25 F. Supp. 2d 421 (S.D.N.Y. 1998), reaff'd on reargument, 36 F. Supp. 2d 191 (S.D.N.Y. 1999) [*Bridgeman*], photographs seeking faithfully to reproduce public domain artworks lacked originality and thus copyright under both U.S. and U.K. law, despite the great care and work needed to achieve faithful reproduction, rejecting (correctly?) *Re Graves* (1869), L.R. 4 Q.B. 715.

3   *Martin v. Polyplas Manufacturers Ltd.*, [1969] N.Z.L.R. 1046 at 1049–50 (S.C.).

potentially marketable commodity.[4] Production and distribution finance can then be attracted from investors who know that their outlay cannot be undercut by cheap copies. Second, the insistence that a work not be copied and that it emanate from an "author" prevents photocopiers, reprinters, tracers, or computer scanners from claiming copyright for mechanical work or for simply making material more available without added value.[5] Third, originality helps police the borders between copyright and other rights. Words used as trade-marks, slogans, or titles for books, films, and songs have all been called unoriginal, however much effort went into devising or researching them.[6] This task of border patrol is, however, too great for originality to perform alone. Judges unversed in art are sometimes too impressed by the effort in producing trivial matter — for example, the sloping VISA mark or the magazine title WOMAN in sloping sans-serif lower-case font — and seem loath to let trade-mark law alone do the job that is its *raison d'être*.[7]

In fact, originality's requirement of some intellectual effort has caused it to lose its way in the twentieth century. As usual, operations at either end of the spectrum are relatively uncontroversial. Originality is rarely questioned where someone has done a translation, written her own computer program, composed her own song or painting, drafted her own engineering drawings, selected and arranged the best work of a single author or group of authors into an anthology, or even written a book on copyright law. At the other end of the spectrum, originality also serves a useful purpose in guarding against over-easy extensions or grants of copyright when work is in, or about to go into, the public domain. Strategies concocted to extend copyrights beyond the fifty years after an author's death by bringing out "new editions" can be

---

4   At least enough to make copyright something other than a cure for any act of unfair competition or misappropriation, torts the federal parliament cannot constitutionally enact: *Macdonald v. Vapor Canada Ltd.* (1976), [1977] 2 S.C.R. 134. The constitutionally unrestricted U.K. view that anything beyond a "single straight line drawn with the aid of a ruler" (*British Northrop Ltd. v. Texteam Blackburn Ltd.* (1973), [1974] R.P.C. 57 at 68 (Ch.) [*British Northrop*]) may be original may therefore need reconsideration in Canada, since it seems little more than a rule against people reaping where they have not sown.

5   *The Reject Shop Plc. v. Manners*, [1995] F.S.R. 870 (D.C.); *Bridgeman*, above note 2.

6   For example, *Exxon Corp. v. Exxon Insurance Consultants International Ltd.* (1981), [1982] Ch. 119 (C.A.); *Sinanide v. La Maison Kosmeo* (1928), 139 L.T. 365 (C.A.); *Jacob v. Boisseau* (16 April 1996), A.Q. 911 (S.C.).

7   *Visa International Service Assn. v. Auto Visa Inc.* (1991), 41 C.P.R. (3d) 77 at 87 (Que. S.C.); *IPC Magazines Ltd. v. MGN Ltd.*, [1998] F.S.R. 431 at 438–39 (Ch.); *Motel 6 Inc. v. No. 6 Motel Ltd.* (1981), [1982] 1 F.C. 638 (T.D.); see section A(9)(c), "Mediating Artistic Practice: Parody and Postmodernism," in chapter 5.

policed by insisting on substantial — not merely cosmetic — changes before a new copyright is allowed over the new matter. Changing a single word — however important — in a poem cannot create a fresh copyright for the poem or the word.[8] Other trivialities are also routinely denied copyright: (re-) arranging existing material in obvious ways, listing starters for a competition, composing a few sentences for an advertisement, producing simple application forms, shortening books with scissors and paste (or their electronic equivalent), or making minor changes to drawings without affecting their overall visual impact.[9]

But, while a low threshold test of originality may protect artists in their livelihood, it does not carry over well into the world of commerce. There it supports almost irresistible pressures to call virtually anything original and protected. Overprotection is then controlled through a sliding standard of infringement: the less original a work, the more exact must be the copying for there to be infringement; the more original the work, the less that need be taken for infringement to be found.[10] So, if someone wants to pay a lot of money for an amateur home video — perhaps because, like Zapruder, the photographer happened to have his camera rolling when President Kennedy was assassinated — then, so the argument goes, surely the filmer must have "rights" in it. Or if time and money is spent scanning public domain material into a databank and making the result publicly available for a fee, surely the scanner must have "rights" in this material. So, why not a *copy*right?

How copyright deals with transcriptions of speeches or interviews is symptomatic. Perhaps a transcriber who turns incoherent babbling into polished prose may deserve to have her work called original. What, though, of the transcriber who, like a tape recorder, provides an accurate transcript, perhaps with only the occasional correction for grammar or syntax? In the Commonwealth, this version is considered original because it protects the transcriber's investment of skill, time,

---

8   *Black* v. *Murray & Son* (1870), 9 Macph. 341 (Ct. Sess., Scot.), where one (albeit critical) word changed in a poem in the second edition of Walter Scott's novel *Antiquary* was not enough to create a new copyright in the poem or the book.

9   For example, *Commercial Signs* v. *General Motors Products of Canada Ltd.*, [1937] O.W.N. 58 (H.C.J.), aff'd without written reasons [1937] 2 D.L.R. 800 (Ont. C.A.); *Interlego AG* v. *Tyco Industries Inc.* (1988), [1989] A.C. 217 (P.C.); *FAI Insurances Ltd.* v. *Advance Bank Australia Ltd.* (1986), 68 A.L.R. 133 at 140–41 (Austl. Fed. Ct.); compare *Caron* v. *Assoc. de Pompiers de Montréal Inc.* (1992), 42 C.P.R. (3d) 292 (Fed. T.D.) [*Caron*] (pocket scheduler original).

10 *Land Transport Safety Authority of New Zealand* v. *Glogau*, [1999] 1 N.Z.L.R. 257 (C.A.) [*Glogau*].

and labour.[11] In the United States, the opposite holds: a court reporter there apparently has no copyright in his transcript of evidence.[12]

The problem with originality therefore starts from its own internal incoherence. Although all concur that the author has to exercise some skill, ingenuity, judgment, labour, or expense (or some combination of these) in making the work, the type and amount of effort is left unclear. Courts often fudge matters by saying that it is all a question of degree and fact; that quality matters more than quantity; and that what qualifies as original for one class of work (say, compilations) is not the same as for another (say, painting). On the degree of work, some would require "little more than negligible" work, others "substantial." On the type of work, some seem happy with industry or even experience; others demand "creativity" or the expression of the author's own thoughts. On the latter theory, a judge's written reasons for judgment would no doubt be original, while the listing of subscribers in a white or yellow pages telephone directory would not.[13] How short e-mail messages or the written "conversations" that occur on Internet "chat corners" may fare is unclear.[14]

Most recently, the Federal Court of Appeal has followed the stricter line adopted in the United States, insisting that originality implies creativity and ingenuity. The routine compilation of data in a yellow pages business directory, though no doubt industrious, was labelled as merely mechanical work and unoriginal. The court insisted that prior judgments equating originality with "skill, judgment or labour" required these words to be read conjunctively. Mere labour without creative skill or judgment was not enough.[15] Such views have elsewhere thrown the protection of electronic databases into doubt and

---

11 *Express Newspapers* v. *News (UK) Ltd.,* [1990] 3 All E.R. 376 (Ch.) [*Express*];
    Gould Estate v. *Stoddart Publishing Co.* (1996), 30 O.R. (3d) 520 (Gen. Div.), aff'd
    (1998), 161 D.L.R. (4th) 321 (Ont. C.A.) [*Gould*]; compare *Cala Homes (South)*
    Ltd. v. *Alfred McAlpine Homes East Ltd.,* [1995] F.S.R. 818 at 835 (Ch.) [*Cala*].

12 *Lipman* v. *Massachusetts,* 475 F.2d 565 (1st Cir. 1973) (Mary Jo Kopechne inquest).

13 For example, *Tele-Direct (Publications) Inc.* v. *American Business Information Inc.*
    (1997), 76 C.P.R. (3d) 296 (Fed. C.A.) [*Tele-Direct*], and *Caron*, above note 9;
    compare *Feist Publications Inc.* v. *Rural Telephone Service Co.,* 499 U.S. 340 (1991)
    [*Feist*]; *C Act*, above note 1, s. 2, def. "compilation." But what if the telephone
    directory were exhibited as an artwork, as A.C. Danto playfully suggested in *The*
    Transfiguration of the Commonplace: A Philosophy of Art (Cambridge, Mass.:
    Harvard University Press, 1981) at 136–38?

14 It is questionable, in the first place, whether these communications qualify as
    literary work.

15 *Tele-Direct*, above note 13, following *Feist*, above note 13.

have prompted an international movement, spearheaded by the European Union, to introduce a special right to protect unoriginal databases for fifteen or more years.[16]

While the comments of the Federal Court of Appeal may ring true for compilations, they hardly reconcile all the cases — for example, those where trite personal or business correspondence has been protected without qualm.[17] Similarly, ordinary photographs, "réalisée au hasard, sans recherche et sans cadrage particulier," have been found original, although sometimes reluctantly.[18] In any event, nobody can tell in advance what quality or quantity of work, skill, judgment, research, or time a court will demand before calling something original. Thus, one judge, relying on the Federal Court of Appeal's test, held that a compiler who combed a white pages telephone directory for Italian-sounding names to produce a telephone directory of (he hoped) Italian-descent subscribers had used enough skill and judgment to create an original compilation.[19] But just a few months later, the selfsame judge, while admitting that the production of headnotes and other editorial material accompanying reports of court decisions requires much labour, skill, and judgment, concluded that this material was unoriginal because it lacked "imagination" or "creative spark."[20] The effort in producing an accurate précis of an obscure judicial decision may well involve imagination or creativity. To say that this involvement occurs more or less often when a

---

16 See, for example, EC Directive 96/9/EC of 11 March 1996 on The Legal Protection of Databases, implemented in the United Kingdom in 1998 as a new fifteen-year "database right"; WIPO Draft Treaty on Intellectual Property in respect of Databases 1996, found at <http://clea.wipo.int/lpbin/lpext.dll>. See R. Howell, "Database Protection and Canadian Laws" (October 1998), prepared for Industry Canada and Canadian Heritage, at <http://strategis.ic.gc.ca/SSG/it04771e.html>.

17 See also *Hager* v. *ECW Press Ltd.* (1998), 85 C.P.R. (3d) 289 (Fed. T.D.) [*Hager*], holding that *Express* and *Gould*, both above note 11, remain good law despite *Tele-Direct*, above note 13.

18 *Ateliers Tango argentin Inc.* v. *Festival d'Espagne et d'Amérique latine Inc.,* [1997] R.J.Q. 3030 (S.C.), citing earlier Canadian case law. The comments in *Ateliers Tango* were made in passing: the court applied a "personal creativity" test of originality to protect photographs that were taken during a shooting session lasting between three and four hours under the direction of a professional photographer; compare *Bridgeman*, above note 2 (photographs of public domain artwork held unoriginal).

19 *Ital-Press Ltd.* v. *Sicoli* (1999), 86 C.P.R. (3d) 129 (Fed. T.D.), Gibson J. (appeal filed).

20 *CCH Canadian Ltd.* v. *Law Society of Upper Canada* (9 November 1999), (Fed. T.D.) [unreported], Gibson J. (appeal filed). Other legal texts and monographs, including the annotations to *Martin's Ontario Criminal Practice 1999*, had enough "originality, creativity and ingenuity."

thematic telephone directory is being compiled than when a headnote is being composed, or that the former activity is somehow different in the extent or quality of creativity from the latter, is to engage in riddles.

Such decisions re-emphasize how much originality in copyright law depends on value judgments flowing from unarticulated assumptions. Judge Jerome Frank once said that, to the casual observer, the decisions of courts about non-obviousness — originality's counterpart in patent law — were "the adventures of judges' souls among inventions."[21] So, too, do decisions about originality seem to be the adventures of judges' souls in the realm of literary and artistic work. A possible way towards greater coherence might involve the application of an incentive-based test — requiring evidence that, without the stimulus of copyright, the work would not have been created[22] — as more consistent with overall copyright policy; but the law, as presently understood, would need realignment, and a number of precedents, such as those finding originality in ordinary personal and business correspondence, would have to be overruled.

This preoccupation with originality has had at least one adverse result. It has tended to divert attention from other possibly more critical issues, such as when, by whom, and how far copyright should be asserted. The resolution of future disputes might be easier if more thought was given to providing guidance on these issues than on the elusive height of the copyright threshold.

2) Fixation

The Act nowhere specifies that fixation is a general condition of protection. Sometimes this condition is explicit for particular classes of work. Choreography, mime, or recitation pieces must have their "scenic arrangement or acting form" fixed in writing or otherwise. Live broadcasts or telecasts are considered fixed if they are recorded while being transmitted. Computer programs may be "expressed, fixed, embodied or stored in any manner," although what the virtual synonyms of "fixed" add is unclear.[23] At other times, fixation is implicit, as

---

21 *Picard* v. *United Aircraft,* 53 U.S.P.Q. 563 at 569 (2d Cir. 1942), quoted with approval in *Farbwerke Hoechst AG* v. *Halocarbon (Ontario) Ltd.* (1974), 15 C.P.R. (2d) 105 at 112 (Fed. T.D.), aff'd (1979), 42 C.P.R. (2d) 145 (S.C.C.), rev'g (1976), 28 C.P.R. (2d) 63 (Fed. C.A.).

22 J.S. Wiley Jr., "Copyright at the School of Patent" (1991) 58 U. Chi. L. Rev. 119 at 145–54.

23 *C Act,* above note 1, s. 2, defs. "dramatic work" and "computer program," & s. 3(1.1).

for photographs. In fact, most works are fixed in some way — in writing or on tape or computer disk.

From all these considerations, one court deduced that "for copyright to subsist in a 'work' it *must* be expressed to some extent at least in some material form, capable of identification and having a more or less permanent endurance."[24] This proposition is a *non sequitur*. The fact that some, even most, works are so fixed does not mean that all are or must be. After all, every work is supposedly protected "whatever may be the mode or form of its expression": this language is expansive enough to cover oral works, too.[25] Thus, "lectures, addresses, sermons and other works of the same nature" are protectable under the *Berne Convention*, even though they are expressed in sign language or an oral "mode or form."[26] By not explicitly requiring fixation for these works, the *Copyright Act* may as plausibly imply that these and other works are protected without fixation.

This potential flexibility seems to have disappeared in Canada, albeit with little substantial argument. Thus, courts have, perhaps too readily, held that all oral conversation lacks copyright.[27] Allowing some flexibility on the fixation issue may nevertheless sometimes be beneficial. Even in the print era, which gave birth to the notion, fixation was an ambiguous concept. Literary critics point to the difficulty of establishing a "fixed" version of a work that has gone through various revisions by the writer and her editors. Digital technology makes the point more starkly: How is an electronic database, on which the data change by the minute, "fixed"? Far from being a general precondition for protection, fixation may function better simply by providing evidence of the existence or character of a work. Otherwise, much improvisational, performance, and kinetic art, as well as interactive art generated by "virtual reality" products, may end up unprotected.[28] Distinguishing

---

24   *Canadian Admiral Corp.* v. *Rediffusion Inc.,* [1954] Ex. C.R. 382 at 394 [*Canadian Admiral*] [emphasis added].

25   *C Act*, above note 1, s. 2, def. of "every original literary, dramatic, musical and artistic work," tracking the *Berne Convention for the Protection of Literary and Artistic Works* (Paris, 1971), 9 September 1886, 828 U.N.T.S. 221 [*Berne*], art. 2(1), although art. 2(2) allows states optionally to make fixation a precondition of protection. *Berne* is found at <http://clea.wipo.int/lpbin/lpext.dll>.

26   *Berne, ibid.,* art. 2(1); S.P. Ladas, *The International Protection of Literary and Artistic Property* (New York: Macmillan, 1938) at 216–17.

27   *Gould*, above note 11. Some oral expression may qualify as a "performer's performance" and have copyright under this head. See section B(11)(b), "Performances," in chapter 2.

28   *Komesaroff* v. *Mickle* (1986), [1988] R.P.C. 204 at 210 (Vic. S.C.), refusing protection to a moving sand sculpture.

between fixed and unfixed material may discriminate among artistic endeavours that, on the face of them, seem equally worthy.

One major effect of fixation is to distribute rights among competing claimants. Thus, in a spontaneous interview, the interviewee currently has no copyright in his or her words, however mellifluous, because they are unfixed; nor may the interview itself qualify as a performance. No copyright will belong to the interviewee. On the other hand, if the interview is for television and is simultaneously taped, the television studio or production company, which employs the director or camera operator involved in the taping, will own copyright in the videotape as a cinematographic work. Anyone, including the interviewee herself, who wants to re-record or broadcast the interviewee's words will need the consent of the studio or production company. The operation of the criterion of fixation thus marginalizes those who provide a work's substance, while celebrating those who provide its routine form. If rights should flow from such an event — and the present consensus seems to be that they should — a case must surely exist for extending rights to the interviewee, perhaps as a co-owner of copyright in a work of joint authorship.[29] Film-makers and reporters may protest the inconvenience of having to clear one more copyright, but clearances are a commonplace in their industry, and one more is hardly a burden.

The fixation requirement does, it is true, add some certainty to the law. It prevents arguments that spontaneous activity, signing, and oral conversation automatically qualify for protection and helps identify (although sometimes artificially) who can claim to be the author of a work.[30] But the whole concept of fixation needs to be rethought. A rule of convenience need not also be a rule of occasional injustice.

3) Connection with Canada, or with a *WTO Agreement*, *Berne Convention*, or *UCC* State

Works created by a Canadian national or a usual resident of Canada (e.g., a landed immigrant or even a refugee claimant), or works first published in Canada, should obviously be protected in Canada. But copyright eligibility extends well beyond this definition. Virtually every original literary, dramatic, musical, or artistic work qualifies for Canadian protection. It does not matter when or where it was first published (indeed, whether it is published at all), and what its author's nationality was.

---

29   See section A(1)(c), "Joint Authors," in chapter 4.

30   Thus, in *Gould*, above note 11, the reporter to whom Glenn Gould gave an oral interview had copyright in his transcript, while Gould had no rights at all.

Until very recently, it was impossible to generalize in this way. Even after *NAFTA* compelled clearer eligibility criteria to be introduced in 1994, a work's eligibility for copyright still depended on poorly drafted provisions dating from the 1921 Act. This restriction was swept aside after 1 January 1996 by Canada's implementation of the *Agreement on Trade-Related Aspects of Intellectual Property Rights* [*TRIPs*]. A work is now protected in Canada if its author was, when the work was made, a citizen, subject, or ordinary resident of a *Berne Convention, Universal Copyright Convention* [*UCC*], or *WTO Agreement* state.[31] Alternatively, the work is protected if it is first published[32] in a *Berne, UCC, WTO,* or Commonwealth country by issuing enough copies to satisfy reasonable public demands. Publication in different countries within thirty days of the actual first publication is treated as simultaneous publication in all, apparently allowing the copyright owner to choose any as the country of origin.[33] Films are protectable on yet another optional basis: if the maker has its corporate headquarters in a *Berne, UCC,* or *WTO* country or, if an individual, is a citizen, subject, or ordinary resident there.[34]

It used to be critical to know what a work's country of origin was because works made or published before the country joined the *Berne Convention* or the *UCC* fell into and remained in the public domain in Canada. This knowledge is important now only to find out whether the work was still in copyright in the country of origin when it joined *Berne* or the *WTO*. If so, the work is now automatically protected in Canada even if it was made before the country joined.[35]

---

31   The alternative criterion of residence in a Commonwealth state was abolished in 1997: *C Act*, above note 1, s. 5(1)(a), as amended by *An Act to Amend the Copyright Act*, S.C. 1997, c. 24 [*1997 Act*]. This change should be of little consequence, since most Commonwealth states qualify as treaty countries.

A person is ordinarily resident wherever he has voluntarily and habitually been living, even if his residence is short (e.g., a month) and even if it is interrupted by accidental or temporary absences: *Neesa v. Chief Adjudication Officer*, [1999] 1 W.L.R. 1937 (H.L.)

32   "Publication" has a technical meaning: *C Act, ibid.*, s. 4(1) & (2): see section A(1), "First Public Distribution," in chapter 5.

33   *C Act, ibid.*, ss. 5(1)(c)(i) & 5(1.1). The "reasonable public demand" criterion does not apply to the construction of architecture or the incorporation of artwork in architecture: s. 5(1)(c)(ii).

34   *C Act, ibid.*, s. 5(1)(b). The film's "maker" is whoever undertook the arrangements necessary for its making (*C Act*, s. 2, def. "maker"); typically, a film production company, but sometimes an individual producer.

35   *C Act, ibid.*, ss. 5(1.01) to 5(1.03). Transitional provisions apply to protect reliance on a work's previous lack of copyright: ss. 33 & 78.

Since almost every significant state belongs to at least one of the *WTO, Berne,* or *UCC,* few works fall outside the net of protection. For those that do, the minister of industry can, by notice in the *Canada Gazette,* extend protection if a non-treaty state protects Canadians similarly to its own nationals.[36]

B. SOUND RECORDINGS, PERFORMANCES, AND BROADCASTS

Sound recordings, performances, and broadcasts have different copyrightability criteria from traditional works. Since they are not works, the *Berne Convention* does not apply to them. There is no need to isolate authorship or to find any originality. The following discussion deals mainly with transitional questions and connecting factors.

These issues are more complicated than their counterparts for works. Not every sound recording, performance, or broadcast is protected in Canada, or at least protected to the same degree. From 1924, Canada extended protection to sound recordings that were made by *Berne* or Commonwealth members, or that were simultaneously first published in a *Berne* or Commonwealth country. Performers and broadcasters were completely unprotected. The *1997 Act* changed this policy. Canada now retrospectively protects almost all sound recordings, but the rights granted differ depending on the nationality of the sound recording maker or on the country where the records were made. Performers and broadcasters are also now retrospectively protected, but coverage is not complete.

The key factor throughout is reciprocity. Canada fully protects Canadian sound recordings, and performances and broadcasts occurring in Canada. Foreign material is protected only so far as the country of origin of the item similarly protects comparable Canadian items. The main obligation to protect sound recordings, performances, and broadcasts springs from the *Rome Convention* of 1961, which over fifty countries have joined. Notably absent is the United States. Less intensive protection for this material is mandated by *TRIPs.* So *Rome* members automatically get the rights guaranteed by the *Rome Convention,* and *WTO Agreement* members automatically get

---

36   *C Act, ibid.,* s. 5(2). This power existed under the original 1921 Act, and works protected on this basis (i.e., U.S. works since 1924) continue with this protection, too.

the lesser rights guaranteed by *TRIPs*. Further rights are extended only if the country involved grants similar rights to Canadians.

In 1996 the World Intellectual Property Organization promoted the *WIPO Performances and Phonograms Treaty* to protect sound recordings and performances. This convention, signed by some fifty countries, was a sort of "*Rome*-plus" treaty; it built on and improved on the rights that performers and record makers had under the *Rome Convention*, and meant to encourage the many *Berne Convention* members who have not joined the *Rome Convention* to reconsider their position.[37] The United States passed implementing legislation in 1998[38] and will no doubt pressure the rest of the world to follow suit.

The relevant copyrightability criteria are now more closely examined.

1) Sound Recordings

A sound recording is protected in Canada on three possible bases. First, its maker must be a citizen or permanent resident of Canada or of a *Berne Convention, Rome Convention,* or *WTO Agreement* state when the record was first fixed. Alternatively, if its maker is a corporation, the corporation's headquarters must be in Canada or a *Berne, Rome,* or *WTO* state when the record was first fixed. Lastly, if neither of these conditions is met, the sound recording is protected if it was first published in a *Berne, Rome,* or *WTO* state in such a quantity as to satisfy reasonable public demand.[39]

The person who undertook the arrangements necessary to first fix the sounds qualifies as the maker of the sound recording.[40] The maker has rights to first distribute, reproduce, rent, or authorize these acts. He may also, on fulfilling some stricter criteria, qualify for rights of remuneration on sales of blank audio recording media and for public performance or telecommunication of the recording.[41]

---

37 J. Reinbothe, M. Martin-Prat, & S. von Lewinski, "The New WIPO Treaties: A First Resume" [1997] 4 E.I.P.R. 171. The *WIPO Treaty* is found at <http://clea.wipo.int/ lpbin/lpext.dll> at links "Intellectual Property" and "Texts of WIPO-Administered Treaties."

38 *Digital Millennium Copyright Act* of 1998 (H.R. 2281, 105th Cong.).

39 *1997 Act*, above note 31, s. 18(2). First publication in a treaty country occurs even if an earlier publication occurred elsewhere within thirty days: s. 18(3).

40 *1997 Act, ibid.,* s. 2, def. "maker." For a discussion of "maker" and of remastered sound recordings, see section A(4)(a), "Sound Recordings," in chapter 4.

41 *1997 Act, ibid.,* ss. 18(1) & 19, and Part VIII. See section B(1), "Sound Recordings," in chapter 5. For the meaning of the right to first distribute, reproduce, etc., see relevant subsections in section A, "Literary, Dramatic, Musical, and Artistic Works," in chapter 5.

Recordings made before 1 September 1997, are similarly protected. The same connecting factors of nationality and publication in a *Berne, UCC,* or *WTO* state apply.[42] However, since pre-1997 sound recordings were treated like traditional works, proof of both originality and of authorship was required. Originality — presumably some intellectual effort in the act of recording — was easily found. Authorship was fictionally attributed to the "maker" of the recording — namely, the person who undertook the arrangements necessary to make it.[43] Before 1994, the fictional author was whoever made the initial plate (matrix, tape, etc.) from which the recording was directly or indirectly derived. For the usual run of commercial records, these fictional authors usually correspond to the person the Act now calls the maker of the recording, but the occasional exception may be found.

2) Performances

Different copyright protection applies to performers, depending on whether the claim for protection is based on *TRIPs* or on the *Rome Convention*. Since 1 January 1996, performers are protected against unauthorized fixation, reproduction, or broadcast of their live performances if the performance occurred before or after 1996 in a *WTO Agreement* state.[44] Since 1 September 1997, performers connected to a *Rome Convention* state have broader rights that cover rental, public performance, broadcast, and authorization.[45] To be protected, the performance must occur in Canada or in a *Rome* state, or it must be simultaneously broadcast from Canada or from a *Rome* state by a broadcaster headquartered there. For performances fixed on sound recordings, the record must be protected by copyright in Canada through its connection with Canada or a *Rome Convention* state: that is, the maker must be headquartered there or be a citizen or a permanent resident of that state, or first publication must take place there.[46]

---

42 *C Act,* above note 1, ss. 11 & 2, def. "maker," & s. 5(4) (all since repealed except for transitional purposes: *1997 Act, ibid.,* above note 31, ss. 55(1) & (2)). See section A(3), "Connection with Canada, or with a *WTO Agreement, Berne Convention,* or *UCC* State," in this chapter.

43 *1997 Act,* above note 31, ss. 11 & 2, def. "maker" as inserted by *NAFTA Implementation Act,* effective 1 January 1994.

44 *1997 Act, ibid.,* s. 26 (*TRIPs* protection).

45 For the meaning of rental, public performance, etc., see chapter 5, "Owners' Rights."

46 *1997 Act,* above note 31, s. 15(2). See section B(1), "Sound Recordings," in this chapter.

To qualify for the blank audio recording media levy, the performer must be a citizen or a resident of Canada.[47]

3) Broadcasts

Broadcasters with their headquarters in a *WTO Agreement* or *Rome Convention* state have a copyright in signals broadcast from that state.[48]

4) Additional Powers of the Minister

The minister of industry may extend the rights given to performances, sound recordings, and broadcasts to other *NAFTA* members, or to other states, on a reciprocal basis.[49] The minister may also eliminate the broadcaster's right in respect of television programs shown wherever the public is charged an entrance fee to view signals coming from countries that do not grant a similar right to Canadians in their legislation.[50]

FURTHER READINGS

HOWELL, R., "Database Protection and Canadian Laws" (October 1998), prepared for Industry Canada and Canadian Heritage, available at <http://strategis.ic.gc.ca>

HOWELL, R., AND Y. GENDREAU, "Qualitative Standards for Protection of Literary and Artistic Property," in Canadian Comparative Law Association, *Contemporary Law 1994* (Cowansville, Que.: Yvon Blais, 1994)

HUGENHOLTZ, P.B., "Implementing the European Database Directive," in J.J.C. Kabel & G.J.H.M. Mom, *Intellectual Property and Information Law: Essays in Honour of Herman Cohen Jehoram* (The Hague: Kluwer, 1998)

KRAUSS, R., *Originality of the Avant-Garde and Other Modernist Myths* (Cambridge, Mass.: MIT Press, 1985)

O'CONNOR, M.J., "Squeezing into Traditional Frames: Intellectual Property Law in the Shadow of the Information Society" (1998) 12 I.P.J. 285

---

47 *1997 Act, ibid.,* s. 79, def. "eligible performer."
48 *1997 Act, ibid.,* s. 21. See section B(3), "Broadcasts," in chapter 5.
49 *1997 Act, ibid.,* ss. 17(4), 20(2), 22, & 85.
50 *1997 Act, ibid.,* ss. 21(1)(d) & 21(3).

CHAPTER 4

TITLE AND DURATION

A. TITLE

The author owns the moral rights in a work and usually first owns the copyright, too. To market their work, however, authors may have to waive their moral rights or transfer copyright to a distributor. If the author is employed, her employer usually owns the copyright automatically, but the position with freelancers and with firms acting as independent contractors is different. Paying a freelancer or a firm does not by itself give the customer full rights to the work.[1] The livelihood of freelancers or such firms may depend on the copyright inventories they maintain. The Act therefore allocates first ownership to them, rather than to the client who hires them.[2]

Unfortunately, there is little consensus internationally on ownership rules. Most states adopt the *Berne Convention*'s rhetoric, which makes the author the central figure on the copyright stage, but then adopt legal rules or practices that quickly allow him to be pushed out

---

1   The exceptions are industrial designs and integrated circuit topographies (ICTs), where the person ordering the work under contract is the first owner of the design or ICT, whether the maker is an employee or a freelancer: *Industrial Design Act*, R.S.C. 1985, c. I-9 [*ID Act*], s. 12(1); *Integrated Circuit Topography Act*, S.C. 1990, c. 37 [*ICT Act*], s. 2(4).

2   Compare section A(3) "Changing Copyright Ownership and Implying Rights of Use," in this chapter.

of sight.[3] In the United States, for example, many freelancers can, by simple signed agreement, be assimilated to employees; so a person or a corporation ordering such a "work made for hire" from them automatically becomes both the author and the first copyright owner.[4] The U.S. owner who sues for infringement in Canada will, however, fail unless it is the owner according to Canadian law or it joins whoever is the owner.[5] This unattractive rule may no longer apply in the United States. If Canada is the country most significantly related to the copyright and the parties — for example, if the work was created in Canada by a Canadian national and first published in Canada by a Canadian company — a U.S. court has recently accepted a rule that would allocate copyright title as provided by Canadian law. Had the parties been U.S. nationals and had the events all occurred in the United States, title may well have been allocated differently by U.S. law; but that is the very reason why Canadian, not U.S., law should apply in the former case.[6] Whether this reasoning or *NAFTA* may prompt Canadian courts to take a different approach for U.S. and Mexican works from that taken to date remains to be seen.[7] Meanwhile, Canadian owners who try to enforce their copyrights abroad (at least elsewhere than in the United States) may have to comply with the foreign forum's law on ownership.[8]

---

3   *Berne Convention for the Protection of Literary and Artistic Works* (Paris, 1971), 9 September 1886, 828 U.N.T.S. 221 [*Berne*], art. 5(1); J. Seignette, *Challenges to the Creator Doctrine* (Deventer: Kluwer, 1994) [Seignette].

4   *Copyright Act*, 17 U.S.C. [*Copyright Act 1976*], ss. 101 ("work made for hire") & 201(b); similarly for ICTs in Canada (*ICT Act*, above note 1, s. 2(4)). Compare section A(1), "Author," in this chapter.

5   *Frank Brunckhorst Co. v. Gainers Inc.* (1993), 47 C.P.R. (3d) 222 (Fed. T.D.).

6   *Itar-Tass Russian News Agency v. Russian Kurier Inc.*, 153 F.3d 82 (2d Cir. 1998). It is yet unclear how far this rule will gain acceptance outside the Second Circuit (i.e., New York and part of the northeastern United States.)

7   The *North American Free Trade Agreement*, 17 December 1992, Can. T.S. 1994 No. 2 [*NAFTA*], art. 1705(3)(b), provides that "any person acquiring or holding such economic rights by virtue of a contract, including contracts of employment underlying the creation of works and sound recordings, shall be able to exercise those rights in its own name and enjoy fully the benefits derived from those rights." No amendment to the Act reflects this provision.

8   *Enzed Holdings Ltd. v. Wynthea Pty. Ltd.* (1984), 57 A.L.R. 167 at 179–81 (Austl. Fed. Ct.); Seignette, above note 3 at 74–79.

1) Author

Who is an "author"? The term compendiously describes whoever writes a book, letter, or play, as well as every other producer of creative work: scriptwriters, music composers, artists, choreographers, and computer programmers alike. But the label will not attach to someone such as a child who parrots back, albeit in her own words, a story the teacher has earlier related to the class. On such facts, an Irish court said that authorship does not involve merely "the good memory, verbal acuity, and gift of articulation of the bright child who entertainingly recounts a story she has been told."[9] Note, however, that the child, while not qualifying as an author, might qualify as a "performer," with a fifty-year copyright in her performance.[10] In practice, the line between authorship and performance will often blur. Thus, the instrumentalist or vocalist who expands on a piece of music will usually be a mere performer, but sometimes he may add or change so much as to qualify as an author or co-author of a new piece of music. The nature and degree of the additions or changes, the reaction of the first author, and expert evidence from experienced musicians and performers may help draw the line; but the result may appear arbitrary and not always satisfactory.[11]

Authorship in Canada is reserved to the individual who actually makes the work. A corporation can author a traditional work in only one case: that of a photograph. Nothing of course prevents it from being a copyright owner.[12] In fact, worldwide, the vast majority of copyrights of both traditional and non-traditional material are owned by corporations.

a) The Unoriginal Author

Some say that "author" and "original work" are "correlative; the one connotes the other."[13] It has even been said that "the word 'author' conveys a sense of creativity and ingenuity."[14] These comments are not

---

9 *Gormley* v. *EMI Records (Ireland) Ltd,* [1998] 1 I.L.R.M. 124 (Ire. H.C.), aff'd [1999] 1 I.L.R.M. 178 (Ire. S.C.).
10 See section B(11)(b), "Performances," in chapter 2.
11 *Hadley* v. *Kemp* (30 April 1999), (Ch.D.) [unreported] [*Hadley*], a dispute between members of the pop group Spandau Ballet.
12 *Massie & Renwick Ltd.* v. *Underwriters' Survey Bureau Ltd.,* [1940] S.C.R. 218 at 232–34 [*Massie & Renwick*]. See section A(4), "Sound Recordings, Performances, and Broadcasts," and section B(1)(e), "Photographs," in this chapter.
13 *Sands & McDougall Pty. Ltd.* v. *Robinson* (1917), 23 C.L.R. 49 at 55 (Austl. H.C.). See section A(1), "Originality," in chapter 3.
14 *Tele-Direct (Publications) Inc.* v. *American Business Information Inc.* (1997), 76 C.P.R. (3d) 296 at 308 (Fed. C.A.) [*Tele-Direct*].

entirely accurate, nor do they make originality a tautologous condition. The Act's reference to "author" requires the discovery and isolation of the person or persons who have actually done the original work that attracts copyright. The person who draws a straight line may be an "author," but his effort is too trivial to be called "original." Similarly, the person who uses a computer to draw or write may be an author, but the result may be unoriginal if all he does is push a couple of keys while a standard computer program does the rest.

A person who does fresh work on an existing work may claim to be author of the resulting product. So a musical arranger may claim authorship and copyright in her arrangement and sue those who infringe it, even if she failed to get clearance for her activity from the source work's copyright owner.[15]

b) Idea Providers Generally Not Authors

Copyright exists in the expression of ideas, not in the ideas themselves. An author is the person who puts ideas into their copyright form: the painter of a canvas, the sculptor of a monument, the architect of a building, or the engineer of its structural work, but not the builder who executes the architect's or the engineer's instructions.[16] "Ideas people" are generally not authors. In finding that an interviewer was the author of her notes and that the interviewee whose words were recorded was not an author at all, one court said:

> A person may have a brilliant idea for a story, or for a picture, or for a play, and one which appears to him to be original; but if he communicates that idea to an author or an artist or a playwright, the production which is the result of the communication of the idea to the author or the artist or the playwright is the copyright of the person who has clothed the idea in form, whether by means of a picture, a play, or a book, and the owner of the idea has no rights [i.e., copyright] in that product.[17]

---

15   *Redwood Music Ltd.* v. *Chappell & Co. Ltd.* (1980), [1982] R.P.C. 109 at 120 (Q.B.).

16   *New Brunswick Telephone Co.* v. *John Maryon International Ltd.* (1981), 33 N.B.R. (2d) 543 (Q.B.), varied (1982), 141 D.L.R. (3d) 193 (C.A.) [*John Maryon*].

17   *Donoghue* v. *Allied Newspapers Ltd.* (1937), [1938] 1 Ch. 106 at 109. The idea provider might, however, claim an equitable interest or constructive trust in the copyright. He or she might also have rights other than copyright — for example, those arising from an express or implied contract, or from a relationship of trust or confidence. *Gould Estate* v. *Stoddart Publishing Co.* (1998), 80 C.P.R. (3d) 161 (Ont. C.A.) [*Gould*], suggests that such cases are exceptional unless the interviewee expressly imposed conditions when consenting to the interview; but this suggestion is questionable.

A lawyer drafting an agreement on a client's instructions should be its author, even though the client has sent her specimen forms as aids. But if the lawyer simply approves or makes minor corrections to a draft the client has sent, the client should remain the author; the lawyer may be legally responsible for the document's inadequacies, but that may not make her an author, any more than a libel lawyer passing a book for publication becomes its author.[18]

c) Joint Authors

The rule that the provision of ideas can never count as authorship is coming under siege. Much work is the result of team, rather than individual, effort. Even a simple song may involve the intermingled contributions of a tunesmith, lyricist, and arranger. A collaboration of this kind may produce a work of joint authorship, with one copyright co-owned by the co-authors. If the contributions are distinct, each author has a separate copyright in her contribution.[19] The participants' conduct may help establish their relationship. So if A and B sign an exploitation agreement stating they are co-authors or, with their knowledge, are so named on their publication or in promotional material, they may be precluded from denying co-authorship, at least in any dispute between themselves.[20] Conversely, a claim of co-authorship becomes implausible where the claimant admits that co-authorship "never crossed his mind" at the time that the work was being created.[21]

What contribution warrants co-authorship may be contentious. Trivial editing is obviously not enough. Correcting punctuation, grammar, and syntax in another's manuscript before publication should not qualify; nor should providing chapter titles, suggesting a few ideas or lines, or requiring additions and alterations as part of the process of approving a work under statutory authority. The provision of interoperability criteria or beta-testing feedback for computer programs also

---

18   D. Vaver, "Copyright in Legal Documents" (1993) 31 Osgoode Hall L.J. 661 at 665–66; compare *Delrina Corp.* v. *Triolet Systems Inc.* (1993), 47 C.P.R. (3d) 1 (Ont. Gen. Div.).

19   *Copyright Act*, R.S.C. 1985, c. C-42 [*C Act*; unless otherwise indicated, references to the Act are as amended], s. 2, def. "work of joint authorship"; *Ludlow Music Inc.* v. *Canint Music Corp.*, [1967] 2 Ex. C.R. 109 at 124–25.

20   *Prior v. Lansdowne Press Pty. Ltd.* (1975), 12 A.L.R. 685 at 688 (Vic. S.C.).

21   *Land Transport Safety Authority of New Zealand v. Glogau*, [1999] 1 N.Z.L.R. 257 (C.A.) [*Glogau*].

cannot make the provider a co-author.[22] On the other hand, contributions to a work's expression that would independently create an original work are obviously enough. In between these two extremes is the case, for example, where A supplies B with all the ideas for the plot of a play and B turns them into a finished work. This collaboration has sometimes not counted as joint authorship unless A's ideas were independently copyrightable[23] — a result that may promote certainty but that still seems hard. There would have been no play at all without A's input. To elevate B's contribution and entirely discount A's may discourage some fruitful collaborations. It may also undesirably invite a minute examination and dissection of who said and did what, often long after the event when memory is unreliable. Any substantial intellectual contribution to a work's composition pursuant to a common design — not just the product of the relationship of master and scribe — should, in principle, count as co-authorship. A house designer whose detailed instructions to the drafters enabled them to draw the house plan was thus held to be a co-author with the drafters.[24]

An apparent reluctance on the part of some courts to admit joint authorship may spring partly from the romantic view of the author as Lone Genius, or from a more pragmatic desire to avoid problems that plague co-ownership generally but that are particularly acute for copyright.[25] Some of these problems are now examined.

---

22 *Dion v. Trottier* (23 July 1987), (Que. S.C.) [unreported] at 29–31; *Boudreau v. Lin* (1997), 150 D.L.R. (4th) 324 at 332–33 (Ont. Gen. Div.); *Seshadri v. Kasraian*, 130 F.3d 798 at 803 (7th Cir. 1997) [*Seshadri*]; *Fylde Microsystems Ltd. v. Key Radio Systems Ltd.*, [1998] F.S.R. 449 at 457–60 (Ch.); *Ray v. Classic FM Plc.*, [1998] F.S.R. 622 (Ch.) [*Ray*]; *Glogau, ibid.*; *Hadley*, above note 11.

23 *Kantel v. Grant*, [1933] Ex. C.R. 84; *Ashmore v. Douglas-Home* (1982), [1987] F.S.R. 553 at 560 (Ch.).

24 *Cala Homes (South) Ltd. v. Alfred McAlpine Homes East Ltd.*, [1995] F.S.R. 818 at 835–37 (Ch.) [*Cala*]; *Najma Heptulla v. Orient Longman Ltd.* (1988), [1989] F.S.R. 598 at 609 (India H.C.); *Ray*, above note 22; *Neudorf v. Nettwerk Productions Ltd.* (10 December 1999), (B.C.S.C.) [unreported] (contributions to Sarah McLachlan songs did not entitle contributor to copyright co-ownership because parties lacked common design to be co-authors). The common law could partly mitigate the results of denying co-authorship — for example, through principles of unjust enrichment, trust, confidence, or implied agreement: see *Promotivate International Inc. v. Toronto Star Newspapers Ltd.* (1985), 53 O.R. (2d) 9 (H.C.J.); *Seshadri*, above note 22.

25 B. Torno, *Ownership of Copyright in Canada* (Ottawa: Consumer & Corporate Affairs, 1981) at 63–67.

i) Co-ownership

The Act has no special provisions regulating co-ownership of copyright. Provincial law therefore governs. Co-ownership may arise not only from co-authorship but from other relationships and transactions. For example, two or more persons may become co-owners if they jointly order a photograph, engraving, or portrait for value, or if a copyright is transferred to them jointly.

In the common law provinces, there are two sorts of co-ownership for land and personal property: co-ownership "in common" and "joint ownership." An owner "in common" holds an undivided share in the property, and that share can be freely transferred without the other co-owners' consent. On the owner's death, the share goes to his estate. By contrast, "joint" owners each own the whole property indivisibly, and all must consent to any disposition. On death, a "right of survivorship" arises; the joint owner's interest disappears entirely, thus benefiting the surviving co-owner(s).

In practice, either form of co-ownership bristles with technical problems. As for co-owners in common, in what shares do they hold? If one co-author contributed more than another, does she deserve a greater share? How is "more" to be assessed, without encountering aesthetic difficulties? Even though one co-owner in common can transfer her interest without asking permission, is there any limit on the identity or number of transferees? For example, may she assign to two or more co-assignees or must she transfer only to one?[26] And what if one co-owner refuses to agree on whether or how to exploit a work? Can the court partition the property or order a sale? If there is a partition, what part goes to which owner, and how can exploitation practically occur without affecting the other owner's interest?

Some of these latter issues may be sidestepped by adopting the prevalent British rule that no co-owner may exploit the copyright by herself. Each co-owner may prevent licensing and may obtain an injunction and her share of damages or profits from infringements, even against a co-owner who tries to exploit the copyright without the consent of all other co-owners.[27] United States law, by contrast, allows one co-owner to exploit a work by non-exclusive licensing without the

---

26 The latter rule has been applied to patents, to minimize dilution of the other co-owner's rights: *Forget v. Specialty Tools of Canada Inc.* (1995), 62 C.P.R. (3d) 537 (B.C.C.A.).

27 For example, *Cescinsky v. George Routledge & Sons Ltd.*, [1916] 2 K.B. 325 at 329–30; *Redwood Music Ltd. v. B. Feldman & Co.*, [1979] R.P.C. 1 (Ch.); *Ray*, above note 22; similarly in Canada, *Massie & Renwick*, above note 12.

other co-owners' consent, subject to accounting to the others for their share of the proceeds.[28] Neither approach, if rigidly followed, is satisfactory. The British rule lets one co-owner play "dog in the manger." The U.S. rule allows her to interfere with possibly better marketing and management strategies that other co-owners wish to pursue.

Co-ownership rules were initially developed long ago in connection with the feudal system of landholding. They may work well for copyright only if one constantly remembers that copyright differs from land or other tangible property and that feudalism is no longer with us.[29] Moreover, to impose inflexible rules on a relationship is less satisfactory than to allow the relationship itself to generate the rules that should govern it. Signs of some such approach appear especially in recent case law. Thus, while joint authors or co-owners usually hold copyright in common in equal shares,[30] this presumption may be displaced. For example, where copyright in wedding photographs and portraits is co-owned by the spouses, a court inferred that their common intention was that the surviving spouse would own the whole copyright on the other's death. Treating the spouses as "joint" owners, with an automatic mutual right of survivorship, accorded with their presumed common intention.[31] Similarly, an Australian court thought that copyright in artistic works made by aboriginal band members using the band's communal knowledge should be co-owned by the band, rather than by any individual member.[32]

Transfer documents should also be interpreted without preconception so as to accord with the parties' presumed intent. "Joint" ownership should not automatically be assumed if one finds a copyright transfer made out to A and B "jointly." Ownership "in common" is more likely where the transfer is part of a business deal, especially

---

28   U.S. Senate, Subcommittee on Patents, Trademarks and Copyrights, *Joint Ownership of Copyrights* (*Study No. 12*), by G.D. Cary (U.S.: Comm. Print, 1958) at 85.

29   Such existing common or joint ownership rules as best fit that relationship could be used to achieve this goal: *Powell* v. *Head* (1879), 12 Ch.D. 686 at 688 [*Powell*]; *Lauri* v. *Renad*, [1892] 3 Ch. 402 at 412–13, aff'd *ibid.* 419 (C.A.).

30   *Powell, ibid.*; *Dixon Projects Pty. Ltd.* v. *Masterton Homes Pty. Ltd.* (1996), 36 I.P.R. 136 at 141 (Austl. Fed. Ct.).

31   *Mail Newspapers* v. *Express Newspapers* (1986), [1987] F.S.R. 90 at 93 (Ch.) [*Mail Newspapers*].

32   *Bulun Bulun* v. *R. & T. Textiles Pty. Ltd.* (1998), 41 I.P.R. 513 at 527 (Austl. Fed. Ct.) (customary law required aboriginal members to use clan knowledge with the clan's permission, and so imposed a fiduciary duty on the members and made the clan equitable owners of copyright in the resulting work).

where one of the transferees is a corporation. Ownership in common may indeed be assumed in most other situations, unless the accompanying circumstances clearly indicate a common intent that A would get the whole property on B's death despite any later desire by B to bequeath it differently.[33] It is, of course, best to avoid ambiguity by using language like "to A and B, with right of survivorship," if joint ownership is really intended. If ownership in common is intended, language like "to A and B in [equal] [60:40] shares" or "to A and B without right of survivorship" should do. Non-lawyers may nevertheless not appreciate such subtleties. Courts should then try not to thwart the parties' intent by the application of ancient precedents beyond the knowledge of most lawyers, let alone laymen.

A flexible approach may also help the resolution of disputes among co-owners. The parties' presumed common intention at the time they started collaborating is usually a sound guide, at least where their intent is not against any public policy. For example, one would usually expect joint authors of academic research to intend early publication of their data and conclusions. If one co-author disagreed about the work, she might reasonably expect that her name be removed and an appropriate disclaimer be entered on the paper. Neither co-author would intend that the other could prevent publication altogether, nor would such a ban be consistent with the public interest in having early access to the fruits of academic research. A court could therefore allow publication of the work by one co-author with appropriate disclaimers, even over the later objection of another co-author. By contrast, a jointly authored confidential document that was meant to be used for one purpose should not usually be published or exploited for a different one. All the co-authors may agree to remove the ban from themselves or from other confidants, but unanimity may not always be necessary. Suppose management employees co-author a corporate buy-out plan. Despite the initial collaboration, the group credo may be "every man for himself and Devil take the hindmost." Consistently with that ethos, any co-author may exploit the plan to her own advantage without the

---

33   *National Society for the Distribution of Electricity by Secondary Generators* v. *Gibbs*,
     [1899] 2 Ch. 289 at 299–300 (patents); *Re Sorensen & Sorensen* (1977), 90 D.L.R.
     (3d) 26 at 38–39 (Alta. C.A.). A joint will or mutual wills by joint owners may be
     effective to pass the share as intended.

consent of any other, let alone a majority, of her co-authors.[34] If, however, the group credo runs closer to the Three Musketeers' — "one for all and all for one" — the result would be different. Conceivably, all, or at least a majority, of the group would have to concur in the exploitation of the plan.

d) Photographs

An unusual ownership provision applies to photographs. The owner of the initial negative or plate (or, if none, of the photograph) is also the author and first copyright owner. The author and first owner may therefore be a corporation.[35] Presumably, the person whose photo is taken in a coin-operated automatic photograph booth is the author of the photo, since the payment made by or for her would usually cover ownership of the negative.

The Act says that the owner of the initial photograph at the time it was "made" is its author. The reference is presumably to the owner of the physical material on which the photograph was taken. Whether the photograph was then visible or not, or how it later was made visible (e.g., through use of a computer) should be irrelevant. Similarly, where the photograph derives from a negative or plate, the "making" of the initial negative or plate presumably refers to the exposure of the film by clicking the camera's shutter, not to the later processing of the film, which could occur years later by someone else at a time when the ownership of the film had changed. The owner of the film at the time of its exposure should therefore be the author of the photograph.

The rule as to who qualifies as the author of a photograph is far from standard worldwide. In Australia, for example, the author is whoever takes the shot; the identity of the owner of the physical film is irrelevant. In the United Kingdom, the author is whoever created the photograph. Depending on the circumstances, this person may be the one who takes the shot, the one who sets the scene that he directs another to shoot, or both the scene arranger and the photographer if

---

34   *Murray v. Yorkshire Fund Managers Ltd.*, [1998] 1 W.L.R. 951 at 959 (C.A.) (a breach of confidence case with copyright lurking in the wings). The legal techniques used to adjust rights between clients and freelancers may be equally used here: see section A(3)(b), "Freelancers: Implied Use Rights for Clients," in this chapter.

35   *C Act*, above note 19, s. 10(2). See section A(2)(b)(i), "Engravings, Photographs, and Portraits," in this chapter.

each collaborates in producing the final result.[36] Canada may have the worst of all possible both worlds. While the rules noted above apply to decide authorship for the purpose of allocating the first ownership of copyright, something like the U.K. rule may have to be applied to determine the duration of copyright — for example, in cases where the photographer is the majority shareholder in a corporation that owns the physical photograph or negative.[37]

e) Films

The authorship of a film — dubbed a "cinematographic work" by the Act — is not elaborated anywhere in the Act. Authorship is nonetheless relatively clear in at least one situation. For an unedited movie of live events shot before 1994, the position is the same as for photographs: the owner of the initial negative is the author, as the movie was then considered merely a series of photographs.[38] Such movies are now classed as dramatic works, even if their "arrangement or acting form or the combination of incidents represented [do not] give the work a dramatic character."[39] Their author would presumably be whoever shoots the film, for he or she is the "effective cause of the representation when completed."[40] Whether scenes taken by an automatic surveillance camera are authored by anyone is doubtful: the person responsible for positioning the camera is no Atom Egoyan. Such authorless films may have no copyright at all.[41]

The question of who can be called the author of a regular commercial movie, cartoon, or television drama has rarely been litigated in

---

36 *Creation Records Ltd.* v. *News Group Newspapers Ltd.* (1997), 39 I.P.R. 1 at 5–6 (Ch.) [*Creation*]; *Ateliers Tango argentin Inc.* v. *Festival d'Espagne et d'Amérique latine Inc.*, [1997] R.J.Q. 3030 (S.C.) [*Ateliers Tango*].

37 See section B(1)(e)(iii), "Photographer-Owned Corporations," in this chapter.

38 *Canadian Admiral Corp.* v. *Rediffusion Inc.*, [1954] Ex. C.R. 382 at 401 [*Canadian Admiral*]; *North American Free Trade Agreement Implementation Act,* S.C. 1993, c.44, s. 75(2).

39 *C Act*, above note 19, s. 11.1. See section B(5)(a), "Film, Video, and Formats," in chapter 2.

40 Compare *Nottage* v. *Jackson* (1883), 11 Q.B.D. 627 at 637 (C.A.) [*Nottage*], on old-time photography.

41 Such films can now be protected in the United Kingdom without proof of originality. The person making the necessary arrangements for the taking of the film is there fictionally deemed to be the author: *Copyright, Designs and Patents Act*, 1988 (U.K.), c. 48, ss. 1(1)(b), 5(2), 9(2)(a); *Hyde Park Residence Ltd.* v. *Yelland*, [1999] R.P.C. 655 (Ch.), protecting videotape and stills taken from a security camera recording the last visit of Princess Diana and Dodi Al Fayed to the Al Fayed home in Paris.

Canada. Such works — unlike the products of the amateur with a handycam — do have an original "dramatic character" resulting from their "arrangement or acting form or the combination of incidents represented." In principle, therefore, the author should be whoever was responsible for creating this original dramatic character.[42] This person will usually be the director.

This result, although not stated specifically in the Act, is most consistent with the principles of copyright as they have developed in Canada. The comparison with building construction is instructive. The architect who gives a building its artistically distinctive design characteristics is recognized as its author. Neither the bank that finances the project nor the builder who follows the architect's plan and organizes the trades does any act of authorship. Neither has a copyright interest in the finished building.[43] Similarly, with a film, the director creates its overall design and original dramatic character. He may be a different person from the "maker" of a cinematographic work, whom the Act elsewhere defines as the person who undertakes the arrangements necessary for the making of the film. If such arrangements involve merely raising finance and organizing the production, without the input of any relevant intellectual creativity into the film itself, the maker cannot be an author, or even a co-author with the film's director.[44] Similarly, the various people who produce the numerous elements that are incorporated into a film are not authors of the final product and have no copyright interest in it. Such people may have individual copyrights in their creative contributions — for example, in scripts, screenplays, camera work, set design, music, and soundtracks. But a movie is more than the sum of these parts. Its copyright is different from the copyright of the elements incorporated into it. Its authorship is different from that of the initial creators of these elements.[45] The copyrights in the elements may often end up, by contract or transfer, in the hands of the "maker" of the film, but that is a different issue.

This analysis of the Canadian position does not necessarily hold elsewhere. The *Berne Convention* has no mandatory rule. So, for example, in the United States, a film is considered to be jointly authored by those who work on it; but, in practice, the movie studio becomes the first

---

42   *Australian Olympic Committee Inc.* v. *The Big Fights Inc.*, [1999] F.C.A. 1042, para. 42 (Austl. Fed. Ct.), reaches this conclusion on the comparable U.K. 1911 Act.

43   *John Maryon*, above note 16 at 244 (D.L.R.).

44   *C Act*, above note 19, s. 2, def. "maker"; compare s. 2.11. A maker may be a corporation. Under the Act, the maker's identity is relevant only to qualify a work for Canadian copyright: ss. 5(1)(b) & 34.1(2)(c).

45   *Jean-Claude Chehade Inc.* v. *Films Rachel Inc.*, [1995] A.Q. 1550 (Que. S.C.).

author through the peculiar U.S. rule that makes the employer of creative workers both the owner and the author of their work. In the United Kingdom, the person who in Canada is called the film's "maker" is there by legislation called its author, with the principal director being deemed to be a co-author. More generally in Europe, the principal director of a film is its author, but co-authorship is permitted and is quite common. Thus, co-authorship is presumed in France. There, the screenplay writer, the author of the adaptation from any work on which the film is based, the author of any such pre-existing work, the author of the dialogue, and the author of any music specially composed for the film may count among the film's co-authors. Even this list is not exhaustive, for any individual adding intellectual creativity to the film may be admitted.[46]

The French approach, with its detailed legislative provision on the modalities of authorship, may appear inconvenient to some observers, in that the definition of what is creative and what is not often seems blurry. Is the contribution of the lighting technician always merely technical or may it sometimes, even often, be considered to be creative? It seems possible for virtually anyone on (or perhaps even off) the long list of credits at the end of the typical commercial movie to show some creative contribution that may warrant a finding of co-authorship. The preferable Canadian position suggested above, though simple, results in only one person qualifying as the author of a cinematographic work (except in cases of co-directorship). Issues of ownership, duration of copyright, and moral rights are therefore more straightforwardly resolved than where co-authorship is involved.[47]

Ultimately, these variants may derive less from pure logic than from pragmatic considerations and the underlying social and economic factors of a particular country's film industry and cultural aspirations.

2) Ownership of Copyright

The author usually first owns the copyright of any work she creates, including preparatory and unfinished material,[48] and may transfer the right by written assignment as she wishes.[49] The author may, however, not be the first owner where she is an employee or where she is commissioned to create certain classes of work.

---

46   M. Salokannel, *Ownership of Rights in Audiovisual Productions: A Comparative Study* (The Hague: Kluwer, 1997) at 120, 135–36.

47   See section A(1)(c), "Joint Authors," in this chapter.

48   *Art Direction Ltd. v. USP Needham (N.Z.) Ltd.*, [1977] 2 N.Z.L.R. 12 at 18 (S.C.).

49   *C Act*, above note 19, s. 13(1). See section B(2), "Assignments," in chapter 8.

a) Employees

An author who is employed under a contract of service or apprentice-ship, and makes a work in the course of that employment or appren-ticeship, does not usually first own the copyright. Instead, her employer does. This standard position may, however, be changed by agreement.[50]

The standard position squares with the common expectation under capitalist modes of production. A person hired to produce material as part of her work normally expects copyright to be her employer's; for, without the hire, the work would probably not have been produced at all. Where expectations are different or the work would have been pro-duced anyway, it would be consistent with copyright policy to leave ownership with the author.

i) Contract of Service

The employer first owns the copyright only if the author is employed under a contract of service. The author must be an employee, not a freelancer. This distinction involves interpreting the parties' relation-ship according to familiar principles of labour law. As more employees work from home and many consultants come to the workplace, the actual site where work is done tells little about whether the worker is an employee or a freelancer. Instead, the hiring contract and the surround-ing circumstances must be examined to see how the worker is treated. If she is called an employee and treated as part of the staff, is paid a salary with income tax deducted at source, is given pension and other benefits, has to attend staff meetings or report on how she spends her time, the worker will probably be found to be an employee. The fewer such fac-tors are present, the more likely the worker will be found to be a freelancer, who *prima facie* owns the copyright in her work product.[51]

Prisoners: Establishing a worker's status has been likened to deter-mining the subject of an impressionist painting which is built up from

---

50   *Ibid.*, s. 13(3) (apprentices are not separately considered). See section A(3), "Changing Copyright Ownership and Implying Rights of Use," in this chapter; generally, see also K. Puri, "Copyright and Employment in Australia" (1996) 27 I.I.C. 53, where similar principles apply.

51   For other factors, see the standard labour law cases. Copyright cases include *Goldner* v. *Canadian Broadcasting Corp.* (1972), 7 C.P.R. (2d) 158 at 161–62 (Fed. T.D.) (television consultant not employee); *Stephenson Jordan & Harrison Ltd.* v. *MacDonald & Evans* (1951), [1952] 1 T.L.R. 101 (C.A.) [*Stephenson*] (management consultant partly employee, partly freelancer); *Community for Creative Non-violence* v. *Reid*, 490 U.S. 730 (1989) (sculptor freelancer); *Ray*, above note 22 (music consultant freelancer). See also Y. Gendreau, "La titularité des droits sur les logiciels créés par un employé" (1995) 12 Can. Intell. Prop. Rev. 147 at 149ff.

an accumulation of detail.[52] Unfortunately, such a painting may strike different viewers differently. Thus, the inmate of a federal penitentiary was recently held to be not only an involuntary tenant of Her Majesty but also (unbeknownst to him) her employee too — paid $6 a day. The government of Canada therefore owned the copyright in a painting he had done as part of his rehabilitation, as well as the painting itself. After serving his time and opening an art business, the painter was not allowed even to photograph the work for his portfolio![53]

Australia has adopted a rather more sensible approach in the analogous case of patents. Two prisoners, who had developed an invention during their confinement, were found to be the legal owners of the resulting patent. The allowance they were paid was not equated with wages or salary. They were not employees, since employment is a relationship freely entered into with contractual intent. Imprisonment involves no bargain; its terms are imposed. The prison could not therefore claim any interest in the patents by calling inmates employees and by asserting that any creative or inventive work they did during rehabilitation was really a service arising from employment. Personal intellectual property rights do not stop at the prison gate.[54]

One-person corporations: Problems of copyright ownership also arise in cases involving senior officers of corporations, especially presidents or chief executives of closely held companies. These officers sometimes do not reduce to writing their status or obligations to the corporation, which they often regard as their *alter ego* or instrument. The officer will also usually be an employee of the company, whether or not a written contract of service exists. Copyright in most work produced for the company's benefit will therefore be owned by the company, as is also true for comparable work done by lower-level employees. Thus, the copyright in design and art work produced for the business in the course of running a one-person corporation is typically owned outright by the corporation.[55] The entrepreneur who tries to have it both ways — to benefit from the limited liability that incorporation

---

52   *Hall (Inspector of Taxes)* v. *Lorimer,* [1992] 1 W.L.R. 939 at 944 (Ch.), aff'd (1993), [1994] 1 W.L.R. 209 (C.A.).

53   *Hawley* v. *Canada* (1990), 30 C.P.R. (3d) 534 (Fed. T.D.) [*Hawley*].

54   *Kwan* v. *Queensland Corrective Services Commission* (1994), 31 I.P.R. 25 (Austl. P.O.). I am indebted to Professor Kamal Puri for this reference.

55   *Netupsky* v. *Dominion Bridge Co. Ltd.* (1969), 5 D.L.R. (3d) 195 at 213 (B.C.C.A.), rev'd on other grounds (1971), [1972] S.C.R. 368; *Centre de Location Ravary (Laval) Ltée* v. *Télé-Direct (Publications) Inc.,* [1995] R.J.Q. 1245 at 1249 (S.C.); *Gardex Ltd.* v. *Sorata Ltd.,* [1986] R.P.C. 623 at 640–41 (Ch.); *Hutchison Personal Communications Ltd.* v. *Hook Advertising Ltd.,* [1996] F.S.R. 549 at 557 (Ch.).

offers, while trying to keep, on bankruptcy, all the intellectual property generated within the corporation — will face some daunting obstacles.[56]

ii) Work Produced in the Course of Employment

Not everything an employee does for her employer is necessarily done "in the course of [her] employment" under her contract. The contract may not compel a work to be created at all or in a form that attracts copyright. A worker who then chooses to produce in that form does so outside the course of her employment. The copyright may then be hers. Two questions are relevant: (1) Would the worker have broken her contract by not producing the work in the form she did? (2) Would the acquisition or retention of copyright by the worker be inconsistent with her duty of good faith and loyalty to her employer? If either question is answered yes, the employer should own the copyright. If both questions are answered no, the copyright belongs to the worker.

The standard case applying these principles involved the *Financial Times* of England and one of its journalists. The *Times* asked its employee, after receiving bids from him and others, to translate an advertisement from Portuguese into English for the paper. The employee did so outside office hours for an agreed fee. The advertisement ran with the translator's byline, but was lifted by another newspaper with the advertiser's consent. The translator won substantial damages for infringement against the second paper. He, not the *Financial Times*, owned the copyright in his translation. The work had been done under a separate contract outside the journalist's regular employment contract.[57]

iii) Employees in the Educational Sector

The application of these principles in one sector, education, is illuminating not only because employees there often produce job-related work indifferently at home or at their place of employment, but also because the applicable principles there may carry over equally to other sectors.

The issue of who owns the copyright — the employer, the employee, or both — should first be approached by looking at the contract of employment. Parties are free to negotiate whatever allocation of copyright they wish. This negotiation often occurs through collective agreement or through written policies developed by institutions, often in consultation with their employees. Any applicable binding agreement will govern the situation. Unwritten or implied agreements and customs can also be effective. For example, all persons in an institution

---

56   *Orwin v. A-G.,* [1998] F.S.R. 415 (C.A.).
57   *Byrne v. Statist Co.,* [1914] 1 K.B. 622 [*Byrne*].

may understand — without the need for a written policy — that they have no legal interest in such things as committee reports and minutes; the copyright in these items will therefore belong to the institution. Such an understanding, once proved, can amount to an implied agreement that is as effective as a signed written contract.

The contract of employment is important even if it says nothing about copyright, for it may indicate what the employee's job obligations are. Suppose a researcher is hired as an employee specifically to produce a teaching manual. This work would be produced "in the course of his employment," because the researcher is contractually bound to produce it. The copyright will therefore belong to the employing institution.

Suppose, however, that a high school teacher, using the school's facilities, writes a manual for her students or school, or for more general publication. Unless her contract (unusually) required her to write manuals, the activity is carried on, consistently with her duty of good faith to her employer, outside the course of her employment. Whether she decided to work of her own accord or at the urging of her principal is irrelevant: either way, the copyright is hers, not the school's.[58] Had the principal asked the teacher to write the manual for money, the work would likely be considered to have been done under a separate contract. Like the *Financial Times* translator,[59] the teacher would, in effect, be acting as a freelancer on this project. She should own the copyright, unless a different agreement was negotiated or could clearly be inferred from past dealings or understandings.

This analysis holds true of lecture notes or course books produced by teachers or professors. Her employment contract may compel an educator to teach, but it leaves how she does that — spontaneously, from jotted notes, or from fully prepared text — entirely up to her. The copyright in any lecture notes or text she prepares should *prima facie* be hers. Educators can therefore object to the unauthorized publication of any notes that students take in class. Such a publication may infringe the educator's copyright and may also breach the implied obligation, arising from the student-teacher relationship, that notes are intended only for the student's own education.[60] This rule allocating copyright to

---

58   *Hays* v. *Sony Corp. of America*, 847 F.2d 412 at 417 (7th Cir. 1988) [*Hays*].

59   *Byrne*, above note 57.

60   H.S. Bloom, "The Teacher's Copyright in His Teaching Materials" (1973) 12 J. Soc. Pub. T.L. 333 at 341; *Caird* v. *Sime* (1887), 12 App. Cas. 326 (H.L.); *Stephenson*, above note 51; *Williams* v. *Weisser*, 78 Cal. R. 542 (2d Dist. 1969); *Noah* v. *Shuba*, [1991] F.S.R. 14 (Ch.) [*Noah*]; *Greater Glasgow Health Board's Application* (1995), [1996] R.P.C. 207 at 222–24 (Pat. Ct.) (applying copyright approach to patents).

the educator can also be supported for policy reasons. Were the copyright the employer's, incentives for the production of worthy work would be reduced; employers would receive a windfall; employee mobility would be reduced, for educators could not effectively deploy their expertise elsewhere once they lost copyright in their course material to their institution; and employers, who typically are responsible for preparing job descriptions, can always bargain for a different result.

The copyright in scholarly articles, textbooks, treatises, and artwork produced by faculty members in educational institutions also belongs initially to the member. Take the university professor whose job is to teach copyright law. His contract may oblige him also to do research, but he usually breaks no obligation of his contract if he does not publish (although he risks losing promotion, tenure, or contract renewal). Similarly, he breaks no contract or obligation of good faith to his employer by writing fiction or newspaper articles, or by drawing and publishing cartoons, on the side. The copyright in all this work belongs to the professor, not his institution, unless the parties have agreed differently.[61]

Copyright also affects students. Students obviously own the copyright in original papers and theses that they submit for course and degree requirements.[62] This ownership should hold true even where the student has a job outside the university and brings his experience into his writing; the external employer should not usually have any copyright claim in the student's work. What is true for the externally employed student also holds true for students who are internally employed as research assistants by a university or an individual professor. The student who simultaneously writes up her research as part of her thesis owns copyright in the thesis, because this work is not part of her research contract. The professor for whom the student worked may have provided the inspiration, but that gives him no right to treat the thesis as his own. Without the student's consent, the professor cannot publish an abridged version under his own name; nor may he deliver it at a conference, unless he is a joint author and a common intention to allow such an act can be inferred.[63]

---

61   *Ibid.*; also *Hays*, above note 58, and *Weinstein v. University of Illinois*, 811 F.2d 1091 at 1094 (7th Cir. 1987), both authored by former law professors at the University of Chicago (Easterbrook and Posner JJ.).

62   *Breen v. Hancock House Publishers Ltd.* (1985), 6 C.I.P.R. 129 (Fed. T.D.); *Boudreau v. Lin* (1997), 150 D.L.R. (4th) 324 at 334 (Ont. Gen. Div.) [*Boudreau*].

63   *Goswami v. Hammons* (29 October 1982), (Ch.) [unreported], aff'd (1985) 129 Sol. Jo. 653 (C.A.); *Boudreau*, above note 62; section A(1)(c)(i), "Co-ownership," in this chapter.

The educational institution will usually own copyright in committee reports, minutes, and administrative memoranda produced by its employees. It may also own other copyrights. Thus, a university was held to own copyright in computer programs developed by programmers employed in the university's computer lab who were using the university's time and facilities. Their work was authorized by the lab director, who intended to exploit the programs privately and rewarded the programmers separately. Although the director may have been entitled, with the university's knowledge, to carry on such outside activities for personal profit, nothing displaced the presumption that the copyright in the programs belonged to his employer, the university.[64] He could not therefore rely on a university policy that entitled him to acquire copyright in programs developed on the side. To change this position, the employees would, presumably, have had to have agreed more explicitly before the event with their employer that they would own the copyright in any future programs developed by them.

A university, like any other employer, may therefore hold copyright in work done by its employees in breach of their obligation of good faith or loyalty to their employer. The work may be treated as having been done in the course of employment under the employee's contract of service, just as an employee who breaks work rules can still be found to be acting in the course of his employment if he carelessly injures someone. If the work is jointly authored with someone who owes no comparable duty of loyalty to the employer, the latter will be entitled only to the copyright share that the defaulting employee would otherwise have held.

iv) Journalist Employees

Copyright law treats journalist employees differently in one respect from other employees. For articles or other contributions (e.g., cartoons) to a newspaper, magazine, or similar periodical, the author retains "a right to restrain" publication of the work otherwise than as part of a newspaper, magazine, or similar periodical. This appears to be only a right of veto. The author has no positive right to publish. Still, unless the journalist has waived the right, the employer or any other

---

64   *Hanis* v. *Teevan* (1998), 162 D.L.R. (4th) 414 at 428–32 (Ont. C.A.), rev'g [1995] O.J. 981 (Gen. Div.) (a somewhat surprising result, if the employer knew of and acquiesced in the employee's "moonlighting"). See also *Electrolux Ltd.* v. *Hudson*, [1977] F.S.R. 312 at 326 (Ch.) (patents); compare *Missing Link Software* v. *Magee*, [1989] 1 F.S.R. 361 at 367 (Ch.).

person may be unable to republish the work in book or any other non-periodical form (e.g., on an electronic database) without first coming to terms with the author. Cartoonists may also use their right of veto to reap some benefit from their characters' popularity on T-shirts and other bric-à-brac.[65]

b) Commissioned Works

i) Engravings, Photographs, and Portraits

Freelancers usually first own copyright in work they produce, even on order. A special rule, however, applies to ordered engravings, photographs, and portraits. If the original, or the negative or matrix from which it derives, is created by a freelancer to fulfil an order given for valuable consideration, the customer is the first copyright owner of the work, any images made from it, and any preparatory material.[66] This rule includes cases where the customer is liable to pay a reasonable price because she has impliedly requested the work. Someone who asks that his photograph be taken does not automatically get the copyright; this happens only if he became expressly or impliedly liable to pay for the original or the prints. Just making oneself available for a photo session may not be enough.[67] With wedding photos, the bride or groom who places the order with the photographer usually does so for both of them. The copyright may then be owned jointly by the spouses.[68]

Material ordered from 1 July 1998 comes under a new rule. The promised consideration must actually be "paid" before the customer becomes the first owner of the copyright.[69] This provision was a late amendment to the bill that became the *1997 Act* and seems ill-considered. It is not evenhanded, as it treats unpaid freelancers better than unpaid employees. It presupposes that all consideration consists of

65   *C Act*, above note 19, s. 13(3); *Sun Newspapers Ltd.* v. *Whippie* (1928), 28 S.R. (N.S.W.) 473 (Eq. Ct.). Compare *De Garis* v. *Neville Jeffress Pidler Pty. Ltd.* (1990), 18 I.P.R. 292 (Austl. Fed. Ct.); K. Puri, "Journalists' Copyright in Australia" (1994) 9 I.P.J. 90.

66   *C Act*, ibid., s. 13(2); *James Arnold & Co. Ltd.* v. *Miafern Ltd.*, [1980] R.P.C. 397 at 403–4 (Ch.) [*Arnold*]; *Planet Earth Productions Inc.* v. *Rowlands* (1990), 73 O.R. (2d) 505 (H.C.J.). This position can be modified by simple agreement: see section A(3), "Changing Copyright Ownership and Implying Rights of Use," in this chapter.

67   *Sasha Ltd.* v. *Stoenesco* (1929), 45 T.L.R. 350 (Ch.); *Arnold*, ibid. at 404.

68   *Mail Newspapers*, above note 31. See section A(1)(c)(i), "Co-ownership," in this chapter.

69   *C Act*, above note 19, s. 13(2), as amended by *An Act to Amend the Copyright Act*, S.C. 1997, c. 24 [*1997 Act*], s. 10(1); P.C. 1998-364, 132 Can. Gaz. (Pt. II) 1149.

money, which is not so. The provision leaves unclear whether a freelancer may waive payment (presumably he may). The provision also suggests that two different people can be "first" owners: the freelancer so long as he is unpaid, and the customer once the freelancer is paid. So if, before payment, the copyright is disposed of by the freelancer, his trustee in bankruptcy, or a sheriff seizing it to satisfy a judgment debt, does title stay where it is if the customer pays later, or does it then vest in the customer?

Freelancers sometimes think that, because they own the copyright, they can do what they like with a work. This view is not true. For example, a photographer has no business giving or selling prints or negatives of commissioned photographs to a newspaper, where the subjects later come into the public limelight. Conduct like this, while not infringing copyright, may violate a duty of confidentiality, privacy, or implied contractual obligation of exclusivity owed to the subject or the customer, and may expose the photographer and possibly the newspaper to an injunction and damages.[70] Conversely, Glenn Gould's estate could not stop the use of photographs of the pianist in a biography about him. Gould had not imposed any conditions on the use of the photographs when the shots were taken for a magazine article. The photographer could therefore reuse or license reuse of the photographs for other purposes.[71] The court deciding the case, however, went too far in suggesting that Gould had no right to complain of any use that might be made of the photographs. The photographer could not, for example, have licensed advertisers to use the photographs to endorse a product. Had this been done, Gould could have sued both the photographer and the advertiser for damages and an injunction.[72]

---

70 *Pollard* v. *Photographic Co.* (1888), 40 Ch.D. 345; see also *Cala*, above note 24 at 836 (drafter producing design for home builder). British Columbia, Manitoba, Newfoundland, Quebec, and Saskatchewan have special privacy legislation that might also be violated by such actions: see, for example, in Quebec, *Aubry* v. *Éditions Vice-Versa Inc.* (1998), 78 C.P.R. (3d) 289 (S.C.C.). In Ontario, such action may breach a common law right of privacy: *Saccone* v. *Orr* (1981), 34 O.R. (2d) 317 (Co. Ct.).

71 *Gould*, above note 17.

72 For example, *Krouse* v. *Chrysler Canada Ltd.* (1973), 1 O.R. (2d) 225 (C.A.); *Athans* v. *Canadian Adventure Camps Ltd.* (1977), 34 C.P.R. (2d) 126 (Ont. H.C.); *Joseph* v. *Daniels* (1986), 11 C.P.R. (3d) 544 (B.C.S.C.). The trial judge in *Gould*, *ibid.*, thought that a product endorsement occurring after Gould's death could have been stopped by his estate (but this point is still unsettled in Canada).

ii) Government Work

Federal, provincial, and municipal governments, as well as Crown corporations, may own and acquire copyrights, just as any private employer may. Thus, the copyrights in work produced by municipal employees as part of their duties belong to the municipality. The copyright in such disparate material as departmental memoranda, cabinet or policy documents, prison manuals, and, more dubiously, artwork produced by a federal prisoner as part of his rehabilitation also has been held to belong to the government as employer.[73]

The Act also vests copyright ownership of any work prepared or published "by or under the direction or control of Her Majesty or any government department" in the federal or provincial government.[74] This provision avoids the need to identify the relevant author or authors. It has caught artwork produced by employees or commissioned from freelancers, and reports written by government employees and published under the aegis of their departments.[75] Apart from such obvious cases, it is difficult to know what this provision is supposed to cover. Its obscurity has often been criticized and it was eventually dropped from the 1988 U.K. legislation. The tendency is to interpret "direction or control" narrowly. So a work is not made under the government's direction or control simply because the government can demand changes, veto publication, or refuse to accept the work for any reason.[76] Extraordinarily, however, the government may own copyright in a freelance work that is published, although not prepared, under its direction or control.[77] To avoid such unexpected results, freelancers dealing with government departments must be constantly vigilant to ensure that the copyright status of any commissioned work is clearly defined.

---

73   For example, *Ontario (A.G.) v. Gowling & Henderson* (1984), 47 O.R. (2d) 449 (H.C.J.); *Australia v. John Fairfax & Sons Ltd.* (1980), 147 C.L.R. 39 (Austl. H.C.) [*Fairfax*]; *Hawley*, above note 53.

74   *C Act*, above note 19, s. 12; B. Torno, *Crown Copyright in Canada: A Legacy of Confusion* (Ottawa: Consumer & Corporate Affairs, 1981). This position can be modified by simple agreement: see section A(3), "Changing Copyright Ownership and Implying Rights of Use," in this chapter.

75   *Kerr v. R.* (1982), 66 C.P.R. (2d) 165 (Fed. T.D.) [*Kerr*]; *R. v. James Lorimer & Co.*, [1984] 1 F.C. 1065 at 1069 (C.A.) [*James Lorimer*].

76   *Glogau*, above note 21; *Kalamazoo Ltd. v. Systems Africa Ltd.*, [1973] East Africa L.R. 242 at 244–45 (Kenya H.C.), rev'd on other grounds [1974] East Africa L.R. 21 (Kenya C.A.); D. Vaver, "Copyright and the State in Canada and the United States" (1996) 10 I.P.J. 187, 190–92 [Vaver, "State"]

77   *Ironside v. A.G.*, [1988] R.P.C. 197 at 202–3 (Ch.).

In addition, "any rights or privileges of the Crown" are specifically preserved.[78] This language refers to the government's prerogative power to control publishing. In seventeenth-century Britain, when talk of treason and sedition was rife, the power was asserted as a form of censorship over everything published. Three centuries later, a Canadian court gave this power a more limited range. It now encompassed only "a somewhat miscellaneous collection of works, no catalogue of which appears to be exhaustive."[79] One of the most important items today may be legislation. Both the provincial and the federal governments continue to claim a perpetual monopoly in statutes, proclamations, orders in council, and regulations.[80] This monopoly may operate loosely in practice, as legislation is made available online and on compact disk, and what users do with it becomes less traceable.

It is interesting to note that the Crown today still claims a prerogative power over publishing judicial decisions. The power may be exercised through delegates such as provincial law societies. The idea may have seemed plausible when the monarch claimed to rule by divine right and the publication of judicial proceedings in the House of Lords was punishable as a contempt of Parliament. It seems less plausible today, especially in light of the untrammelled rise of private law reporting in Britain since at least the mid-eighteenth century. No European state, other than the United Kingdom, Eire, and Italy, claims to protect "official texts of a legislative, administrative and legal nature, and . . . official translations of such texts."[81] Nor does the United States. Judges there have since the nineteenth century asserted that the people's laws belong to the people. In the United States, there is therefore no copyright on federal and state court opinions and legislation as a matter of public policy.[82] U.S. copyright may, however, exist

---

78   *C Act*, above note 19, s. 12.

79   *R. v. Bellman*, [1938] 3 D.L.R. 548 at 553 (N.B.C.A.) (hydrographic and admiralty charts of the Bay of Fundy).

80   Upheld in *New South Wales (A.G.) v. Butterworth & Co. (Australia) Ltd.* (1938), 38 S.R. (N.S.W.) 195 (Eq. Ct.), although the New South Wales government recently waived its rights over this material and s. 182A of the *Copyright Act*, 1968 (Austl.) now allows limited reprographic copying of legislation and judgments.

81   *Berne*, above note 3, art. 2(4); see also J.A.L. Sterling, "Crown Copyright in the United Kingdom and Other Commonwealth Countries" (1996) 10 I.P.J. 157. As from 27 October 1999, U.K. copyright in legislation is waived if accuracy is maintained: see HMSO Guidance Note 6 at <www.hmso.gov.uk/guides.htm>.

82   This policy may, however, not extend to assertions of copyright in such material outside the United States: Vaver, "State," above note 76.

in added value such as headnotes, annotations, indexes, and compilations, but probably not pagination.[83]

The U.S. and majority European position seems more compatible with the idea of a modern democracy. When or whether Canada's provincial governments will eventually see things this way is a matter for speculation. The federal government led the way in 1997 by allowing anyone to reproduce federal legislation and the judgments of federal courts (including the Supreme Court of Canada) and federal administrative tribunals, so long as the copy is not distorted or represented to be an official version.[84] In 1999 Ontario announced that it will follow suit, but Quebec still seems determined to maintain its monopoly.[85]

3) Changing Copyright Ownership and Implying Rights of Use

Copyright may always be transferred by written assignment.[86] Two special cases where this rule is qualified should be noted.

a) Changing First Ownership by Simple Agreement

First ownership may be varied by simple agreement in the three situations just discussed: employees; government works; and freelance engravings, photographs, and portraits. So the *prima facie* rule that an employer owns the copyright in works employees produce on the job can be changed with no formality at all before the work is begun or even (possibly) completed. An oral agreement may work; so may an agreement implied or inferred from conduct. No special rules govern the terms and duration of the agreement, which needs to be established according to standard common or civil law principles. The person

---

83   *Howell* v. *Miller*, 91 F. 129 (6th Cir. 1898) (state statutes); *Banks* v. *Manchester,* 128 U.S. 244 (1888); *Callaghan* v. *Myers*, 128 U.S. 617 (1888) (judicial decisions); *Matthew Bender & Co.* v. *West Publishing Co.*, 158 F.3d 693 (2d Cir. 1998), allowing scanning of judgments (without copying headnotes or arrangement) from West law reports into electronic database, not following *West Publishing Co.* v. *Mead Data Central Inc.*, 799 F.2d 1219 (8th Cir. 1986), cert. denied 479 U.S. 1070 (1987); see also L. Patterson & C. Joyce, "Monopolizing the Law: The Scope of Copyright Protection for Law Reports and Statutory Compilations" (1989) 36 U.C.L.A. L. Rev. 719.

84   Section B(1)(d), "Federal Law and Court Judgments," in chapter 7.

85   *Wilson & Lafleur Ltée* v. *Société québécoise d'information juridique*, [1998] A.Q. 2762 (S.C.)

86   See section B, "Assignments and Licences," in chapter 8.

alleging a variation from the standard position established by the Act carries the burden of proving the variation.[87]

One major area where copyright ownership is often reallocated in this way is in the business of photography. Independent studios may, for example, have their customers sign an agreement allocating copyright to the studio, to prevent rival studios from making cheaper prints and enlargements from the negatives. In a recent interesting case, a freelance photographer took a photograph of Member of Parliament Sheila Copps at the request of *Saturday Night* magazine. The photograph turned up on the cover of the magazine and the photographer was duly paid. The *Toronto Star* newspaper later reproduced the magazine cover, without anyone's consent, for a story it ran on Copps. The photographer sued the *Star*. The court accepted evidence of a trade custom — an implied agreement contrary to the standard position — under which freelancers doing such media work continued to own copyright in their work. In ordinary circumstances, *Saturday Night* could use the photo once, but would have to get the freelancer's consent for reuse and pay customary reuse fees. However, an appeal court held, somewhat charitably, that the *Star* could rely on a fair dealing defence to avoid payment. Without such a defence, it would have had to pay the photographer damages for infringing his copyright.[88]

b) Freelancers: Implied Use Rights for Clients

Many people contracting with freelancers are but dimly aware, if at all, of their copyright position. They may think that, having paid for the work, they can do what they like with it — that they own the full copyright. Firms paying for a computer program to be upgraded have sometimes been surprised to find that the programmer owns the copyright on the upgrade and can even sell it to the firm's competitors.[89] Courts have sometimes tried, within the Act's framework, to avoid such results and to produce instead an outcome that meets their perception of the parties' expectations and the equities of the situation. Techniques such as express or implied agreements, trusts, estoppels, waivers, implied licences, proved trade custom, and finding the client to be a joint copyright owner have all been used. For example, engineers or architects hired to produce plans for a building usually keep their

---

87   *Noah*, above note 60 at 25–27.

88   *Allen v. Toronto Star Newspapers Ltd.* (1997), 152 D.L.R. (4th) 518 (Ont. Div. Ct.), rev'g (1995), 63 C.P.R. (3d) 517 (Ont. Gen. Div.). See section B(11), "Fair Dealing," in chapter 7.

89   *Amusements Wiltron Inc. v. Mainville* (1991), 40 C.P.R. (3d) 521 at 525ff (Que. S.C.).

arrangement either in-house through its employees or through independent contractors.

Who made the record and who undertook the arrangements necessary for its making are both factual questions. Suppose a record company hires a freelancer to make a record. Paying him and giving him his working instructions can amount to undertaking "the arrangements necessary" for the making of the record. Other variants are possible. When the British ice-skating duo Torvill and Dean asked their agent — an employee of their service corporation — to have two musical works recorded for them to use in their routines, the freelancer who was hired by the corporation for a flat fee was held to "make" the record. There was more to making a record than ensuring the tape was running while the music played. The freelancer had commissioned and paid for appropriate arrangements of the music. He also had hired and paid musicians, a studio, and technicians to turn out the end-product under his direction. All this activity was part of making the record. But it was the service corporation that had undertaken the arrangements necessary for the making to occur. The corporation was therefore the copyright owner, and it could prevent the unauthorized marketing of a video of the skaters' performance that included the recorded music.[98]

b) Performances

A performer is the first owner of the copyright and of the rights of remuneration in his or her performance.[99] The Act does not define "performer." Anyone treated as a performer under the *Rome Convention* presumably qualifies. The list there includes "actors, singers, musicians, dancers, and other persons who act, sing, deliver, declaim, play in, or otherwise perform" literary, dramatic, artistic, or musical works.[100] The material may be in or out of copyright, or it may be improvised and thus apparently incapable of having copyright as a "work" because it is not fixed in a tangible form.[101]

The list in the *Rome Convention* is not exhaustive. The conductor and her orchestra or choir, the television announcer reading the news, the comedian executing her patter are all obviously performers. Equally obviously, the football or baseball player is not a performer

---

98   A. & M. Records Ltd. v. *Video Collection International Ltd.*, [1995] E.M.L.R. 25 (Ch.).

99   *C Act*, above note 19, ss. 24(a) & 26(1).

100   *Rome Convention for the Protection of Performers, Producers of Phonograms and Broadcasting Organisations* (26 October 1961) [*Rome*], art. 3(a).

101   *C Act*, above note 19, s. 2, def. "performer's performance." See section A(2), "Fixation," in chapter 3.

because no "work" is performed. Generally, anyone providing "individual input into the production of a work which imbues it with the personality of the artist" may claim the status of a performer under *Rome*.[102] The theatrical stage director, the ballet master, or even the sound or lighting technician whose work may transcend the technical into the realm of personal creativity are all possible candidates.[103]

Such an amorphous test may obviously cause arguments about who does or does not qualify as a performer. Such disagreements are best resolved among the participants before the performance occurs. The performers may more likely then agree among themselves how to split any royalties from exploitation of the performance. Impresarios should also ensure that all potential performers join in signing the relevant contracts. Otherwise, exploitation may stall as a neglected performer later refuses consent.

c) Broadcasts

The broadcaster is the first owner of the signal it broadcasts.[104] A broadcaster is defined as a body that, in the course of operating a broadcasting undertaking, broadcasts a communication signal in accordance with the law of the country where the undertaking is carried on. An entity whose primary activity is the retransmission of such signals does not qualify as a broadcaster.[105] A cable company that incidentally transmits some programming that originates in-house will therefore not qualify as a broadcaster. Its primary activity still remains retransmission rather than broadcasting.

B. DURATION

1) Literary, Dramatic, Musical, and Artistic Works

Copyright terms have grown over the years. What started in early eighteenth-century Britain as a twenty-eight-year term (fourteen years plus an optional fourteen years' renewal) was added to incrementally over the years until, by the early twentieth century, it had internationally

---

102 W. Nordemann, K. Vinck, & P.W. Hertin, English version by G. Meyer (based on trans. R. Livingston), *International Copyright and Neighboring Rights Law* (New York: VCH Publishers, 1990) at 356.

103 *Ibid.* at 355–58.

104 *C Act*, above note 19, s. 24(c).

105 *C Act, ibid.*, s. 2, def. "broadcaster."

become the life of the author plus fifty years. Before 1924, Canada's term mirrored the maximum forty-two year term (twenty-eight years plus an optional fourteen years' renewal) that prevailed in the United States until 1909. Since 1924, Canada's term for most works has been the standard *Berne Convention* term of life of the author plus fifty years.[106] The period runs to 31 December of the year in which it is due to expire. So the term of copyright for an author who died on 1 January 1956 expires immediately after midnight on 31 December 2006.[107]

Calls for longer, even perpetual, periods of protection continue. Europe recently increased its standard term to seventy years past the author's death, while refusing to protect foreign works beyond the term in their country of origin. The United States followed suit in 1998 by adding twenty years retroactively to all its existing and future copyrights.[108] Copyright owners elsewhere now clamour for their governments to follow the European and U.S. leads. The public today pays for recycled work where it previously had cheaper or even free access. One unintended consequence may be that the production and distribution of new works is discouraged as copyright holders instead wring the last drop of benefit from existing inventory. How far authors or their descendants benefit from longer terms, either absolutely or relatively to distributors, is also a contentious question.

The *1997 Act* continued Canada's trend to bring most work under the standard life-plus-fifty-year rule. Many discrepancies remain, including some arising from transitional measures for work made before the *1997 Act* was proclaimed into force. These variations complicate assessments about whether a work is protected or whether it has fallen into the public domain. Complications multiply when a work is exploited abroad, for terms are not uniform worldwide.

The more important discrepancies in Canada are the following:

a) Jointly Authored Works

Copyright in a jointly authored work lasts until fifty years after the last author dies.[109] There is one qualification in section 9(2) of the Act: any author who is a national of a country that provides a shorter term of

---

106   *C Act, ibid.,* s. 6. Compare *Berne,* above note 3: (1908), art. 7, & (1971), art. 7.

107   *C Act, ibid.,* s. 6. This "year's end" formula is repeated throughout the Act for all work and other subject matter.

108   *Sonny Bono Copyright Term Extension Act* of 1998 (105th Cong., 2d Sess., s. 505).

109   *C Act,* above note 19, s. 9(1). See section A(1)(c), "Joint Authors," in this chapter. An elderly author would do well to choose a young, but risk-averse, collaborator, should he wish to prolong the term of a copyright.

protection cannot claim a longer term in Canada. The United States and Mexico, as *NAFTA* countries, were exempted from this "rule of the shorter term" as from 1994.[110]

Section 9(2) has little impact on most current jointly authored work, since most countries apply the *Berne* minimum of fifty years past the death of the last-to-die author. At first sight, one affected category could be jointly authored photographs. Some countries protect photographs for a shorter period than fifty years past the death of the last-to-die author, the new standard for photographs in Canada.[111] Nonetheless, although jointly authored photographic works may benefit in Canada from this new term for the first time, the rule of the shorter term in section 9(2) should not apply to them. The *Berne* provision from which section 9(2) is copied was not intended to catch photographs, and section 9(2) should therefore be correspondingly interpreted similarly.[112]

The rule of the shorter term may still affect old works, especially those made or published before a country joined *Berne* or *NAFTA*. Such work may be unprotected in Canada if all the joint authors came from a country where the term of protection for the work had expired before the country joined the treaty, even though the same work, had it been made by Canadian nationals, would have been fully protected in Canada.

However, if even only one joint author was a national of Canada or of a country with an equal term of protection, the work would be fully protected in Canada. Only the author from the country where the copyright had expired, and those deriving title from him, would be unable to assert copyright in Canada. So the Canadian or other equal-term author, and those deriving title from him, could obtain an injunction in Canada against a continuing infringement, but monetary recovery should be limited according to the qualifying author's interest. The

---

110   *C Act, ibid.*, s. 9(2). Calculating the shorter term by reference to the country of the author's nationality, instead of the country of the work's origin, results from the mistaken inclusion of art. 7*bis*(2) in *Berne* (1928): S. Ladas, *The International Protection of Literary and Artistic Property* (New York: Macmillan, 1938), vol. 1 at 327 [Ladas]. The mistake is corrected in *Berne* (1971), art. 7(8), which applies to joint works. Canada's retention of s. 9(2) therefore technically contravenes its *Berne* (1971) obligation.

111   See section B(1)(e), "Photographs," in this chapter, where the exceptions to this rule are also noted.

112   A. Raestad, *La Convention de Berne révisée à Rome 1928* (Paris, 1931) at 177; Ladas, above note 110, vol. 1 at 327–28. On interpreting the Act to conform with *Berne*, see, for example, *National Corn Growers Assn. v. Canada (Import Tribunal)*, [1990] 2 S.C.R. 1324; *Milliken & Co. v. Interface Flooring Systems (Canada) Inc.* (1994), 58 C.P.R. (3d) 157 (Fed. C.A.).

Canadian or other equal-term author who has only a 25 percent stake in the copyright should therefore get only 25 percent of the recoverable damages or profits. The co-author, whose copyright has expired in his country of nationality, has no legal copyright interest in Canada and therefore cannot legally be harmed.

b) Anonymous and Pseudonymous Works

Copyright in anonymous and pseudonymous works lasts for the shorter of fifty years from first publication or seventy-five years from the making of the work. However, if during that period the author's identity becomes commonly known, the standard life-plus-fifty-year term applies.[113]

c) Unexploited Works

Until 1999, copyright was perpetual for many works that were not exploited at the time of the author's death. This class comprised literary, dramatic, and musical works that were not published, performed in public, or telecommunicated to the public, and engravings that were not published. Once an engraving was published, or the other work was exploited by publication, performance in public, or telecommunication to the public, the copyright ceased fifty years later.[114]

Researchers, historians, and archivists chafed under this rule, which made the copying or publication of much nineteenth-century and even earlier material risky. Tracing descendants who could give valid consents was either costly or impossible.[115] Additionally, what moral claim remote descendants might exercise over historical research on their forbears was often obscure.

Something almost unheard of in copyright annals occurred in the *1997 Act*: a copyright term was rolled back. From 1 January 1999 the standard author's-life-plus-fifty-year term applies to all such new works, whether or whenever they are first exploited after the author's death. Copyright in existing works is phased out in the following way:

---

113 *C Act*, above note 19, s. 6.1. These rules also apply to jointly authored work (s. 6.2), subject to the rule of the shorter term in s. 9(2): see authorities in note 112 above.

114 *C Act, ibid.*, s. 7, as it stood before *An Act to Amend the Copyright Act*, S.C. 1997, c. 24 [*1997 Act*].

115 The consent of unlocatable owners is sometimes unnecessary, if a copy of a work in a non-profit archive is to be made: *C Act, ibid.*, s. 30.2(5); see section B(12)(e), "Archival Copying" in chapter 7. The Copyright Board cannot help in other cases where a copyright owner is unlocatable because its powers apply only to published works: see section B(14)(e), "Unlocatable Owners," in chapter 7.

- For a work first exploited after the author's death but before 1999, copyright will expire fifty years after the exploitation. The pre-*1997 Act* position continues for these works.
- For an unexploited work whose author died less than fifty years before 1999, copyright will expire fifty years from 1999 — on 31 December 2049 — whether or whenever the work is later exploited.
- For an unexploited work whose author died more than fifty years before proclamation, copyright will expire at the end of 31 December 2004, whether or whenever the work is exploited.[116]

d) Films

The usual cinema movie or cartoon is protected for the standard period of life of its author (presumably the director) plus fifty years.[117] An attempt, when *NAFTA* was implemented in 1993, to cut this term down to a flat fifty years, as some countries provide, was successfully resisted by the Canadian film industry, and is not likely to be repeated soon.

Only films that lack a dramatic character arising from their arrangement, acting form, or combination of incidents (e.g., unedited, and perhaps even many edited, films of live events)[118] are protected for a straight fifty-year period running from when the film was made. If, however, the film was first published during this period, the copyright is prolonged to fifty years past that publication. These rules also apply to a compilation of non-dramatic films.[119]

The copyright term of works or other subject matter incorporated into a film is unaffected by the film's term of protection. Suppose copyright in a musical work expires at the end of 1999, fifty years after the composer's death in 1949. The inclusion of the music on a dramatic film's soundtrack in 1996 does not change the musical work's copyright term. The music will fall into the public domain on 1 January 2000, even though the film's copyright will expire much later that century. Similarly, copyright in an existing sound recording that is incorporated in the film's soundtrack will, despite the incorporation, still expire fifty years after the record's earlier first fixation. After that

---

116   *C Act, ibid.*, s. 7, as amended by *1997 Act*, above note 114; proclaimed into force as of 1 January 1999 by SI 98-45, 132 Can. Gaz. (Pt. II) 1149 (1 April 1998).

117   See section B(1)(d), "Films," in this chapter.

118   *Australian Olympic Committee Inc.* v. *The Big Fights Inc.*, [1999] F.C.A. 1042, para. 42 (Austl. Fed. Ct.), holds that an edited film of live events may become a dramatic work only where (perhaps) the editing creates a story or drama that was not otherwise present in the raw film.

119   *C Act*, above note 19, s. 11.1.

expiry, anyone may, without infringing copyright, copy the recording or perhaps even the soundtrack, even though the recording fell under the film's copyright on incorporation in the film.[120]

e) Photographs

Before 1999, copyright in photographs lasted for fifty years from when the initial photograph, negative, or plate was made.[121] Since the *Berne Convention* mandates only a minimum term of twenty-five years for photographs, the Canadian term more than amply protected the average domestic snap or news shot. But, as from 1 January 1999, the *1997 Act* lengthens protection to fifty years past the author's death for many new and existing photographs.

The new provisions, introduced after the second reading of Bill C-32, broadly follow a worldwide pattern of increasing protection for photographs. The *WIPO Copyright Treaty* of 1996[122] mandates the standard copyright term for photographs. In this respect, the Treaty reflects the law long applied in the United States, and also in Europe for photographs reflecting some intellectual creativity (whatever that is). On the other hand, Yousuf Karsh's famous photographic portrait of Winston Churchill, taken in 1941, fell into the Canadian public domain in 1992 while Karsh was still very much alive and in business.

The policy decision to increase Canadian protection to fifty years past the author's death faced some technical difficulties. The Act fictionally calls someone the "author" of a photograph if he owns the negative from which the photograph is derived. The fictional author can therefore be a corporation, which may "live" forever. A policy of avoiding potentially perpetual copyright protection for corporations could have been implemented simply by eliminating the corporate-author fiction.[123] Photographs would then, like every other work, have been capable of being authored only by humans. This course was not taken. Instead, the *1997 Act* tries to mix and match new and old provisions. It grants human authors a life-plus-fifty-year term, while retaining the flat fifty-

---

120   *C Act, ibid.*, s. 2, defs. "sound recording" (which excludes "any soundtrack of a cinematographic work where it accompanies the cinematographic work") and "cinematographic work" (which includes works "whether or not accompanied by a soundtrack").

121   *C Act, ibid.*, s. 10.

122   The *WIPO Copyright Treaty* of 1996, art. 9, requires ratifying states not to apply the shorter *Berne Convention* term for photographs.

123   Canada may eliminate this complicating fiction when implementing the obligations of the *WIPO Copyright Treaty* of 1996.

year term for corporate authors. The scheme applies both to photographs taken as from 1 January 1999 and also to pre-1999 photographs that were still in copyright at that date — those taken after 31 December 1948.[124] A photograph taken before 1 January 1949, such as Karsh's Churchill photograph, therefore remains in the public domain, although Karsh's post-1948 work benefits from the new extended protection.

The scheme operates as follows:

i) Human Author

The human author of a photograph has copyright for life plus fifty years after his death.[125] The identity of this "author" is not changed by the *1997 Act*. It is whoever owned the initial physical negative, plate, or photograph at the time it was made.[126] Joint owners of the physical material are presumably also its joint authors.[127]

ii) Corporate Author

A corporation can still be an author. The term then remains at fifty years from the making of the initial negative or plate. If there is no negative or plate, the fifty years runs from the making of the photograph.[128]

iii) Photographer-Owned Corporations

One major exception, introduced by the *1997 Act*, to the flat fifty-year term for corporate authors aims to make photographers who work through corporations that they control no worse off than photographers who do not incorporate. This laudable aim is, however, imperfectly realized, since many anomalies and arbitrary distinctions have been created along the way.

The idea is that the new term of life-of-the-author-plus-fifty-years should apply where the "real" flesh-and-blood author owns a majority of the voting shares in the corporation. The relevant life is then that of the "real" human author. However, while the duration of the copyright is measured by reference to the "real" author's life, for all other pur-

---

124   *1997 Act*, above note 114, s. 54.1 (transitional). Photos taken at a 1949 New Year's celebration may have copyright, depending on when they were taken — before or after midnight on 31 December 1948.

125   *C Act*, above note 19, s. 6, now applies to photographs, except to the extent modified by the new s. 10.

126   See section B(1)(e), "Photographs," in this chapter.

127   On whether a joint author from a foreign country that grants a shorter term of protection may claim the longer term in Canada, see section B(1)(a), "Jointly Authored Works," in this chapter.

128   *C Act*, above note 19, s. 10(1), inserted by *1997 Act*, above note 114, s. 7.

poses the corporation is still deemed to be the author of the photograph and its first copyright owner. Parity with the case where the photograph's author is a flesh-and-blood person is therefore not achieved. For one thing, the copyright may still revert to an author's estate where the author is human, but not where the author is a corporation.[129] Further, a different test must necessarily be used to identify the "real" author for the purpose of calculating the duration of copyright. The "real" author is "the natural person who will have qualified as the author of the photograph" were it not for the provision that fictionally allocates authorship to the owner of the physical negative.[130] This test may require the application of case law going back to the birth of photography.

Under the old law, financing the photographic enterprise, supplying ideas or commissions, or owning the photograph or negative did not produce authorship. Instead, the author was whichever individual was responsible for the photograph's composition.[131] These principles were difficult enough to apply in the nineteenth century; they are no less difficult now. Thus, it will not always be the person clicking the shutter on the camera who will qualify as the author of the photograph. Suppose that A requests bystander B to photograph a group which includes A. If B poses the group, B will be the photograph's author. If A poses the group, A will be the author. If both A and B jointly pose the group, the work would ordinarily be jointly authored.[132] The concept of joint human authorship, however, fits poorly into the new scheme. The language of the new provisions simply does not seem to contemplate it. The temptation to allocate sole authorship to either A or B, according to whoever was most responsible for the work's composition, may therefore be almost irresistible.

Yet another difficulty relates to the provision that establishes the longer life-plus-fifty-year term only where the author holds a majority of the voting shares in the corporation. This linking of protection to shareholding may create arbitrary distinctions. For example, the longer term will not apply where the photographer uses a corporation as his *alter ego*, but lacks the necessary type or amount of shares at the time the photograph is taken. The term will also not wholly apply where the corporation comprises two photographers working in unequal partner-

---

129   See section B(2)(b), "Exceptions," in this chapter.

130   *C Act*, above note 19, ss. 10(1.1) & 6; *1997 Act*, above note 114, s. 54.1(b).

131   *Nottage v. Jackson* (1883), 11 Q.B.D. 627 at 632, 635, & 637 (C.A.); *Bauman v. Fussell* (1953), [1978] R.P.C. 485 (C.A.); *Ateliers Tango*, above note 36.

132   *Creation*, above note 36 at 5–6.

ship. If one photographer holds 51 percent of the voting shares, his work will benefit from the longer term, but his partner's work will not.

f) Government Works

Copyright in works that are prepared or published by or under the direction or control of the federal or provincial government, and that are first owned by it, lasts until fifty years have elapsed past first publication.[133] Copyright in a work that is prepared under the government's direction or control, but that is never published, may therefore be perpetual, even if the government later transfers the copyright to someone else.

This rule of perpetual copyright should have been abolished at the same time that the *1997 Act* repealed perpetual copyright in unpublished works authored in the private sector. Such a move would have eliminated the further anomaly that allows the government to change this potentially perpetual term by a simple, even an implied, agreement. The present Act lets a government agree that the author will become the first copyright owner of a work that is prepared under the government's direction or control.[134] In such a case, the ordinary life-plus-fifty-year term automatically applies to the work. Provisions like this, allowing copyright periods to be shortened or lengthened by a voluntary agreement, seem objectionable in principle.

It would be simpler if a straight fifty-year term from the date of making of the work were instituted. The term could extend to municipal governments, which presently hold copyright in work produced for them by their employees for the quite illogical period of fifty years after the death of the particular employee.

A final anomaly is that no term is specified at all for works falling under the Crown prerogative.[135] If, as governments claim, all the statute law of the land comes under this power, the result is that every pre- and post-Confederation statute, regulation, and order in council, whether repealed or still in force, is still under the exclusive control of the federal and provincial governments.[136] The governments could, of course, abandon these claims with the stroke of a pen or bring them under the ordinary term applying to government copyrights.

---

133   *C Act,* above note 19, s. 12. Municipalities are not included.
134   *Ibid.*
135   See section A(2)(b)(ii), "Government Work," in this chapter.
136   In 1997 the federal government issued an open invitation for anyone to use this material, but (Ontario apart, since 1999) the provinces have been more reticent. See section B(1)(d), "Federal Law and Court Judgments," in chapter 7.

g) Shorter Duration for Foreign Works

Berne Convention and *WTO Agreement* countries grant foreign works the minimum periods of copyright protection that *Berne* mandates. On first joining *Berne* or the *WTO*, a country must apply this principle to existing foreign works connected with another *Berne* or *WTO* country, except those works whose term of protection has expired in their country of origin. This "rule of the shorter term" is an optional exception to *Berne*'s national treatment principle, namely, that foreign works must be treated the same as local works.[137] European countries, in particular, apply the rule of the shorter term rigorously to prevent foreign works from benefiting from Europe's term of seventy years past the author's death, unless the foreign country has an equivalent term.[138]

The Canadian *Copyright Act* that took effect in 1924 did not contain any rule of the shorter term. A version of the rule, applying only to jointly authored works, was, however, introduced in 1931 to mirror a *Berne* (1928) provision, but Mexico and the United States, as *NAFTA* partners, were exempted from its operation in 1994. The occasional joint work may nonetheless still be caught by the rule.[139]

Apart from this exception, Canada traditionally has not cared whether or how a foreign work was protected in its country of origin. The only relevant question was whether the country belonged to the *Berne Convention* or benefited from a Minister's Notice extending protection to that country.[140] So an action for infringing copyright in Charlie Chaplin's film *The Gold Rush* succeeded in Canada, even though the film's copyright had expired in the United States, its country of origin. The court held that the copyright status of a work in its country of origin or elsewhere was irrelevant to the existence and term of Canadian copyright.[141] The result was that a film that was circulating freely in the

---

137   See *Berne* (1971), above note 3, art. 7(8) (allowing shorter terms), which derogates from art. 5(1) (national treatment). Article 19 allows greater protection to be granted.

138   The European Union's stance was successfully used by U.S. right-holders to persuade the U.S. Congress in 1998 to increase the duration of U.S. copyrights retrospectively by twenty years.

139   See section B(1)(a), "Jointly Authored Works," in this chapter.

140   *C Act*, above note 19, s. 5(2). Notices were issued if the foreign country granted reciprocal protection to Canadian nationals. Some Notices were issued *ad hoc*; others were issued for those *UCC* members who were not also members of *Berne*. See, for example, "Foreign Countries to Which the Canadian Copyright Act Extends" (1987) 3 I.P.J. 226.

141   *Roy Export Co. Establishment v. Gauthier* (1973), 10 C.P.R. (2d) 11 (Fed. T.D.).

United States could not be exhibited in Canada even to private film clubs. What exactly Canada gained from such a policy is unclear.

This policy changed only slightly in 1996, when the *WTO Agreement* amendments to the *Copyright Act* took effect. Canada now applies the rule of the shorter term to works whose copyright expired in their country of origin before the country joined *Berne* or the *WTO*.[142] Even this application of the rule of the shorter term is less draconian than at first sight appears.

Take the case of Chaplin's film *The Gold Rush*, mentioned earlier. Chaplin died in 1977, so his Canadian copyrights expire at the end of 2027. The United States first joined *Berne* in 1989, at a time when U.S. copyright in *The Gold Rush* had expired.[143] If the rule of the shorter-term rule applies, Canadian copyright in *The Gold Rush* terminated in 1996. This result, however, follows only if the claim for protection is made on the basis of the work's connection with *Berne* or the *WTO/ TRIPs Agreement*.

The claim need not be made on this basis. Instead, *The Gold Rush* may rely for its protection on the Minister of Trade's Notice of 1923, which extended Canadian copyright to the United States as from 1 January 1924.[144] Protection under this Notice is distinct from the protection available to the United States through its accession to *Berne* or *TRIPs*. Since protection under a Minister's Notice is "not affected by reason only of the country in question becoming a treaty country,"[145] *The Gold Rush* is not caught by the shorter-term rule. Nor is any other work that can rely for its protection on a Minister's Notice.

In practice, therefore, the major impact of Canada's version of the rule of the shorter term may fall on the newer adherents to the copy-

---

142 *C Act*, above note 19, ss. 5(1.01) to 5(1.03).

143 Before 1977, the copyright term in the United States was twenty-eight years, with a right of renewal for another twenty-eight years. Copyright was not renewed for Chaplin's film, which accordingly then fell into the U.S. public domain. The U.S. *Copyright Act* of 1976 adopted a life-plus-fifty-year term and also extended protection for existing in-copyright works to seventy-five years from when they first acquired copyright.

144 Can. Gaz., 29 December 1923. Canadian works were reciprocally protected in the United States from 1 January 1924, by a U.S. Presidential Proclamation of 27 December 1923. See R.M.W. Chitty, "Copyright in Canada" [1926] 2 D.L.R. 753 at 758ff.

145 *C Act*, above note 19, s. 5(7), to which s. 5(1.2) is apparently subject. The relevant treaties are *Berne*, the *UCC*, and the *WTO/TRIPs Agreement*: ibid., s. 2, def. "treaty country." The validity of all existing Minister's Notices was confirmed by s. 54 of the *1997 Act*.

right treaties, such as developing nations. Whether this impact is consistent with Canada's usual stance of relative generosity to such nations raises an interesting question of foreign policy.

2) Reversion

Any assignment or grant of interest in copyright in a work (e.g., an exclusive licence) by an author ends automatically twenty-five years after his death, and the entire copyright becomes vested in the estate.[146]

The exceptions to this rule are noted below. Those apart, reversion cannot be overridden by agreement. The aim is to enable the estate to benefit directly from the copyright and to free itself of any bad deal the author may have made.[147] If the author has made no assignment or grant, obviously nothing reverts; on the author's death, the whole copyright passes immediately to the estate, which may deal with it as with any other personal property.

Borrowed from the virtually identical provision in the 1911 United Kingdom Act, reversion was originally introduced in Canada in 1924 to complement the new longer copyright term also enacted at that time. Before then, Canadian copyright ran for a maximum of forty-two years: an initial twenty-eight-year period, with a further fourteen-year right of renewal granted to the author or his estate. The new 1924 term ran for the author's life plus another fifty years. The avowed purpose was to benefit the author's surviving family, and reversion was supposed to turn purpose into practice. It was presumably thought that grantees who dealt decently with the author and the estate, and who worked effectively to exploit the copyright, would have little to fear from reversion, since the estate would want to keep dealing with them. This presumption has been largely so in practice. Estates may invoke reversion where they think the copyright is worth significantly more than is provided for in the original contract. On the other hand, grantees who suspect that an estate may want to switch can strategically seek to drive down the value of the copyright as reversion time approaches.

---

146 *C Act, ibid.*, s. 14. Somewhat anomalously, the *NAFTA* amendments extending copyright periods to 31 December of each year did not touch this provision. So copyright in a book whose author died on 1 January 1996 lasts until 31 December 2046, but the estate benefits from reversion as from 1 January 2021.

147 *Chappell & Co. Ltd. v. Redwood Music Ltd.*, [1980] 2 All E.R. 817 at 828–29 (H.L.) [*Chappell*].

Reversion has been criticized as an undue interference with freedom of contract. When the U.K. reversionary provision was first debated, one legislator denounced it as "a new species of entail . . . putting authors in leading strings, and treating them as persons who cannot take care of their own interests."[148] Such criticisms may now have support from *NAFTA*, which insists that economic rights should be freely transferable and that transferees should "enjoy fully the benefits derived from those rights."[149] A convincing argument is available that reversion contradicts this obligation, at least for copyrights arising after 1 January 1994. The argument would equally impugn the comparable reversionary provision in section 203 of the U.S. *Copyright Act* of 1976, putting both Canada and the United States in breach of their *NAFTA* obligations.

The argument, if correct, does not mean the reversionary provisions are ineffective. It merely means that a complaint could be referred to a *NAFTA* trade panel, which could direct both countries to repeal their provisions. Repeal would certainly eliminate the complexities and uncertainties surrounding reversion. It would, however, also undercut the legitimacy of a copyright term that is based on an intent to benefit authors' estates, but from which many authors' estates will not obtain any benefit in fact.

a) What Interests Revert

Partial, as well as whole, assignments and grants revert, as does the copyright in jointly authored works.[150] Any non-exclusive irrevocable licence should also terminate, since irrevocability may create an interest in copyright. Logically, other licences should come to an end at this time as well, but the Act is not explicit on this point.

Reversion also applies to non-dramatic films. True, these films are protected for only a flat fifty years, which may expire even before the author dies, whereas reversion is geared mainly to works with a term of life-plus-fifty years. Yet reversion clearly applied to works with a longer term: for example, works unpublished at the author's death, which until

---

148   U.K., H.L., *Debates* (14 November 1911) at 158.

149   *NAFTA*, above note 7, art. 1705(3).

150   *Redwood Music Ltd.* v. *Francis, Day & Hunter Ltd.*, [1978] R.P.C. 429 at 449 (Q.B.) (partial); *Redwood Music Ltd.* v. *B. Feldman & Co.*, [1979] R.P.C. 1 at 14–15 (Q.B.), aff'd [1979] R.P.C. 385 (C.A.) (joint). Copyright in a joint work reverts twenty-five years after the last joint author dies: *C Act*, above note 19, s. 9(1), concluding words. See section A(1)(c), "Joint Authors," and section B(1)(a), "Jointly Authored Works, " both in this chapter.

1999 could be protected forever. It should therefore apply equally to works with shorter terms.[151]

The Act says nothing about further assignments, grants, sub-licences, and permissions that are made or given by the initial grantees from the author or later grantees; but since no one can pass greater rights than he acquires, such later dispositions should also terminate with the original grant. Similarly, although nothing is said about moral rights, any waiver of such rights ought to terminate when the copyright reverts, since their duration is inextricably linked to the duration of the copyright.[152] Whether an author's waiver of post-reversion moral rights binds the estate is less clear. In principle, it should not bind, since there seems little point in leaving a grantee with a waiver but no copyright. Moral rights should therefore descend to the estate, despite any prior waiver, so that the estate may exercise or waive them anew on reversion.

The estate may benefit immediately from a reversion. Thus, although the author could not have raised money by selling his expectation of reversion, the executor or administrator can sell the expectancy immediately to pay off creditors if the estate is insolvent. Whether a particular grant transfers the reversion depends on the interpretation placed on the language of the grant. Foreign, as well as Canadian, contracts may validly transfer a Canadian reversion. A U.S. composer's executor once granted a U.S. music publisher "all rights whether now known or unknown, which the grantor has or which she may be entitled to for all countries outside the United States which the grantor can convey, transfer or grant." This language was found effective to transfer the U.K. (and, no doubt, also any Canadian) reversionary interest in the composer's musical works to the publisher. Whether the grantor or grantee had known or thought about foreign reversionary rights was irrelevant.[153] Unless the contract itself can be vitiated for some reason (e.g., misrepresentation, mistake, or unconscionability), this result

---

151 Parliament clearly believed so when it enacted transitional provisions for pre-1997 sound recordings, which then were protected for fifty years from the date of making the underlying matrix: *1997 Act*, above note 114, s. 55(3). Comparable transitional provisions also appeared when reversion was abolished in the United Kingdom (1956), New Zealand (1962), and Australia (1968).

152 *C Act*, above note 19, s. 14.2(1). In contract law, a contractual waiver typically terminates with its contract: *Chomedy Aluminium Co.* v. *Belcourt Construction (Ottawa) Ltd.* (1979), 97 D.L.R. (3d) 170 at 179 (Ont. C.A.), aff'd (1980), 116 D.L.R. (3d) 193 (S.C.C.) (waiver of building lien).

153 *Redwood Music Ltd.* v. *Francis, Day & Hunter Ltd.*, above note 150 at 459 & 461; *Chappell*, above note 147.

seems correct in principle and, indeed, the parallel Canadian dispute was settled by agreement on this basis.[154]

The reversion rule primarily targets Canadian copyrights. An author who assigns her worldwide copyright forever will effectively dispose fully of the copyright in those countries that have no reversion law. Canadian copyright will, however, automatically revert twenty-five years after the author's death. An author who wants foreign copyrights to revert with her Canadian copyright needs to spell this point out clearly in the contract, and should also check that the laws governing the foreign copyrights recognize the validity of such a provision.

One practical problem with reversion is that people often forget about it. The grantee may continue paying royalties to the estate according to the old agreement, and the estate may blissfully accept them without knowing copyright has reverted to it. When it finds out, however, the estate may demand that the grantee negotiate a new agreement if the latter wants to continue using the copyrights. The grantee must stop using the rights, at least on receiving reasonable notice, but its activities till then may be treated as non-infringing and impliedly licensed by the estate.[155]

b) Exceptions

Copyright does not revert to the estate in the following cases:

i) Author Not First Copyright Owner

Copyright will not revert where the author is not the first copyright owner. This may occur in three situations:

- The work is produced by an employee as part of her duties. The employer then first owns copyright.
- A photograph, engraving, or portrait is made for valuable consideration by a freelancer or independent contractor and is paid for. The client then first owns copyright.
- The work is made by or under the direction or control of federal or provincial government or a government department. The government then first owns copyright.[156]

---

154   *Redwood Music Ltd. v. Bourne Estate* (1995), 63 C.P.R. (3d) 380 at 404 (Ont. Gen. Div.), aff'd (1999), 84 C.P.R. (3d) 414 (Ont. C.A.).

155   *Redwood Music Ltd. v. Chappell & Co. Ltd.* (1980), [1982] R.P.C. 109 at 102ff (Q.B.).

156   *C Act*, above note 19, ss. 13(3), 13(2), & 12; see section A(2), "Ownership of Copyright," in this chapter. Reversion does not apply to works falling under the Crown prerogative of exclusive publication, which is technically not a "copyright." See section B(1)(f), "Government Works," in this chapter.

In any of these cases, the author may become the first copyright owner by an agreement made between the parties before the work is produced. Reversion will apply in such a case.

ii) Corporate Author of Photograph[157]

Reversion applies only to human authors — those who are capable of dying and of leaving estates. A corporation is by definition excluded. So reversion does not apply where a corporation is fictionally classed as the author of a photograph. Thus, somewhat anomalously, reversion does not apply in some cases where a photographer runs his own business through a one-person corporation and the copyright term lasts for fifty years past his death.[158]

iii) Item Is Not a Work

Performances, sound records, and broadcasts are not "works." Therefore their copyright does not revert, except for one minor case. Before 1997, sound recordings were classed as "works" with "authors." Reversion therefore applies to an assignment or grant made before 1 September 1997 by an individual (not a corporation), who then qualified as the "author" of a sound recording.[159]

iv) Collective Works

Reversion does not apply to (1) the assignment of the copyright in a collective work, or (2) a licence to publish a work or part of a work as part of a collective work.[160] A collective work is defined as "(a) an encyclopaedia, dictionary, year book or similar work; (b) a newspaper, review, magazine or similar periodical, and (c) any work written in different parts by different authors, or in which works or parts of works of different authors are incorporated."[161]

These exceptions are poorly thought out and their interpretation is difficult. The exception in case (2) above — where a licence to publish a work or part of a work as part of a collective work is involved — means that there is no reversion for a contribution to an encyclopedia, newspaper, or anthology, where the publisher has been granted an exclusive or (presumably) irrevocable licence to publish the item as part of the larger work. But reversion does apply if the copyright in the

---

157   C Act, ibid., s. 10; see section B(1)(e)(iii), "Photographer-Owned Corporation," in this chapter.

158   C Act, ibid., s. 10(1.1); see section B(1)(e)(iii), "Photographer-Owned Corporation," in this chapter.

159   1997 Act, above note 114, s. 55(3). See C Act, above note 19, ss. 11, 23, & 25.

160   C Act, ibid., s. 14(2).

161   C Act, ibid., s. 2, def. "collective work."

contribution is transferred — not just licensed — to the publisher.[162] Moreover, case (2) will not cover the licence to publish that is granted in a typical publishing agreement for a novel or non-fiction work, for the licence does not relate to a "collective work." Reversion presumably applies here. On the other hand, reversion may not apply if the work is in fact included in an anthology produced under such a licence granted during the author's lifetime.[163]

The exception in case (1) above excludes from reversion only assignments of copyright in the collective work itself, not assignments in contributions included in the collective work.[164] So an assignment of copyright in an individual item included in an encyclopedia or newspaper as a compilation will revert, whereas assignments of copyright in the compilation itself will not. Why the estate of the contributor of an item to an encyclopedia should be better off where the contributor assigned, rather than merely exclusively licensed, the copyright is unclear.

The exceptions apply only if there is copyright in the collective work — for example, where it is an original compilation. Music publishers once argued that the copyright in a song did not revert in cases where the composer and lyricist were different people who had assigned their rights, because the songs were said to fall under paragraph (c) of the above definition of "collective work." The argument failed. The court held that a tune may have copyright as an original musical work and that its lyrics may have copyright as an original literary work, but that meshing the two together did not produce a third original collective work with its own copyright. The copyright of each work reverted twenty-five years after the death of the respective author, so the publishers were forced to renegotiate their lapsed deals with each author's estate if they wanted to continue exploiting the music.[165]

These views probably also represent Canadian law, with one caveat. It has been suggested that a song can, in Canada, be a collective work because a musical work is defined to include compositions "with or without words."[166] But this suggestion is implausible. The definition of musical work merely recognizes that words can be part of a musical

---

162   See section B(2), "Assignments" and section B(3), "Licences," in chapter 8.
163   *Chappell*, above note 147 at 830.
164   *Ibid.* at 827 & 831.
165   *Ibid.* at 826 & 830–31. The collective works exception was inserted as an amendment after the bill was reported out of a U.K. House of Commons committee, but no debate on it is recorded: U.K., H.C., *Debates* (1911) at 1978, 2134, & 2192; U.K., H.L., *Debates* (1911) at 486.
166   *C Act*, above note 19, s. 2, def. "musical work." The United Kingdom lacks this definition.

work, whether or not they are themselves separately protected by copyright. The definition does not imply that a third copyright arises. Meshing lyrics with music may sometimes involve considerable skill; yet there seems no reason to isolate this activity from the overall process of composition, to create a third copyright that serves only to complicate dealings with the composite work.

v) Wills and Intestacies

Reversion does not apply to dispositions of copyright made by the author in his will.[167] The beneficiary receives whatever the will directs. Similarly, where the author dies without a will and without having earlier assigned or granted any interest in copyright by licence, the estate's administrator can deal with the copyright free of any reversion. If the author has made an assignment or grant, the estate obviously gets the reversionary interest, but any specific bequest of copyright should pass the reversion to the named beneficiary. The law of the country where the author died domiciled should determine the beneficiaries, whether the author dies with or without a will.

Grantees who want the full benefit of copyrights may occasionally try to prevail on authors to bequeath them the reversion. This strategy is not foolproof, since an author can change her will at any time. Even if the author contracts not to change his will, this may be ineffective. The requirement that the copyright "shall" devolve on the estate "notwithstanding *any* agreement to the contrary" should catch such a circumvention.[168]

3) Sound Recordings, Performances, and Broadcasts

Straight fifty-year terms of protection apply to the extended rights under the *1997 Act* for sound recordings, performances, and broadcasts. As with all other copyright terms, protection covers both new and pre-1997 items, and expires on 31 December of the relevant

---

167   *C Act, ibid.*, s. 14(1).

168   *C Act, ibid.* Parliament clearly intended to prevent all avoidance strategies. Thus, a proposal to except joint works was dropped; otherwise, reversion "would become nugatory, because all you would need to do would be to put in a nominal joint author": U.K., H.L. *Debates* (14 November 1911) at 161 (Viscount Haldane). Compare the more explicit U.S. provision: "Termination of the grant may be effected notwithstanding any agreement to the contrary, including an agreement to make a will or to make any future grant": *Copyright Act 1976*, above note 4, s. 203(5).

year.[169] Copyright will not automatically revert twenty-five years after the author's death, except in one minor transitional case, noted below, relating to sound recordings.

Sound recordings connected with new *Berne Convention, WTO Agreement,* and *Rome Convention* members are automatically covered, but they may fall under the rule of the shorter term in one respect. Canadian rights are denied if the term of protection for the item had already expired in that country on its becoming a *Berne, WTO,* or *Rome* member.[170]

The date when the fifty-year term starts running for these items is as follows:

a) Sound Recordings

The fifty-year term runs from the date the sound recording was first fixed, whether before or after 1997.[171] This modernizes the old rule under which the fifty years was said to run from when the initial plate (e.g., matrix, tape) of the recording was made.[172] Under no circumstance do assignments and exclusive licences made after 31 August 1997 automatically terminate twenty-five years after the author's death, with copyright reverting to the author's estate.[173]

Since the term runs from "the first" fixation, it follows that a second or later fixation of the same sounds in another recording will not restart the fifty-year term. This idea makes sense, especially where the recording is of a performance, since the rights in both the recording and the performance it fixes are interconnected and so should usually start and end together. The idea also discourages strategies designed to turn limited-term protection into perpetual protection. However, old records that are remixed or remastered enough for a new set of sounds to result may acquire a new fifty-year term from the first fixation of the remix or

---

169 *C Act, ibid.,* ss. 23(1) & (3).

170 *C Act, ibid.,* ss. 23(4) & (5). On the operation of rule of the shorter term, compare section B(1)(g), "Shorter Duration for Foreign Works," in this chapter. Presumably, the shorter-term rule applies only to countries that did in fact grant such rights; otherwise the reference to "the term of protection [having] expired" is otiose. On the other hand, the reference in ss. 23(4) & (5) to *Berne* is not otiose; it contemplates *Berne* countries such as Canada, which voluntarily protected material (such as sound recordings) that technically falls outside *Berne*: D. Vaver, "Copyright in Foreign Works: Canada's International Obligations" (1987) 66 Can. Bar Rev. 76 at 78–79 & 106ff.

171 *C Act, ibid.,* s. 23(1)(b); *1997 Act,* above note 114, ss. 55(1) & (2).

172 *C Act, ibid.,* s. 11 (pre-1997).

173 *1997 Act,* above note 114, s. 55(3). See section B(2)(b)(iii), "Item Is Not a Work," in this chapter.

remaster. Originality is no longer a copyright requirement for post-1997 recordings. Yet some looser concept of originality may prove helpful in sorting out which recordings deserve new protection and which do not. If a substantial amount of skill and judgment went to create the new recording, a fresh term of protection may be warranted.[174]

b) Performances

The time from which the fifty-year term for performers runs depends on whether the performance qualifies for *WTO Agreement* or *Rome Convention* protection.[175] The term of a *WTO* performance runs from when the performance took place.[176] The same live performance gets a fresh term of protection each time it is repeated. Both these features are also true of a live *Rome* performance that is not fixed in a sound recording. If, however, the *Rome* performance is so fixed, the fifty-year term runs from the date of first fixation.[177] So, for example, if a sound recording is later made off the soundtrack of a videotaped live performance, the *Rome* term restarts from the date the sound recording is first made, but the *WTO* term continues to run from the earlier date of the live performance.[178]

Protection for a performance that occurred in a country that is both a *Rome* and a *WTO* member can be claimed on either basis, but performers will usually prefer *Rome* protection because of the greater benefits extended under *Rome*.

c) Broadcasts

The fifty-year term for the communication signals that a broadcaster transmits runs for fifty years from the date when the signal was broadcast.[179] A repeat of the same signal is technically another signal, and it seems that a fresh term of protection will therefore attach to it.

---

174   Compare section A(1), "Originality," in chapter 3.
175   See section B(1), "Sound Recordings," in chapter 3.
176   *C Act*, above note 19, s. 26(5).
177   *C Act*, ibid., s. 23(1)(a).
178   *C Act*, ibid., s. 2, where the definition of "sound recording" excludes a soundtrack when it accompanies a film.
179   *C Act*, ibid., s. 23(1)(c).

FURTHER READINGS

BLOOM, H.S., "The Teacher's Copyright in His Teaching Materials" (1973) 12 J. Soc. Pub. T.L. 333

CHITTY, R.M.W., "Copyright in Canada" [1926] 2 D.L.R. 753

FROW, J., "Public Domain and Collective Rights in Culture" (1998) 13 I.P.J. 39

GENDREAU, Y., "La titularité des droits sur les logiciels créés par un employé" (1995) 12 Can. Intell. Prop. Rev. 147

GENDREAU, Y., A. NORDEMANN, & R. OESCH, eds., *Copyright and Photographs: An International Survey* (London, The Hague, Boston: Kluwer International, 1999)

GRAPHIC ARTISTS GUILD (U.S.), *Graphic Artists Guild Handbook: Pricing and Ethical Guidelines,* 8th ed. (New York: Graphic Artists Guild Inc., 1997)

HOWELL, R., "Database Protection and Canadian Laws" (October 1998), prepared for Industry Canada and Canadian Heritage, <http://strategis.ic.gc.ca>

MONOTTI, A.L., "Ownership of Copyright in Traditional Literary Works within Universities" (1994) 22:2 Federal Law Review 340, <http://uniserve.edu.au/law/pub/edinst/anu/flrv22/ownershi.htm>

PURI, K., "Copyright and Employment in Australia" (1996) 27 I.I.C. 53

PURI, K., "Journalists' Copyright in Australia" (1994) 9 I.P.J. 91

PURI, K., "The Term of Copyright Protection — Is It Too Long in the Wake of New Technologies?" [1990] 12 E.I.P.R. 12

RICKETSON, S., "The Copyright Term" (1992) 23 I.I.C. 753

SALOKANNEL, M., *Ownership of Rights in Audiovisual Productions: A Comparative Study* (The Hague: Kluwer, 1997)

VAVER, D., "Copyright in Foreign Works: Canada's International Obligations" (1987) 66 Can. Bar Rev. 76

VAVER, D., "Canada," in P. Geller, ed., *International Copyright Law and Practice*, 10th update (New York: Matthew Bender, 1998) ss. 3 & 4

CHAPTER 5

OWNERS' RIGHTS

A. LITERARY, DRAMATIC, MUSICAL, AND ARTISTIC WORKS

The list of activities set out in the *Copyright Act*[1] over which the copyright owner has control has grown longer over the years and will likely continue to do so as right-holders try to tighten their grip over the newer forms of electronic delivery. The *1997 Act*[2] is part of this trend. When Parliament baulks, owners sometimes try to achieve their ends by persuading courts to interpret already listed items expansively; for unless an activity is listed, it is no infringement to do it, however harmful, immoral, or unfair right-holders might think the use is.[3] Since it is easy for a product to qualify for copyright, courts should exercise great care in delineating protection suitable for that type of product. As suggested earlier,[4] a lottery ticket may not merit the same extent and intensity of protection as a book or a computer program. These distinctions must be borne in mind when one interprets whether a user has a formal

---

1   *Copyright Act*, R.S.C. 1985, c. C-42 [*C Act*; unless otherwise indicated, references to the Act are as amended].

2   *An Act to Amend the Copyright Act*, S.C. 1997, c. 24 [*1997 Act*].

3   *CBS Songs Ltd.* v. *Amstrad Consumer Electronics,* [1988] A.C. 1013 (H.L.) [*CBS Songs*].

4   See section B(1), "Literary, Dramatic, Musical, and Artistic Works," in chapter 2.

justification[5] and whether an activity falls under the copyright owner's control in the first place: "the too rigorous application of legal logic" should not replace "common sense," as one court chose to put it.[6]

In the list of activities that follows, anyone doing any of them for whatever reason without the owner's consent may infringe copyright.[7] The owner may or may not give its consent as it wishes, and may impose whatever conditions it wishes. The consent does not have to be in writing. An oral consent will do. Consent may even be implied or inferred from the circumstances.[8]

At least a part of the activity must occur in Canada to be within the owner's control. An offshore Internet service making copyright material available to Canadian subscribers may need Canadian copyright clearance. So may a Canadian user who uploads or downloads material coming from a foreign server.[9] However, as far as musical works on the Internet are concerned, the Copyright Board held in 1999 that only the operators of Internet servers or mirror sites located in Canada would be liable to SOCAN (Society of Composers, Authors and Music Publishers of Canada, the Canadian performing right society) for making such works available for downloading from their sites.[10] Similarly, a Canadian composer may not be able to sue in Canada for any unauthorized reproduction of her music in the United States, even if the copier's company is located in Canada: a U.S. copyright is infringed only in the United States.[11]

1) First Public Distribution

The copyright owner has the right to first distribute an unpublished work — to "mak[e] copies . . . [of it or a substantial part] available to

---

5   See section A(1), "Approach," in chapter 7.

6   *Autospin (Oil Seals) Ltd.* v. *Beehive Spinning,* [1995] R.P.C. 683 at 700 & 701 (Ch.).

7   *C Act,* above note 1, ss. 27(1) & 3(1).

8   *Noah* v. *Shuba,* [1991] F.S.R. 14 at 27 (Ch.). As to *Competition Act* constraints, see section B(3)(a), "Exclusive, Sole, and Non-exclusive Licences," in chapter 8.

9   *C.A.P.A.C.* v. *International Good Music Inc.,* [1963] S.C.R. 136 at 143 (border television station).

10 *Statement of Royalties to Be Collected for the Performance or the Communication by Telecommunication, in Canada, of Musical or Dramatico-Musical Works (Tariff 22), Phase I: Legal Issues,* Copyright Board Decision of 27 October 1999 [*Tariff 22*].

11 *Def Lepp Music* v. *Stuart-Brown,* [1986] R.P.C. 273 (Ch.); *Pearce (Gareth)* v. *Ove Arup Partnership Ltd.,* [1999] F.S.R. 525 (C.A.); *Coin Controls Ltd.* v. *Suzo International (U.K.) Ltd.,* [1998] 3 W.L.R. 420 at 426–27 (Ch.). See section A(5), "Telecommunication," in this chapter.

the public."[12] Once the first copies of a work have been put on the market, the first distribution right has gone for those works and all other copies of the work. The owner cannot control later distribution of copies of the work, whoever puts them on the market.[13] Similarly, once the person who has been granted the first publication right for a work has published the work, his right is exhausted. Therefore an article first published in a magazine cannot, without the copyright owner's further consent, be put into digital form and posted on an electronic database accessible to the public.[14]

Some jurisdictions — for example, Chile, California, and many European Union states — allow artists to recapture a percentage of an artwork's price on resale. Pressure is mounting to make this right (sometimes called *droit de suite*) more widespread. No such right presently exists in Canada.[15]

The Act confusingly calls the right to distribute a right of publication, reflecting the Act's print bias. "Publication" here has nothing to do with publication as the concept is understood in, say, the law of defamation. Performing, exhibiting, broadcasting, or otherwise telecommunicating a work may publicize it, but does not technically publish it.[16] A question arises whether the presence of the word "copies" (plural) in the above definition requires more than one copy to be made available. The plural form traces back to a *Berne* provision that has given equal trouble internationally.[17] "Copies" is capable of meaning "copy";[18] and one copy of a piece of serious music, a movie, a dreary book, or any posting on the Internet may be quite enough to satisfy public demand. This usage suggests that "copies" may well include a

---

12   *C Act*, above note 1, ss. 3(1), 4(1) & (2).

13   *Infabrics Ltd. v. Jaytex Ltd.* (1981), [1982] A.C. 1 (H.L.); *Avel Pty. Ltd. v. Multicoin Amusements Pty. Ltd.* (1990), 171 C.L.R. 88 (Austl. H.C.). See section A(10), "Distributing and Importing Infringing Copies: Secondary Infringement," in this chapter.

14   *Tasini v. New York Times Co.*, 972 F. Supp. 804 (S.D.N.Y. 1997), aff'd 52 U.S.P.Q.2d 1186 (2d Cir. 1999).

15   For a critique, see J.H. Merryman, "The Wrath of Robert Rauschenberg" (1993) 40 J. Copr. Soc. U.S.A. 241.

16   *C Act*, above note 1, s. 4(1)(d) to (g). Sculpture or architecture is also not published by issuing photographs or engravings of it: s. 4(1), closing words.

17   *Berne Convention for the Protection of Literary and Artistic Works* (Paris, 1971), 9 September 1886, 828 U.N.T.S. 221 [*Berne*], art. 4(3), def. "published works"; S. Ricketson, *The Berne Convention for the Protection of Literary and Artistic Works, 1886–1986* (London: Centre for Commercial Law Studies, Queen Mary College, 1987) at 182–86.

18   *Interpretation Act*, R.S.C. 1985, c. I-21 [*I Act*], s. 33(2).

single copy. The key is whether it is made available "to the public." This requirement is not satisfied by making it available to a restricted group of people; this use may be "private," not "public."[19] So first publication occurs only when at least one physical copy is made publicly available free or for sale or hire, with or without advertising or dispositions occurring.[20] Work available online or sitting in a public database may therefore be considered "published."[21] In Germany, the entrepreneurs who sold graffiti art taken from the demolished Berlin Wall were found to have infringed the artists' right of first public distribution and had to compensate the artists accordingly.[22]

2) Reproduction

A central right is "to produce or reproduce the work . . . in any material form whatever."[23] To come under this right, the owner's work must be copied. This means copying the form in which the ideas are expressed — not the ideas themselves, which are free to all. Thus, one filmmaker cannot prevent another filmmaker from copying the first's camera and editing techniques or his choice of subject matter, any more than one painter can stop others from copying his use of colour or brush technique. These elements are the author's style or ideas, which are free for all to imitate, at least if the second comer does not pass his work off as that of the earlier author.[24] It is the film or painting itself that is the

---

19 These disclosures, if unauthorized, may amount to an actionable breach of confidence (see Glossary), but that is another matter.

20 *Massie & Renwick Ltd.* v. *Underwriter's Survey Bureau Ltd.*, [1940] S.C.R. 218; *British Northrop Ltd.* v. *Texteam Blackburn Ltd.* (1973), [1974] R.P.C. 57 (Ch.). Exceptionally, to construct architecture or to include artwork incorporated into architecture is also to publish the architecture or artwork: *C Act*, above note 1, s. 4(1)(b). This provision contravenes *Berne*, above note 17, art. 3(3).

21 *C Act, ibid.*, ss. 4(1)(a) to (c); Information Highway Advisory Council, *Final Report of the Copyright Subcommittee: Copyright on the Information Highway* (Ottawa: The Council, 1995) at 11; compare *R.* v. *M.* (*J.P.*) (1996), 67 C.P.R. (3d) 152 at 156 (N.S.C.A.) [*M.* (*J.P.*)], where a seventeen-year-old computer bulletin board operator who made infringing copies of computer software available to selected users was held guilty of the criminal offence of "distribut[ing]" them to the copyright owner's prejudice: *C Act, ibid.*, s. 42(1)(c). Compare *Tariff 22*, above note 10: making a work "available" is different from, and precedes, its "communication."

22 *Wall Pictures* (1997), 28 I.I.C. 282 (German Fed. Sup. Ct., 1995).

23 *C Act*, above note 1, s. 3(1).

24 *Norowzian* v. *Arks Ltd.* (*No. 2*), [1999] F.S.R. 79 (Ch.), aff'd *The [London] Times*, 11 November 1999 (C.A.). Passing-off is, however, a separate wrong, with criteria distinct from those for copyright infringement.

author's expression, and it is this that cannot be copied without the first author's consent.

There may be a "reproduction" even if the source work has not been seen by its copier. An engraver may, for example, produce an artwork according to a third party's verbal description of the original, as happened with "knock-offs" of Hogarth's engravings in the eighteenth century; or a photographer may infringe copyright in boat plans by photographing the boat itself. A copy of a copy is still a copy.[25] Nor do minor changes avoid a charge of copying. A "colourable imitation" is as much a reproduction as a direct photocopy.[26]

The process by which a work is made is critical in deciding if a reproduction has occurred. For example, no historian can monopolize her research and sources: a second comer can write a similar history relying on those sources, among others, but she must check them out independently.[27] Similarly, a filmmaker cannot base his treatment on the incidents, dialogue, and treatment of a historical event as interpreted by just one historian, without getting her prior consent.[28] Compilers of information or anthologies may take the idea of making a compilation from previous sources, but they must do their own work. They can use earlier work only to ensure that their own is complete; they cannot proceed the other way round and take a substantial part of the earlier compilation's original selection or arrangement, even if they add their own material.[29]

"Any material form whatever" has been interpreted broadly to cover all forms in which a source work is recast, however much work went into the transformation. So changing direct speech to indirect speech, transcribing a work into or out of code, braille, or shorthand, video- and audiotaping, or scanning work into a computer have all been held to reproduce the source works, whether or not the new for-

---

25   *Dorling v. Honnor Marine Ltd.* (1964), [1965] Ch. 1 at 22–23 (C.A.).

26   *C Act*, above note 1, s. 2, def. "infringing"; *Bouchet v. Kyriacopoulos* (1964), 45 C.P.R. 265 at 278–79 (Ex. Ct.), aff'd, *ibid.*, 281 (S.C.C., 1966).

27   *Jarrold v. Houlston* (1857), 3 K. & J. 708 at 714–17, 69 E.R. 1294 (Ch.).

28   *Harman Pictures NV v. Osborne*, [1967] 2 All E.R. 324 (Ch.) [*Harman Pictures*]. Compare *Hoehling v. Universal City Studios Inc.*, 618 F.2d 972 (2d Cir. 1980): facts and information have no copyright; infringement occurs only when actual expression is lifted.

29   *Macmillan & Co. Ltd. v. Cooper* (1923), 93 L.J.P.C. 113 at 117–21; compare *Cambridge University Press v. University Tutorial Press* (1928), 45 R.P.C. 335 (Ch.): an annotated compilation of thirteen Hazlitt essays with notes was not infringed by a later compilation of twenty essays that included the same thirteen, but differently arranged and annotated.

mat was immediately humanly perceptible as a copy.[30] Similarly, two-dimensional artwork is "reproduced" in three dimensions, and vice versa, if the copy looks like its source. So the copyright owner of a cartoon character may control the making of toy doll replicas from it. Similarly, *tableaux vivants* may infringe a painting, and a building may infringe drawings or plans.[31]

Whether such transformed work should legally infringe the source work is another question. Too often courts mechanically assume that any unauthorized reproduction must be an infringement, whatever the nature and extent of the transformation. Thus postmodernist artist Jeff Koons was found by a U.S. court to have infringed copyright in a commonplace photograph by mimicking it in a large sculpture he designed and exhibited, even though the sculpture was meant to critique modern culture.[32] A century ago, when art flourished at least as much as today, this result would have been unthinkable.[33] And had law like this been applied in Shakespeare's time, a very different opus from the Bard would be with us now. In deciding issues of infringement, especially in an era of high experimentation with digital technology, courts must consider not only the parties' immediate interests but also how any decision may affect future artistic behaviour.[34] So, in Koons's case, why postmodernism had to suffer at the hands of modernism certainly requires explanation, if not justification.

a) Computer Programs and Files

Copying source or object codes may reproduce the program as a literary work. The fact of reproduction may be demonstrated through expert evidence. Even rewriting code to achieve the same effect as a previous program may "reproduce" the latter. Thus, non-literal copy-

---

30   *C Act*, above note 1, s. 2, def. "infringing"; *Apple Computer Inc.* v. *Mackintosh Computers Ltd.*, [1990] 2 S.C.R. 209; *Phillips* v. *Kidsoft L.L.C.*, 52 U.S.P.Q.2d 1102 (D.C. Md. 1999). The *1997 Act*, above note 2, s. 32, would allow works to be put in more suitable format for the blind in some circumstances. See section B(7), "Perceptual Disability," in chapter 7.

31   *King Features Syndicate Inc.* v. *O. & M. Kleeman Ltd.*, [1941] A.C. 417 (H.L.); *Bradbury, Agnew & Co.* v. *Day* (1916), 32 T.L.R. 349 (K.B.); *Netupsky* v. *Dominion Bridge Co. Ltd.*, [1972] S.C.R. 368.

32   *Rogers* v. *Koons*, 960 F.2d 301 (2d Cir. 1992) [*Rogers*]; K. Bowrey, "Copyright, the Paternity of Artistic Works, and the Challenge Posed by Postmodern Artists" (1994) 8 I.P.J. 285 at 311ff.

33   *Hanfstaengl* v. *Empire Palace,* [1894] 3 Ch. 109 (C.A.).

34   See R. Posner, *Law and Literature: A Misunderstood Relation* (Cambridge, Mass.: Harvard University Press, 1988) at 343ff.

ing of a program's structure — for example, its flow charts and organization of modules — has been held to "reproduce" the program, just as a dramatic work can be infringed by adopting its overall structure, characters, plot development, and dénouement.[35] Similarly, the displays of a videogame may be protected as an artistic or dramatic work.[36] But any idea or "any method or principle of manufacture or construction"[37] is not protectable, so any features of a program dictated by functional considerations can be copied. Copyright in a user interface and screen display has therefore been denied, for there were only a few ways to design these elements. To force later programmers to design around them would indirectly protect the underlying ideas.[38] More recently, a U.S. court held the menu command tree on the Lotus 1-2-3 program an unprotectable "method of operation." Without the commands, the program was as useless as a VCR with no operating buttons.[39]

Computer files are certainly "reproduced" when copied to a computer's permanent memory (hard disk, tape, or diskette). U.S. courts have even held that it is infringement to download a file into temporary volatile memory so it may be viewed on a monitor — thereby creating for works in electronic form a new right: the exclusive right to read. On this theory, the movement of files between Internet servers and the viewing of the files by users fall under the copyright owner's control because such activity requires temporary reproductions of the material — "caching" — to be made within a server or a user's machine before the material can be viewed. One hopes that this theory will be avoided in Canada, but one cannot be confident.[40]

---

35   *Computer Associates International Inc.* v. *Altai Inc.*, 982 F.2d 693 (2d Cir. 1992).

36   *Stern Electronics Inc.* v. *Kaufman*, 669 F.2d 852 at 855 (2d Cir. 1982).

37   *C Act*, above note 1, s. 64.1(1)(d); *Agreement on Trade-Related Aspects of Intellectual Property Rights, Including Trade in Counterfeit Goods* (1994), 25 I.I.C. 209 [*TRIPs*], art. 9(2).

38   *Delrina Corp.* v. *Triolet Systems Inc.* (1993), 47 C.P.R. (3d) 1 at 44 (Ont. Gen. Div.) [*Delrina*].

39   *Lotus Development Corp.* v. *Borland International Inc.*, 49 F.3d 807 (1st Cir. 1995), aff'd by equally divided court, 116 S.Ct. 804 (1996).

40   *MAI Systems Corp.* v. *Peak Computer Inc.*, 991 F.2d 511 (9th Cir. 1993) [*MAI*], criticized by J. Litman, "The Exclusive Right to Read" (1994) 13 Cardozo Arts & Ent. L.J. 29 at 40; D. Vaver, "Rejuvenating Copyright, Digitally," in *Symposium of Digital Technology and Copyright* (Ottawa: Department of Justice, 1995) 1 at 3–5. Compare Information Highway Advisory Council, *Final Report: Connection, Community, Content: The Challenge of the Information Highway* (Ottawa: The Council, 1995) at 114–15 ["Challenge"] (copyright owner should be able to control "browsing").

The concept of reproduction in relation to works in electronic form raises many difficulties. For example, artwork scanned into a computer file may be converted into a binary form that does not look at all like the source, but the artwork is probably "reproduced" in the file. But what if the file is later electronically manipulated so that the artwork no longer looks like its source? It should no longer be a "reproduction" of the former artistic work if the result is judged visually. But what if substantial parts of the underlying binary code are still the same? Can this be a reproduction of the underlying literary work? One trusts not. An impressionist painter may copy another's brushstrokes, and yet produce a painting that would strike the ordinary art lover as quite different. Why should this painting be held a "reproduction" of the first work, just because an art expert can trace the influences? The brushstrokes, like the electronic bits and bytes, are a means to an end. Art may best be judged by its impact on its intended market — typically, art buyers and spectators, not experts on artistic technique.

b) Subconscious Copying[41]

Reproduction implies that there is a causal connection between an earlier and a later work, although the copier may not have intended to reproduce or may not have known he or she was doing so. Moreover, close similarity between the two works, if the defendant had access to the first, presents a *prima facie* case the defendant must answer to avoid infringement.[42]

In combination, these two rules create a dilemma for anyone who may have seen or heard a work long ago, retained it in his subconscious memory, and later reproduced a major part without knowing it. A U.S. court found infringement in such a case against ex-Beatle George Harrison for subconsciously copying the Chiffons' 1962 hit "He's So Fine" in his 1970 composition "My Sweet Lord."[43] In upholding a substantial award of damages against Harrison, the appeal court said that "as a practical matter" any other rule "could substantially undermine" copyright protection.[44]

---

41 See generally, B. Green, "Haven't I Heard This Song Before?" Subconscious Plagiarism in Pop Music and the Infringement of Copyright — Towards a Partial Defense of Cryptomnesia" (1998) 13 I.P.J. 53.

42 *Francis Day & Hunter Ltd.* v. *Bron*, [1963] Ch. 587 (C.A.).

43 *Bright Tunes Music Corp.* v. *Harrisongs Music Ltd.*, 420 F. Supp. 177 (D.N.Y. 1976); compare *Gondos* v. *Hardy* (1982), 38 O.R. (2d) 555 (H.C.J.).

44 *ABKCO Music Inc.* v. *Harrisongs Music Ltd.*, 722 F.2d 988 at 999 (2d Cir. 1983). The tunes may be aurally compared at <http://www.benedict.com> under "Glam: Famous Copyright Infringements," "George Harrison."

The issue is more complex than it would appear: cryptomnesia — involuntarily recalling something one's memory chose to retain — is not uncommon today, when so much of the manufactured environment to which everyone is daily exposed is protected by copyright. All authorship has even been called the "astigmatic repackaging of others' expression."[45] The problem is the defendant's lack of moral culpability: his subconscious, not he, was in control, without his knowing or being able to influence it. Society does not usually hold people legally responsible where their mind does not prompt or direct their actions. Sleepwalkers, automatons, the very young, and the insane are not usually liable for assaults or trespasses because they cannot appreciate the nature or quality of what they are doing. The same sort of "somewhat uneasy compromises"[46] struck for such people may need to evolve for cryptomnesiacs. The copyright owner may sometimes perhaps deserve protection, but it seems hard to justify the full schedule of remedies against the "infringer": perhaps at most an injunction and an account of profits, deducting any added value. As copyright-protected material comes to occupy more and more of everyone's physical and mental space, copyright holders as a group may have to make do with a lower overall level of protection if society is to be allowed to function reasonably or at all. This relaxed approach may not, of course, apply against the habitual involuntary recaller: courts will no doubt help him "get out of the author business and go to digging ditches, where his mind will not be able to pilfer."[47]

3) Subsidiary Rights

Some rights are variants on the right to reproduce.

a) Abridgments and Abstracts

Abridgments and condensations are within the owner's right to "reproduce . . . [a] substantial part" of the work.[48] This category includes both

---

45   J. Litman, "The Public Domain" (1990) 39 Emory L.J. 965 at 1011.

46   *Williams v. Williams* (1963), [1964] A.C. 698 at 752 (H.L.) (insanity). The fear that cryptomnesia will become a defence *à la mode* is unrealistic, any more than insanity or somnambulism have become such defences in civil cases.

47   E.P. Butler, "'Pigs Is Pigs' and Plagiarists Are Thieves," in M. Salzman, *Plagiarism: The "Art" of Stealing Literary Material* (Los Angeles: Parker, Stone & Baird, 1931) at 70.

48   *C Act*, above note 1, s. 3(1); D. Vaver, "Abridgments and Abstracts: Copyright Implications" [1995] 5 E.I.P.R. 225.

"scissors and paste" versions (e.g., trimming a seven-volume report down to one volume) and *Coles' Notes*–like condensations.[49]

Abstracts are usually more condensed than abridgments. Those that just whet the reader's appetite, such as the abstracts or catchlines found at the head of articles in many periodicals, should not usually be treated as reproductions. Such abstracts present the essential ideas of a work in short form, but are not concerned to preserve any element of the source work's form or expression. An abridgment, on the other hand, usually draws on the source work's form or expression. It also typically differs in purpose from an abstract. An abridgment of a play is designed to be read or performed as a lighter substitute for the full work: for example, Charles and Mary Lamb's *Tales from Shakespeare* (1807), which made the Bard accessible to the juvenile market. By contrast, an abstract gives "just enough information to put the reader upon inquiry, precisely as the syllabus of a law report, the review of a book or the description of a painting induces the reader to examine further,"[50] and so does not infringe. Today, however, headnotes or syllabuses of law reports may run into three or four pages of small type, instead of the three or four lines of yore. Yesterday's abstract may have become today's abridgment. If the abstract substitutes for the original, it may infringe. Thus, a newspaper's systematic abstraction of analyses from a financial newsletter "suck[ed] the marrow from the bone" of the source work and was enjoined.[51]

Abridgments were not always thought of as infringements. Samuel Johnson did say in 1773, in reply to Boswell's quip that an abridgment "was only cutting the horns and tail off the cow," that "No sir, 'tis making the cow have a calf."[52] But Johnson had earlier defended abridg-

49   *R. v. James Lorimer & Co.*, [1984] 1 F.C. 1065 (C.A.) [*Lorimer*]; *Sillitoe v. McGraw-Hill Book Co. (U.K.) Ltd.*, [1983] F.S.R. 545 (Ch.) [*Sillitoe*].

50   *G. Ricordi & Co. v. Mason*, 201 F. 182 at 183 (S.D.N.Y. 1911), refusing a pretrial injunction for half-page abstracts of forty-six-page opera). The claim was finally dismissed, *ibid.*, 184 (S.D.N.Y. 1912), aff'd 210 F. 276 (2d Cir. 1913). Ricordi similarly failed in England to stop even fuller extracts that appeared in a record company's catalogue: *Valcarenghi v. The Gramophone Co. Ltd.*, [1928–1935] MacG. Cop. Cas. 301 (Ch.).

51   *Wainwright Securities Inc. v. Wall Street Transcript Corp.*, 418 F. Supp. 620 at 625 (D.N.Y. 1976), aff'd 558 F.2d 91 (2d Cir. 1977); *Nihon Keizai Shimbun Inc. v. Comline Business Data Inc.*, 49 U.S.P. Q.2d 1517 at 1519–20 (2d Cir. 1999) [*Nihon*] (abstracts that mimic same structure and organization of facts of source work infringe; those that repeat facts but rephrase and rearrange them do not infringe).

52   Z.H. Chafee Jr., "Reflections on Copyright Law" (1945) 45 Columbia L.R. 503 at 511, citing an incident in 1773 from Pottle & Bennett, eds., *Boswell's Journal of a Tour to the Hebrides with Samuel Johnson* (New York: Literary Guild, 1936) at 49.

ments as a public benefit when he dealt with a complaint concerning an abridgment that condensed a thirty-seven-page work down to thirteen pages: "The design of an abridgment is to benefit mankind by facilitating the attainment of knowledge; and by contracting arguments, relations or descriptions into a narrow compass, to convey instruction in the easiest method, without fatiguing the attention, burdening the memory, or impairing the health of the student."[53] To Johnson, an abridger did a public service in condensing the verbose writer; indeed, without the threat of abridgment, writers would have no incentive to be brief! The work before Johnson was a fair abridgment, not a scissors-and-paste affair that just took the choicest selections from its source.

Johnson's later views came to prevail in law but they took a century to gain acceptance. Not until the third quarter of the nineteenth century did abridgers start to lose their image of public benefactors and begin being treated as infringers.

b) Translation

Translation is expressly included as an owner's right in the Act.[54] It encompasses changing a work in one language or dialect into another. Even some computer programming may be included — for example, changing code from Pascal to Fortran.[55] But just as changing text into braille is reproduction, not translation, converting source to object code should not be translation either: one set of symbols is simply switched for another or for electrical circuitry.

Complications arise with multiple translations. Suppose A's work is translated by B from English to French, and C translates the French back into English. C must get clearance from both A and B, or he will infringe two copyrights: B's translation right and A's reproduction right. If D copies C's unauthorized work, A and (presumably) B can sue D, but C cannot sue D. C should have no copyright in a reproduction of A's work, even though the back-translation may not read word for word the same as A's original.

---

53   E.L. McAdam Jr., *Dr. Johnson and the English Law* (Syracuse, N.Y.: Syracuse University Press, 1951) at 13–14, indicating Johnson's opinion was first published posthumously in *Gentleman's Magazine* in 1787.

54   *C Act*, above note 1, s. 3(1)(a); D. Vaver, "Translation and Copyright: A Canadian Focus" [1994] 4 E.I.P.R. 159.

55   *Prism Hospital Software Inc. v. Hospital Medical Records Institute* (1994), 57 C.P.R. (3d) 129 at 278 (B.C.S.C.).

Translators may consult and use other sources if they act fairly. The National Film Board once produced an English/French glossary of terms used in Canadian cinematography. A film lab published the glossary without the NFB's authority, claiming the NFB had no copyright because 228 of the 775 words had been taken from an American handbook on cinematography. The court disagreed, finding the NFB's work to be original. In doing so, the judge added some comments that, though directed to originality, are also pertinent to the question of what sources a translator may legitimately use:

> No doubt the original list of words and many of the translations were obtained from other sources, but, in examining these various sources and making a selection from them and then adding independent translations some knowledge and judgment was involved. Anyone who has had any experience in translation from one language to another realizes that selection of the most appropriate or apt translation for any given word frequently involves both considerable research and discussion with other translators.[56]

A translator's duty, if not specified in the contract, has been said to be "to express the idea or mood of the original work in a style appropriate to the subject. In a proper translation, the translator, however, must be content with his role and not attempt to rewrite, revise or alter the ideas, mood or style of the original."[57] This standard, formulated in the case of a literary translator, may be easier to state than to apply. For example, may a rhyming poem be translated into either free verse or prose? Or must its rhyme (perhaps foreign to the target language) be respected, often at the expense of fidelity to the source language? The standard quoted above may not, in any event, be universal.[58] For example, a lyricist who is asked to prepare a French version of an English hit song for the mass market is, in practice, permitted greater liberties than a translator dealing with a technical safety manual.

---

56   *National Film Board* v. *Bier* (1970), 63 C.P.R. 164 at 174 (Ex. Ct.).

57   *Seroff* v. *Simon & Schuster Inc.* (1957), 162 N.Y.S.2d 770 at 773 (S.C.), aff'd (1960), 210 N.Y.S.2d 479 (A.D.).

58   See, for example, the offbeat but entertaining book by D.R. Hofstadter, *Le Ton beau de Marot: In Praise of the Music of Language* (London: Bloomsbury, 1997), where dozens of widely disparate styles of translating Clément Marot's short and apparently simple poem *À une Damoyselle malade* (1537) appear. In chapter 9, Hoftstadter criticizes Vladimir Nabokov's free-verse translation of Pushkin's *Eugene Onegin* for preferring the letter of Pushkin's work to its spirit.

Canada introduced translation rights early on in its copyright law of 1868. Before the nineteenth century, authors were typically unconcerned about the lack of such rights. In 1752 cleric Johannes Stinstra translated Samuel Richardson's *Pamela* into Dutch without even thinking to ask the author. Far from objecting when he found out, Richardson was so pleased that he offered to buy four copies of the translation, and even persuaded Stinstra to arrange a translation of Richardson's next work, with no thought of payment! A century later, Harriet Beecher Stowe was less sanguine when a U.S. publisher produced an unauthorized German translation of *Uncle Tom's Cabin* that competed with Stowe's authorized translation. Her competitor could not, however, be stopped. The U.S. copyright statute then forbade only the making of "copies." This, a U.S. judge held, meant only transcripts in the same language.[59] As late as the 1890s, courts in India also held that translations from English into Hindi, and from one Indian language into another, did not violate copyright.[60] The United States partly changed its law in 1870 and eventually granted full translation rights in 1909. The United Kingdom followed in 1911, to implement its obligations under the *Berne Convention*.

c) Novelization, Dramatization, and Movie Adaptation

Novelization, dramatization, and movie adaptation are separate rights in the Act.[61] They can cover quite unusual cases. Thus, *Coles' Notes'* version of Shaw's *St. Joan* infringed the novelization right by converting the play into a non-dramatic work. The summary was in indirect speech, interspersed with criticism, and intended as a study aid; but none of this mattered.[62] More typically, making a play or a movie will usually engage these rights. Taking a substantial part of either the dialogue or the plot of the source work may then infringe. Just taking one or two ideas or situations may not be enough, but reproducing the combination and sequence of incidents and characters has been held to be infringement.[63]

---

59   *Stowe v. Thomas*, 23 Fed. Cas. 201 at 208 (E.D. Pa. 1853).

60   *Macmillan v. Khán Bahádur Shamsul Ulama M. Zaka* (1895), 19 India L.R. (Bombay) 557.

61   *C Act*, above note 1, ss. 3(1)(b), (c), & (e).

62   *Sillitoe*, above note 49 at 550–51.

63   *Kelly v. Cinema Houses Ltd.* (1932), [1928–1935] MacG. Cop. Cas. 362 (Ch.), aff'd (1932), [1928–1935] MacG. Cop. Cas. 371 (C.A.) [*Kelly*]; *Harman Pictures*, above note 28 (John Osborne filmscript for *The Charge of the Light Brigade* infringed Cecil Woodham-Smith's book.)

The protectability of characters alone has been much debated. Cartoon characters are usually more easily recognizable, and hence protectable, in movie or other adaptations than are literary characters. So Walt Disney has stopped Goofy, Mickey, and other characters from being recast in counter-culture comic books and films.[64] Courts are more reluctant to protect literary characters, even "obvious" copies of characters "as distinctive and remarkable" as Falstaff, Tartuffe, or Sherlock Holmes. A U.S. judge put it neatly:

> If Twelfth Night were copyrighted, it is quite possible that a second comer might so closely imitate Sir Toby Belch or Malvolio as to infringe, but it would not be enough that for one of his characters he cast a riotous knight who kept wassail to the discomfort of the household, or a vain and foppish steward who became amorous of his mistress. These would be no more than Shakespeare's "ideas" in the play, as little capable of monopoly as Einstein's Doctrine of Relativity, or Darwin's theory of the Origin of Species. It follows that the less developed the characters, the less they can be copyrighted: that is the penalty an author must bear for marking them too indistinctly.[65]

A Canadian court also indicated its willingness to protect the characters in a script for a science fiction movie if they were "sufficiently clearly delineated," but found they did not meet this test on the facts.[66] A more favourable conclusion for character protection was reached in a case where a colourable parody in adult movies of archetypical characters drawn from a well-known television soap opera was disallowed.[67]

d) Film, Audio, and Video Recording

These "mechanical" rights are part of "the sole right . . . to make any sound recording, cinematograph film or other contrivance by means of which the [literary, dramatic, or musical] work may be mechanically reproduced or performed."[68] Video recordings are obviously cinematographic films or contrivances, while record pressers, film processors,

---

64 *Walt Disney Productions* v. *Air Pirates,* 581 F.2d 751 (9th Cir. 1978).

65 *Nichols* v. *Universal Pictures Corp.,* 45 F.2d 119 at 121 (2d Cir. 1930) [*Nichols*], criticized as involving vague aesthetic judgment by F.M. Nevins Jr., "Copyright + Character = Catastrophe" (1992) 39 J. Copr. Soc. U.S.A. 303 at 309ff.

66 *Preston* v. *20th Century Fox Canada Ltd.* (1990), 33 C.P.R. (3d) 242 at 275, aff'd (1993), 53 C.P.R. (3d) 407 (Fed. C.A.) (Ewoks in *Return of the Jedi*).

67 *Productions Avanti Ciné-Vidéo Inc.* v. *Favreau,* [1999] J.Q. 2725 (Que. C.A.), rev'g (1997), 79 C.P.R. (3d) 385 (Que. S.C.) [*Avanti*].

68 *C Act,* above note 1, s. 3(1)(d).

and the persons ordering the pressing or processing are among those who "make" such material.[69] Even ephemeral recordings, such as those a broadcaster makes for technical reasons, have fallen under this right. So a broadcaster who transfers a work, for which it has telecommunication rights, onto a more suitable medium for broadcast in a different time zone has to pay an additional fee to the owner of the mechanical reproduction right.[70] The *1997 Act* allows broadcasters to make certain ephemeral recordings of live performances and also to transfer sound recordings to more appropriate media for broadcast. However, the broadcaster can do so freely only if no collective society authorized to license these activities exists.[71]

4) Public Performance

Public performance is a major means by which copyright owners may make money from music, drama, novels, and movies.[72] Both live and recorded performances are included, since a performance is defined as "any acoustic representation of a work or any visual representation of a dramatic work." Performance therefore includes whatever is seen or heard when a radio, television set, or an audio or video player is turned on.[73]

Actors and musicians obviously qualify as performers, but so may anyone who causes a performance to be represented. This group includes everyone from the owner of the cabaret where the band or radio plays, down to the person who actually switches on the radio or television set.[74] Broadcasters and cablecasters also perform in public where a studio audience is present, but not when they transmit their programming: a separate right of public telecommunication[75] is designed not to overlap with public performance.[76]

A special provision extends liability where theatres and other places of entertainment are used for profit for a public performance. If

---

69 *Warner Brothers–Seven Arts Inc.* v. *CESM-TV Ltd.* (1971), 65 C.P.R. 215 at 241 (Ex. Ct.); *Compo Co.* v. *Blue Crest Music Inc.* (1979), [1980] 1 S.C.R. 357, 105 D.L.R. (3d) 249 [*Compo*].

70 Compare *Bishop* v. *Stevens*, [1990] 2 S.C.R. 467.

71 See section B(6), "Ephemeral Recording," in chapter 7.

72 *C Act*, above note 1, s. 3(1). The right also encompasses public delivery of lectures, addresses, speeches, sermons, and the like.

73 *C Act, ibid.*, ss. 3(1) & 2, def. "performance."

74 *Vigneux* v. *Canadian Performing Right Society*, [1945] A.C. 108 (P.C.) [*Vigneux*].

75 See section A(5), "Telecommunication," in this chapter.

76 *C Act*, above note 1, s. 3(4), overruling *Canadian Cable Television Assn.* v. *Canada (Copyright Board)*, [1993] 2 F.C. 138, 46 C.P.R. (3d) 359 (C.A.) [*Canadian Cable*].

the performance has no copyright clearance, anyone "permitting" the premises to be used for it also infringes copyright, unless he was unaware and had no reasonable ground for suspecting the lack of clearance. Simply leasing or licensing premises to a performing group is not in itself "permission"; there must be some control over the performers, knowledge of the particular work or subject matter to be performed, and permission to use the premises for that performance.[77]

Everyone is of course fully entitled to play records or to switch on the radio in private. What is not permissible is to perform a work "in public" without the copyright owner's consent. The decision on whether a performance in public has occurred has been left, over the past century, for courts to work out, with little guidance from legislatures. A large, often inconsistent, jurisprudence has developed on the point. One reason for this phenomenon has been strategic behaviour by powerful copyright interests with worldwide inventories, particularly musical performing rights societies, who stand to gain from a broad interpretation of public performance. Such groups spend much time and money in analyzing judicial trends, and in choosing what case to bring before which jurisdiction to produce the desired result. Other jurisdictions may then be persuaded, by a system of "log-rolling," to accept the favourable precedent obtained by the group. The precedent will then be publicized and used to cover new situations, while unfavourable precedents will be denigrated or distinguished as decisions on special facts.[78]

One standard test to decide whether a performance is "in public" is to consider the character of the audience. On this test, private or domestic performances are excluded. This exclusion should cover performances in private homes and apartments, or in rooms hired for weddings, confirmations, or batmitzvahs, where the guests are family and friends and the premises are an extension of the host's home. A slightly different test holds that performances occurring "openly, without concealment and to the knowledge of all" will be found to be "in public," whether or not anyone intends to make money from the performance. This approach would bring within the concept of public performance the use of works and other subject matter in restaurants, cabarets, arenas, members' clubs open to invited guests, and offices,

---

77 C Act, ibid., s. 27(5); Corporation of the City of Adelaide v. Australasian Performing Right Assn. Ltd. (1928), 40 C.L.R. 481 (Austl. H.C.); de Tervagne v. Beloeil (Town), [1993] 3 F.C. 227 (T.D.). See also section A(8), "Authorization," in this chapter.

78 For example, Performing Right Society Ltd. v. Rangers F.C. Supporters Club, [1975] R.P.C. 626 at 640 (Ct. Sess., Scot.) [Rangers].

factories, or elevators where music plays to relax staff or customers.[79] So to play music softly at the back of a store in a way that makes it audible to only the owners of the store would be to perform the music in private. Raising the volume so that customers and staff can also hear the music may produce a performance in public.[80]

Grey areas abound with either test. What of a performance at a firm's Christmas party: Are the employees there privately or as members of the public? An Australian case, interestingly, suggests the latter. An employer who played an instructional video at the workplace to a small group of employees was found to have put on a public performance. The ties that bind employees were thought to be commercial, not private or domestic.[81]

What of hotels that rent movies to guests to play in their rooms? In Australia the hotel was said to be causing public performances; not so in the United States.[82] The U.S. rule seems preferable. The guest is, in relation to the hotel, certainly a member of the public; but the performance is surely in private because the hotel room is merely a person's temporary home. Had the guest hired the movie from a separate rental store, the performance in her room would have been "in private." How can the identity of the supplier change the character of the performance? Finding the performance to be private nonetheless creates an anomaly: rental gets a competitive edge over in-house cable delivery systems that must pay copyright fees for "[tele]communicat[ing] to the public."[83] Substitute delivery systems should compete on their merits. Either both or neither should pay. Copyright law here should strive for technological neutrality.

---

79 *Canadian Cable,* above note 76; *Rangers, ibid.* ; compare *North American Free Trade Agreement,* 17 December 1992, Can. T.S. 1994 No. 2, art. 1721, defining "public." There is no additional requirement that the performance be "for profit," except under the provisions that extend liability to persons who "permit" a theatre or other place of entertainment to be used for a public performance: *C Act,* above note 1, s. 27(5), discussed in the previous paragraph.

80 *South African Music Rights Organisation Ltd.* v. *Trust Butchers (Pty.) Ltd.* (1978), 1 S.A.L.R. 1052 (S. Afr., E.C.D.).

81 *Australasian Performing Right Assn. Ltd.* v. *Commonwealth Bank of Australia* (1992), 40 F.C.R. 59 (Austl. Fed. Ct.).

82 *Rank Film Production Ltd.* v. *Dodds* (1983), 76 F.L.R. 351 (N.S.W.S.C.); compare *Columbia Picture Industries Inc.* v. *Professional Real Estate Investors Inc.,* 866 F.2d 278 (9th Cir. 1989).

83 *Canadian Cable,* above note 76; see section A(5), "Telecommunication," in this chapter.

The Australian movie rental case is part of a recent discernible trend to equate any performance that results in profit or commercial advantage with a performance in public. So, in the United States, a video store that provides private cubicles for individual members of the public to view films or to listen to music has been said to give a public performance.[84] Similarly, in Australia, performances in a "commercial setting" are considered public performances because courts say that copyright owners may reasonably expect payment from such uses.[85] Canadian courts need not follow this trend. The Canadian Act could have been written so as to include any performance "for motive of gain" or "for profit" within the concept of "performance in public." In fact, those concepts have been kept separate.[86] It follows that a concert given in a public square should be a performance in public, even if the performers work for free and the audience pays nothing. Equally, a lesson given by a music teacher in a private salon should not be a performance in public, even if the teacher is paid, more than one pupil participates simultaneously in the lesson, and the pupils are professional musicians. Adding motives of profit in the first case and subtracting them in the second case should not logically change the character of the performance. To say otherwise comes close either to arguing in a circle or to rewriting the Act.

5) Telecommunication

The similar expansive trends that operate in respect of the public performance right appear, for similar reasons, in respect of the right to communicate "to the public by telecommunication," and are open to similar objections.[87] The public telecommunication right covers transmission by "wire, radio, visual, optical or other electromagnetic system."[88] Sending works by radio, television, cable, fax, modem, satellite, or microwave therefore involves telecommunication. But, to attract lia-

---

84   *Columbia Pictures Industries Inc.* v. *Aveco*, 800 F.2d 59 (3d Cir. 1986).

85   *Telstra Corp. Ltd.* v. *Australasian Performing Right Assn. Ltd.* (1997), 38 I.P.R. 294 at 303–4 (Austl. H.C.) [*Telstra*].

86   See, for example, *C Act*, above note 1, ss. 27 (5) (permitting certain public performances "for profit" is infringement), and 29.3(1) & 29.5 (preventing public performances for educational or training purposes if carried out "for motive of gain"). See section B(13)(b)(iv), "Performances for or by Students," in chapter 7.

87   See section A(4), "Public Performance" in this chapter.

88   *C Act*, above note 1, s. 3(1)(f); s. 2, def. "telecommunication."

bility, the communication must be "to the public."[89] This communication should exclude such activities as point-to-point e-mails and faxes, and transmissions between a network and its affiliate television stations.[90] It would, however, include programming — ordinary, scrambled, or interactive — delivered by cable to private subscribers.[91] These copyright rules are bolstered by non-copyright provisions that let distributors of pay television programming prevent both the unauthorized decoding of their scrambled signal and also the supply of unauthorized decoders to the public.[92]

A mass unsolicited faxing of material to telephone subscribers may be included within the telecommunication right. So may data posted on, or at least downloaded from, such publicly accessible electronic bulletin boards as the Internet, even if people access the data at different times from different places.[93] This principle was applied in Australia to music played over mobile telephones where a caller was placed on hold. This activity was held to involve telecommunication to the public by the telephone company, even though the music could be heard by only one caller at a time. The court said that a communication in a "commercial setting" was usually directed towards a section of the copyright owner's anticipated public. Callers on hold could therefore be treated as part of the copyright owner's public "not because they themselves would be prepared to pay but because others are prepared to bear the cost of them [sic] having that facility."[94] The criticisms

---

89   Perhaps broader than the corresponding words "*in* public" [emphasis added] in the public performance right: *Canadian Cable*, above note 76, at 148–49 (cited to F.C.).

90   *CCH Canadian Ltd.* v. *Law Society of Upper Canada* (9 November 1999), (Fed. T.D.) [unreported] [*CCH*]. A public communication occurs only when the affiliate airs the program; the network and the affiliate are then jointly liable: *CTV Television Network Ltd.* v. *Canada (Copyright Board)*, [1993] 2 F.C. 115 (C.A.) [*CTV*]; *C Act*, above note 1, s. 3(1.4). The provider of the means of carrying the communication is not liable: *C Act*, *ibid.*, s. 3(1.3).

91   *CTV, ibid.* This programming includes a communication exclusively to occupants of apartments, hotel rooms, or dwelling units in the same building: *C Act*, *ibid.*, s. 3(1.2).

92   *N.I.I. Norsat International Inc.* v. *Express Vu Inc.* (1997), 81 C.P.R. (3d) 345 (Fed. C.A.), applying *Radiocommunication Act*, R.S.C. 1985, c. R-2, s. 9(1).

93   Compare "Challenge," above note 40 at 114; *Tariff 22*, above note 10; *CCH*, above note 90; *M. (J.P.)*, above note 21, where a computer bulletin board operator, who made infringing copies available to selected users, was found guilty of "distribut[ing]" them to the copyright owner's prejudice, contrary to s. 42(1)(c) of the *C Act*, above note 1.

94   *Telstra*, above note 85.

made earlier in respect of the concept of public performance — that in Canada this approach may apply a circular test or may read into the Act words that are not there[95] — apply here as well.

Special schemes regulate the licensing and payment for cable retransmissions and music used in public telecommunication.[96] Indeed, the Society of Composers, Authors and Music Publishers of Canada recently filed a proposal with the Copyright Board to require Internet providers of musical works to pay royalties from 1996 at the greater of the rate of twenty-five cents per month per subscriber or 3.2 percent of gross revenue from advertising. At time of writing, the Copyright Board had not ruled on what royalty rate should apply. In 1999, however, it decided that liability may attach to whoever posts music on an Internet Web site or bulletin board with the intention of making the work accessible to the public because the posting constitutes an authorization to communicate the work to the public by telecommunication. Internet service providers (ISPs) may be liable, depending on what they do in relation to the posted material. A passive ISP that merely provides the means of communication is no more liable than the telephone company that carries infringing material faxed by one subscriber to others. On the other hand, an ISP that "posts content, associates itself with others to offer content, creates embedded links or moderates a newsgroup," or which "creates a cache for reasons other than improving system performance, modifies the contents of the cached material or interferes with any means of obtaining information as to the number of 'hits' or 'accesses' to the cached material" may come under copyright liability.[97]

6) Public Exhibition of Artwork

The copyright owner of an artistic work (except a map, chart, or plan) has the right to present it "at a public exhibition," other than for sale or hire. This right applies to works made after 7 June 1988, the date the right was first introduced.[98] Galleries and museums that exhibit such

---

95 See section A(4), "Public Performance," in this chapter.

96 See section B(14), "Paying Uses," in chapter 7.

97 *Tariff* 22, above note 10, esp. at 41 of the unreported decision; *C Act*, above note 1, s. 2.4(1)(b). This approach resembles that proposed in the European Union: D. Vaver, "Copyright in Europe: The Good, the Bad and the Harmonised" (1999) 10 Aust. I.P.J. 185.

98 *C Act*, above note 1, s. 3(1)(g). See W. Noel, *The Right of Public Presentation: A Guide to the Exhibition Right* (Ottawa: Canadian Conference of the Arts, 1990).

works are typically included; dealer galleries are not, unless the work is there purely for exhibition. Works hanging in public lobbies may not be covered either, although the point is unclear.[99] Whether finger-paintings hung in school hallways come under the right is a problem that caused some school boards initial anxiety, but no budding Picasso has yet come forward to sue.

Like the public performance right, this right is supposed to return some benefit to artists for the public exposure of their work. It is often more symbolic than practical. Institutions may be loath to exhibit a work unless the artist waives her right to demand a fee. If the artist holds out, there is usually plenty of pre-1988 material that can be shown free.

7) Rental

Canadian authors have, since 1987, received money from a fund administered by the Public Lending Rights Commission (now under the Canada Council) to compensate for book loans made through public libraries. Around $8 million per year is distributed to some 12,000 writers. The scheme does not operate within the copyright system, partly to avoid any obligation to pay foreign authors.

No right to control renting exists under copyright, except for computer programs rented out "for motive of gain."[100] Only easily reproducible over-the-counter operating or application programs are targeted. Videogame cartridges, encrypted programs reproducible only by experts, or hard-wired programs that help run items like dishwashers or automobiles are outside the right. For programs that are caught, all types of rental (including sham transactions) should be encompassed. Loss leading and cross-subsidization practices may not avoid liability; businesses that try to attract custom by offering free rentals are obviously pursuing a motive of gain, for their purpose is to profit financially.[101] Genuine sales or inventory financing involving lease-back or rent-to-own schemes should, however, be excluded. So should

---

99   Compare French version of *C Act*, *ibid.*, art. 3(1)g): "présenter [une oeuvre artistique] au public lors d'une exposition"; literally, "to show [an artistic work] to the public during an exhibition."

100   *C Act*, *ibid.*, ss. 3(1)(h) & 3(2); D. Vaver, "Record and Software Rentals: The Copyright Spin" (1995) 10 I.P.J. 109. A similar rental right also applies to sound recordings: *C Act*, *ibid.*, ss. 5(4) to (6); see section B, "Sound Recordings, Performances, and Broadcasts," in this chapter.

101   Compare *C.A.P.A.C. v. Western Fair Assn.*, [1951] S.C.R. 596 [*Western Fair*].

loans by non-profit libraries, members' clubs, or other cases where no more than a cost recovery, including overhead, charge is made.[102]

The rental right is an exception to the rule that copyright owners cannot control dispositions past the first public distribution.[103] It was created because the computer industry claimed that renting cut into sales, since some renters illicitly copied programs before returning them. So far, this right is used by owners more to close down operations than to provide an alternative means of exploiting their products. This practice may change as owners experiment with rental as one form of delivery on the Internet. Pressure may also mount to extend the rental right more generally to other copyright material such as movies and videogames, or even across the board.

8) Authorization

The owner can "authorize" any of the above rights that fall under the definition of copyright.[104] In practice, the authorization right attaches liability to people beyond those who actually commit the infringing act. Thus, whoever grants, or purports to grant, expressly or impliedly, the right to reproduce or perform a work in public has been held to "authorize" the reproduction or performance. The authorizer is then as liable as the reproducer or the performer.[105] A publisher or a record company placing orders with a printer or a presser has been found to "authorize" the reproduction. Someone hiring a dance orchestra and giving it full discretion to play whatever the conductor chooses also impliedly authorizes the performance. A cablecaster, too, has been held liable for impliedly authorizing bars that are its subscribers for the public performance that occurs when the television set is turned on for the patrons to watch cable.[106] Liability attaches only if the "authorized" act occurs, although *quia timet* relief is available where the act authorized has not yet been committed.

Buyers of blank tapes sometimes use them to record music without authority. Similarly, VCR users sometimes record programming off air

---

102   *C Act*, above note 1, ss. 3(2)(a) & (3).

103   See section A(1), "First Public Distribution," in this chapter.

104   *C Act*, above note 1, s. 3(1), closing words; see section A(4), "Public Performance," in this chapter.

105   *Muzak Corp. v. C.A.P.A.C.*, [1953] 2 S.C.R. 182 at 189 [*Muzak*].

106   *Compo*, above note 69 at 255 (cited to D.L.R.); *Canadian Performing Right Society Ltd. v. Yee* (1943), 3 C.P.R. 64 (Alta. Dist. Ct.); *Canadian Cable*, above note 76 at 371–72 (cited to C.P.R.).

or from other tapes. It is, of course, difficult and politically embarrassing to pursue individual private users. A blank audio recording media levy introduced by the *1997 Act* took effect in 1999 to overcome the logistical problem of remunerating copyright owners for unauthorized recording of sound recordings. Copyright owners had till then been unsuccessful in holding manufacturers and sellers or lenders of records, blank tapes, and copying and recording machines liable for the infringing acts of buyers or hirers.[107] Courts said that merely to provide the means of infringement was not the same as authorizing it, any more than someone selling a gun thereby authorizes a buyer to hunt without a licence or to commit a crime.[108] A supplier of a jukebox and records at a fixed rental to a restaurant was found not to authorize the hirer to publicly perform the music on the records.[109]

For a time, "authorize" was equated with "sanction, approve, and countenance" or even "permit."[110] "Authorize," "sanction," or "approve" may be close paraphrases, but "countenance" is too wide since it connotes condonation, and to condone is not to authorize.[111] So this equation fell out of favour in the United Kingdom in the 1980s: attempts to turn passivity into authorization were rejected. The broader meaning, however, led to liability in Australia against a university library that let photocopying occur on its premises without taking reasonable steps to discourage suspected infringements.[112] This is doubtful law in the United Kingdom and probably in Canada, too. The Copyright Board has favoured the U.K. view, in holding that an Internet service provider (ISP) does not commit the wrong of authorizing infringement simply by letting users post infringing material on a Web site. The ISP is entitled to assume that users will act legally. On the other hand, a newsgroup moderator who filters or edits messages reaching the group's members may be found to authorize the communications accessed by

---

107   *CBS Songs*, above note 3; *Sony Corp. of America* v. *Universal City Studios Inc.*, 464 U.S. 417 (1984).

108   *Muzak*, above note 105.

109   *Vigneux*, above note 74. The hirer and its customers, however, both performed the work in public. Had the supplier told the hirer that public performances could occur without fee, or if they were partners or joint venturers, authorization might have been found: *Muzak, ibid.* at 189.

110   *Falcon* v. *Famous Players Film Co.*, [1926] 2 K.B. 474 at 491 (C.A.); *Muzak, ibid.* at 193.

111   *Amstrad Consumer Electronics Plc.* v. *British Phonographic Industry Ltd.*, [1986] F.S.R. 159 at 207 (C.A.), aff'd (*sub nom. CBS Songs*), above note 3.

112   *Moorhouse and Angus & Robertson (Publishers) Ltd.* v. *University of New South Wales*, [1976] R.P.C. 151 (Austl. H.C.).

members. The facts of each case must be examined to see whether or not the impugned activity amounts to granting or purporting to grant the right to do an act within the copyright owner's control. If so, authorization may be found.[113] Facts nevertheless remain doubtful until they have been authoritatively "found" by a court, and doubts also remain about how far the Board's views on authorization can be safely applied outside the sphere of performing rights unless they receive endorsement from a Canadian appeal court.

The *1997 Act* has not removed these doubts. It eliminated the risk of liability in certain cases for non-profit educational institutions, libraries, archives, and museums that operate photocopiers on their premises. The main qualification is that the institution has taken or is negotiating for a licence from a reprographic collecting society. A suitable copyright notice must be displayed beside the machine.[114] The Act continues to say nothing about whether a non-complying institution would be liable in the first place. The risk that authorization may occur in these and other situations therefore remains.

9) Substantial Infringement

A copyright owner controls what may be done not only with her whole work but with any substantial part of it.[115] Taking half a book may be infringement; so, too, may changing direct to indirect speech or even paraphrasing every sentence, as these acts change nothing of substance. A substantial part of a book may be not merely its collocation of words but its structure: its relationship of characters, incidents, and development. To lift this structure is as much infringement as lifting a chapter bodily. But structure cannot be abstracted too highly: had William Shakespeare and Leonard Bernstein been contemporaries, *West Side Story* should have opened despite its being inspired by *Romeo and Juliet*. The general stock of incidents in fiction or drama is free for all to use — a substantial part of everyone's culture, not of any one individual's work. What is substantial for one category of work may be unsubstantial for another. A set of numbers may form a substantial part of a table of statistics because of the skill and work that went into their

---

113   *Tariff 22*, above note 10.

114   *C Act*, above note 1, ss. 30.3 & 30.4. See section B(12)(d), "Self-Service Photocopiers," in chapter 7.

115   *C Act*, above note 1, s. 3(1), refers to "any substantial part" of a copyright work only in reference to the opening rights (reproduce, publish, publicly perform), but it applies to *all* the rights: for example, *Kelly*, above note 63 at 371.

production and compilation. The same numbers, if used in a locking routine in a computer program, may be an unsubstantial part of the program if they are simply arbitrary numbers generated from a commonplace algorithm.[116] "Substantial part" thus polices the line dividing what belongs to one and what belongs to all — and what, normatively, should so belong.

Nineteenth-century copyright statutes did not usually include any "substantial part" language, but judges nevertheless rightly wrote it into the law. Infringement then was a question of fact, often decided by a jury. The questions asked interchangeably were whether a taker had "unfairly" or "wrongfully" appropriated a claimant's labour and skill, or whether he had "unfairly used" a claimant's material. Clearly, a value judgment was being made, depending on a number of considerations. Judges who today say that infringement is "all a question of fact and degree" mean much the same.

a) Taking a Particle Does Not Infringe

One should first screen out what cannot in law be a substantial part. "Part" means portion, not "particle."[117] A copyright owner cannot therefore control every particle of her work, any little piece the taking of which cannot affect the value of her work as a whole. So to carry two minor scenes from one play into another was found not to infringe copyright. More recently, transferring 60 of 14,000 lines of computer program source code into another program was found not to take a substantial part of the former work, especially since writing this routine material from scratch would have taken a competent programmer twenty minutes.[118] The occasional hyperbole to the contrary — that the taking of even a single sentence from the likes of a Dickens or a Shakespeare may infringe[119] — is simply nonsense. It falsely supports more mischievous assertions, such as that the inclusion in an audio recording of a single sound, however distinctive, from an earlier record infringes copyright. Two or three seconds from a three-minute record-

---

116   *Data Access Corp.* v. *Powerflex Services Pty. Ltd.* (1999), 45 I.P.R. 353 (Austl. H.C.)

117   *Chatterton* v. *Cave* (1878), 3 App. Cas. 483 at 492 (H.L.) [*Chatterton*].

118   *Ibid.*, at 495: "their extent was so slight, and their effect so small, as to render the taking perfectly immaterial"; *Delrina*, above note 38.

119   For example, *Rockford Map Publishers* v. *Directory Service Co. of Colorado Inc.*, 768 F.2d 145 at 148–49 (7th Cir. 1985): "Dickens did not need to complete *Bleak House* before receiving a copyright; every chapter — indeed every sentence — could be protected standing alone," citing (of course) no authority. *Nihon*, above note 51 at 1520, corrects this tendency: taking one out of six factual paragraphs from the source work was held insubstantial quantitatively.

ing is a mere particle; the sound, while perhaps of value to the taker, should not affect the value of the source work as a whole and so should be outside the copyright owner's control. Performers and record companies nevertheless continue to make such claims.[120]

b) Taking an Essential or Material Part Infringes

All concede that "substantial" connotes quality as much as or even more than quantity: so taking a material or essential part alone infringes another's copyright. A line or note count is relevant, but not conclusive. On the one hand, to take a major chapter from a novel must be infringement except in the rarest of cases.[121] So is the taking of a few bars from the refrain of a popular song — presumably more than the few notes necessary for anyone to "name that tune" — for what else is left?[122] On the other hand, to take four lines from a poem may not infringe: the context in which they are put may be critical. To feature the lines in an advertisement would most likely infringe; to stand them at the head of a magazine article probably would not.[123] Asking whether the part taken could have been protected on its own, as sometimes happens, is not helpful. Let us admit that *haiku* can be protected. How does that answer the question whether what *this* defendant did in taking *these* four lines from *this* poem infringes *this* claimant's rights?

What activities have been found to infringe or not to infringe has been indicated during the discussion on owner's rights.[124] Matters are

---

120 *Grand Upright Music Ltd.* v. *Warner Bros. Records Inc.*, 780 F. Supp. 182 (D.N.Y. 1991), finds unauthorized sampling to be an infringement, but the part taken appears to have been substantial. *Jarvis* v. *A & M Records*, 827 F. Supp. 282 (D.N.J. 1993), suggests that a distinctive bridge and keyboard riff may be a substantial part of a musical work.

121 Compare *Hager* v. *ECW Press Ltd.* (1998), 85 C.P.R. (3d) 289 (Fed. T.D.) [*Hager*]: taking a third of a chapter on pop singer Shania Twain from compilation of biographies for another biography of Twain held infringement; a second edition that removed all direct quotes, but retained some colourable imitations, was held not infringement.

122 *Hawkes & Son (London) Ltd.* v. *Paramount Film Service Ltd.*, [1934] Ch. 593 (C.A.); compare *G. Ricordi & Co. (London) Ltd.* v. *Clayton & Waller Ltd.* (1930), [1928–1935] MacG. Cop. Cas. 154 (Ch.): taking eight bars, a fourth of the waiting motif in *Madam Butterfly*, may not infringe if "not the most distinctive or important part of that air."

123 Compare *Kipling* v. *Genatoson* (1920), [1917–1923] MacG. Cop. Cas. 203 (Ch.) with *Chappell & Co. Ltd.* v. *D.C. Thompson & Co. Ltd.* (1934), [1928–1935] MacG. Cop. Cas. 467 (Ch.). Compare the fair dealing defence, "How Much and What Is Used," section B(11)(b)(iii), in chapter 7.

124 See section A, "Literary, Dramatic, Musical, and Artistic Works," in this chapter.

often judged by how the ordinary reasonable buyer or user would react on seeing the two products involved together. Expert evidence may be needed to put the court in the position of someone reasonably versed in the relevant art or technology, so it may view the products through the eyes of such a person.[125] The following factors then become relevant in reaching a decision on infringement:[126]

- Is the part taken distinctive — something on which the first author spent much skill, effort, or ingenuity? The simpler a work, and the closer the line between its idea and its expression, the less need there is to grant broad control — indeed, the greater the care that must be taken that ideas do not end up being protected.
- Does the author merit the degree of protection sought, to her and others, to produce works of that sort? Would takings of this kind significantly impair the incentive to create for other similarly placed authors?
- Has the claimant's present or future ability to exploit her work been substantially affected?
- Is the user unfairly enriching himself at the author's expense? Has he saved himself much time, trouble, or expense by taking the features that make the claimant's work what it is?
- Do the two works compete for much of the same market? Is the market for the user's work one that ought fairly to belong to the author?

The more one answers these questions in the affirmative, the more likely one should find infringement. Since the variables differ from case to case, decisions on ostensibly similar facts may also — perhaps frustratingly — differ. The overall goal is to ensure that any decision furthers copyright as a means to encourage the production and dissemination of valuable creative work. At the same time, public access to and use of a work for socially desirable ends should not be unduly fettered. A balance must be struck between these two objectives.[127]

c) **Mediating Artistic Practice: Parody and Postmodernism**
In deciding whether an activity infringes, courts should be careful not to interfere with fair artistic practices and trends. Substantiality can act

---

125   *Tele-Direct (Publications) Inc.* v. *American Business Information Inc.* (1997), 76 C.P.R. (3d) 296 (Fed. C.A.) [*Tele-Direct*]; *Ancher, Mortlock, Murray & Wooley Pty. Ltd.* v. *Hooker Homes Ltd.*, [1971] 2 N.S.W.L.R. 278 (S.C.); *Nichols*, above note 65.

126   Compare the list in *U & R Tax Services Ltd.* v. *H & R Block Canada Inc.* (1995), 62 C.P.R. (3d) 257 at 268 (Fed. T.D.); *Hager*, above note 121.

127   *Pink Panther Beauty Corp.* v. *United Artists Corp.*, [1998] 3 F.C. 534 (C.A.), leave to appeal granted (19 November 1998), Doc. 26689 (S.C.C.).

as a rough mediator between what is and what is not acceptable. For example, parody should be given wide leeway when practised by writers, artists, and performers, except in the rare case where the parody is meant to, and does, substitute for its target, or where people do not realize the work is a parody and think it is actually produced by the person it is spoofing.[128] Purely commercial parodies could be more strictly controlled. So, for example, advertisers taking others' music for their jingles could be held to be taking a substantial part, even when they parody the music. Takings of these kinds directly interfere with a composer's livelihood and the stream of income she can expect from having her work exploited.[129]

Other interferences seem less justifiable. Spoofs of trade-marks and labels that were found to be protected by copyright have been held to be infringements. Unions were forbidden from caricaturing the St-Hubert rooster logo or the "Michelin Man," even though the activities were part of an ongoing labour dispute with the mark owner. Similarly, Schweppes successfully asserted copyright in its tonic-water label to stop a firm from marketing SCHLURPPES "tonic bubble bath" under a similar label, even though the product did not compete with tonic water and Schweppes lost no sales. Neither free speech nor free trading were found important enough interests to outweigh the court's desire to protect a trade-mark from having its value diluted. The strange thing is that trade-mark law was not violated by these acts; so copyright, as applied, has produced a result apparently at odds with trade-mark policy.[130] Free speech values would likely exonerate similar activities in the United States,[131] but even U.S. courts have a patchy record in this respect. Thus,

---

128 *Clark* v. *Associated Newspapers Ltd.*, [1998] R.P.C. 261 (Ch.) (no copyright infringement, but passing-off found).

129 *Glyn* v. *Weston Feature Film Co.*, [1916] 1 Ch. 261; *Joy Music Ltd.* v. *Sunday Pictorial Newspapers (1920) Ltd.*, [1960] 2 Q.B. 60; *Campbell* v. *Acuff-Rose Music Inc.*, 114 S.Ct. 1164 (1994) (rap treatment of Roy Orbison's "Oh Pretty Woman"); compare *Avanti*, above note 67 (adult movie not allowed to spoof soap opera characters); *MCA Canada Ltd. (Ltée)* v. *Gilbery & Hawke Advertising Agency Ltd.* (1976), 28 C.P.R. (2d) 52 (Fed. T.D.) (parody for jingle admittedly infringement).

130 *Rôtisseries St-Hubert Ltée* v. *Syndicat des Travailleur(euses) de la Rôtisserie St-Hubert de Drummondville* (CSN) (1986), 17 C.P.R. (3d) 461 (Que. S.C.) [*St-Hubert*]; *Cie générale des établissements Michelin/Michelin & Cie* v. *CAW Canada* (1996), 71 C.P.R. (3d) 348 (Fed. T.D.); *Schweppes Ltd.* v. *Wellingtons Ltd.* (1983), [1984] F.S.R. 210 (Ch.).

131 For example, *International Association of Machinists & Aerospace Workers, AFL-CIO* v. *Winship Green Nursing Center,* 914 F. Supp. 651 (D. Me. 1996), aff'd on other grounds, 103 F.3d 196 (1st Cir. 1996); *United We Stand America Inc.* v. *United We Stand, America New York Inc.*, 44 U.S.P.Q.2d 1351 (2d Cir. 1997).

a U.S. court's decision to brand a whole postmodernist artistic practice — appropriating and recontextualizing previous artwork — as copyright infringement is dubious: postmodernism will go its own way whatever four New York judges say or do.[132] Courts as much as right-holders may need to be constantly reminded to "lighten up."

Unfortunately, many courts still work on the "rough practical test," frequently trotted out by claimants' lawyers, that "what is worth copying is prima facie worth protecting."[133] As a legal invitation, this is too crude to be overtly accepted. Taken literally, it begs all questions of copyrightability, infringement, and substantiality.[134] More often, however, the "test" operates covertly, directing action from the wings rather than taking centre stage. The upshot is that, in practice, people regularly seek permission to carry on arguably non-infringing activities because the cost of permission is usually less than the cost and inconvenience of going to court. But right-holders may refuse permission. When they do, the effect may be to eliminate a socially beneficial, or at least not socially harmful, practice. The uncertainties surrounding substantial infringement work very much to the advantage of powerful right-holders, and quite often to the disadvantage of the general community and the values of free expression.

10) Distributing and Importing Infringing Copies: Secondary Infringement

Anyone can usually sell, resell, and rent lawfully acquired works and non-infringing copies without worrying about copyright.[135] But copyright owners can control the distribution of infringing copies in Canada or unauthorized parallel imports. Someone who knows or should have known that a work infringes copyright, or knows or should have known that it would infringe had it been made in Canada, has to get the copyright owner's consent to deal with the work. Otherwise, he infringes copyright if he does any of the following: sells or rents out the work; exposes it by way of trade, or offers it for sale or rental; distributes it for

---

132   *Rogers*, above note 32.

133   *University of London Press Ltd.* v. *University Tutorial Press Ltd.*, [1916] 2 Ch. 601 at 610.

134   *Ibcos Computers Ltd.* v. *Barclays Mercantile Highland Finance Ltd.* (1994), 28 I.P.R. 25 at 37 (Ch.); *National News Ltd.* v. *Copyright Agency Ltd.* (1996), 34 I.P.R. 53 at 71 (Austl. Fed. Ct.).

135   An exception is renting computer programs and sound recordings. See section A(7), "Rental," and section B, "Sound Recordings, Performances, and Broadcasts," in this chapter.

the purposes of trade or so as to affect the owner of the copyright prejudicially; by way of trade exhibits it in public; possesses the work for any
of these purposes; or imports it into Canada for sale or rental.[136] These
activities — as well as making an infringing work for sale or rental, pos-
sessing plates specifically designed or adapted to make infringing copies, or performing works in public for private profit — are sometimes
called "secondary infringements." They may also amount to criminal
acts if knowingly committed. On conviction after indictment, they can
attract penalties of up to a $1 million fine and/or five years' jail.[137]

Three issues are pertinent to this discussion: parallel imports, the
knowledge requirement, and exclusive book distribution.

a) Parallel Imports

The provision that a person who handles a work, knowing that it
"would infringe copyright if it had been made within Canada," operates
to prevent the import and commercial handling of unauthorized copies
made outside Canada. Works made offshore without anyone's consent
are obviously caught. Indeed, the Canadian owner or exclusive licensee
who suspects that such goods are about to be imported can obtain a
court order directing Customs to stop them at the border.[138] But the
former provision also targets goods legitimately made abroad that are
imported into Canada. The idea is not to strike at the inadvertent or
otherwise innocent importer. To be liable, the importer must know, or
should have known, that the Canadian copyright owner would not have
consented to the making of the works had they been made in Canada.[139]
This provision may even be used to stop the import of non-copyright
goods. Since copyright may exist in the trade-marks, labels, packaging,
or even computer programs associated with goods (e.g., a computer
chip that helps run a car or a microwave), the copyright owner may stop
the parallel import of the non-copyright goods because the copyright in
the associated matter would be infringed by this act.[140]

---

136   *C Act*, above note 1, ss. 27(2) to (4).
137   *C Act, ibid.*, ss. 42(1) & (2). The criminal provisions extend also to sound
recordings and fixed performances and communication signals.
138   *C Act, ibid.*, s. 44.1.
139   *Clarke, Irwin & Co. v. C. Cole & Co.*, [1960] O.R. 117 (H.C.J.); *Fly by Nite Music
Co. v. Record Wherehouse Ltd.*, [1975] F.C. 386 (T.D.).
140   For example, *Frank & Hirsch (Pty.) Ltd. v. A. Roopanand Brothers (Pty.) Ltd.*
(1993), 29 I.P.R. 465 (S. Afr. S.C.(A.D.)) (TDK blank audio tapes). Removal of the
offending trade-mark or part, if possible, may avoid infringement. In 1998
Australia and New Zealand amended their copyright laws to prevent the use of
copyright in this way to stop the import of non-infringing goods.

Apart from the case of books, exclusive selling agents or distributors cannot use these provisions because these dealers typically have only contractual rights that create no interest in copyright.[141]

b) Knowledge

Whoever personally makes or authorizes the making of an infringing copy of a work infringes.[142] But, as already noted, those who deal (by sale, rental, import, etc.) with an infringing copy that they have not personally made infringe copyright only if they know or should have known they are dealing with infringing copies.

Before 1997 the Act required such dealers to have actual knowledge. The 1997 Act also imposed liability on dealers who "should have known" they were dealing with infringing goods. Previously, the Act was lenient with the ignorant, the careless, and the unsophisticated. Claimants wanting to reach such dealers often needed to inform the trade or a targeted dealer of their allegations and would have to back them up fully, for proceedings issued before an innocent acquirer had a reasonable time to investigate the allegations risked dismissal with costs. Turning a blind eye to the obvious can, however, amount to actual knowledge. A person is assumed to have "the ordinary understanding expected of persons in his line of business, unless by his or other evidence . . . [the court] is convinced otherwise."[143] Sometimes, knowledge only of the facts constituting infringement was found enough to constitute the necessary actual knowledge, and an honest but mistaken belief that the goods did not infringe was thought irrelevant.[144] Since 1997 the doubt surrounding this interpretation of the Act is removed. Those who "should have known" that the copies were infringing are equally liable with those who actually know so.[145]

c) Exclusive Book Distribution

Under the 1997 Act, sole distributors for books in Canada or any part of Canada, or for any particular sector of the Canadian market (e.g., education), can stop anyone from importing a book coming under

---

141 *Maison du livre français de Montréal Inc.* v. *Institut littéraire du Qué. Ltée* (1957), 31 C.P.R. 69 (Que. S.C.). See section A(10)(c), "Exclusive Book Distribution," in this chapter.

142 There may, however, also be liability on other grounds — for example, vicarious liability. See section B, "Whom to Sue," in chapter 9.

143 *RCA Corp.* v. *Custom Cleared Sales Pty. Ltd.* (1978), 19 A.L.R. 123 at 126 (N.S.W.C.A.).

144 *Sillitoe,* above note 49.

145 *C Act,* above note 1, ss. 27(2) & (3).

their distribution agreement if the intending importer has been previously notified in writing of the fact that the book is so covered. Unauthorized importation, or the knowing distribution or possession for distribution of an unauthorized importation, is an infringement of copyright. The Customs authorities may also be enlisted to stop imports at the border. The ban became effective on the coming into force of the *Book Importation Regulations* of 1999.[146]

These distributors' rights are connected to copyright only in that they apply to in-copyright books. Their object is less to encourage creativity than to reinforce the way in which book publishers find it congenial to partition the Canadian market. The scheme expressly allows distributors — both Canadian and foreign-owned holders of sole Canadian book distribution rights, including local affiliates of foreign publishers or distributors — to charge more for an imported book than the price at which legitimate copies can be acquired abroad. Canadian businesses who try to save money by "buying around" are now deemed to be copyright infringers.

i) Scope of Distribution Right

While the Act says that "any" person may infringe these provisions, the word "any" cannot be taken literally. Elsewhere in the Act, non-profit libraries, archives, museums, or educational institutions are allowed to import a single copy of a book without going through the exclusive distributor. Similarly, anyone — including, apparently, a corporation — can import two copies of a book for his own use, and government departments may import as many copies as they like.[147] The targets of the right are further restricted by the *Book Importation Regulations*. These regulations provide that the critical written notice, without which no infringement can occur, may be given to booksellers, others who sell books in the operation of a business, nonprofit and for-profit libraries, but to nobody else.[148] If the *Regulations* are valid in this respect, it follows that no mechanism has been provided for exclusive distributors directly to ban imports by persons or institutions outside these categories. Presumably, bodies such as archives,

---

146   *C Act, ibid.*, ss. 27.1 & 44.2; *Book Importation Regulations*, SOR/99-324, 133 Can. Gaz. (Pt. II) 2050 [*Book Regs.*], made under *C Act*, ss. 2 (def. "exclusive distributor") and 27.1(6). Criminal prosecution is not possible: *C Act*, s. 42(5).

147   *C Act, ibid.*, s. 45(1). See section B(9), "Imports," in chapter 7.

148   *Book Regs.*, above note 146, s. 4. A for-profit library is rather oddly called an "institution established or conducted for profit that maintains a collection of documents."

museums, and educational institutions were not seen as threatening the proposed system.

The distribution right applies to books in English or French or to Canadian editions in any language — namely, editions published abroad under an agreement that confers a separate right to reproduce the book for the Canadian market.[149] "Book" is expansively defined to include any volume or part or division of a volume in printed form, but excludes items such as pamphlets; newspapers, reviews, magazines, or other periodicals; separately published maps, charts, plans, and sheet music; and instruction or repair manuals that accompany products or services.[150] The distribution right does not extend to the importation of leased books; books intended solely for re-export; remaindered books that have been offered as such abroad for at least sixty days and importation of which has been notified to the Canadian distributor; books marked as "damaged" by the importer or retailer; and used scientific, technical, or scholarly texts for use in non-profit or for-profit educational institutions.[151]

ii) Conditions Imposed on Distributor

The distributor's right is subject to a number of conditions. The distributor must be appointed in writing by the copyright owner or exclusive licensee of the book in Canada. He must notify potential importers in writing of the distributorship and what books it covers.[152] He must meet complicated pricing and performance criteria that vary according to the book's origin, language, and availability. For example, an order for a French-language book from Europe must be filled within five days if the book is in stock in Canada, but within sixty days if it is not in stock. The criteria for English-language books are split into two. One covers the first twelve months after the *Book Importation Regulations* of 1999 took effect on 1 September 1999, and a stricter set applies from then on. Before 1 September 2000, an imported English-language book must be supplied within five days of order if it is in stock. Later orders must be filled within three days. For books not in stock, European imports must arrive within thirty-five days until 1 September

---

149   *Book Regs.*, *ibid.*, ss. 1 (def. "Canadian edition") & 2(1). Presumably, the targeted agreement will grant either a licence or an assignment for a stated period of the Canadian reproduction right.

150   *C Act*, above note 1, s. 2, def. "book."

151   *Book Regs.*, above note 146, ss. 7, 8, & 10.

152   The contents of the notice and how it should be sent are set out in *Book Regs.*, *ibid.*, s. 4.

2000, but cannot exceed thirty days past then. Orders for U.S. imports must be filled initially within fifteen days, but after 1 September 2000 must be filled within twelve days.[153]

iii) Premium Chargeable

The premium the exclusive distributor can charge for U.S. books is 10 percent over the U.S. list price — the price listed on the book cover — minus any applicable discounts. The premium for other books is 15 percent over the list price in the country of export, whatever discounts are usually offered. These premiums may be exacted, whatever the exclusive distributor actually pays for the book and whatever the book can be actually bought for abroad.

These percentages are said to represent the average actual costs paid by book importers for transportation and related expenses.[154] Since the percentages are only averages, clearly some, perhaps many, exclusive distributors incur lower costs than these, but now have little incentive to pass savings on to buyers. Canadian policy on exclusive book distribution thus differs markedly from recent initiatives taken by comparable net book importing countries such as Australia and New Zealand, which have allowed parallel importing of books precisely to keep prices down. It will be interesting to see how Canadian consumers will react to the new scheme, and whether it will, in any event, survive the inroads into traditional bookselling created by the increased individual use of the Internet for online book purchasing and downloading.

B. SOUND RECORDINGS, PERFORMANCES, AND BROADCASTS

Complicated sets of rights apply particularly to sound recordings and performers' performances. The complications arise because not all countries grant a full range of rights to these items. Those that do grant such rights do not always apply national treatment to foreign-based record producers, or to foreign performances connected to countries that do not grant similar rights to equivalent persons connected with Canada.

---

153   *Ibid.*, s. 5; *C Act*, above note 1, s. 2 (def. "exclusive distributor").
154   According to the Regulatory Impact Analysis Statement accompanying the *Book Regs.*, above note 146.

1) Sound Recordings

Copyright for sound recordings includes first distribution, reproduction, rental, and authorization rights, as well as rights over unauthorized distribution or importation of sound recordings. Rights of remuneration for public performance or telecommunication of the record, and on sales of blank audio recording media (e.g., audiotapes and disks), exist for sound-recording makers who fulfil the following further three criteria:[155]

- The maker must be closely involved in the making of the sound recording. He must have arranged the performers' contracts, or undertaken the financial or technical arrangements necessary for the sounds to be first fixed.[156]
- For the public performance and telecommunication rights, the maker of the record must have its corporate headquarters in Canada or a *Rome Convention* country, or must be a citizen or permanent resident of one of them at the time the record was first fixed. Alternatively, all the records must have been made in such a country.[157] The minister of industry may, by a statement published in the *Canada Gazette*, extend these benefits reciprocally to persons similarly connected with countries that grant substantially equivalent benefits to Canadian citizens, permanent residents, or corporations headquartered in Canada.[158]
- To qualify for the blank audio recording media levy, the record must be first fixed by a Canadian citizen, permanent resident, or record company with its headquarters in Canada. The minister may extend this right to other countries on a reciprocal basis.[159]

The levy and the public performance and broadcast royalties, although first introduced by the *1997 Act*, also apply to records made before 1 September 1997.

---

155   *C Act*, above note 1, ss. 18(1), 19(1), 27(2) to (4), & 81(1). For the content of these rights, see the corresponding headings under section A, "Literary, Dramatic, Musical, and Artistic Works," in this chapter; also section B(14)(c), "Blank Audio Recording Media Levy," in chapter 7.

156   *C Act, ibid.*, s. 2.11 (the French version is clearer than the English on the mandatory character of this requirement).

157   *C Act, ibid.*, s. 20(1).

158   *C Act, ibid.*, ss. 22 & 85.

159   *C Act, ibid.*, s. 79, def. "eligible maker." Presumably, this person cannot be different from the sound-recording maker who was responsible for qualifying the record for Canadian protection in the first place.

2) Performances

Two classes of performances qualify for copyright or rights of remuneration: those connected to *WTO Agreement* states and those connected to *Rome Convention* states. Canadian performers, as well as other performers based on reciprocity, may also benefit from a blank audio recording media levy.[160]

WTO performances attract a more limited set of rights than do *Rome* performances. A performer who qualifies under either *WTO* or *Rome* criteria may, presumably, choose whichever set of rights benefits him most in a particular instance.

a) *WTO Agreement* Performances

Copyright for performers from *WTO* states comprises a right to fix their performance on a record, a reproduction right over records containing unauthorized fixations, a telecommunication right over their live performance, and an authorization right.[161] They also have rights, like those of copyright owners over traditional works, in respect of unauthorized distribution and importation of fixed performances.[162]

b) *Rome Convention* Performances

Performers whose performance is connected to a *Rome* state have the following copyrights:

- For unfixed performances, a telecommunication right, and a public performance right where the performance is telecommunicated to the public other than by a communication signal (e.g., by cable).
- For fixed performances, a reproduction right over fixations made without their authority; a right to prevent the use of authorized fixations beyond the purpose the performer authorized; a right over unauthorized reproductions taken from a copy made pursuant to a user's right or the blank audio recording media exemption, if the reproduction itself does not come under a user's right or the exemption; a right over unauthorized distribution and importation of fixed performances, akin to the similar right of copyright owners over traditional works.

---

160   *C Act, ibid.*, ss. 81ff. See section B(14)(c), "Blank Audio Recording Media Levy," in chapter 7.

161   *C Act, ibid.*, s. 26.

162   *C Act, ibid.*, ss. 27(2) to (4). See section A(10), "Distributing and Importing Infringing Copies: Secondary Infringement," in this chapter.

- A rental right over sound recordings of their performance.
- An authorization right.[163]

The *Rome* performer also has rights of equitable remuneration for public performance and telecommunication if the performance is embodied in a published sound recording.[164]

3) Broadcasts

Broadcasters have rights to fix their transmissions, reproduction rights over unauthorized fixations, performance rights over television programs played in places where the public pays an entrance fee to view, an authorization right over these acts, and also a right to authorize simultaneous retransmission by other broadcasters. They also have rights, like those of copyright owners over traditional works, in respect of unauthorized distribution and importation of fixed communication signals.[165]

FURTHER READINGS

BOWREY, K., "Copyright, the Paternity of Artistic Works, and the Challenge Posed by Postmodern Artists" (1994) 8 I.P.J. 285

FAWCETT, J.J., & P. TORREMANS, *Intellectual Property and Private International Law* (Oxford: Clarendon, 1998)

GREEN, B., "'Haven't I Heard This Song Before?': Subconscious Plagiarism in Pop Music and the Infringement of Copyright — Towards a Partial Defense of Cryptomnesia" (1998) 13 I.P.J. 53

HAYES, M.S., "Copyright Infringement on the Internet," in M. Racicot et al., *The Cyberspace Is Not a "No Law Land": A Study of the Issues of Liability for Content Circulating on the Internet* (February 1997), available at <http://strategis.ic.gc.ca>

---

163   *C Act, ibid.*, ss. 15(1) & 27(2) to (4). For the content of these rights, see the corresponding headings under section A, "Literary, Dramatic, Musical, and Artistic Works," and section A(10), "Distributing and Importing Infringing Copies: Secondary Infringement," in this chapter.

164   *C Act, ibid.*, ss. 19 & 20.

165   *C Act, ibid.*, ss. 21(1) & 27(2) to (4). For the content of these rights, see the corresponding headings under section A, "Literary, Dramatic, Musical, and Artistic Works," and section A(10) "Distributing and Importing Infringing Copies: Secondary Infringement," in this chapter.

INFORMATION HIGHWAY ADVISORY COUNCIL, *Final Report: Connection, Community, Content: The Challenge of the Information Highway* (Ottawa: The Council, 1995) 112 ff.

KARJALA, D.S., "A Coherent Theory for the Copyright Protection of Computer Software and Recent Judicial Interpretations" 66 Cincinnati L. Rev. 53 (1997)

LITMAN, J., "The Exclusive Right to Read" (1994) 13 Cardozo Arts & Ent. L.J. 29

NEVINS JR., F.M., "Copyright + Character = Catastrophe" (1992) 39 J. Copr. Soc. U.S.A. 303

SPENCE, M., "Intellectual Property and the Problem of Parody" (1998) 114 L.Q.R. 594

SPURGEON, C.P., "Digital Networks and Copyright: Licensing and Accounting for Use — The Role of Copyright Collectives" (1998) 12 I.P.J. 225

TAKACH, G.F., *Computer Law* (Concord, Ont.: Irwin Law, 1998)

ULLMANN, D., "Liability Issues in Providing Musical Content to the Internet Community" (1997) 76 C.P.R. (3d) 417

VAVER, D., "Abridgments and Abstracts: Copyright Implications" [1995] 5 E.I.P.R. 225

VAVER, D., "Canada," in P. Geller, ed., *International Copyright Law and Practice*, 10th update (New York: Matthew Bender, 1998) §8[1]

VAVER, D., "The Protection of Character Merchandising — A Survey of Some Common Law Jurisdictions" (1978) 9 I.I.C. 541

VAVER, D., "Record and Software Rentals: The Copyright Spin" (1995) 10 I.P.J. 109

VAVER, D., "Rejuvenating Copyright, Digitally," in *Symposium on Digital Technology and Copyright* (Ottawa: Department of Justice, 1995) 1

VAVER, D., "Translation and Copyright: A Canadian Focus" [1994] 4 E.I.P.R. 159

WEATHERALL, K., "An End to Private Communications in Copyright? The Expansion of Rights to Communicate Works to the Public" [1999] E.I.P.R. 342 (Part I), 398 (Part 2)

CHAPTER 6

AUTHORS' MORAL RIGHTS

Authors have "moral rights" in respect of their works, quite apart from any copyright. The word "moral" is somewhat misleading. These rights are legally enforceable.[1] They are based on the idea that an author's work is an extension of the author and that any assault on it is as much an attack on the author as a physical assault. Parting with the copyright does not lessen the author's personal attachment to the work, and the author should have recourse against those who present the work differently from the way the author originally intended.[2]

A. GENERAL FEATURES

The Act recognizes three rights: attribution, integrity, and association. Other analogous author interests are protected through common and civil law doctrines. The rights provided by the Act are intimately linked with copyright. They apply only to authors who have produced an original work protected by copyright, whether or not they still own the copy-

---

1   The term is a poor translation of *droits moraux*, roughly "personal" or "intellectual" rights.

2   Performers, sound-recording makers, and broadcasters are not "authors" and do not create "works"; hence they have no moral rights. Article 5 of the *WIPO Performances and Phonograms Treaty* of 1996, <http://clea.wipo.int/lpbin/lpext.dll>, proposes moral rights for performers akin to authors' moral rights.

right.[3] The rights last as long as the copyright and descend to an author's estate. Otherwise, they are personal: they can be waived, but not assigned.[4] The usual schedule of remedies applies, but it is discretionary.[5]

Moral rights theory emanated from nineteenth-century Europe and became internationally entrenched in the *Berne Convention*'s 1928 revision. Canada legislated the *Berne* provision (art. 6*bis*) into the *Copyright Act* in 1931, later clarifying and expanding its operation in 1988. But moral rights were recognized even earlier in a 1915 *Criminal Code* amendment. This made it an offence either to change anything in a copyright-protected dramatic, operatic, or musical work that was to be publicly performed for profit or to suppress its title or authorship, unless the author or her legal representative consented. A filmmaker who took a play, changed its title, and suppressed the dramatist's name was successfully prosecuted in 1916.[6] This criminal provision was moved to the *Copyright Act* in 1921. Though still on the books, it has lain unused for at least the last half century.[7]

Authors' interests may also be protected through common and civil law doctrines. This protection was pointed out as long ago as 1911, when the Supreme Court forced a publisher to return the author's only copy of a rejected manuscript. One judge said:

> I cannot agree that the sale of a manuscript of a book is subject to the same rules as the sale of any other article of commerce, *e.g.*, paper, grain or lumber. The vendor of such things loses all dominion over them when once the contract is executed and the purchaser may deal with the thing which he has purchased as he chooses. It is his to keep, to alienate or to destroy. But it will not be contended that the publisher who bought the manuscript of "The Life of Gladstone," by Morley, or of Cromwell by the same author, might publish the manuscript, having paid the author his price, with such emendations or additions as might perchance suit his political or religious views and give them to the world as those of one of the foremost publicists of our day. Nor could the author be denied by the publisher the right to

---

3   See section A(1), "Author," in chapter 4, and section A(1), "Originality," in chapter 3.

4   *Copyright Act*, R.S.C. 1985, c. C-42 [*C Act*; unless otherwise indicated, references to the Act are as amended], ss. 14.1, 14.2, 28.1, & 28.2. See also section B(2)(a), "What Interests Revert," in chapter 4.

5   See section G, "Remedies for Infringement of Moral Rights," in chapter 9.

6   *Joubert v. Géracimo* (1916), 35 D.L.R. 683 (Que. C.A.).

7   *C Act*, above note 4, s. 43. The penalties for violation — maximum $250 or $500 fines, and two to four months' jail in addition for repeat offences — have not changed since 1921.

make corrections, in dates or otherwise, if such corrections were found to be necessary for historical accuracy; nor could the manuscript be published in the name of another. After the author has parted with his pecuniary interest in the manuscript, he retains a species of personal or moral right in the product of his brain.[8]

Sentiments like these may underpin authors' actions for passing-off, misappropriation of personality, or breach of contract when their interests are affected. Such claims, interestingly enough, have met with more success than assertions of the moral rights the Act provides.

B. MORAL RIGHTS

The following moral rights are now examined: attribution, integrity, association, and others.

1) Attribution

The Act entitles an author to remain anonymous. It also entitles an author to be associated with the work by name or under a pseudonym, "where reasonable in the circumstances," when an act within copyright occurs (e.g., reproduction, translation, or telecommunication to the public).[9] So, a professional photographer was recently awarded $2000 when another photographer, working under instructions, usurped the former's authorship.[10] Falsely attributing work to someone else — for example, saying that a work is "by X" when X had nothing to do with it — falls outside this right, but X may, in some cases, obtain redress against this form of passing-off in a provincial court.[11]

The "reasonableness" qualification, introduced in 1988, has not been judicially discussed. It is presumably there for the sake of flexibility and to deter trivial complaints. For example, producing a music video, an advertising campaign, or a complex computer program may involve inputs from many people. Demands for attribution could pro-

---

8   *Morang & Co.* v. *Le Sueur* (1911), 45 S.C.R. 95 at 97–98, Fitzpatrick C.J.C., relying on civil law doctrine in an Ontario appeal.

9   *C Act*, above note 4, s. 14.1(1). The "reasonableness" qualification does not seem to apply to the right to remain anonymous.

10 *Ateliers Tango argentin Inc.* v. *Festival d'Espagne et d'Amérique latine Inc.*, [1997] R.J.Q. 3030 (S.C.).

11 *Clark* v. *Associated Newspapers Ltd.*, [1998] R.P.C. 261 (Ch.).

duce a list as long as that found at the end of a movie. The difficulties of deciding who did what and how it contributed to the final product may make it unreasonable for anybody to demand credit. This is certainly the way many advertising agencies and software companies proceed, preferring to stress their ownership rather than actual authorship. Presumably, too, the reasonableness qualification is what allows broadcasters not to mention composers or lyricists when playing records on air, while, perhaps paradoxically, often mentioning the names of the performers, who have no statutory moral rights.

The qualification is unclear about whether it is supposed to reinforce or to undermine respect for contractual provisions that deal explicitly with credit. Suppose two people collaborate on a work, but only one is named co-author. In the absence of any agreement on the point, the omitted person is entitled to credit. A court may give damages for the past breach and order an appropriate credit line to be inserted. For example, if Martha thinks up a short story and takes it to John, a script doctor, to put into literary shape, Martha and John may technically be joint authors.[12] An appropriate credit line might be "by Martha and John" or, perhaps, *vice versa*. But if Martha's contribution is relatively more important, the credit line might better read "by Martha, with John."[13] Suppose, however, the contract said that John would get no credit. Would it be "reasonable in the circumstances" to enforce this agreement and perpetuate the lie that the work was a sole production? Or would it be more reasonable to refuse to enforce the provision and let the truth out? Since the Act specifically allows moral rights to be waived,[14] one suspects that contract may be allowed to trump truth.

2) Integrity

The right of integrity stops work from being "distorted, mutilated or otherwise modified," but only if this prejudices the author's honour or reputation.[15] Theoretically, then, the author may control the way her work is presented, at least to some extent, though this control should not prevent reasonable adaptations and changes over time. So, for example, even "faithful" cinematic adaptations of a book rarely trans-

---

12   See section A(1)(c), "Joint Authors," in chapter 4.

13   *Courtenay v. Polkosnik* (1983), 77 C.P.R. (2d) 140 at 144 (Ont. H.C.J.); compare *Goulet v. Marchand* (18 September 1985), (Que. S.C.) [unreported]: part compiler of legal text entitled to co-author credit.

14   See section C, "Waiver," in this chapter.

15   *C Act,* above note 4, ss. 14.1(1) & 28.2(1).

pose the literary medium directly into a visual one; so long as the book's theme and spirit are fairly interpreted and presented, an author may not be able to complain if whole scenes and characters are omitted. Similarly, an artist's natural sensitivity should not interfere with the sort of experimentation that is the hallmark of much artistic progress. Where would parody, jazz, or techno be if authors could complain about the way a parodist, jazz musician, or techno group handled their work?[16] The reputation of both Leonardo da Vinci and the *Mona Lisa* remains intact, despite Marcel Duchamp's representation of her with an added moustache and goatee, and our understanding of art is enriched by the implications of Duchamp's iconoclasm.

Concerns like these may underlie the often sceptical reception with which moral rights are greeted in Canada. The scrawler of graffiti on a public sculpture may, on one view, be infringing the sculptor's moral rights. On another view, he may be exercising, however crudely, rights of free speech and comment. In any event, he is untraceable, and courts have not visited his delinquency on art owners, who have been held under no duty to preserve or restore inventory. Courts have even held that total destruction may not violate moral rights. Thus, when a town's clean-up crew dumped public sculptures in the local river after the works had deteriorated through vandalism and neglect, the Quebec courts dismissed the sculptors' claims against the town. The artists' reputation could hardly suffer from works that were out of sight and out of mind.[17] At the other extreme, a choreographer's claim that the ballet he composed could not be staged without his participation was also dismissed. Others could direct the work competently and not "every step or nuance of movement in every performance" need be duplicated. Near enough was good enough.[18] Against unpromising jurisprudence like this, a case where Michael Snow forced the Eaton Centre in downtown Toronto to remove Christmas decorations with which the centre's management had bedecked his Canada geese sculpture comes as somewhat of a surprise. The court there found that the work had indeed been distorted or modified to the prejudice of the artist's honour or reputation.[19]

---

16 Compare *Schott Musik International GmbH & Co.* v. *Colossal Records of Aust. Pty. Ltd.* (1997), 38 I.P.R. 1, esp. at 17 (Austl. Fed. Ct.), holding that a techno version of the "O Fortuna" chorus from Carl Orff's *Carmina Burana* did not "debase" Orff's original work, but was a new genre with its own integrity.

17 *Gnass* v. *Cité d'Alma* (3 June 1977), (Que. C.A.) [unreported] [*Gnass*], discussed in D. Vaver, "Authors' Moral Rights in Canada" (1983) 14 I.I.C. 329 at 341ff.

18 *Patsalas* v. *National Ballet of Canada* (1986), 13 C.P.R. (3d) 522 at 528 (Ont. H.C.J.).

19 *Snow* v. *Eaton Centre Ltd.* (1982), 70 C.P.R. (2d) 105 (Ont. H.C.J.) [*Snow*].

Snow would have an even easier ride today because prejudice to an artist's honour or reputation is now "deemed to have occurred" whenever a painting, sculpture, or engraving is distorted, mutilated, or otherwise modified.[20] One trusts this "deeming" presents only a rebuttable presumption; otherwise, a modern-day da Vinci would have a clear claim against a follower of Duchamp who dared to interfere with even a print purchased from a museum gift shop. The Act also provides that merely changing a work's location or making good-faith efforts to preserve it is not automatically a distortion.[21] The right of owners of public artwork to relocate works to placate offended public sensibilities is therefore confirmed, at least if the new site still allows some public viewing. No attempt is made, however, to reconcile these provisions with the case earlier noted, in which public sculptures were relocated at the bottom of the local river.[22] Total destruction apparently continues to be less offensive than relocation to an obscure warehouse or handing the work back to the artist. The views of those who produced the now dismantled or crumbling sculptures of Lenin throughout Eastern Europe would be interesting on this point.

Proving prejudice to honour or reputation outside these "deemed" cases continues to be difficult. In *Snow*, the court said that considerable weight may be given to the artist's opinion if "reasonably arrived at."[23] But, more recently, "objective" evidence of prejudice has been insisted on. A novelist's moral rights claim that his work had been poorly anthologized by a copyright infringer was dismissed because the claimant's view was unsupported by expert opinion and his career had continued to flourish despite wide distribution of the repugnant work.[24] This approach may help stem some dubious claims — for example, where employers enlist their employees' moral rights as a tactic against

---

20 *C Act*, above note 4, s. 28.2(2).

21 *C Act*, *ibid.*, s. 28.2(3).

22 *Gnass* in Vaver, above note 17 at 338.

23 *Snow*, above note 19 at 106; see D. Vaver, "Snow v. The Eaton Centre: Wreaths on Sculpture Prove Accolade for Artists' Moral Rights" (1983) 8 Can. Bus. L.J. 81.

24 *Prise de Parole Inc. v. Guérin, Éditeur Ltée* (1995), 66 C.P.R. (3d) 257 at 266 (Fed. T.D.), aff'd (1996), 73 C.P.R. (3d) 557 (Fed. C.A.) (a copyright infringement claim, however, succeeded); similarly *Gnass*, above note 17, where the sculptors' defamation claim equally failed.

competitors.[25] At the same time, it may turn aside legitimate complaints from artists with well-established reputations: the da Vincis that even Duchamps cannot shake.

3) Association

The author may also control the use of the work "in association with a product, service, cause or institution." This right is part of the integrity right and so is infringed only if the use prejudices the author's honour or reputation.[26] An advertiser may therefore be unable to use a Gordon Lightfoot composition in a commercial, even if the copyright owner (typically the music publisher) agrees, unless Lightfoot also agrees. If he never appears in commercials, Lightfoot could argue that any use of his work in advertising is in itself offensive. That apart, whether Lightfoot has a right to refuse may depend on the commercial involved. His honour or his reputation could still be prejudiced if the music is badly presented, the lyrics are distorted, or the commercial is distasteful (e.g., for toilet cleaners rather than an anti-drug campaign).

4) Other Rights

The Act recognizes no other moral rights, although under the *Berne Convention* an author can prevent "derogatory action" in relation to her work beyond attribution, integrity, and association right infringements. The sort of derogatory action recognized in European states that take moral rights seriously may, however, also be recognized by the common or the civil law. For example, authors are said to have the right to create or to refuse to create a work; this right is reflected at common law in rules that invalidate unreasonable restraints on the right to work and that allow dilatory authors under contract to plead "writer's block" to specific performance (but not damages) actions brought by publishers.

---

25   Nintendo tried this tactic in seeking to block *Game Genie*, a third-party cartridge that fitted a Nintendo computer and improved the way Nintendo videogames ran. The complaint of Nintendo's staff videogame designer that his artistic integrity had been compromised because of the new antics Super Mario and Donkey Kong were made to perform did not impress Canadian courts much: *Nintendo of America Inc. v. Camerica Corp.* (1991), 34 C.P.R. (3d) 193 (Fed. T.D.), aff'd (1991), 36 C.P.R. (3d) 352 (Fed. C.A.), refusing interlocutory relief.
26   *C Act*, above note 4, ss. 14.1(1) & 28.2(1)(b).

In Europe, artists are also said to have a right to prevent excessive criticism of their work. This right may be vindicated in Canada through defamation law. European authors may also usually decide when or whether to make a work public. This feature is part of copyright in Canadian law — the first public distribution right.[27] Even the right, recognized in France, to withdraw a work from circulation or disavow it if it no longer represents the author's views may be recognized at common law. This author's right is rarely exercised in France because publishers can insist on being indemnified for the cost of existing stock. Common law courts could presumably develop a similar right subject to similar conditions. There is unfavourable old case law. For example, British poet laureate Robert Southey found he could not suppress distribution of a youthful poem he no longer believed in.[28] But is it really possible that a newspaper today could publish, with impunity, a letter to the editor, over the objections of a sender who has since found out that his facts are wrong and the letter is defamatory?[29]

C. WAIVER

One reason moral rights are more talked about than exercised in Canada is because the Act explicitly allows their waiver.[30] While assignments or exclusive licences for copyright need to be in writing, waivers of moral rights do not. A waiver may even be implied. No such implication arises simply because a copyright is assigned or licensed. Indeed, an obligation to respect moral rights should usually be inferred where a written assignment or licence says nothing about them.[31] Still, a waiver was implied against an engineer who tried to complain about changes made in his design work for public safety reasons, even though his

---

27   C Act, ibid., s. 3(1). Being a copyright, however, it can be exercised by the owner against an author's interests. This may happen when the copyright has been assigned or has first vested in someone other than the author (e.g., her employer). See also section A(1), "First Public Distribution," in chapter 5.

28   Southey v. Sherwood (1817), 2 Mer. 435, 35 E.R. 1006 (Ch.).

29   This result was unlikely even in the nineteenth century: Davis v. Miller & Fairly (1855), 17 D. 1166 (Ct. Sess., Scot.).

30   C Act, above note 4, s. 14.1(2). The waiver prima facie also benefits later copyright owners and licensees: s. 14.1(4).

31   C Act, ibid., s. 14.1(3); Blair v. Osborne & Tomkins, [1971] 2 Q.B. 78 (C.A.) (implied licence to copy architect's drawings does not waive architect's moral rights).

contract said nothing about moral rights.[32] Although the implication was fairly made in that case, the principle that allows waivers to be implied may be applied in rather less obvious cases.

Exploitation agreements often contain provisions under which authors expressly waive their moral rights in perpetuity. This practice has long been common, for example, in the motion picture industry; writers whose books, plays, or scripts are used for a film inevitably sign a standard form that lets the film company do what it likes with the material. The heirs of Victor Hugo cannot complain about Disney's animated version of *The Hunchback of Notre Dame* because the book is long out of copyright; but had Hugo been alive today he would have had no claim, either, because any contract he would have signed with a North American film company would have required him to waive all moral rights. Courts may sometimes restrict a waiver by construing it to cover only changes that do not prejudice the author's honour or reputation. But explicit language can presumably oust this qualification.[33] Otherwise, trying to invalidate such waivers is as difficult as avoiding any other contract provision for some abuse of power (fraud, misrepresentation, restraint of trade, unconscionability, etc.).

D. JUSTIFICATION AND PROBLEMS

How, then, can moral rights be theoretically justified? Metaphysical reasoning about the intimate link between an author and her work seems about as persuasive as attempts to base copyright protection on everyone's "natural" right to the fruits of his labour. A more plausible case for moral rights could draw on four sources:

- "Truth-in-marketing": Like trade-marks, moral rights help assure the public that the works it has come to associate with a particular author are indeed that author's genuine product.
- Social reward: Authors merit whatever reward (or lack of it) their work may bring, and that merit is in the work as they have issued it.
- Author empowerment: Moral rights give authors a bargaining chip which, given the greater power generally wielded by entrepreneurs, allows the former some say over the manner in which their work is later exploited.

---

32 *New Brunswick Telephone Co. v. John Maryon International Ltd.* (1981), 33 N.B.R. (2d) 543 (C.A.).

33 *Kerr v. R.* (1982), 66 C.P.R. (2d) 165 (Fed. T.D.).

- Cultural preservation: The public interest in a continuous record of its culture justifies giving authors some control over their works as a private right to be exercised for the public good.

In practice, however, there are enormous difficulties in enforcing moral rights in a digital era. They may be enough to cause the "moral" in "moral rights" to take on its more common meaning as an opposite of "legal," since moral suasion may come to replace legal enforceability on the Internet. How may an author stop a user from altering and redistributing work that has been downloaded from the Internet? How can he stop still later users altering it further? How can authorship in a composite work be traced and established? When practical problems such as this combine with the scepticism with which North Americans treat moral rights, the threat to moral rights is clear.[34] By contrast, Europeans have tended to treat moral rights more reverentially. The notion of the Author as Romantic Genius may still linger there. Whether this respect will hold true much longer, except as a form of academic nostalgia, is an interesting question.

Meanwhile, how moral rights will play out in Canadian courts is uncertain. Take the problem of colourizing black-and-white movies. After initial hostility during the late 1980s from many film directors and actors, this practice has become so accepted in North America that a moral rights claim is almost inconceivable except against a totally incompetent adaptation. By contrast, in 1991 John Huston's heirs convinced France's highest court to stop a television screening of a colourized version of *The Asphalt Jungle*. Huston may have had no integrity right in the United States when the film was made, but the French court was willing to teach Americans a lesson in how to preserve a culture they did not recognize they had. The right of a film director and his estate to prevent modifications of his *oeuvre* which would prejudice his honour or reputation was affirmed.[35]

The reaction of Canadian courts to a case like Huston's would be interesting. Their overall record to date has, with few exceptions, shown little inclination to press moral rights liability much beyond what the common law or the civil law would have imposed anyway. Claims relying purely on the Act may therefore be risky propositions unless strong common or civil law support is also available.

---

34 A typical U.S. response to moral rights is to call them "elitist and despotic," "special-interest legislation . . . for the benefit of a minority who feel better knowing that the owner is not allowed to act in an uncultured way": S.L. Carter, "Owning What Doesn't Exist" (1990) 13 Harv. J.L. & Pub. Policy 99 at 100–1.

35 Y. Gendreau, "The Continuing Saga of Colourization in France" (1993) 7 I.P.J. 340.

FURTHER READINGS

ASSOCIATION LITTÉRAIRE ET ARTISTIQUE INTERNATIONALE, *Le droit moral de l'auteur/The Moral Right of the Author*, Congress of Antwerp, 19–24 September 1993 (Paris, 1994)

D'AMATO, A., & D.E. LONG, eds., *International Intellectual Property Law* (London: Kluwer, 1997) c. 6

GENDREAU, Y., "The Continuing Saga of Colourization in France" (1993) 7 I.P.J. 340

GRABER, C.B., & G. TUBNER, "Art and Money: Constitutional Rights in the Private Sphere?" (1998) 18 Ox. J. Leg. Stud. 61

VAVER, D., "Authors' Moral Rights in Canada" (1983) 14 I.I.C. 329

VAVER, D., "Authors' Moral Rights and the Copyright Law Review Committee's Report: W(h)ither Such Rights Now?" (1988) 14 Monash U. L. Rev. 284

VAVER, D., "Authors' Moral Rights — Reform Proposals in Canada: Charter or Barter of Rights for Creators?" (1987) 25 Osgoode Hall L.J. 749

VAVER, D., "Moral Rights Yesterday, Today and Tomorrow" (1999) 7 Int'l J. Info. Tech. and Law 270

VAVER, D., "Snow v. The Eaton Centre: Wreaths on Sculpture Prove Accolade for Artists' Moral Rights" (1983) 8 Can. Bus. L.J. 81

USERS' RIGHTS

International law allows fairly wide leeway for limitations or exceptions to copyright, if these are confined to "certain special cases which do not conflict with a normal exploitation of the work and do not unreasonably prejudice the legitimate interests of the right holder."[1] User rights in Canada changed little from 1924 until the *1997 Act*,[2] which introduced a new set to counterbalance the new rights and remedies that copyright holders had gained since 1988. The new user rights, although not overly generous, reflect prevailing trends among developed nations. Sometimes users can act without paying; more often, some payment must be made to a copyright holder or collective society acting on his behalf. Courts have also, over the years, created

---

1   This formula, found in the *Agreement on Trade-Related Aspects of Intellectual Property Rights, Including Trade in Counterfeit Goods* (1994), 25 I.I.C. 209 [*TRIPs*] and the *North American Free Trade Agreement*, 17 December 1992, Can. T.S. 1994 No. 2 [*NAFTA*], is based on the *Berne Convention for the Protection of Literary and Artistic Works* (Paris, 1971), 9 September 1886, 828 U.N.T.S. 221 [*Berne*], which left most exceptions then found in national laws unaffected: see *TRIPs*, art. 13, and *NAFTA*, art. 1750(5), generalizing from *Berne*, art. 9(2), which applied only to the reproduction right. See also the *Rome Convention for the Protection of Performers, Producers of Phonograms and Broadcasting Organisations* (26 October 1961) [*Rome*], art. 15; S. Ricketson, *The Berne Convention for the Protection of Literary and Artistic Works, 1886–1986* (London: Centre for Commercial Law Studies, Queen Mary College, 1987) at 9.6.
2   *An Act to Amend the Copyright Act*, S.C. 1997, c. 24 [*1997 Act*].

additional user rights in particular cases, using common or civil law techniques such as estoppel, waiver, implied licence, or principles of public policy. But the role of the courts has been relatively limited. Their overall mission is to adjust the often competing claims of owners and users fairly in the public interest, without letting copyright laws become "instruments of oppression and extortion."[3] But courts cannot expand a user right beyond what the Act says, nor may they refuse to enforce a copyright simply on grounds of unfairness.[4] Fairness in copyright law and policy is, after all, a variable ideal. Its implementation has rightly been left largely to legislatures.

We shall look first at some general matters, and then particularly at the rights that are found in the new Act or that have been developed by courts.

A. GENERAL MATTERS

1) Approach

Any use that falls under a statutory exception does not infringe copyright, and so may fairly be called a "user right." Such uses are sometimes referred to as "exceptions" or "exemptions." Logically, however, these "exceptions" define the outer limits of owner rights. If O equals the initial allocation of rights (R) that the Act grants to an owner, and E equals exceptions therefrom, then $R = O-E$. Put another way, owners cannot control acts falling under the exceptions because their rights do not extend that far.[5] The label put on E does not matter so long as it does not mislead. The use of "exception" or "exemption" may, however, be objectionable if it implies that all uses should be within the copyright holder's control, and that any departure from this position is abnormal. Copyright holders have naturally sought to promote such

3   *Hanfstaengl* v. *Empire Palace*, [1894] 3 Ch. 109 at 128 (C.A.) [*Hanfstaengl*], followed in *Vigneux* v. *Canadian Performing Right Society Ltd.*, [1943] S.C.R. 348 at 353–54 (dissent), rev'd [1945] A.C. 108 (P.C.) [*Vigneux*], approving the S.C.R. dissent; and *Canadian Assn. of Broadcasters* v. *Society of Composers, Authors & Music Publishers of Canada* (1994), 58 C.P.R. (3d) 190 at 196 (Fed. C.A.); *Pro Sieben Media A.G.* v. *Carlton U.K. Television Ltd.*, [1999] F.S.R. 610 (C.A.) [*Pro Sieben*].
4   *Pro Sieben, ibid.*, aff'g on this point [1998] F.S.R. 43 at 49 (Ch.)
5   Similarly, a compulsory patent licence does not "take away" the patentee's property: rather, the "original grant is of a limited character": *Smith, Kline & French Laboratories Ltd.* v. *Canada (A.G.)* (1985), 24 D.L.R. (4th) 321 at 351 (Fed. T.D.), aff'd (1986), 34 D.L.R. (4th) 584 (Fed. C.A.) [*Smith Kline*].

views. The occasional court has even suggested that "owner rights" should be interpreted expansively, while "user exceptions" should be interpreted narrowly.[6]

This latter approach is bad law and bad policy. It runs counter to decisions such as the Supreme Court's reversal of a trial judgment that equated a user benefit with the "taking" of copyright property.[7] Moreover, the policy of copyright law has always been to balance competing owner and user interests according to both contemporary exigencies and transcendental imperatives such as free speech and free trade. Without a corresponding user benefit, an owner's right may never have been enacted or retained in that form. User rights are not just loopholes. Both owner rights and user rights should therefore be given the fair and balanced reading that befits remedial legislation.[8]

A narrow approach to user rights also overlooks the fact that some exceptions in the Act are there largely for the sake of caution and to avoid argument. For example, one exception allows a non-profit library, archive, or museum to copy material for the purposes of police investigations.[9] Nevertheless, it seems inconceivable that a private citizen or even a for-profit library that copied for this purpose would be found to have infringed copyright, even though no specific exception for such users appears in the Act. Yet a narrow interpretation of "user exceptions" might wrongly cause infringement to be found in such a case. A narrow approach may, furthermore, overlook the fact that the user rights included in the Act are cumulative and sometimes overlap. An activity that does not qualify under one right can, therefore, without incongruity qualify under another.

---

6   *Cie générale des établissements Michelin/Michelin & Cie* v. *CAW Canada* (1996), 71 C.P.R. (3d) 348 at 381 (Fed. T.D.) [*Michelin*]; *CCH Canadian Ltd.* v. *Law Society of Upper Canada* (9 November 1999), (Fed. T.D.) [unreported] [*CCH*].

7   *Vigneux* v. *Canadian Performing Right Society Ltd.*, [1942] Ex. C.R. 129 at 138, aff'd [1943] S.C.R. 348 at 356 (dissent), rev'd on this point [1945] A.C. 108 at 123 (P.C.); *C.A.P.A.C.* v. *Siegel Distributing Co. Ltd.*, [1959] S.C.R. 488 (interpreting an exemption broadly to include jukebox systems within "gramophone") [*Siegel*]; *Smith Kline*, above note 5. Compare *Statement of Royalties to Be Collected for the Performance or the Communication by Telecommunication, in Canada, of Musical or Dramatico-Musical Works (Tariff 22), Phase I: Legal Issues*, Copyright Board Decision of 27 October 1999 [*Tariff 22*], claiming that *Michelin*, above note 6, states only that exceptions should not be "read into the Act."

8   *C.A.P.A.C.* v. *Western Fair Assn.*, [1951] S.C.R. 596 at 601 [*Western Fair*]; *Interpretation Act*, R.S.C. 1985, c. I-21 [*I Act*], s. 12. See also *Pro Sieben*, above note 3 (fair dealing defence "should be interpreted liberally").

9   *Copyright Act*, R.S.C. 1985, c. C-42 [*C Act*; unless otherwise indicated, references to the Act are as amended], s. 30.1(1)(e).

2) Burden of Proof

In civil cases, user rights may technically be classed as defences, justifi-cations, or excuses, which become relevant only after a claimant has alleged and *prima facie* proved infringement. It is then up to the defen-dant to plead and prove a reason — a defence, justification, or excuse — allowing him to avoid liability and to produce the evidence in sup-port.[10] If the evidence falls short in any respect, the defendant, however well intentioned, may be found to have infringed copyright. Any copies he made will be infringing copies that are liable to be seized.[11]

A defendant may be somewhat better off in a criminal proceeding, for there it seems that the Crown must prove a lack of justification as an element of the offence. So a defendant need not prove that he has dealt fairly with a copyright; it is for the Crown to prove that he did not, or the case will be dismissed.[12]

3) Customary Practices

Copyright law does not recognize what one Australian judge has dis-paragingly called "the *Cosi Fan Tutte* defence (everybody's doing it)."[13] Just because a particular class of users has acted in a particular way for years without objection does not mean the usage is legal. News and other print publishers seem particularly inclined to make this sort of argument, although with little success. A recent example was the Brit-ish newspaper that brazenly asserted as common practice a right to republish any photograph published in any other newspaper. The paper's operating principle was that the copyright owner, having con-sented once, would likely consent again to a republication. The court disagreed and found copyright infringement. The newspaper's asser-tion was rejected as "plainly unjustified and unlawful."[14]

---

10   *L.B. (Plastics) Ltd. v. Swish Products Ltd.,* [1979] F.S.R. 145 at 152 (H.L.); *Avel Pty. Ltd. v. Multicoin Amusements Pty. Ltd.* (1990), 171 C.L.R. 88 at 94–95 & 119–20 (Austl. H.C.).

11   *C Act,* above note 9, s. 2, def. "infringing." See section F, "Delivery and Seizure," in chapter 9.

12   *R. v. Laurier Office Mart Inc.* (1994), 58 C.P.R. (3d) 403 at 416 (Ont. Prov. Div.), aff'd (1995), 63 C.P.R. (3d) 229 (Ont. Gen. Div.) [*Laurier*]; see text accompanying above note 5.

13   *Flocast Australia Pty. Ltd. v. Purcell* (1997), 39 I.P.R. 177 at 184 (Austl. Fed. Ct.); *Hager v. ECW Press Ltd.* (1998), 85 C.P.R. (3d) 289 (Fed. T.D.) [*Hager*] (accord).

14   *Banier v. News Group Newspapers Ltd.,* [1997] F.S.R. 812 at 815 (Ch.) [*Banier*].

Of course, if a copyright owner is aware of a practice and does nothing where action would normally be expected, it may temporarily be barred from complaining about the practice. The owner should, however, be able to change its mind by putting the user on notice that, as from a certain date, the practice will no longer be tolerated. A user who disregards such a warning acts at his own risk.

B. PARTICULAR USER RIGHTS

The following user rights appear in the *Copyright Act* or have been developed by the courts:

1) Literary Work

a) Computer Programs
The owner of a physical copy of a computer program can make a backup copy if none is supplied. She may also make the program compatible with her own computer. In either case, she must delete the copy or adaptation on ceasing to own the program.[15] A user cannot, under this exemption, copy a program to disassemble and analyze it for the purpose of producing another functionally similar program.[16]

b) News Reporting of Political Speeches and Public Lectures
Any person may make or publish, for the purposes of news reporting or summary, reports of addresses of "a political nature delivered at a public meeting," and also reports of public lectures, addresses, sermons, or speeches. The second class of report is, however, prohibited if a conspicuous notice prohibiting reports is kept at the main entrance of the building and, unless the building is being used for public worship, near the speaker.[17] Whether this prohibition can stand with the *Charter* guarantee of freedom of expression is doubtful. Reports, including those made in defiance of a prohibition, may nevertheless themselves have copyright.[18]

---

15 *C Act*, above note 9, ss. 27(2)(1) & 27(2)(m).

16 *Creative Technology Ltd.* v. *Aztech Systems Pty. Ltd.* (1996), [1997] F.S.R. 491 at 508–10 (Singapore C.A.). But see section B(11)(b)(i), "Research or private study," under "Fair Dealing," in this chapter.

17 *C Act*, above note 9, ss. 32.2(c) & (e).

18 See section A(1), "Originality," in chapter 3.

c) Public Recitation of Published Work

Anyone may read or recite in public a reasonable extract from a published work.[19] Private correspondence, being unpublished, does not fall under this exemption. Nor do readings or recitations that are broadcast, since a telecommunication "to" the public is distinct from a performance — a reading or recitation — "in" public.[20]

d) Federal Law and Court Judgments

Federal legislation and the judgments of federal courts and administrative tribunals may be reproduced without payment or the prior permission of the government (indeed, much of this, as well as provincial, material has been made available on the Internet). This policy took effect in 1997 after longstanding criticism of the federal government's previous claims of control over this material. The Order implementing the new policy reads as if it has almost constitutional status. It declares in its preamble the "fundamental importance to a democratic society that its law be widely known and that its citizens have unimpeded access to that law." The Order then provides:

> Anyone may, without charge or request for permission, reproduce enactments and consolidations of enactments of the Government of Canada, and decisions and reasons for decisions of federally-constituted courts and administrative tribunals, provided due diligence is exercised in ensuring the accuracy of the materials reproduced and the reproduction is not represented as an official version.[21]

The following points are worth noting:

- The Order does not apply to provincial legislation or judgments of provincial tribunals and courts, including superior courts with federally appointed judges.[22] Yet knowledge of, and unimpeded access to, provincial law is as fundamental to a democratic society as is knowledge of, and uinimpeded access to, federal law. Provinces should now find it harder to provide respectable reasons for their claims to control publication of provincial laws and court decisions.

---

19   *C Act*, above note 9, s. 32.2(1)(d).

20   Compare *C Act, ibid.*, s. 2.3; *Bishop* v. *Stevens*, [1990] 2 S.C.R. 467 [*Bishop*].

21   *Reproduction of Federal Law Order*, SI/97-5, 131 Can. Gaz. (Pt. II) 444 (8 January 1997). See also section B(10), "Public Interest," in this chapter.

22   Legislating by way of Order rather than through Parliament meant that the federal government was constitutionally constrained from treading on the jurisdiction or prerogative power of the provinces.

Indeed, in 1999 Ontario announced that it would follow the federal government's lead, but Quebec continues to maintain its monopoly.[23]

* The word "enactment" in the Order must carry its standard meaning of "Act of Parliament or regulation." "Regulation" includes the following:

> an order, regulation, rule, rule of court, form, tariff of costs or fees, letters patent, commission, warrant, proclamation, by-law, resolution or other instrument, made or established
>
> (a) in the execution of a power conferred by or under the authority of an Act, or
>
> (b) by or under the authority of the Governor in Council.[24]

Commission reports and government correspondence would not likely be included.

* The word "reproduce" is not defined, but it must at least include "reproduction in any material form whatever," the formula used in the *Copyright Act*.[25] An even wider meaning is justified. The Order is partly made under the prerogative power, which extends beyond "reproduction" in this technical sense. The Order also aims to make the law "widely known" and to let citizens have "unimpeded access" as fundamentally important features of a democratic society. Copies in hard copy, digital form, and CD-ROM should therefore be included. So should copies uploaded, downloaded, or otherwise accessed and distributed on the Internet, although in copyright law these activities may also involve telecommunication of a work to the public or acts other than reproduction. However, the power of the government to charge for hard copies of legislation and judgments ordered from it seems unaffected.

* Although the Order applies primarily to activities in Canada, the government will not likely object to similar acts committed offshore. The goal of making the laws as fully accessible to Canadians as possible is advanced whether Canadians are in the country or abroad, whether the material comes from an offshore Internet site or a local one, and whether or not foreigners also incidentally benefit from access.

* Non-compliance with the dual proviso in the Order — to exercise due diligence in ensuring accuracy and not to represent the copy as an official version — presumably makes the offender an infringer, but of

---

23 *Wilson & Lafleur Ltée* v. *Société québécoise d'information juridique*, [1998] A.Q. 2762 (S.C.)

24 *I Act*, above note 8, s. 2, defs. "enactment"and "regulation."

25 See section A(2), "Reproduction," in chapter 5.

what? The Order presupposes that legislation and judgments are subject to government copyright, Crown prerogative, or both.[26] Whether these suppositions are true still awaits authoritative decision.

2) Musical Work

a) Exhibitions and Fairs

Musical works may be freely performed — live or off a record or the radio — at any agricultural, agricultural-industrial exhibition, or fair that receives a grant from a federal, provincial, or municipal authority, or that is held by its directors under such authority. The performance must, however, be "without motive of gain."[27] This exemption is rarely available because a motive of gain has been found where any musician is paid to perform, or where the music is designed to attract people to the event or to any special exhibition at it.[28]

b) Public Performance by Radio

Theatres that play radios have to pay the applicable SOCAN tariff if the theatre is ordinarily and regularly used for entertainment and charges admission.[29] Otherwise a radio may be played anywhere without infringing public performance rights in music. Compensation for the activity is theoretically included in the SOCAN tariff payable by radio broadcasters.

Not all countries have this exemption, and some that do try to limit it. Thus, in the United States, premises having only "a single receiving apparatus of a kind commonly used in private homes" were exempt until 1998, when large stores were also allowed to use up to six loudspeakers, without payment, to play music.[30] By contrast, Canada allows public performance of musical works "by means of any radio receiving set," without qualification. This language should be interpreted broadly, in the same way as courts interpreted "gramophone" when this item appeared in the pre-*NAFTA* exemption. Under this now

---

26   The Order is stated to be made under "other than statutory authority." This cryptic formula is typically used by government drafters to signal that the government is relying at least partly on the Crown prerogative, as well as legislation (here, the *Copyright Act*), as authority for its actions.

27   *C Act*, above note 9, s. 32.2(2).

28   *Western Fair*, above note 8.

29   *C Act*, above note 9, s. 69(2); *Vigneux*, above note 3.

30   *Copyright Act*, 17 U.S.C. [*Copyright Act 1976*], § 110(5), as amended by the *Fairness in Music Licensing Act* of 1998 (105th Cong., 2d Sess., s. 505). In 1999, the European Union formally complained to the WTO that the U.S. amendment violated the *Berne Convention*, and hence *TRIPs*, art. 9(1), both above note 1.

repealed exemption, a Wurlitzer system that featured a single turntable wired to coin-operated speakers in individual booths in a restaurant was allowed to operate without payment of royalties. The music remained gramophonic, whether the restaurant had one system or six record players scattered around the room.[31] The line was drawn at a Muzak service with a central turntable wired to 600 speakers and 190 amplifiers in multiple locations in multiple buildings. "Gramophone" in ordinary speech did not encompass something resembling a cable diffusion system. At least the same entity had to control the music at the point of emission and reception.[32]

An approach like this would today cover a commercial sound system connected to a single radio receiver servicing a multi-floor department store or perhaps even the common areas of a shopping plaza controlled by a single landlord. It would probably not cover a system carrying sound among differently owned premises, or by coaxial cable or satellite.

c) Charitable, Educational, and Religious Objects

Musical works may be performed — live or off a record or the radio — if the performance furthers a religious, educational, or charitable object, and is given by a religious organization or institution, or non-profit educational institution, or a charitable or fraternal organization.[33]

Who, besides these organizations or institutions, is sheltered by this "worthy causes" exemption is unclear. The minister, congregants, and church choir who sing hymns during the service are presumably as free of liability as the church itself; otherwise the exemption has little point. The position of the guest singer brought in by the church to lead the singing seems less certain. The Act extends other educational exemptions involving an educational institution to "a person acting under its authority."[34] The lack of comparable language in the worthy causes exemption suggests that such a person may be liable to pay a performance fee if SOCAN demands one, although no fee would probably be demanded of a performer who worked for free.

---

31 *Siegel*, above note 7 at 491.
32 *Associated Broadcasting Co. Ltd.* v. *C.A.P.A.C.* (1954), [1955] 2 D.L.R. 452 at 456 (P.C.), aff'g (*sub nom. C.A.P.A.C.* v. *Associated Broadcasting Co. Ltd.*) (1952), 16 C.P.R. 33 (Ont. C.A.).
33 *C Act*, above note 9, s. 32.2(3). See also section B(13)(b)(iv), "Performances for or by Students," in this chapter.
34 For example, the exemptions in *C Act, ibid.*, ss. 29.4 to 29.9.

In another respect, the worthy causes exemption is not as wide as it looks. The Kiwanis Club was not allowed to use it to justify the public dances it ran at Casa Loma in Toronto, even though the proceeds went to charity. Fearing that a wide reading would let charities run dance halls and opera houses without paying composers a cent, the court said the exemption covered only performances that furthered the worthy object and were a "participating factor" in it or in an activity "incidental" to it. The sort of events that the exemption therefore envisages are performances as part of church services, educational meetings "with musical interpolations," or music played at Christmas dinners for the poor.[35] School concerts could also qualify because their major purpose is to further the students' musical education and performance abilities.[36]

The exemption has a further oddity. The provision states that no named institution "shall be held liable to pay any compensation" for doing the stated acts, while other exemptions simply say that "it is not an infringement of copyright" to do the stated acts. This wording seems a distinction without a difference. A performing right society (a predecessor of SOCAN) once claimed an injunction against a particular performance because the relevant exemption said only that "no fees, charges or royalties shall be collectable" from the performers. This, the society said, took away only its right to collect money, not an injunction. The courts disagreed. A performance that by law did not have to be paid for must be lawful, which therefore meant that copyright was not infringed and the society could get no injunction.[37] The comparable language in the worthy causes exemption should equally exonerate beneficiaries from all copyright liability.

3) Artistic Work

a) Recycling Ideas

Artists who do not own the copyright in a work may continue to use preparatory material — moulds, casts, sketches, etc. — from their earlier works for new projects, if the main design of the earlier work is not repeated. The exception seems to reflect two principles: first, that no copyright exists in ideas and, second, even where copyright does exist,

---

35   *C.A.P.A.C.* v. *Kiwanis Club of West Toronto*, [1953] 2 S.C.R. 111 at 114 & 115.

36   See section B(13)(b)(iv), "Performances for or by Students," in this chapter.

37   *Vigneux*, above note 3 at 122 & 124 (cited to A.C.). A common result should flow from both these exemptions because both were initially enacted together: see *Copyright Amendment Act*, S.C. 1938, c. 27, ss. 4 & 5. See also *C Act*, above note 9, s. 32.3, which assumes that s. 32.2(3) refers to non-infringing acts.

no transfer of copyright nor employment relationship should inhibit an author from deploying his talents to produce new work from old preliminary material. So, had Monet sold the copyright in his first Rouen cathedral painting, he could have used its preparatory material for later paintings of the same subject without objection, so long as he was just doing variations on the theme and not repeating the main design of the first work.[38] More recently, a court, partly relying on the exception by analogy, allowed a computer programmer to retain and use his working notes as against his former employer, who continued to own the copyright in the program developed from the notes.[39]

b) Works Derived from Public Art

Paintings, drawings, engravings, photographs, or films can be made and published of certain works: architecture, sculpture, and works of artistic craftsmanship. A limitation for architecture is that the derivative work cannot itself be an architectural drawing or plan; for sculpture or works of artistic craftsmanship, the item must be permanently situated in a public place or building.[40] Presumably, this definition includes works in a gallery's permanent collection, though not currently exhibited.

4) Copying Authorized by Legislation

Copying material under the *Cultural Property Export and Import Act*, *Access to Information Act*, federal and provincial *Privacy Acts*, and the *National Archives of Canada Act* is allowed.[41] Other legislation requiring or allowing copying may also implicitly exempt that act from infringing. For example, copying material from public registries may be allowed; this may also be true for material produced on discovery in litigation or to comply with a court order. The copying would have to be consistent with the reason for having the registry or the discovery in the first place. A manuscript that is produced on discovery may therefore be copied for purposes relevant to the litigation, but cannot be distributed for sale.[42]

---

38 *C Act, ibid.*, s. 32.2(1)(a); compare *Franklin Mint Corp.* v. *National Wildlife Act Exchange Inc.*, 575 F.2d 62 (9th Cir. 1978).

39 *Canavest House Ltd.* v. *Lett* (1984), 2 C.P.R. (3d) 386 (Ont. H.C.J.).

40 *C Act*, above note 9, s. 32.2(1)(b).

41 *C Act, ibid.*, ss. 27(2)(h) to (k) & 28.02(2)(c).

42 *Home Office* v. *Harman*, [1981] Q.B. 534 at 558–59 (C.A.), aff'd on other grounds (1982), [1983] 1 A.C. 280 (H.L.); *Wall* v. *Brunell* (1997), 75 C.P.R. (3d) 429 (Fed. T.D.) [*Wall*].

5) Incidental Inclusion

Copyright works or subject matter may be "incidentally and not deliberately" included in other works or subject matter.[43] This new exemption recognizes the difficulties of avoiding copyright-protected matter in everyday life, especially with the greater range of activities the *1997 Act* now brings under the control of copyright owners. To allow owners to control every exposure of their material in other media would be oppressive and extortionate. Suppose that a television crew films a street parade or news event. Can the studio reasonably be expected to clear copyright in advance with all billboard advertisers, corporate logo owners, and street performers in the vicinity? What is to be done if an owner or performer refuses consent or demands prior payment? The exemption overcomes such difficulties. A parade or news event may be filmed without the producer's worrying over what performers or owners of any copyright in advertisements and logos that happen to be captured on film may think about their inclusion.

Two key provisos, however, narrow the scope of exemption so much that its practical utility seems doubtful. First, the included material must be incidental — "casual, inessential, subordinate or merely background"[44] — to the subject of the film. Second, the inclusion must not be deliberate. A television program that features billboards, corporate logos, or street performers as its subject is obviously not exempted. Even a shot that lingers too long over an initially innocently incorporated item may make the inclusion deliberate or non-incidental. In the United States, the use of a poster as a set decoration in an episode of a television show was held to infringe copyright in the poster, even though the item was visible for a total of less than half a minute in the background of one scene.[45] Similarly, in Britain, the inclusion in a television commercial of a magazine cover to promote a rival magazine was found to be not incidental but "an essential and important feature" of the advertisement. Copyright in the cover was therefore infringed.[46] The results in Canada should be comparable. The poster in the U.S. case would probably not qualify in Canada as an incidental inclusion; even if it did, its appearance in the television episode

---

43   *C Act*, above note 9, s. 30.7(a). Compare the *Copyright, Designs and Patents Act*, 1988 (U.K.), c. 48 [*UK Act*], ss. 31(1) & (3).

44   *IPC Magazines Ltd v. MGN Ltd.*, [1998] F.S.R. 431 at 441 (Ch.) [*IPC*].

45   *Ringgold v. Black Entertainment Television Inc.*, 126 F.3d 70 (2d. Cir. 1997), refusing to find fair use.

46   *IPC*, above note 44.

was as deliberate as the appearance of the magazine cover in the British commercial. Both activities would equally infringe copyright in Canada.

A related exemption allows further dealing with the work or other subject matter that includes the exempt material. The dealing must, however, itself also be incidental and not deliberate.[47] This exemption is very narrow. It might, for example, cover a simultaneous or slightly delayed broadcast of the film of the street parade or news event mentioned earlier. Presumably, the studio need not prove that the broadcast itself was "incidental and non-deliberate," for the exemption would then have no practical application: only studios that broadcast accidentally or without cognition would benefit. So the exemption should cover a simultaneous broadcast that is planned as part of the initial filming, so long as nothing can practicably be done to edit out the innocently included material as it is being broadcast.

The exemption allowing further dealing would not, however, authorize the making of copies of the film for sale. This reproduction, being quite deliberate, would require clearance unless it fell under some other exemption.

6) Ephemeral Recording

The *1997 Act* contains exemptions for broadcasters to make temporary recordings in two narrowly defined cases.

a) Live Performances
The ephemeral recording exemption deals with cases like that of the broadcaster who wishes to broadcast a performance live (e.g., a concert or street parade) and who has the necessary consents to broadcast from all interested copyright holders. The broadcaster may wish to record the event simultaneously — for example, to transmit a delayed broadcast to another time zone. The broadcaster will typically have a blanket broadcast licence from SOCAN and the collective societies representing performers and record producers. The right to record will be held by other entities, which may not themselves be collective societies. A licence to broadcast does not in itself authorize the recording of the broadcast.[48] The ephemeral recording exemption, proclaimed into effect as from 1 October 1999, deals with such a case. It allows a temporary recording to be made of a live performance, including any

---

47   *C Act*, above note 9, s. 30.7(b). Compare 1988 *UK Act*, above note 43, s. 31(2).
48   *Bishop*, above note 20.

accompanying work or sound recording, to facilitate later transmission by the broadcaster or its network, where the broadcaster already has the authority to broadcast.[49]

b) Transfer of Medium

A transfer-of-medium exemption, introduced during the late stages of Bill C-32 in the Commons, is designed to cope with modern technologies for broadcasting sound recordings. Little programming today involves spinning records on a turntable. More often, records are assembled into convenient compilations and are electronically retrieved and played by the presenter. As noted earlier, a licence to broadcast a recording does not automatically authorize the recording of the broadcast.[50] As from 1 October 1999, the transfer-of-medium exemption therefore allows a sound recording owned by a broadcaster to be temporarily copied to a more appropriate format for broadcasting.[51]

c) Restrictions

These two exemptions, both introduced after Bill C-32's second reading in the Commons, are modest in scope and purpose. They apply only to broadcast undertakings licensed under the *Broadcasting Act*.[52] The broadcaster must itself make the recording for its own broadcast, although a network may also do this for a projected network broadcast. Neither activity can be contracted out.[53] The recordings cannot be synchronized with other material or used in advertising.[54] They cannot be archived in the broadcaster's archives. Indeed, only ephemeral recordings of an "exceptional documentary character" may be archived at all, and then only in the National Archives of Canada or an official provincial archive.[55] All recordings must be deleted within thirty days unless the copyright holder says otherwise. Records of activities under the exemptions must be kept for the inspection of copyright holders.[56] No cinematographic work — for example, movie or television progam — can be recorded.[57] A slip in any respect may cause copyright to be

---

49   *C Act*, above note 9, s. 30.8.
50   *Bishop*, above note 20; see section B(6)(a), "Live Performances," in this chapter.
51   *C Act*, above note 9, s. 30.9.
52   *C Act*, *ibid.*, ss. 30.8(11) & 30.9(7).
53   *C Act*, *ibid.*, ss. 30.8(1)(b), 30.8(9), & 30.9(1)(c).
54   *C Act*, *ibid.*, ss. 30.8(1)(c) & (d); ss. 30.9(1)(d) & (e).
55   *C Act*, *ibid.*, ss. 30.8(6) & (7); see *Berne*, above note 1, art. 11*bis* (3), & *Rome*, above note 1, art. 15(1)(c).
56   *C Act*, *ibid.*, ss. 30.8(2) to (4) & ss. 30.9(2) to (4).
57   *C Act*, *ibid.*, s. 30.8(1).

infringed.[58] Most important, neither exemption applies where a collective society can license the exempted activities.[59]

In practice, these exemptions will save some search and transaction costs. Broadcasters may not need to negotiate another line of text relating to temporary recording in their agreements. They will also not have to chase multiple copyright owners for clearances. If there is a collective society around, the broadcaster will have to deal with it alone. If there is no collective around, he pays nothing and simply relies on the exemption.

7) Perceptual Disability

a) Background
Some activities designed to make material accessible to people with a disability that prevents or inhibits them from reading or hearing such material in its original format are allowed under the *1997 Act*. The target group includes those who cannot see, hear, or understand such material very well, including dyslexics and people who find it hard to hold or turn the pages of a book.[60]

Subject to a condition of commercial availability,[61] the material that falls under this exemption is quite comprehensive. Any literary, musical, dramatic, or artistic work is included, but no sound recording, broadcast, extemporary performance, or cinematographic work.[62] Nor may a large-print book be made, even if this format is unavailable anywhere.[63] The consent of the copyright holder or its collecting society is needed in such cases.

The groups who may make material accessible are also quite comprehensive: non-profit organizations acting for the disabled — such as the Canadian National Institute for the Blind — or anyone else acting, for profit or for free, at the disabled person's request.[64] Surprisingly, the Act does not say that a disabled person may make material accessible for himself, but this power may be implied. It would be nonsensical — and against the principles of equality and non-discrimination found in

---

58   *C Act, ibid.*, s. 30.8(10); *Phonographic Performance Ltd. v. A.E.I. Rediffusion Music Ltd.*, [1997] 3 W.L.R. 982 (Ch.).

59   *C Act, ibid.*, ss. 30.8(8) & 30.9(6).

60   *C Act, ibid.*, s. 2, def. "perceptual disability."

61   Section B(7)(b), "Commercial Availability," in this chapter.

62   *C Act*, above note 9, s. 32(1)(a).

63   *C Act, ibid.*, s. 32(2).

64   *C Act, ibid.*, s. 32(1), opening words.

the *Canadian Charter of Rights and Freedoms* and in human rights codes — if a person could not do for himself what he can ask others to do on his behalf for profit.

b) Commercial Availability

The exemption does not mean to cut into the sale of existing alternative format material on the market. Copies cannot be made of a work that is already commercially available in a format specially designed to meet the relevant person's needs. Before a user can rely on the exemption, he must make reasonable efforts to locate an appropriate alternative format copy on the Canadian market. If a reasonably priced copy is locatable within a reasonable time, that copy must be bought and no private copy can be made. Any known or reasonably likely Canadian distributors of the work in question should be checked, although scouring the world should not be necessary.[65] If such a copy is not located, the user may make his own copy without seeking a licence from a collecting society.

This condition of commercial availability will need to be sensibly applied. Suppose, for example, that two different formats can meet the needs of a person with poor eyesight. She prefers one format over another. Must she nonetheless buy the available format even though another suits her more? It seems so, for the Act speaks of works designed to meet a person's "needs," not merely her preferences. So if the person can read large-print books or listen to a reading with equal facility, and the work is readily available in Canada on tape, she may have to buy the tape even though she likes large print better. If she still wants a large-print book, she must seek a licence from the copyright owner, who may grant or refuse consent as it chooses. If the opposite situation prevails — the book is available in large print but not in audio form, and the user prefers audio to print — she must buy the large-print book or seek a licence from the copyright owner to put the book on tape.

At some point, of course, a person's strong preference will become a "need." If someone's reading pace is slow compared to what she can absorb by listening, it seems reasonable to accept that her "needs" can be met only by an audio version. The perceptual disability exemption has, presumably, at least two aims: to achieve and maintain equality of opportunity and dignity between people with different physical or cog-

---

65   *C Act, ibid.*, ss. 32(3) & 2, def. "commercially available" (para. (a)). See further on "commercially available," section B(12)(b)(i), "Fragile and Obsolete Formats," in this chapter.

nitive abilities, and to encourage copyright holders to meet the market preferences of all Canadians, including those with disabilities. These aims are best furthered by assessing the "needs" of such people sympathetically in the light of their expressed strong preferences.

c) Permissible Alternative Formats

Once it is established that an appropriate version of a work is not commercially available, an alternative means of making it accessible may be pursued. The means allowed are the following:

- Making one or more copies or sound recordings. The copy may be made in any format — for example, in digital text.[66]
- Using sign language to translate, adapt, or reproduce a literary or dramatic work.
- Using sign language to perform a literary or dramatic work in public, either live or in an alternative format.

It should be re-emphasized that sound recordings, broadcasts, extemporary performances, and cinematographic works are excluded from the exemption. Signing, close-captioning, or producing alternative formats for these items requires the consent of the copyright owner or its collective society.

8) Repairs and Modifications

The owner of an article has, at common law, the right to repair, modify, or destroy it if he wishes. This right may conflict with the copyright or moral rights applicable to a particular article, so some accommodation may need to be reached among these rights.[67] The landmark case involved British Leyland's attempts in the 1980s to prevent the third-party aftermarket manufacture and sale of spare parts for the motor vehicles it made and sold. Leyland's spare parts were made from engi-

---

66   *C Act, ibid.*, s. 32(1), refers to "a" copy or recording, but the singular includes the plural because (a) this is the normal rule (*I Act*, above note 8, s. 33(2)); (b) the exemption was initially confined to a "single" copy or sound recording, but "single" was dropped in committee and does not appear in the *C Act*; and (c) where the *C Act* intends to exempt the making of single copies only, it is explicit: see *C Act*, ss. 29.6(1)(a), 29.7(1), 30.2(4)(b), 30.21(3)(c), & 30.6. A reference to a tariff for multiple copies inadvertently remains in *C Act*, s. 73(1)(a)(i), but it is otiose because the authority to apply for it was also deleted in committee: compare *C Act*, s. 71(1)(d), at first reading (referring to an eliminated s. 32(5)) with s. 71(1) in the committee and final version of Bill C-32.

67   See also section B(2), "Integrity," in chapter 6.

neering drawings, so the manufacturer who copied a muffler *prima facie* infringed copyright in the underlying drawing, despite never having seen it. The House of Lords nevertheless held that the right of every buyer to repair a product that he owns prevailed over Leyland's copyright. This right of repair would be useless if third-party spare-parts manufacturers could not anticipate it. As a matter of public policy, Leyland could therefore not eliminate or abridge this right by contract or any other device.[68]

In Canada, such parts, comprising designs applied to mass-produced articles of utility, would not be protected through copyright at all.[69] The *Leyland* principle may apply in other cases, but its extent is ill-defined and controversial. Repairs to avoid danger to the user or to the public should nonetheless be allowed on public policy grounds. Buyers should also be able to bring products up to the standard that a seller has expressly or impliedly promised but not met, even where the defect is not dangerous.[70] In the United States, on the other hand, sellers have, through copyright, until recently been able to keep lucrative rights to repair items such as computer programs to themselves. By restricting, through a clause in the software licence, the right to reproduce the program, the copyright owner could stop the temporary downloading of a program, even where such a reproduction is necessary to diagnose defects. Acting outside the licence infringed copyright in the program. Legislation passed in 1998 overrode this device and allowed repairers to make temporary copies of a program in the course of repair.[71]

The U.S. legislation seems correct in principle. The vice might be avoided in Canada by a judicious use of *Leyland*. A supplier of a computer program should not, as a matter of public policy, be able to prevent the acquirer from repairing the program or from modifying it to suit her needs. The buyer of a program is not buying a fancy box with a bunch of exclusion clauses. She is buying a tool designed to function as advertised. If it does not, she should be able to repair it; if she wants it to work better, she should equally be entitled to try to make it do that. What the buyer may do by herself, she may do through an agent. Third

---

68   *British Leyland Motor Corp. Ltd.* v. *Armstrong Patents Co. Ltd.,* [1986] A.C. 577 (H.L.) [*Leyland*].

69   *C Act,* above note 9, s. 64(2). See section B(7), "Industrial Design" in chapter 2.

70   *New Brunswick Telephone Co.* v. *John Maryon International Ltd.* (1982), 43 N.B.R. (2d) 469 (C.A.); compare *Saphena Computing Ltd.* v. *Allied Collection Agencies Ltd.* (1988), [1995] F.S.R. 649 (C.A.).

71   *Digital Millennium Copyright Act 1998* (105th Cong., 2d Sess.), ss. 301–2, rev'g the effect of *MAI Systems Corp.* v. *Peak Computer Inc.,* 991 F.2d 511 (9th Cir. 1993).

parties may anticipate her wants by advertising and providing repair and modification services. Any attempt by the program copyright holder to withdraw, restrict, or interfere with such rights should be treated as void either by application of the *Leyland* principle or as thwarting the public interest in having competitive repair and after-market sectors. These points gain cogency with the coming of the "Millennium bug," the program defect that may cause malfunctioning in computers that have not been adjusted to deal with dates beyond 1999. Users need surely not wait for the suppliers that created this defect to remedy it. They should be entitled to take whatever steps they think fit to correct it, without either them or any repairers they engage having to worry that the act of repair itself may constitute copyright infringement.

Meanwhile, the act of repair has been distinguished from the supply of items like razor blades, which are designed to wear out and be replaced. Thus, copyright has been used in Hong Kong to prevent the manufacture of toner cartridges for printers. The result was justified on the basis that there was no danger of monopoly in the aftermarket because of the presence of companies which refilled and resold used cartridges in competition with new cartridges. Moreover, the seller was pursuing a reasonable business plan under which printers were priced low and cartridges were priced high. This strategy both maximized the seller's profits and brought printing to the widest possible range of buyers, who effectively paid according to the intensity with which they used their printers.[72] Whether a danger of monopoly, combined with an unreasonable pricing strategy, might have caused the court to create another exception to copyright is doubtful. These issues, involving economics and the public interest, belong more to the competition authorities than to the courts, which are less well equipped to investigate them.

9) Imports

Imports of the following are allowed:[73]

- up to two copies of any work or other subject matter for the importer's own use;
- any number of copies of a work or other subject matter for use by a federal or provincial government department;

---

72 *Canon Kabushiki Kaisha* v. *Green Cartridge Co. (Hong Kong) Ltd.*, [1997] 3 W.L.R. 13 (P.C.). Razor blades would not usually carry copyright protection in Canada: see section B(7), "Industrial Design" in chapter 2.

73 *C Act*, above note 9, s. 45(1).

- a single copy of a book for the use of a non-profit library, archive, museum, or educational institution;[74]
- any number of copies of a work or other subject matter (other than a book) before the item is made in Canada, if these are required for the use of a non-profit, library, archive, museum, or educational institution;[75] and
- any number of used books.[76]

Importing beyond these limits may infringe the rights of a copyright holder or exclusive Canadian book distributor.[77] The Customs authorities may also halt the import unless they have satisfactory evidence that it is allowable under the above rules.[78] The item must in all cases be a legitimate copy. It cannot infringe copyright in its country of manufacture. It may presumably be imported as accompanying baggage, by an order placed from Canada, or by an agent on the prior request of the person or institution proposing to use it.[79]

10) Public Interest

At common law, a person with a "good cause or excuse" to deal with material as a matter of public interest will not infringe copyright. For example, promoting the administration of justice falls squarely within this interest. Thus, a client who, anticipating litigation, copies a file to put before his solicitors for safe-keeping should not feel inhibited from doing so by the law of copyright.[80] Copying a judge's reasons for judg-

---

74 For a fuller definition of what libraries, archives, museums, or educational institutions qualify, see sections B(12)(a), "Eligible Institution," and B(13), "Education," in this chapter. The definition of "book" is noted in section A(10)(c), "Exclusive Book Distribution," in chapter 5.

75 See previous note.

76 Used textbooks of a scientific, technical, or scholarly nature for use within an educational institution in a course of instruction were originally excluded from this exemption. The government, however, had second thoughts and in 1999 decided that such used textbooks could be imported for both non-profit and for-profit educational bodies: *Book Importation Regulations*, SOR/99-324, s. 8. See section A(10)(c), "Exclusive Book Distribution," in chapter 5.

77 See section A(10), "Distributing and Importing Infringing Copies: Secondary Infringement," in chapter 5.

78 *C Act*, above note 9, s. 45(2).

79 This result follows because the exemptions apply not only to individuals but also to corporations, which can act only through agents; and what applies to a corporation must apply equally to an individual.

80 *Wall*, above note 42.

ment (assuming these have copyright at all) may also be acceptable under this head.[81] The copying of any value-added material such as headnotes (assuming these have copyright) falls outside this exception.[82] All levels of government should nevertheless place standards of fair play above bureaucratic convenience when raising issues of copyright in their dealings with the public. Thus, a provincial fire marshal was criticized for insisting on compliance with the standards of a fire protection code, while citing copyright as a reason for not supplying the public with the relevant parts of the code. The copyright objection was spurious if the province owned the copyright or had an express or implied licence to reproduce provisions of the code while carrying out its duties. Copies of the law should be easily available, at least for a reasonable price, so that the public obligation to obey the law of the land is not inhibited by the unreasonable exercise of private copyrights.[83]

Whistleblowers are sometimes excused from infringing copyright when they copy private documents and hand them over to a newspaper for publication. The exposure must first be found to be in the public interest — for example, if criminal or disgraceful conduct or matters affecting others' life or liberty are disclosed.[84] Celebrities may also have difficulty in preventing the media from publishing stories about their private lives and public conduct. Those in public life who concoct a public image have been told that they cannot complain if the truth comes out, even in breach of confidence: "As there should be 'truth in advertising,' so there should be truth in publicity."[85] But an explicit moderately drawn contractual clause in the employment contracts between a celebrity and her retinue restricting disclosure will probably be enforced: the public interest in keeping promises and in personal privacy may be at least as important as the public's interest in a celebrity's goings-on and the media's need to keep its reader and audience ratings high.

Merely making public information more accessible more cheaply has not been thought important enough to justify the production of an abridgment that infringed copyright. The *Charter* right of free expression

---

81   *British Columbia Jockey Club* v. *Standen* (1985), 8 C.P.R. (3d) 283 at 288 (B.C.C.A.).

82   *CCH*, above note 6.

83   *McKenna's Furniture Store* v. *Office of the Provincial Fire Marshal, Department of Provincial Affairs* (2 April 1997), [P.E.I.S.C., T.D.] [unreported] at 11: the marshal's "copyright concern is an internal matter which should be remedied by the [marshal] so that it does not in future adversely affect those whom it regulates."

84   *Lion Laboratories Ltd.* v. *Evans*, [1985] Q.B. 526 (C.A.) [*Lion*].

85   *Woodward* v. *Hutchins*, [1977] 1 W.L.R. 760 at 764 (C.A.).

was, perhaps surprisingly, found irrelevant, even though the original material was produced under the aegis of the Canadian government, which claimed it wanted the material to be widely circulated.[86] Similarly, a Quebec court has rejected the relevance of *Charter* guarantees where a publisher unsuccessfully claimed free access to the judgments of the Quebec courts. Free press and speech do not mean free — that is, unpaid — access to the law.[87] A cognate view was taken in Britain, where a news service that published detailed data taken from a specialized financial newsletter was found to infringe copyright in the data even though wider dissemination desirably promoted transparency in commodity markets.[88]

11) Fair Dealing

Anyone may deal fairly with any item for the purposes of private study, research, criticism, review, or news reporting. In the latter three cases, both the source and the name of the author, performer, broadcaster, or sound-recording maker, if given in the source, must be mentioned before the dealing can qualify as fair.[89]

This rigid approach comes to Canada via U.K. law, although the two laws differ in detail. Both contrast sharply with U.S. law, where the "fair use" justification is worded more expansively. The U.S. purposes — "criticism, comment, news reporting, teaching (including multiple copies for classroom use), scholarship, or research"— are non-exhaustive. Even attribution of source is not necessary for a use to be found fair.[90] The U.S. provision is, however, no user's panacea. Parodists may have greater leeway under it than in Canada or the United Kingdom, but fair use has not shielded a U.S. commercial copy shop from liability in producing university course-packs that contained substantial extracts from literary works. In Canada, a similar practice would have equal difficulty passing muster.[91]

---

86   *R. v. James Lorimer & Co.*, [1984] 1 F.C. 1065 (C.A.).

87   *Wilson & Lafleur Ltée v. Société québécoise d'information juridique*, [1998] A.Q. 2762 (S.C.).

88   *PCR Ltd. v. Dow Jones Telerate Ltd.*, [1998] F.S.R. 170 at 187 (Ch.).

89   *C Act*, above note 9, ss. 29, 29.1, & 29.2.

90   *Copyright Act 1976*, above note 30, § 107; *Hager*, above note 13; compare *Michelin*, above note 6 at 379ff.

91   *Princeton University Press v. Michigan Document Services*, 99 F.3d 1381 (6th Cir. 1996) [*Princeton*]; *Boudreau v. Lin* (1997), 150 D.L.R. (4th) 324 at 335 (Ont. Gen. Div.) [*Boudreau*]; compare *Laurier*, above note 12, where a criminal prosecution for infringement against an Ottawa copy shop failed, but the firm nevertheless took a reprography licence from CanCopy to avoid future problems.

The following passage from a U.K. case, where an ex-Scientologist successfully claimed fair dealing in a book critical of Scientology which contained long quotations from the church's teaching material, seems also to represent Canadian law:

> It is impossible to define what is "fair dealing." It must be a question of degree. You must consider first the number and extent of the quotations and extracts. Are they altogether too many and too long to be fair? Then you must consider the use made of them. If they are used as a basis for comment, criticism or review, that may be fair dealing. If they are used to convey the same information as the author, for a rival purpose, that may be unfair. Next, you must consider the proportions. To take long extracts and attach short comments may be unfair. But, short extracts and long comments may be fair. Other considerations may come to mind also. But, after all is said and done, it must be a matter of impression. As with fair comment in the law of libel, so with fair dealing in the law of copyright. The tribunal of fact must decide.[92]

This high level of uncertainty favours mainly those with deep pockets. Parliament has not only passed its responsibility to provide clear rules over to the courts but has let them regulate industries as "a matter of impression." The result has been that people have avoided going to law except as a last resort or to settle a principle regardless of cost: copyright is either ignored or negotiated around by private agreement. The following discussion of the jurisprudence may suggest why.

a)   Factors to Consider

Several factors have been used to determine whether a dealing is fair: the purpose and character of the dealing; the nature of the source work; what and how much has been dealt with, compared with the source work as a whole; the effect of the dealing on the potential market for or value of the source work; whether the source work was available within a reasonable time at an ordinary commercial price; and any reasonable guidelines accepted by joint owner and user interests. Some subsidiary general points have also been made, such as:

- One may deal fairly with even a whole work, sound recording, performance, or broadcast.[93] How else can *haiku*, a photograph, or a minimalist performance artist be sensibly criticized or reviewed? Similarly,

---

92   *Hubbard v. Vosper*, [1972] 2 Q.B. 84 at 94 (C.A.) [*Hubbard*].
93   *Allen v. Toronto Star Newspapers Ltd.* (1997), 152 D.L.R. (4th) 518 (Ont. Div. Ct.).

a whole broadcast may fairly be taped to allow the user to decide what extract from it he wants to use. If the extract is later fairly dealt with, the earlier taping will be equally lawful as part of the same single process.[94] In other situations, however, the longer the item and the more that is taken and ultimately used, the less likely the dealing will be fair, as the owner's market is cut into by the new work.

- The dealing must be fair in relation to its purpose and medium. The fair amount copied for private study may be unfair if copied for criticism. Extracts, too long for a newspaper, may be found fair if used in a television news film. But changing the author's name or meaning is presumed to be unfair.[95]

- The purpose of the dealing need not be directly related to the source work. I may criticize or review work **X** by quoting both from that work and from work **Y**, without infringing copyright in either. I may equally report news or publish research about corporation **A** and reproduce item **B** to support the story or research, whoever owns copyright in item **B** and even if item **B** did not precipitate the story or research.[96] I am inhibited only by my obligation to deal fairly and to attribute sources where the Act requires it.

- Dealings with unpublished material "leaked" in breach of confidence have had difficulty passing the test of fairness. Private-sector leaks that further an important public interest, such as the due administration of justice, have been dealt with more leniently, but the treatment is far from uniform.[97]

- Dealings may be fair even though they are done by a competitor to increase its business at the copyright holder's expense. A broadcaster that aired clips from a rival's live telecast in order to report news was found to have dealt fairly, although both broadcasters competed for audience share with rival news shows.[98]

---

94   *Pro Sieben*, above note 3.

95   *Boudreau*, above note 91 at 335.

96   These conclusions flow from the general language in which ss. 29 to 29.2 are expressed: "Fair dealing for the purpose of [research, private study, criticism, review, or news reporting] does not infringe copyright," subject only to the obligation to cite sources for the last three purposes.

97   Compare *Australia v. John Fairfax & Sons Ltd.* (1980), 147 C.L.R. 39 (Austl. H.C.), *Wigginton v. Brisbane T.V. Ltd.* (1992), 25 I.P.R. 58 (Qld. S.C.), and *B.W. International Inc. v. Thomson Canada Ltd.* (1996), 137 D.L.R. (4th) 398 at 409–10 (Ont. Gen. Div.), rejecting fair dealing for leaked documents, with *Lion*, above note 84, accepting it so as to minimize convictions of innocent defendants.

98   *British Broadcasting Corporation v. British Satellite Broadcasting Ltd.*, [1992] Ch. 141 [*BBC*].

- One may deal fairly only for one's own purposes. A teacher may copy fairly for her own private study; her student may copy fairly for his private study; the student may, if the teacher's employee or agent (e.g., research assistant), copy for his teacher's purpose; but, otherwise, neither teacher nor student may copy for the other's purpose.

- Dealings for mixed purposes seem acceptable. I may criticize a work fairly, even if I mean also to educate, as long as the criticism is not simply a cover for a dealing for educational purposes (not being a purpose specifically allowed by the Act). The overall purpose of the activity is judged objectively: A user's sincere belief that he is criticizing is less important than whether the activity is in fact part of an exercise in criticism. The user's intentions and motives are more relevant to the question of whether the dealing is fair.[99]

b) Specific Cases

A discussion follows of how these general factors apply to specific cases.

i) *Purpose of the Dealing*

Fair dealing can occur only in respect of a closed set of purposes: news reporting, criticism, review, research, or private study. Particular citation practices are mandatory for news reporting, criticism, and review.

News reporting: The 1921 Act, dealing with then current technology, allowed fair dealing only for the purposes of "newspaper summary." This term excluded later different delivery systems such as movie newsreels. Television news programs therefore needed permission from copyright holders for any material that they aired and that fell outside the other relevant fair dealing purposes of criticism or review.

Since 1997 the fair dealing defence applies more generally to "news reporting" if the report mentions the source and other participants in the source work.[100] "News reporting" is broader than "newspaper summary." Reporting can therefore occur in any medium, not just newspapers. It may cover a wider range of formats than mere summaries, and may apply to all forms of news, not just reporting current events (as other countries sometimes prescribe). Investigative journalism, where the newspaper effectively creates the news, may equally be included.[101]

The comparable U.K. provision has allowed broadcasters to tape the highlights from events such as World Cup soccer matches, in which

---

99 *Pro Sieben*, above note 3.

100 *C Act*, above note 9, s. 29.2. See "Mandatory citation practices" below in this section.

101 For example, *Fraser v. Evans*, [1969] 1 Q.B. 349 (C.A.).

a rival broadcaster has exclusive rights, and to exhibit short clips in sports news programs shown within the day following the initial telecast.[102] Later showings would probably be classified as history, rather than news, and would have to be justified, if at all, under such exceptions as fair dealing for criticism or review. Of course, if the clip was not a substantial part of the initial program, it would not infringe copyright in the first place. Such a conclusion is, however, unlikely where the clip relates to scores or attempts on goal, the heart of any game. The conclusion may be plausible where, for example, the clip is just a few seconds long, involves a subsidiary part of the game, and is shown as part of a review of the strategy adopted by a particular team or player.

Criticism or review: "Criticism" and "review" presumably involve analyzing and judging merit or quality. "Review" may also include surveying past events or facts. The substantive fairness of the criticism or review is irrelevant. The only issue is whether too much of the source work has been taken to support the purpose.[103] An attempt to justify *Coles' Notes* study aids as criticisms or reviews failed because criticism did not require as full a condensation of the source work as the *Notes* contained.[104] Similarly, a newspaper that published a story about a celebrity's physical condition failed in its claim that the accompanying unauthorized photograph of the celebrity was for the purpose of criticism or review. The story's real objective was not criticism or review, but simply praise of the subject's courage in posing for the picture.[105] On the other hand, a British television program that criticized a film distributor's decision to stop exhibiting *Clockwork Orange* in the United Kingdom and included extracts totalling some 8 percent of the film was held to be dealing fairly.[106] Another television program that included a thirty-second extract from a rival program as part of a story on the iniquities of "chequebook journalism" was also found to act fairly, despite getting some of the facts wrong.[107]

While U.S. courts have treated parody and satire as forms of criticism,[108] the majority of Canadian courts have not, despite the prevalence of parody and satire as Canadian tropes and despite the enormous cross-

---

102   *BBC*, above note 98.

103   *Hager*, above note 13; *Pro Sieben*, above note 3; compare *Michelin*, above note 6 at 384.

104   *Sillitoe v. McGraw-Hill Book Co. (U.K.) Ltd.*, [1983] F.S.R. 545 (Ch.) [*Sillitoe*].

105   *Banier*, above note 14.

106   *Time Warner Entertainments Co. v. Channel Four Television Corp.* (1993), 28 I.P.R. 459 (C.A.).

107   *Pro Sieben*, above note 3.

108   *Campbell v. Acuff-Rose Music Inc.*, 114 S.Ct. 1164 (1994) (rap treatment of Roy Orbison's song "Oh Pretty Woman").

border flow of media in this vein. One set of cases involved mainly unions that parodied corporate logos during bitter labour disputes, and the court judgments are remarkably unsympathetic in their treatment of such tactics. Most recently, the Michelin tire company obtained an injunction and damages against a union for its parody of the "Michelin Man" logo in pamphlets used during an attempt to unionize a company plant. Interestingly enough, Michelin fared worse in its home country, where a French court denied it relief for a similar parody of the company's alleged anti-social business practices.[109] Moreover, in Canada, the mandatory requirement to mention the source and other participants in the source material works against parody. As a policy matter, it would therefore be better that genuine parody and satire — as distinct from works that "free-ride" on or exploit an earlier work's popularity under the guise of parody or satire — not be held infringements in the first place.[110] The contrary view in the *Michelin* case, with its disturbing assertion that the freedom of expression guarantee in the *Charter of Rights and Freedoms* can never override copyright "property,"[111] should be rejected.

Research or private study: "Research" in this context means investigating or closely studying a subject. "Study," on the other hand, involves applying oneself to acquire knowledge or learning, or examining and analyzing a particular subject.[112] Since the user need not acknowledge sources, it has been suggested that uses that communicate

---

109 *Michelin*, above note 6; compare Judgment of the Cour d' appel (Riom) of 15 September 1994, [1995] Dalloz-Sirey 429 (note, B. Edelman). Presumably the "Michelin Man" logo used in question was not the original logo commissioned in 1898, whose copyright must by now have expired. See also *Rôtisseries St-Hubert Ltée* v. *Syndicat des Travailleur(euses) de la Rôtisserie St-Hubert de Drummondville (CSN)* (1986), 17 C.P.R. (3d) 461 (Que. S.C.) [*St-Hubert*].

110 *Productions Avanti Ciné-Vidéo Inc.* v. *Favreau*, [1999] J.Q. 2725 (Que. C.A.), rev'g (1997), 79 C.P.R. (3d) 385 (Que. S.C.), holding that a pornographic version of the Quebec sitcom *La Petite Vie* infringed the latter's copyright because its purpose was to exploit, not to parody, the source: sometimes a "difficult [line] to trace," as one of the judges admitted.

111 *C Act*, above note 9, s. 29.1; see section A(9), "Substantial Infringement," in chapter 5; see section B(5), "Constitutional Problems," in chapter 1. U.S. courts protect First Amendment values more solicitously in such cases: for example, *International Association of Machinists & Aerospace Workers, AFL-CIO* v. *Winship Green Nursing Center*, 914 F. Supp. 651 (D. Me. 1996), aff'd on other grounds, 103 F.3d 196 (1st Cir. 1996); *United We Stand America Inc.* v. *United We Stand, America New York Inc.*, 44 U.S.P.Q.2d 1351 (2d Cir. 1997).

112 *British Columbia (A.G.)* v. *Messier* (1984), 8 D.L.R. (4th) 306 at 309–10 (B.C.S.C.), followed in *De Garis* v. *Neville Jeffress Pidler Pty. Ltd.* (1990), 18 I.P.R. 292 (Austl. Fed. Ct.); see also G.A. Bloom & T.J. Denholm, "Research on the Internet: Is Access Copyright Infringement?" (1996) 12 Can. Intell. Prop. Rev. 337.

the source material to the public "fall outside" research or private study.[113] This view seems wrong. A doctoral thesis is written for research purposes, even though copies of the thesis are routinely deposited in the National Library and other public libraries.[114] Non-acknowledgment of sources may make a particular dealing "unfair" because of the failure to observe moral rights,[115] but that is a separate question. Although dealing for *private* study only is acceptable, this qualification does not apply to research. Thus, non-private or commercial research may qualify as fair dealing. As a result, not only scholars and students may engage in reasonable discourse, but private sector firms and workers should also be able to further their knowledge and research. Such activities become even more important to achieve national competitiveness in a global market. Firms may also be able to copy news or current affairs articles or programs — for example, to study public attitudes to their business.[116] However, in the United States, a corporation's research workers were not allowed to copy journal articles for future reference where an efficient means of buying copyright clearances existed.[117] The *1997 Act* introduced measures that to some extent clarified the permissible ambit of similar practices in Canada.[118]

Mandatory citation practices: Material used for criticism, review, or news reporting — but not research or private study — can be dealt with fairly only if sources are properly attributed. The "source" of the material must be mentioned; so, too, must the name of any author, performer, sound-recording maker, or broadcaster, if the name appears in the source.[119] Users need not, however, search out the names of anonymous authors or participants.[120]

---

113 *Hager*, above note 13.
114 The judge reached her conclusion partly because "private study" contemplated no public disclosure, and what was true for private study must also be true for its s. 29 companion, "research." This conclusion does not follow. Before 1994, private study and research were grouped in the same section with criticism, review, and newspaper summary, which plainly contemplated public disclosure. The modernization and regrouping of these purposes into three sections (ss. 29, 29.1, and 29.2) show no intent to narrow the character of any purpose.
115 See section B, "Moral Rights," in chapter 6.
116 D. Vaver, "Clipping Services and Copyright" (1994) 8 I.P.J. 379 at 381–82.
117 *American Geophysical Union v. Texaco Inc.*, 37 F.3d 881 (2d Cir. 1994) [*Geophysical*]; compare D. Vaver, "Copyright Inside the Law Library" (1995) 53 Advocate 355.
118 See sections B(12), "Libraries, Archives, and Museums," and B(13), "Education," in this chapter.
119 *C Act*, above note 9, ss. 29.1 & 29.2.
120 *Michelin*, above note 6 at 383.

In the United States, citation is not a precondition of fair use, but merely a factor to consider. A use there may be fair even if sources are not cited fully or at all. In the United Kingdom, source citation is required less often than in Canada; for example, reporting current events by sound recording, film, or telecommunication requires no acknowledgment of source.[121] Why Canada has chosen a stricter course than what both these jurisdictions or international laws mandate is not known.[122] These citation requirements are no doubt supposed to reinforce the moral rights of authors and entrepreneurs, but their implementation is both awkward and irrational.

It is odd that, whereas the only moral rights the Act positively recognizes are those of authors, such rights are extended to performers, broadcasters, sound-recording makers, and publishers through the oblique device of an infringement defence.[123] More seriously, the fair dealing provision allocates the remedy for non-citation to the wrong person: the copyright owner, not the person who is not mentioned. An author may, no doubt, sue separately for the infringement of her moral rights, but she may be unconcerned about the lapse. Why this breach should then also be a copyright infringement actionable by the copyright owner — more often someone other than the author — is far from clear. Where no separate moral rights claim is made or available, the copyright owner will presumably also keep any damages recovered for the infringement.

The fair dealing citation requirements are easily and commonly observed in the print media when literature or art is reviewed or criticized. They are less easily or commonly observed in the broadcast or electronic media. Suppose, for example, that Broadcaster A shows highlights from Broadcaster B's live telecast of a football game for news reporting purposes. Clearly, to avoid infringement, Broadcaster A must refer to Broadcaster B in a way that identifies B to the average viewer, or at least in a way that B usually identifies herself (e.g., by her logo).[124] A need not mention the names of any players: they are not (at least in copyright law) performers. Broadcaster A may, however, be prudent to name the commentators whose voices are heard on the clip, on the off

---

121 *UK Act*, above note 43, s. 30(3).
122 Moreover, international law does not require that non-compliance with source citation should automatically result in a finding of copyright infringement: compare *Berne*, above note 1, arts. 10(3) & 10 *bis* (2), and *Rome*, above note 1, arts. 15(1) & (2), with *C Act*, above note 9, ss. 27(1), 29.1, & 29.2.
123 See section B, "Moral Rights," in chapter 6.
124 *Pro Sieben*, above note 3.

chance that the commentary may be treated as an improvisational performance.[125] Whether Broadcaster **A** must name the director of the program, the record company that made the record of any music heard in the clip, the performers and authors of that music, and the names of the cheerleaders and their choreographers, if their names appear in the credits that run at the end of the telecast, is unclear. At some point, a failure to mention all or even most of the many people whose contribution is reflected in a twenty-second clip must be treated as *de minimis*, lest the fair dealing defence turn out to be meaningless across whole sections of activity.

The comparable U.K. provision is interpreted quite flexibly. True, a U.K. first-instance court found that a British television channel that included a clip from a German news program, showing only the filmmaker's logo, had not adequately identified the film's author and so could not take advantage of any fair dealing defence. The judge said that punctilious citation is demanded if an author is dead or even if he "may have assigned his copyright 100 years ago to someone else or he may be so well known that identifying him is redundant."[126] But this view was reversed on appeal. The filmmaker commonly identified itself simply by its logo; giving more particulars of the author's identity would mean nothing to the intended audience of the film.[127] A similar case in Canada was decided differently. The union that parodied the "Michelin Man" logo was told that it had not dealt fairly because the source of that artistic work — apparently, the Michelin company, rather than the unnamed artist — was nowhere mentioned.[128] The situation was the converse of the U.K. case. There, nobody would have been any the wiser about the author's identity even if more information were given. In *Michelin*, nobody needed any more identification to know precisely what the source of the "Michelin Man" logo was. Had the caricature of the "Michelin Man" been broadcast on national television, few would be unaware of the connection with the Michelin company. Michelin was clearly not prejudiced by the union's failure to inform Michelin workers, to whom alone the parody was circulated, of the obvious. The Canadian court, like the first-instance court in the

---

125   *C Act*, above note 9, s. 2, def. "performer's performance," includes an improvisation of a literary work, whether or not based on a pre-existing work.

126   *Pro Sieben*, above note 4 at 48 (Ch.), rev'd on the facts, *ibid.* (C.A.).

127   *Ibid.*

128   *Michelin*, above note 6 at 382–83.

U.K. case, interpreted the citation requirement too strictly. However, if this view is wrong, then a law that penalizes such trivial lapses so severely needs to be rethought.

ii) Nature of the Work Taken From

Fair dealing applies to both published and unpublished work. Were it otherwise, plays could not sensibly be reviewed.[129] But fair dealing is harder to prove for unpublished documents unless, for example, they expose illegal or unethical practices. Biographers have had a particularly hard time. In the United States, for example, J.D. Salinger's biographer, Ian Hamilton, was forced into paraphrasing his subject's ideas after being enjoined from using direct quotes from Salinger's publicly archived correspondence.[130] Fair dealing is more likely for material with some public circulation (e.g., bulletins sent by a corporation to its stockholders) than for material where the interest in secrecy is higher (e.g., material produced on discovery).

iii) How Much and What Is Used

The amount and substantiality of the material taken from the source work is always relevant: Has the user taken more than reasonably necessary for the purpose? This criterion should be looked at broadly. The copying of very "substantial" extracts or even whole works can be fair, although the burden of justification gets higher the more that is taken.[131] Guidelines settled by owner and user groups may also help if they sufficiently take account of the general public interest. Thus the Australian Parliament has deemed that copying one article from a periodical, or the greater of one chapter or 10 percent of a published edition, is fair dealing for research or study, without precluding other uses from qualifying.[132] A guideline like this may also be acceptable in Canada.

iv) How the Market for, or Value of, a Work Is Affected

It is always important to know what effect a use has on a work's present or reasonably expected future market. A use that substitutes for, or competes with, the copyright work is less likely to be held fair. A maker of instructional films had no trouble stopping buyers from making permanent copies for their convenience: it was being unfairly

---

129   Public performance is technically not a publication: see section A(1), "First Public Distribution," in chapter 5.

130   *Salinger v. Random House Inc.,* 811 F.2d 90 (2d Cir. 1987).

131   *Hubbard,* above note 92 at 98.

132   *Copyright Act,* 1968 (Austl.) No. 63, ss. 40(3) & 10(2).

deprived of a sale or licence fee.[133] Owners may also be entitled to reserve future markets. Thus, a magazine publisher may stop its cartoons from being compiled into a thematic anthology: it may want to develop its own anthology later and so should be entitled to refuse to license a potentially harmful use.[134]

v) Easy Alternative Availability
Copyright owners can hardly complain of unwanted uses if their distribution or permission practices are unfair or inefficient. A U.S. court noted: "It is sensible that a particular unauthorized use should be considered 'more fair' when there is no ready market or means to pay for the use, while such an unauthorized use should be considered 'less fair' when there is a ready market or means to pay for the use."[135]

Such reasoning cannot, however, avoid the question whether payment is fairly due for particular uses in the first place. U.S. courts claim that their insistence on "reasonable, or likely to be developed, markets"[136] avoids the vice of circularity. This claim is not entirely plausible, for a market may develop that includes or posits non-infringing uses, precisely to avoid a definitive court decision on infringement. Requiring entrants into such a market to be licensed extends copyright's reach beyond its legislated limits and makes users pay where the Act does not intend them to.

12) Libraries, Archives, and Museums

The *1997 Act* enacted a set of exceptions for non-profit libraries, archives, and museums (LAMs). For some time, copyright owners had claimed that many activities carried on by or in LAMs infringed owner rights. After 1988, collective societies began to form and to press institutions to enter agreements with them to cover photocopying practices. Some LAMs — especially those in schools, colleges, and universities — became included in agreements with collective societies like CanCopy and Union des écrivaines et d'écrivains québécois (UNEQ), under which fees were paid for library photocopying.

---

133   *Tom Hopkins International Inc. (Tom Hopkins Champions Unlimited)* v. *Wall & Redekop Realty Ltd.* (1984), 1 C.P.R. (3d) 348 (B.C.S.C.), varied (*sub nom. Tom Hopkins International Inc.* v. *Wall & Redekop Realty Ltd.*) (1985), 6 C.P.R. (3d) 475 (C.A.).
134   *Bradbury* v. *Hotten* (1872), L.R. 8 Ex. 1.
135   *Geophysical,* above note 117 at 898.
136   *Ibid.* at 931.

Many people nevertheless felt unhappy with the vagueness of rules, dating back to 1924, that continued to govern, despite enormous intervening technological changes.[137] In proposing copyright amendments in 1987, the government undertook eventually to clarify the position of LAMs by giving them latitude to carry out their vital service of making knowledge and data easily accessible to Canadians. This legislative task required the wisdom of Solomon if copyright owner interests were also to be fairly protected, as the government said they would. The *1997 Act* will require robust interpretation if the structure it sets up is to work smoothly. A particular interpretation may also have wide repercussions, since collective agreements typically do not require payment or clearance for activities that fall within a statutory exception.

a) Eligible Institution

The exceptions apply only to non-profit LAMs, including those in non-profit educational institutions,[138] and to persons acting under their authority. Such persons would include not only employees and volunteers, but also independent contractors such as outside firms acting on specific instructions.

An eligible LAM must hold and maintain a collection of documents or other material that is open to the public or to researchers. The LAM need not be separately incorporated, but it cannot be established or conducted for profit, or be part of a body that is established or conducted for profit; nor can it be administered or directly or indirectly controlled by such a body.[139] Typical qualifying institutions would include federal, provincial, and municipal LAMs, and LAMs run by public schools, colleges, and universities. Non-qualifying institutions would encompass those run by businesses, including law firms. A LAM cannot avoid being for-profit just because it is run by a non-profit corporation. If one or more businesses or for-profit firms directly or indirectly control the non-profit corporation, the LAM does not qualify as non-profit. The status of a LAM run by a professional association such as a law society may therefore depend on such circumstances as how the LAM is established and run. The matter can be clarified by asking the government to issue a regulation confirming the LAM's status as non-profit.[140]

137　See J. McAnanama, "Copyright Law: Libraries and Their Users Have Special Needs" (1991) 6 I.P.J. 225.

138　*C Act*, above note 9, s. 30.4.

139　*C Act, ibid.*, s. 2, def. "library, archive or museum."

140　*C Act, ibid.*, s. 2, def. "library, archive or museum," para. (b).

The world of institutional information is thus divided into the public and private sectors. The public sector is intended to benefit from the special exemptions; the private sector is not. The public sector is, moreover, treated as part of an information network. One non-profit LAM can copy material for another non-profit LAM in the same way as it can for its own use or for its own patrons.[141] Private sector LAMs fall outside this network. Copies they request from one another or from a non-profit LAM are not exempt. Such copies may fall under a collective reprographic agreement.

Unless otherwise noted, the following discussion applies only to qualifying non-profit LAMs.

b) Collection Maintenance and Management

A LAM can make a copy of an item in its permanent collection in certain circumstances for the maintenance or management of its permanent collection. It may equally copy items for the maintenance or management of the collection of another non-profit LAM. Intermediate copies made along the way must be destroyed when no longer needed. The institution must also observe any procedural regulations prescribed by order in council.[142] All material within copyright is included in the exemption: any published or unpublished literary, dramatic, musical, or artistic work, sound recording, performance, or recorded broadcast.

i) Fragile and Obsolete Formats

Some items may be unable to be viewed, handled, or listened to because of their condition or because they must be kept under special atmospheric conditions. An exemption allows a copy for on-site consultation then to be made. Rare or unpublished items may also be deteriorating, damaged, lost, or at risk of becoming so. A copy of such items, presumably for on-site consultation, may also lawfully be made.[143] Other items may be in an obsolete format (for example, low-density floppy diskette) or the technology to use it may be unavailable (for example, a 78 r.p.m. record-player). A copy in an alternative for-

---

141   *C Act, ibid.*, ss. 30.1(1) & 30.2(5). Whether requests from offshore LAMs are covered is doubtful.

142   *C Act, ibid.*, ss. 30.1(1), (3), & (4).

143   This exception may overlap with another allowing restoration: *C Act, ibid.*, s. 30.1(1)(f). See section B(12)(b)(ii), "Administration and Restoration," in this chapter.

mat — for example, compact disk, audiotape, or transfer to computer hard-drive — may then lawfully be made.[144]

These exemptions are all subject to one major qualification. The LAM cannot make a copy if a version of suitable quality for its purpose is "commercially available."[145] The LAM must, however, first use reasonable efforts to locate a suitable copy in Canada. If one is found at a reasonable price, the institution must buy it instead of making its own copy. If no such suitable item is found, the LAM can still not immediately make a copy. It must first try to locate a collective society that is authorized to license the making or use of the appropriate copy. Only if the society does not offer the LAM a licence for a reasonable price and within a reasonable time may the LAM then make its own copy for free.

The procedure just outlined seeks to apply "commercially available" in a practical way, but the actual definition of "commercially available" in the Act is not quite so clear.[146] The following questions may arise:

- What if the LAM reasonably believes a search for a suitable copy on the market would be futile? For example, the LAM may believe that no distributor or collective society exists for a rare work because the publisher has disappeared. Alternatively, the work may be unpublished and therefore is outside a collective society's repertoire. Presumably, the LAM need not go through the motions of search. Any neglect in such a case should be excused on the principle that the law does not compel the doing of useless acts.

- If a search is undertaken, how much must reasonably be done to try to find a suitable copy "available on the Canadian market"? Is it enough to check Canadian distributors? Should the LAM also search the second-hand market?[147] If these efforts are unsuccessful, should the search extend to foreign distributors who may be expected to offer such items for lawful sale in Canada? Should an Internet search be conducted? When the LAM looks for an appropriate collective society, is it confined to Canada, or must it check abroad if no local society can license the needed rights?

---

144   *C Act, ibid.*, ss. 30.1(1)(b), (a), & (c).
145   *C Act, ibid.*, ss. 30.1(2) & 2, def. "commercially available."
146   *C Act, ibid.*, s. 2, def. "commercially available"; the French def., *ibid.*, art. 2 ("accessible sur le marché"), is somewhat clearer.
147   Probably not, because neither copyright holders nor Canadian distributors benefit from the sale of used items.

Presumably, since the Act deals with rights in Canada, reasonable efforts to locate a Canadian distributor or a Canadian collective society should usually suffice, but this is not clear.

- What will be considered an "appropriate" copy, for example, to upgrade an obsolete format? Suppose that the music on an obsolete 78 r.p.m. record in a library is also commercially available on compact disk, but patrons prefer the wider range of frequencies that vinyl provides when compared with the CD. Is the compact disk nevertheless "appropriate"? May the library use a transfer method that produces a higher-quality modern format, even though the collective refuses a licence and directs the library to buy the compact disk? May this not depend as much on the nature of the library and its patrons as on what is available on the market? For example, a copy not appropriate for music students using a university library may be appropriate for the general public using a municipal library, unless the latter library is also a resort of professional musicians with higher demands.

- Having found an appropriate source, how may the LAM tell if the price demanded for an item or a licence is or is not "reasonable"? In the case of a licence offered by a collective society, any charge that is significantly out of line with the society's usual tariff will presumably not be considered reasonable; but there will be other cases where the reasonableness of the asking price may prove more difficult to ascertain and resolve.

ii) Administration and Restoration

The LAM need not check for distributors or collective societies when it wishes to make a copy of an item for any of five purposes: internal record-keeping, internal cataloguing, insurance, police investigations, and restoration.[148] The first four require little comment, except to say that the idea that a non-profit institution — or anyone else — needs a copyright holder's permission to copy anything that may be useful in a criminal investigation is absurd. Any term in a licence that tried to impose such a restriction would surely be against public policy and void.

The ambit of the fifth purpose — making a copy "if necessary for restoration" — is somewhat unclear. The exemption should not be used to evade the cognate one that allows the copying of rare or unpublished original items that are deteriorating, damaged, lost, or at risk of becoming so; for, in these cases, the LAM has to try to buy a

---

148   *C Act*, above note 9, ss. 30.1(1)(d), (e), & (f).

copy or a licence before making its own copy.[149] The restoration exemption should therefore cover only published material that does not qualify as "rare."

Restoration presumably refers to such common practices as replacing torn pages from a book with pages photocopied from another copy. The exemption may, however, extend beyond this limit. Read literally, it could even allow a library to replace the entire inventory it lost in a fire with photocopies made at its request by another library. This unattractive result will no doubt be limited, if not by order in council, then by evidence of reasonable institutional practice. For example, the model collective agreement negotiated between CanCopy and the Association of Universities and Colleges of Canada, which allows copying of up to 20 percent of a work to replace damaged or missing pages, may be some evidence of the practical limits of what is meant by restoration in the context of the statutory exemption.

c) Photocopying Articles

A LAM may make a single reprographic copy from a newspaper or periodical for a patron in certain circumstances:

- The article must be published in a scholarly, scientific or technical periodical. Alternatively, it must have been published over a year earlier in any other periodical or in a newspaper.[150]
- The whole or any part of an article can be copied, as may any work — for example, a photograph, drawing, or table — contained in the article.
- Any sort of article can be copied from a scholarly, scientific, or technical periodical, but no work of fiction or poetry, and no dramatic or musical work, can be copied from any other periodical or from a newspaper.[151]
- The person requesting the copy must intend to use it for research or private study, and must satisfy the LAM that it will be used for nothing else.[152]
- The LAM can order the copy from another institution. It may, presumably, receive the copy by mail, fax, or other electronic means. The copy delivered to the patron cannot, however, be in digital form: the LAM cannot, for example, send the copy by e-mail or on

---

149   See section B(12)(b)(i), "Fragile and Obsolete Formats," in this chapter.
150   C Act, above note 9, s. 30.2(2).
151   C Act, ibid., s. 30.2(3).
152   C Act, ibid., ss. 30.2(2) & (4).

diskette. Any intermediate copy left after delivery (for example, on the hard drive of a LAM's computer) must be destroyed.[153]

- Any fee or mark-up can cover the LAM's costs, including overhead, of providing the service, but the LAM cannot seek to profit beyond that.[154]
- Regulations to clarify procedures and qualifying publications may be made by order in council.[155] Regulations taking effect on 1 September 1999 specify that LAMs must keep records when providing copies and must stamp copies with a legend such as "For Research or Private Study Only. Other Users May Require Copyright Owner's Authorization." Returns must be made, on request, to copyright owners or collectives once a year, and records must be kept for three years.[156]

The rules distinguish between, on the one hand, material appearing in scholarly, scientific, and technical periodicals and, on the other, material appearing in other classes of periodicals and in newspapers. Contributors to the former types of periodical often come from educational institutions or the professions. These authors are typically paid little, if anything, for their contribution and sometimes must transfer copyright to the publisher. Since they write mainly to circulate their ideas as widely as possible, such authors expect their work to be freely copied and generally do not expect or want royalties from this activity. By providing this exemption, the *1997 Act* makes publishers share these expectations as well.

Parliament attributed quite different aspirations to contributors to newspapers and more popular periodicals. It presumed, on the one hand, that copyright owners of fiction, poetry, music, or drama deserve compensation anytime the work is copied. On the other hand, Parliament presumed that copyright owners of artwork or factual writing deserve compensation, at least from library photocopying, only while their work is fresh. It remains to be seen whether those authors who are equally adept in several modes will now foresake factual writing for fiction and poetry, in order to profit from the more favourable benefits the latter categories theoretically enjoy.

These policies are the result of some rather uneasy compromises, but at least LAMs have reasonably clear guidelines to follow. They need not concern themselves with a work's copyright status or with page or

---

153   *C Act, ibid.*, s. 30.2(5) & (5.1).
154   *C Act, ibid.*, s. 29.3.
155   *C Act, ibid.*, s. 30.2(6).
156   *Exceptions for Educational Institutions, Libraries, Archives and Museums Regulations*, SOR/99-325 [*LAM Regs.*].

word counts. Even an article occupying the whole number of a periodical may apparently be copied. Neither the LAM nor the requesting person infringes copyright if the procedures are followed. The LAM should be protected even if the person lies to it about his purpose for requesting the copy, but the liar may not himself be protected. If, for example, he scans the copy of the article onto a Web site, not only will the uploading infringe copyright but the initial photocopy may become infringing and may have to be handed over to the copyright holder on demand.[157]

The exemptions do not authorize the downloading of work from the Internet or an electronic database, even though the article may have also appeared in a newspaper or periodical. This copying is clearly not "reprographic reproduction." Electronic databases that carry newspaper and periodical articles with the copyright owner's consent may therefore set whatever terms they wish for accessing or downloading their contents. They are unaffected by these exemptions.

d) Self-Service Photocopiers

LAMs that put photocopy machines at the disposal of patrons have worried about copyright liability at least since the mid-1970s, when an Australian university was found liable for infringements committed by patrons on coin-operated machines within the library. The Australian High Court held the library had "authorized" infringements by not adequately warning patrons against infringing and by not policing the machines to check that the warnings were working.[158] Whether Canadian courts would go this far is doubtful. Canadian precedents so far seem closer to the British approach, which equates authorization with sanctioning, approving, or granting or purporting to grant authority to do, the infringing act. By contrast, the Australian approach also embraces countenancing, permitting, or even condoning infringements as authorization.[159] Still, the point is arguable in Canada, and collective societies quickly took advantage of the situation to encourage risk-averse institutions to enter agreements covering self-service photocopying. LAMs nevertheless continued to press for exoneration from liability.

---

157   *C Act*, above note 9, s. 2, def. "infringing." The photocopy may have been "dealt with" in contravention of the *C Act* under para. (a) of this definition.

158   *Moorhouse and Angus & Robertson (Publishers) Ltd.* v. *University of New South Wales*, [1976] R.P.C. 151 (Austl. H.C.). See section A(8), "Authorization," in chapter 5.

159   Compare *A.P.R.A. Ltd.* v. *Jain* (1990), 18 I.P.R. 663 (Austl. Fed. Ct.), with *Muzak Corp.* v. *C.A.P.A.C.*, [1953] 2 S.C.R. 182; *Amstrad Consumer Electronics Plc.* v. *British Phonographic Industry Ltd.*, [1986] F.S.R. 159 at 207 (C.A.), aff'd (*sub nom. CBS Songs Ltd.* v. *Amstrad Consumer Electronics*) [1988] A.C. 1013 (H.L.), following *Vigneux*, above note 3.

As first introduced, Bill C-32 seemed to give LAMs all they wanted. Non-profit educational institutions could have photocopiers on their premises for students, instructors, and staff. LAMs could also have photocopiers for their patrons. No such institution would be liable for what users photocopied, if a notice warning about copyright was located as prescribed by regulation.[160]

This simple exemption did not, however, survive in this form. Collective societies attacked it in committee as undercutting their existing agreements and argued that it should either be modified or scrapped. A new set of clauses was added when the bill emerged from committee.[161]

As now written, the exemption applies only to certain non-profit educational institutions and LAMs — namely, those that have

- a reprographic agreement with a collective society;
- a reprographic tariff set or approved by the Copyright Board under the new procedures provided in the Act;
- a reprographic tariff proposal before the Copyright Board;
- an exemption order from the Copyright Board after talks for a collective agreement have been initiated; or
- an individual reprographic agreement with a copyright owner, but only in respect of the copying of works covered by that agreement.

The modified exemption is thus quite modest in scope when compared with the one initially proposed. Institutions with existing collective agreements seem no better off than before; the collective society was already bound under the agreement to indemnify the institution if any non-participating copyright holder sued for infringement. Institutions without a collective agreement or tariff also seem no better off. They continue to be potentially liable for infringements committed by users, depending on the facts and on whether a Canadian court comes closer to the Australian or the British precedents on authorization. The major beneficiaries, perhaps ironically, seem to be the reprographic collective societies. Not only were their licensing drives strongly boosted but, just as important, the Act also relieved them from all liability in respect of self-service photocopying under the indemnity clause in their collective agreements with users. Institutions will no longer ask for indemnity in these cases because they are now themselves exempt from liability under the Act. Nor will societies any longer risk litigation from non-members for participating in, or autho-

---

160 *C Act*, above note 9, ss. 30.3(1) & (5). The form of the Notice is set out in s. 8 of the *LAM Regs.*, above note 156.

161 *C Act, ibid.*, ss. 30.3(2), (3), & (4).

rizing infringements of, non-members' works by the use of self-serve photocopiers in institutions: for a society commits no wrong by participating in, or authorizing, a non-infringing activity.

e) Archival Copying

On its introduction in the House of Commons, Bill C-32 contained no special exemptions for archival copying. Exemptions were included only when the Bill was reported out of Committee. The drafting was somewhat hurried; so, too much should not be made of stylistic differences from other exemptions.

The exemptions are now outlined. A more detailed consideration of their scope and limits then follows.

i) Works Deposited after 1 September 1999

An archive may make a copy of an unpublished work that is deposited after 1 September 1999 in its collection in the following circumstances:

1) The archive is satisfied the patron will use the copy only for research or private study.
2) Only one copy is made for that patron.
3) The copyright owner must not have prohibited copying. If that owner was the depositor, the prohibition can occur only on deposit of the work. Other copyright owners may prohibit copying at any later time, but the archive need not notify them of the deposit.
4) The right to prohibit extends to prohibit copying of the whole or part of a work — for example, particular pages of a document. The copyright owner may lift the prohibition anytime, either for a specific copying or generally.
5) The archive must notify the depositor, when the works are deposited, that the works may be copied. The depositor thus can decide whether to ban the copying of any work in which he owns copyright, and whether to advise other affected persons who may want to consider their options. The archive need not notify any other copyright owner.
6) Any copying fee or mark-up can cover the archive's copying costs, including overhead, but the archive cannot seek to profit beyond that.
7) Regulations prescribing the manner and form of copying may be made by order in council, and these must be observed. Such regulations were made in 1999 and are similar to the general rules for photocopying in libraries, archives, and museums. [162]

---

162   *C Act, ibid.,* ss. 30.21(1) to (4), & s. 29.3; ss. 5 & 6 of the *LAM Regs.,* above note 156.

ii) Works Deposited before 1 September 1999

All the above conditions except number (5) also apply to the copying of unpublished material deposited before 1 September 1999. An archive may have informed pre-1999 depositors of its copying policies and may have some form of written acknowledgment on file from the depositor. But the procedures it followed may have differed from what is now prescribed under the *1997 Act*. Condition (5) therefore does not apply retrospectively.

The archive may have some further obligations where the author is still living, or where he died on or after 1 January 1949. There is no difficulty where a copyright owner has already consented, preferably in a signed writing filed with the archive, to copying for research or private study. But in other cases, the archive must first seek the consent of the relevant copyright owner — not merely the depositor, who may not own the copyright in question. If the owner is located and consents, the copying may go ahead; if he refuses consent, the archive must abide that decision.

Where the archive cannot locate the copyright owner — presumably after reasonable attempts to do so — it may nevertheless go ahead and copy in accordance with conditions (1), (2), (6), and (7), but it must make and keep a record of the copying in the prescribed form.[163]

The obligation to search for copyright owners does not apply where the work is a literary, dramatic, or musical work, or an engraving; the author died before 1949; and the work had not by then been published or publicly performed or telecommunicated. The archive may copy these works by observing all the conditions, except number (5), noted above.[164] Copyright protection of these works does not last beyond 31 December 2004.

iii) Scope and Limits

The following points about the scope and limits of the archival exemptions should be noted.

Copyrights expired or held by archive: The archival exemptions are irrelevant where the relevant copyright has expired or has been abandoned, or where it has been assigned to the archive. Archives can therefore solve some access problems by asking donors irrevocably to renounce all their rights, including copyrights, or to assign all their rights to the archive. Something like this occurred, although somewhat fortuitously, with the 1941 gift to the Quebec archives of the personal

---

163   *C Act, ibid.*, s. 30.21(5) & (6); *LAM Regs., ibid.*, s.5.
164   *C Act, ibid.*, s. 30.21(7).

correspondence of Louis-Joseph Papineau and his wife, Julie. The donor, a descendant of these celebrated figures in Lower Canada and early Quebec politics, had been entrusted with Papineau memorabilia, including the correspondence and its associated copyrights, by family members, to make the material widely available for the benefit of the general public and researchers. When, however, a researcher published an unflattering biography of Julie Papineau, two family members sued, claiming that extracts from archived letters found in the book infringed copyrights that had descended to them. The court disagreed. Although copyright was not specifically mentioned in the discussions between the donor and the officials negotiating for the government, the court held that the intention of the gift was to transfer both the objects and their copyrights to the province.[165]

Material covered: The exemption applies only to "works." Sound recordings, performances, and broadcasts are not mentioned. Only the National Archives of Canada may copy sound recordings or broadcasts for archival purposes, but, even then, no provision specifically allows the Archives to make a further copy, without the copyright holder's consent, for a patron's research or private study purposes.[166] Researchers may no doubt listen to or view an archival recording in private without infringing, but, if they want a copy, they must persuade the archive to let them make their own under the fair dealing exception.[167] Alternatively, the archive may make the copy at a researcher's request as her agent, and may be protected to the same extent as the researcher. A non-profit archive providing this service must keep a record in the form prescribed by regulation,[168] but, somewhat anomalously, a for-profit archive is not subject to this formality. In either case, a researcher who has the archive copy more for her than is necessary for her research purposes may expose both herself and the archive to liability.

Applicability of other obligations: The exemption does not affect obligations arising from other laws. The laws of contract, confidentiality, privacy, and tort may also control access and affect how the material may be used. For example, a depositor may stipulate, as a condition of the deposit, that the archive must notify users that no research resulting from access to the material may be published without his prior consent. The Act contemplates a condition like this only

---

165 *Bourassa v. Ouellet* (8 January 1970), (Que. S.C.) [unreported] [*Bourassa*].

166 *C Act*, above note 9, s. 30.5.

167 See section B(11), "Fair Dealing," and specifically "Research or private study" in section B(11)(b)(i) in this chapter.

168 *C Act*, above note 9, ss. 30.2(1) & (5).

where the depositor owns the copyright.[169] But, even where he does not, such a condition may be effective under provincial law. In this case, an archive that fails to notify a user could be liable for damages for breach of this contract, while a researcher who knowingly violates the condition may be enjoined and may also have to pay damages to the depositor.[170]

Restrictive conditions may be imposed because a donor may fear that the publication of information, which was given to him in confidence, may break a legal or moral obligation of confidence owed to the discloser. The donor may also want to control the revelation or publication of embarrassing material. But users may come under other obligations even where no conditions are imposed on the deposit. Thus, a user may not disclose material that he recognizes or ought to recognize as being confidential (e.g., genuine matters of national security), although this obligation may in time disappear. For example, Cabinet discussions may be highly confidential, but a British court allowed their details to be published by an ex-minister ten years later when no discernible public interest in maintaining confidentiality any longer remained.[171] Other obligations may endure longer. Thus, in the Papineau litigation mentioned earlier, a historian was held liable under Quebec law for defaming Papineau's descendants, by interpreting the family's early history in a way that was found to reflect adversely on them.[172]

Ascertaining copyright ownership: A donor may occasionally own copyright in everything she deposits. For example, a freelance author may deposit her draft manuscripts or other material that she has solely produced; alternatively, all the copyright holders may have assigned their rights to the donor, as was the case with the Papineau correspondence earlier mentioned.[173] Quite often, however, copyrights in deposited material will be held by people other than the donor. For example, someone who deposits a bundle of correspondence may own copyright in the letters and memoranda that he wrote, but the copyright in work produced by him as an employee on the job may belong to his employer. Similarly, copyright in letters sent to the donor may belong to the sender or the sender's employer. The publication of an item may

---

169   *C Act, ibid.*, s. 30.21(3)(a).

170   Compare *Lindsey v. Le Sueur* (1913), 29 O.L.R. 648 (C.A.).

171   *Attorney-General v. Jonathan Cape Ltd.*, [1976] 1 Q.B. 752 (Richard Crossman's diaries).

172   *Bourassa*, above note 165. The damages awarded were modest, but the publisher destroyed remaining stocks to avoid further liability.

173   *Ibid.*

therefore infringe copyright if the consent of the correct copyright owner has not first been obtained.[174]

Persons acting under archive's authority also exempted: Unlike other exemptions relating to LAMs, the archival exemption is not specifically stated to apply both to the institution and to persons "acting under [its] authority."[175] This must nevertheless be its effect, because a linked provision, inserted at the same time the archival exemption was first introduced in the Bill, clearly assumes that the archival exemption extends to a "person acting under [an archive's] authority," and the implementing Regulations assume the same.[176]

13) Education

A set of exemptions in the *1997 Act* now clarifies the copyright position of non-profit educational institutions. Some activities are totally exempt from copyright, but, more commonly, non-profit institutions, like their for-profit counterparts, are encouraged either to buy material that is available on the market or to deal with a collective society for a licence.

As drafted, the exemptions do not always fully capture the wide range and diversity of modern educational practice. Their interpretation will therefore need a heavier-than-usual dose of common sense if they are to work effectively.

a) Eligible Institution

The exemptions apply to non-profit educational institutions and also, as for LAMs, to persons acting under the institution's authority.[177] "Educational institution" is broadly defined. All levels of education — pre-school to tertiary — are included, but the institution must be non-profit and must be licensed or recognized by or under federal or provincial legislation. Non-profit institutions that provide continuing, professional, or vocational education or training are included, if the institution is directed or controlled by a board of education regulated by or under provincial legislation. The government department or agency or non-profit body that controls or supervises the education or training is also included. This extension should cover boards of education and

---

174   *Salinger v. Random House Inc.*, 811 F.2d 90 (2d Cir. 1987). See further section A(2)(a), "Employees," in chapter 4.

175   For example, *C Act*, above note 9, s. 30.2(2), on photocopying by a LAM. See section B(12)(c), "Photocopying Articles," in this chapter.

176   *C Act, ibid.*, s. 29.3(2); see, for example, s. 5 of the *LAM Regs.*, above note 156.

177   See section B(12)(a), "Eligible Institution," in this chapter.

government education departments, as well as professional organizations such as medical associations, engineering institutes, or law societies that run continuing education programs, provided the organization qualifies as non-profit. Any doubts about the eligibility of any institution can be resolved by asking the government to issue a regulation confirming the body's status.[178]

b) Teaching

Some minor uses of material for teaching and examining purposes are exempted. These uses involve teaching aids, tests and examinations, performances for or by students, off-air recording, and compilations for students. The institution or person doing the activity can charge users to recover associated costs, including overhead, but cannot otherwise intend to profit.[179]

First the general limitations on all these uses, and then the permitted uses themselves, are discussed.

i) General Limitations

The education or training to which the activity, to be exempt, is directed must occur on the institution's premises or somewhere controlled or supervised by it.[180] The exemptions therefore do not seem to apply to distance learning, for example, where one-way or interactive television or the Internet is used to transmit material to a student's home or between different institutions. One-off seminars or educational sessions held in rooms booked for the event should, however, be as fully exempt as classes held in schools and institutions, presumably including overflow classes where the instructor is seen on closed-circuit equipment.

An institution with multiple campuses or locations should also benefit from the exemptions. For example, an examiner located in one campus should be able to set an examination for students to sit in another campus or location under the same institution's supervision. Presumably, too, a lesson in a classroom on one campus may be beamed simultaneously by closed circuit signal to a classroom on the second campus. The location and number of classrooms, and the distance between them, seem irrelevant where all are under the same institution's control or supervision.

---

178   C Act, above note 9, s. 2, def. "educational institution."
179   C Act, ibid., s. 29.3.
180   C Act, ibid., ss. 29.4(1), (2), & s. 2, def. "premises."

ii) Teaching Aids

Educators may copy material onto blackboards or flip charts for their classes without infringing copyright. They may also copy works for use on an overhead projector "or similar device."[181] The copying and exhibition should be done manually. The overhead projector exemption needs some elaboration.

Copying for overhead or similar projection: An educator cannot use technology other than a pen or pencil to copy an image for projection without first checking the following:

- Does the copying fall under an existing collective agreement? If so, it can occur only on the terms the agreement prescribes. If not:
- Can an appropriate copy be bought reasonably soon at a reasonable price on the Canadian market?[182] If so, the item should be bought. If not:
- Is there another collective society that can license the making of an appropriate copy in a reasonable time and for a reasonable price? If so, the licence must be bought. If not:
- The work may be transferred onto the appropriate medium for free.

What projection equipment, other than an overhead projector, may be used? A slide projector should be allowed, as it clearly is a "similar device." A laptop computer, into which text and pictures are scanned for projection before a class, may also perhaps qualify as a "similar device." A movie projector or video-cassette player would not qualify, since the exemption seems directed to the copying of still images only.[183]

iii) Tests and Examinations

Any material "as required for a test or examination" may be used without infringing copyright.[184] The policy seemingly allows educators to set tests and students to sit them, without anyone risking infringement. The exemption was drafted to work in tandem with the collective

---

181 C Act, ibid., s. 29.4(1).

182 C Act, ibid., ss. 29.4(3) & 2 (def. "commercially available"). Earlier discussion on the difficulties in interpreting "commercially available" applies here too. See sections B(12)(b)(i), "Fragile and Obsolete Formats," and section B(7)(b), "Commercial Availability," in this chapter.

183 This restriction reflects the distinction the C Act draws throughout between cinematography and still photography. A movie projector is no more like an overhead projector than a video camera is like an ordinary camera. Had copying for movie projection been intended, the reference to "overhead projector or similar device" would presumably have been dropped or drafted differently.

184 C Act, above note 9, s. 29.4(2).

agreements commonly entered into between educational institutions and reprographic collectives.

Anomalies nevertheless remain. Most are avoidable by interpreting the exemption broadly in the light of the imperatives surrounding testing for competency. After all, federal legislation dealing with copyright should not lightly be assumed to have an impact on substantive educational policy, which is a matter typically within provincial jurisdiction.

Among the more obvious problems are the following:

- Only a closed list of uses is exempt: reproduction, translation, public performance, and telecommunication to the public.[185] A strict reading would exclude examinations that require a drama class to précis a play or movie or to dramatize a part of a novel, or that require students of sound engineering to demonstrate their practical skills by making a professional-quality recording. It is to be hoped that "reproduc[tion]" will be interpreted broadly to include such practices.[186]
- Many examinations and tests allow students to work on their answers outside the physical precincts of the institution; yet the exemption lets someone "reproduce, translate or perform in public *on the premises of the educational institution*" only.[187] If the italicized phrase qualifies all that precedes it, no take-home examination in, say, translation could be administered.[188] This absurdity is avoidable if the phrase is read to qualify only the words "perform in public." Thus, not only would examinations involving public performances and telecommunications to the public be placed on a parallel footing,[189] but the legislature would also not be taken to have unduly interfered with common testing practices.
- The exemption is qualified in the same way as the exemption for making copies for overhead projection. Material required for a test or examination cannot be copied or used if it is "commercially avail-

---

185   *C Act, ibid.*, ss. 29.4(2)(a) & (b). These activities in respect of works are found in ss. 3(1), 3(1)(a), & 3(1)(e).

186   Thus, abridgment, dramatization, and sound recording — specifically mentioned in the *C Act, ibid.*, ss. 3(1)(b), (c), & (d) — may perhaps be implicitly included with the concept of "reproduc[tion]" under s. 29.4(2)(a); see *Apple Computer Inc.* v. *Mackintosh Computers Ltd.* (1986), 8 C.I.P.R. 185 at 185 & 188–89 (Fed. T.D), aff'd [1990] 2 S.C.R. 209.

187   *C Act*, above note 9, ss. 29.4(2)(a) & 2 (def. "premises") [emphasis added].

188   Unfortunately, the French version of *C Act, ibid.*, s. 29.4(2)(a), supports this reading.

189   An examination involving telecommunication to the public requires the public to be located on the institution's premises: *C Act, ibid.*, s. 29.4(2)(b).

able in a medium that is appropriate for the purpose."[190] This condition must refer to the questions set by the examiner; students cannot be expected to check for commercial availability of a work before providing their answers!

The good-faith judgment of the examiner on whether alternative material is "appropriate" must carry weight. Clearly, an examiner who wants to play a commercially available piece of recorded music for music students to criticize should buy the record instead of copying it. On the other hand, an examiner may wish to test the proficiency of translation students by asking them to correct a passage that the examiner has deliberately translated poorly. This examination should be exempt even if an excellent translation were available on the market, for the latter would not meet the purpose of the examination. Institutions should also not be forced to deal with a collective society for a licence where the security of an examination may be compromised.

iv) Performances for or by Students

Performing and studying performance are essential to much education, from pre-schoolers singing "Baby Beluga" to conservatory students executing music, drama, and dance to professional standards. The reception of educational and other programming by radio, television, cablecast, and, more recently, the Internet has also been integrated across the entire curriculum. The Act lumps these disparate activities together because all technically involve a performance, however little pre-schoolers' singing may have in common with high-schoolers' viewing television in class or drama students rehearsing a Tomson Highway play.

The *1997 Act* allows the following activities to be carried on under certain conditions on an educational institution's premises for educational or training purposes, without infringing copyright:

- Works (typically music or a play) may be performed live, primarily by students of the institution. Teachers or others may take part, so long as they do not take over.
- Sound recordings may be played.
- Lawfully received television or radio programs may be played live as they are broadcast or transmitted by cable, including pay-per-view programs.

---

190   *C Act, ibid.*, ss. 29.4(3) & 2 (def. "commercially available"). See section B(13)(b)(ii), "Teaching Aids," in this chapter.

- Material available on the Internet may also, possibly, be accessed and displayed simultaneously, if the conditions of reception are observed. This should be true for broadcasts available on the Internet in "real time" — at the same time as they are received on conventional radio and television sets. Whether it is true of other material available on the Internet is as yet unclear.[191]

The following restrictions must be observed:

- The playing or performance must have an educational or training purpose. The satirical reviews that students stage annually may not qualify if entertainment, not education, is their purpose.
- The audience must consist primarily of students, instructors, or persons directly responsible for setting the curriculum for the institution, or any combination of them. The word "primarily" suggests both that these persons should comprise most of the audience, and also that the activity should be mainly for their benefit, although others may incidentally be present.[192] The school concert that is put on mainly for parents, friends, and well-wishers obviously does not qualify.
- The institution or performer cannot profit from the activity. Professional musicians, actors, and dancers who perform for the student body must therefore do so without fee; but there should be no objection if the institution reimburses their travel and lodging, rents a hall, stage-props, or instruments, and recovers these costs from students.[193] Performances for fund-raising purposes will not, however, be exempt.

v) Off-Air Recording

Material can be recorded off-air, under certain conditions, for replaying to an audience consisting primarily of the students of an educational institution. While at the institution, students may listen to or view any broadcast or cablecast, regardless of content. One might therefore have thought that the recording and replaying of such transmissions could equally take place, regardless of content. This policy was, however, not adopted. While anything may indeed be recorded off a lawfully received

---

191   *C Act, ibid.*, ss. 29.5, 29.8, & 2 (def. "premises"). On what constitutes an institution's premises, see section B(13)(b)(iii), "Tests and Examinations," in this chapter. Musical performances may also fall under another exemption: see section B(2)(c), "Charitable, Educational, and Religious Objects," in this chapter .

192   Compare *Canada (Registrar of Trade Marks) v. Coles Book Stores Ltd.*,[1974] S.C.R. 438 on "primarily."

193   *C Act*, above note 9, s. 29.3; *Western Fair*, above note 8.

transmission,[194] only some material — essentially current events — can be replayed without copyright payments, subject to certain time limits, record-keeping, and marking requirements. The institution may, if it wishes, charge students beyond cost recovery for these services.

News programs: The institution may record a news or news commentary program — but not a documentary — off-air for educational or training purposes. Only a single copy may be made, but it can be shown any number of times, for up to a year, to the institution's students. After a year, the institution can retain the copy, but must then pay for and use it according to the terms set by the Copyright Board. Otherwise the copy must be erased.[195]

Current affairs are central to the education curriculum at all levels, and the exemption puts broadcast news and newspapers on a comparable footing. Students can discuss a newspaper easily by passing a copy around, but a fleeting news broadcast is a more difficult subject unless a copy is first made and viewed. The exemption still distinguishes between the two media, for a newspaper may be freely archived indefinitely for later browsing, while a library of recorded broadcasts cannot be created and maintained without payment.

What constitutes news or news commentary programs, and what distinguishes them from documentaries, will sometimes be contentious. Clearly, the CBC's *The National* and SRC's *Téléjournal* are news programs, SRC's *Le Point* is a news commentary program, Newsworld's *The Passionate Eye* is a documentary, and the CBC's satirical fiction series *Newsroom* is presumably none of the above. But what of the CBC's *This Hour Has 22 Minutes* or *The Fifth Estate*? May either qualify as a news or news commentary program, although the former is mainly satirical and the latter is part news and part documentary?

Copying for evaluation: A single copy of any broadcast or cablecast item may be recorded off-air and kept up to thirty days, so that a decision may be made on whether it is worth playing to students for their education or training. If the decision is no, the copy must be erased; if yes, the copy may be kept, but royalties for making and performing the copy to students will have to be paid according to the tariff set by the Copyright Board.[196]

---

194 Whether recording off the Internet is included is unclear. See section B(13)(b)(iv), "Performances for or by Students," in this chapter.

195 *C Act*, above note 9, ss. 29.6, 29.8, & 71 to 76.

196 *C Act, ibid.*, ss. 29.7, 29.8, & 71 to 76.

There is no restriction on what may be copied. Operas for students of music, soap operas for students of popular culture, *The Polka Dot Door* for kindergarteners or education majors, *Cheers* reruns for students training to be bartenders — all may qualify.

Audits: The institution must keep records of its activities under the exemptions and appropriately mark any copies made. Regulations prescribed by order in council or by the Copyright Board (with Cabinet approval) cover specifics such as what details must be kept relating to the making, use, or destruction of copies, and what returns must be made to collective societies.[197]

vi) Compilations

A narrow exemption dating back to 1924 allows short passages from published literary works to be included in a collection for the use of educational institutions.[198] The collection need not be published by the institution itself: the exemption applies equally to a commercial publisher. Whether the collection itself is original enough to have its own copyright as a compilation is irrelevant. The following conditions must, however, be observed:

- The collection must be composed mainly of unprotected material. Thus, the relevant author or authors must have died more than fifty years ago, or copyright never existed or has since been waived or abandoned. The compiler will not lose the exemption by including her own preface and short comments, or by including the occasional protected piece that has been cleared for copyright.
- The collection must be intended for the use of non-profit educational institutions,[199] and must be so described in the title and any advertisement issued by the publisher.
- Only short passages can be taken, and they must come from published literary works that are not themselves published for the use of educational institutions. A page or two from a novel or long essay, or a few verses from a long poem, should be unobjectionable. Photographs cannot be used.

---

197   *C Act, ibid.*, s. 29.9.

198   *C Act, ibid.*, s. 30; compare s. 2, def. "collective work." The previous range of institutions is now broadened beyond just "schools," but coverage is now restricted to non-profit institutions: compare s. 27(2)(d) (repealed) of previous *C Act*.

199   On what comprises an "educational institution," see section B(13)(a), "Eligible Institution," in this chapter.

- The same publisher cannot publish more than two passages from works by the same author within five years. The two passages may presumably appear in the same collection.
- The source of the passages must be acknowledged and the author's name, if there given, must be mentioned.

The exemption may be useful for the publisher who wants to compile, for school or college use, the works of an author or authors who died before the end of World War II, and to include the occasional page or two from a few modern authors. More extensive course-packs will need clearance from CANCOPY, UNEQ (Union des écrivaines et d'écrivains québécois), or from individual copyright holders, who may charge such fees as they wish. A similar position pertains in the United States, where copy shops have had to obtain prior copyright clearances to produce course-packs containing substantial extracts from published literary works for university classes. Whether, without such course-packs, students would have had to buy the relevant books was thought to be of no consequence.[200]

14) Paying Uses

a) Music: Public Performance and Telecommunication
Someone wishing to perform a musical work in public or to communicate it to the public by telecommunication must obtain a licence from the Society of Composers, Authors and Music Publishers of Canada. SOCAN takes assignments of performance and telecommunication rights in musical works from composers and lyricists. It then issues blanket licences for its repertoire, which comprises virtually any piece of music still in copyright.[201] The royalties received from licensing are distributed to composers, lyricists, and music publishers according to rules fixed by SOCAN's board. A 50 percent split of the royalties for original published music always goes to the publisher; the remaining 50 percent goes to the composer or composers. If lyricists are involved, the split is 25 percent to the composer(s) and 25 percent to the lyricist(s). Nothing seems to prevent private rearrangement of this division, even though SOCAN's rules try to discourage it. For example, a music publisher can buy the author's share of SOCAN royalties if the

---

200 *Princeton*, above note 91; compare in Canada the course-pack found objectionable in *Boudreau*, above note 91.

201 A 1998 decision of the Copyright Board allowed broadcasters to negotiate special rates with individual copyright owners outside the blanket licensing scheme.

author goes bankrupt.[202] This practice suggests that a provision in the original publishing agreement, assigning the author's share of royalties to the publisher, may equally be held valid.

The fees SOCAN charges are fixed annually by the Copyright Board after hearing from SOCAN and considering any objections to the proposed tariff advertised in the *Canada Gazette*.[203] In 1994 SOCAN collected domestic fees of $66 million, of which $56 million came from radio and television, and $10 million came from licensing taverns, shopping centres, restaurants, halls, and the like. SOCAN also has affiliation agreements with foreign performing rights societies, and it similarly distributes monies received from foreign performances.

The *1997 Act* made public performance and telecommunication royalties payable also to record companies and performers (50 percent to each side) whenever their commercially released records are played. A society organized on similar lines to SOCAN administers the scheme, with the Copyright Board settling tariffs. Radio broadcasters pay only $100 royalties on the first $1.25 million of advertising revenue. Beyond that, the appropriate rate will be set by the Board. Liability is phased in gradually over three years, with a 33 percent incremental liability each year. Television broadcasters and cable companies transmitting programming that originates in-house also have their liability phased in over three years, but none of their advertising revenue is exempt. Lower rates apply to community broadcast and small cable transmission systems. The former pay a flat $100 per year, while the Copyright Board fixes a preferential rate for the latter.[204]

b) Cable Retransmission

Since 1989, cable retransmitters of television and radio programming have paid royalties fixed by the Copyright Board for copyright material contained in distant broadcasts they retransmit. The Board sets a rate based on what willing sellers and buyers would have agreed to. This rate currently averages fifteen cents per subscriber per month. The lion's share of the $45 million per year this rate costs cable companies is distributed to collecting societies representing U.S. film and television companies (57 percent). Another roughly 13 percent goes to public television and non-U.S. foreign program producers; 12 percent to

---

202   *Éditions MCC Ltée v. Assn. des Compositeurs, Auteurs & Éditeurs du Canada Ltée* (1987), 11 C.I.P.R. 322 (Que. S.C.).

203   *C Act*, above note 9, ss. 67–69.

204   *C Act, ibid.*, ss. 19, 68, & 68.1.

Canadian and U.S. networks; 10 percent to the baseball, hockey, and football leagues; and 3 percent to SOCAN.[205]

c) Blank Audio Recording Media Levy

Since the 1960s, European and other states have established levies on blank audiotapes. Declining record sales during this period were attributed to unauthorized home copying of sound recordings, so a levy on blank audiotapes was supposed to compensate for these losses. An empirical basis for the levy was, however, far from established. The music industry customarily blames lower record sales not on its own poor management, or on the business cycle, or on shifting tastes in leisure activity, but rather on unauthorized copying by those who would otherwise have bought their products. Cyclical declines in record sales continue despite the blank tape levy, but the charge obeys a familiar principle of copyright: an owner's right, once enacted, is never repealed, whether the economic justification for its introduction proves true or false.

The *1997 Act* introduced a blank audio recording media levy into Canada, taking effect as from 1 January 1999. It is now confirmed that copying commercially recorded music, at least for private use, no longer infringes copyright.[206] Makers and importers of any blank "audio recording medium" — mainly audio-cassettes, reel-to-reel tape, and recordable compact disks — must pay a collecting society a levy on every unit sold or, on default, risk a penalty of up to five times this sum.[207] On 17 December 1999, the Copyright Board fixed the "fair and equitable" levy at 23.3 cents for audio-cassettes, 70.8 cents for audio recordable compact disks and MiniDisks, and 5.2 cents for regular recordable compact disks (which are often used for purposes other than recording music). The anticipated levy of $8.85 million for 2000 is to be paid to the Canadian private copying collective, to be split 60.8 percent to authors, 21.5 percent to performers, and 17.7 percent to record makers.[208]

---

205 *Re Royalties for Retransmission Rights of Distant Television Signals 1995–1997* (28 June 1996), (Copyright Bd.) [unreported] [*Royalties 1995–97*], and *FWS Joint Sports Claimants* v. *Canada (Copyright Board)* (1991), [1992] 1 F.C. 487 (C.A.) [*FWS*]. *Royalties 1995–97* sets out the 1995–97 television and radio tariffs. Similar rates have been fixed for later years. Performers and record companies are excluded: *C Act*, above note 9, s. 19(1).

206 *C Act, ibid.*, s. 80(1).

207 See section D(4)(f)(i), "Blank Audio Recording Media Levy," in chapter 9.

208 *Private Copying*, Decision of Copyright Board of 17 December 1999, at <www.cb-cda.gc.ca/decisions/tocopy-e.html> [*Private Copying*]; *C Act,* above note 9, ss. 79, 83, 84, & 88.

The beneficiaries of the levy are carefully targeted. All Canadian composers, lyricists, performers, and record companies qualify, but so do virtually all non-Canadian composers and lyricists: they are "authors" and, if they come from a *Berne Convention* or *WTO Agreement* country, they must share on an equal footing with Canadians. Beyond that, only performers and record companies from countries that grant corresponding benefits to Canadians will receive a share of the levy. The minister of industry designates qualifying states and contours the benefits to achieve reciprocity.[209]

Incongruities remain. Thus, the Act exonerates from liability only those who record music. People who tape drama, comedy, or recitation off records for their private use risk infringing, even though they indirectly pay for a levy that is distributed to the music industry. The contours of what is and is not exempted from the levy are also quite arbitrary. Computer disks and tapes, which can be used to record and play back music, are exempt because they are more often used for other purposes such as recording data generated by the user himself.[210] Blank tape sold to associations representing people with perceptual disabilities — for example, institutes for the blind — is not subject to the levy, presumably because the tapes will mainly be used for exempt activities such as making talking books.[211] The policy to exclude tape used for exempted purposes or to record unprotected material is, however, imperfectly implemented. The individual who buys tape to make a "talking book" for himself, or the friend who buys tape to make the recording for him, must pay the levy. So must anyone who wants to record her own original music, a private performance or entertainment, or an exempted fair dealing. So must the radio station or newspaper that buys tape for its reporters; so must the researcher who uses tape to conduct oral interviews.

Although the underlying principle for the levy is supposedly that of "user pays," the mismatch between payers and payees raises the question of whether the levy is a forced royalty or a disguised tax. In Australia, the distinction proved critical when tape manufacturers attacked a similar levy on constitutional grounds. Under the Australian Constitution, taxation measures must appear in a separate bill and cannot

---

209   *C Act, ibid.*, ss. 79 (defs. "eligible author," "eligible maker," "eligible performer") & 85.

210   *C Act, ibid.*, s. 79, where "audio recording medium" is confined to a medium "of a kind ordinarily used by individual consumers" for the purpose of reproducing sound recordings.

211   *C Act, ibid.*, s. 86.

be mixed up with non-tax measures. The Australian High Court decided that the blank-tape levy really was a tax and was therefore invalid because it was included in a bill that also dealt with copyright matters.[212] A constitutional challenge in Canada on similar grounds is possible, but less plausible because of differences between the two constitutions.[213] The challenge has failed so far.[214] Yet further dangers lurk for a measure that loses its copyright connection. It may, for example, have to pass muster under the general non-copyright obligations of international agreements like the *WTO Agreement*, perhaps including obligations to provide national treatment.

d) Collecting Societies

Other collecting societies based on the SOCAN model have formed to collect royalties for uses in circumstances where individual collection has proved either impossible or extremely costly to monitor and enforce. The collecting society seeks to reach agreements with users on royalties and related terms. Failing this, either party may apply to the Copyright Board.[215] Agreements filed with the board within fifteen days of being concluded are insulated from attack under the *Competition Act*. The competition director may, however, ask the board to examine any agreement thought to be against the public interest. No such request has been made to date.[216]

Operating under these provisions, the Canadian Musical Reproduction Rights Agency Ltd. (CMRRA) has licensed record producers to make sound recordings of the agency's repertoire at a standard negotiated rate. This rate presently is 7.1 cents per work per record, with an added 1.42 cents per minute for works longer than five minutes.[217] Similarly, the Canadian Copyright Licensing Agency (CANCOPY) has concluded agreements with the federal government, universities, copy

---

212 *Australian Tape Manufacturers Assn. Ltd.* v. *Australia* (1993), 25 I.P.R. 1 (Austl. H.C.). This result put the copyright provisions in the Act that dealt with matters other than blank tapes under a cloud of invalidity as well, forcing the Australian parliament to re-enact them: J. McKeough & A. Stewart, *Intellectual Property in Australia*, 2d ed. (Sydney: Butterworths, 1997) at 158, note 153.

213 See further section A(3), "Intellectual Property versus Other Means," in chapter 1.

214 *Evangelical Fellowship of Canada* v. *Canadian Musical Reproduction Rights Agency*, [1999] F.C.J. 1391 (C.A.); *Private Copying*, above note 208. See section B(5), "Constitutional Problems," in chapter 1.

215 *C Act*, above note 9, s. 70.2.

216 *C Act, ibid.*, ss. 70.5 & 70.6.

217 Canadian Musical Reproductions Rights Agency Ltd. at <http://www.cmrra.ca/Mechanical_Licensing/mechanical_licensing.html>.

shops, and other institutions providing for payment of royalties for photocopying from books.

e) Unlocatable Owners

Copyright owners sometimes seem to disappear off the face of the earth, and efforts to locate them to obtain copyright permissions are unavailing. The Copyright Board helps prospective users in such cases, by issuing a non-exclusive licence to use a published work or sound recording, or a fixed performance or communication signal. The user simply writes to the board and documents the steps it has taken to try to locate the missing owner. The board will act if it is satisfied the applicant has made reasonable efforts.

The board's practice is to fix an appropriate royalty for the user to pay to a collecting society. The board then authorizes the society to apply the sum to its general revenue if the copyright owner does not collect the royalty within five years.[218] This practice seems questionable. The board cannot require applicants to make charitable donations as a condition of obtaining licences. A power to authorize copyright collectives to confiscate money is even less plausible. The royalty might better be deposited with the board, which could then return it to the user if the owner does not claim it within five years of the expiry of the licence.

FURTHER READINGS

CANADIAN CONFERENCE OF THE ARTS, *Colloquium on the Collective Administration of Copyright*, Toronto, 31 October 1994 (Ottawa: Canadian Conference of the Arts, 1995)

CANADIAN INTELLECTUAL PROPERTY INSTITUTE, *Copyright in Transition: Enforcement, Fair Dealing and Digital Developments* (Ottawa: The Institute, 1994)

GORDON, W.J., et al., "Virtual Reality, Appropriation, and Property Rights in Art: A Roundtable Discussion" (1994) 13 Cardozo Arts & Ent. L.J. 89

HENDERSON, G.F., ed., *Copyright and Confidential Information Law of Canada* (Toronto: Carswell, 1994)

---

218   *C Act*, above note 9, s. 77; *Re Fritz (Licence to use English Language Instruction Video)* (1995), 62 C.P.R. (3d) 99 (Copyright Bd.).

HOUSE OF COMMONS, Standing Committee on Communications and Culture, *Report of the Sub-Committee on the Revision of Copyright*: *A Charter of Rights for Creators* (Ottawa: Supply & Services, 1985)

HUGENHOLTZ, P.B., "Third Consensus Forum Report: 'Rights, Limitations and Exceptions: Striking a Proper Balance'" (1997) <http://www.imprimatur.alcs.co.uk/download.htm>

INFORMATION HIGHWAY ADVISORY COUNCIL, *Final Report: Connection, Community, Content: The Challenge of the Information Highway* (Ottawa: The Council, 1995) <http://info.ic.gc.ca/info-highway/ih.html>

INFORMATION HIGHWAY ADVISORY COUNCIL, *Final Report of the Copyright Subcommittee*: *Copyright and the Information Highway* (Ottawa: The Council, 1995) <http://strategis.ic.gc.ca/SSG/ih01650e.html>

INSTITUTE FOR INFORMATION LAW, Amsterdam, *Contracts and Copyright Exemptions* (Amsterdam: The Institute, 1997) <http://www.imprimatur.alcs.co.uk/download.htm>

KNOPF, H.P., ed., *Copyright Reform: The Package, the Policy and the Politics* (Toronto: Insight, 1996)

MARTIN, S., "The Impact of the Revision of the Canadian Copyright Act on Educational Institutions" (1999) 33:1 Copyright Bulletin 18

PATRY, W.F., *The Fair Use Privilege in Copyright Law* (Washington, D.C.: Bureau of National Affairs, 1985)

PATTERSON, L.R., & S.W. LINDBERG, *The Nature of Copyright: A Law of Users' Rights* (Athens: University of Georgia Press, 1991)

SINACORE-GUINN, D., *Collective Administration of Copyright and Neighboring Rights* (Boston: Little, Brown, 1993)

SOCIETY OF COMPOSERS, AUTHORS AND MUSIC PUBLISHERS OF CANADA (SOCAN), *SOCAN Facts: A Guide for Composers, Lyricists, Song-writers and Music Publishers* (1990), and *SOCAN Distribution Rules* (1994), available from SOCAN, 41 Valleybrook Drive, Don Mills, ON, M3B 2S6 (Tel. 1-800-55-SOCAN)

U.S.A., *Report of the Working Group on Intellectual Property Rights*: *Intellectual Property and the National Information Infrastructure* (Washington, D.C.: Patent and Trademark Office, 1995) (Chair: U.S. Commissioner of Patents Bruce A. Lehman) <www.uspto.gov/web/offices/com/doc/ipnii/>

CHAPTER 8

MANAGEMENT

A. INTRODUCTION

Copyright has been deliberately organized to facilitate a free national and international market in rights. So, a copyright can be bought and sold separately or in combination with other intellectual property rights. It can be split up horizontally and vertically — by territory, time, market, and so on — and dealt with accordingly. The maximum extraction of rents is thus assured. The right-holder may also transfer or license some rights while retaining others. So the copyright owner of a poem may assign the German translation right for Germany, may license the dramatization right for ten years to someone else, and may assign to yet another person the Canadian blank audio recording media levy right for the poem set to music, while retaining all other rights.[1]

This framework is flexible enough to accommodate changes in practice that respond to new distribution and communication methods. The Internet, for example, provides opportunities for freelance authors to deal directly with users without the intervention of middlemen such as publishers, record companies, or art dealers. In this milieu, speedy standard licences may become more common than signed transfers of rights.

---

1   See sections B(2)(b), "Partial Assignments," and B(3), "Licences," in this chapter.

B. ASSIGNMENTS AND LICENCES

1) Interpretation

What is assigned or licensed is a matter of negotiation, and the ordinary principles of contract interpretation apply to the result. Interpretation is not necessarily a neutral exercise. Continental European judges often take a pro-author stance, construing grants strictly against the grantee and leaving new uses under the control of the grantor (often the author). Some Canadian courts seem similarly inclined, and Parliament has also shown a similar, albeit tentative, inclination.[2] But these swallows do not necessarily make a summer. For example, media distributors with an eye towards electronic delivery and future means of exploitation may ask freelancers to sign contracts that contain a clause transferring "all now or hereafter existing rights of every kind and character whatsoever pertaining to said work, whether or not such rights are now known, recognized or contemplated for all purposes whatsoever" to the distributor. Will Canadian courts "construe" this transfer in a limited way, or will they hold it to mean that the grantor has relinquished all control over the work forever in favour of the distributor?

More grantees than grantors have prevailed throughout the Commonwealth and the United States in such disputes, even where courts claim to apply "neutral" principles of contract interpretation. Thus, the grantee of performing rights under a document signed when cinema was unknown automatically got the film rights when movies appeared, and grantees of motion picture rights acquired during the silent era often found they had also magically acquired the talking pictures rights when "talkies" came along. The same principle applied where the author expressly retained motion picture rights on a grant of dramatic rights, but cases involving such reservations are uncommon.[3]

A judicial stance of neutrality works best where both parties are equally knowledgeable and powerful. When applied to unequals,

---

2   For example, *Bishop v. Stevens*, [1990] 2 S.C.R. 467 [*Bishop*]; *Marquis v. D.K.L. Technologies Inc.* (1989), 24 C.I.P.R. 289 at 295–96 (Que. S.C.)[*Marquis*]; *Comstock Canada v. Electec Ltd.* (1991), 38 C.P.R. (3d) 29 at 51ff (Fed. T.D.) [*Comstock*] (patents and designs). See also section B(2)(d), "New Rights Created by the 1997 Amendments," in this chapter.

3   *Serra v. Famous-Lasky Film Service Ltd.* (1922), 127 L.T. 109 (C.A.); *L.C. Page & Co. Inc. v. Fox Film Corp.*, 83 F.2d 196 (2d Cir. 1936); *J.C. Williamson Ltd. v. M.G.M. Theatres Ltd.* (1937), 56 C.L.R. 567 (Austl. H.C.) (reservation of cinematographic and film production rights); *Board of Governors of the Hospital for Sick Children v. Walt Disney Productions Inc.*, [1967] 1 All E.R. 1005 at 1009 & 1017 (C.A.).

neutrality simply produces more inequality. A recent U.S. decision illustrates the point. In 1939 Igor Stravinsky sold the right to use the musical work *The Rite of Spring* in the animated film *Fantasia* to the Walt Disney Corporation for $6000. Nearly sixty years later, a U.S. court found that this sale of "motion picture" rights could "reasonably" be interpreted to include the right to market the movie on home video. The court said it was up to Stravinsky to have expressly excluded home video from the grant if that was his intention. Disney produced evidence that a "nascent market" in 1939 for home viewing of feature films existed, so home video was then a "reasonably foreseeable" development. It did not matter that Disney knew of this market and Stravinsky did not, nor that this "nascent" market was nothing like the home video market explosion of the 1970s. Disney did not tell Stravinsky what he was potentially selling, nor did it have to.[4]

This reasoning applies neutral principles of interpretation with a vengeance. It inevitably favours distributors, who will know more than authors about likely market and technological shifts. Distributors will also likely have good lawyers to draft contract language that will sweep up new uses that are "foreseeable" to distributors, but that may be unknown to authors or their agents. The author's estate may sometimes be able to renegotiate the deal when the rights revert twenty-five years after the author's death, but a strategic distributor could act in anticipation so as to drive down the value of the reversion.[5]

Traditional contract principles allow courts to take into account that freelancers are often economically dependent on media distributors and so are unequal when bargaining with them.[6] Whether this allowance will help freelancers much will depend on the case. There may be room for manoeuvre if the contract is entered irregularly — for example, if reasonable steps were not taken to bring onerous boilerplate to the other party's attention before the contract was concluded. This omission may invalidate the typical "shrink-wrap" licence found in a pre-packaged computer program.[7] But, in the end, an agreement that a transferor had ample time to read or get legal advice on before signing will usually be enforced. Avoidance is likely only where there

---

4   *Boosey & Hawkes Music Publishers Ltd.* v. *Walt Disney Co.*, 145 F.3d 481 (2d Cir. 1998).

5   See section B(2) "Reversion," in chapter 4.

6   See authorities in note 2 above.

7   Compare *North American Systemshops Ltd.* v. *King* (1989), 97 A.R. 46 at 51 (Q.B.) (unenforceable), with *ProCD Inc.* v. *Zeidenberg*, 86 F.3d 1447 (7th Cir. 1996) (enforceable).

was misrepresentation, fraud, undue influence, unreasonable restraint of trade, unconscionability, or a breach of trust. Only a union or the occasional persistent author or assignee with a deep pocket and a finely honed sense of grievance will likely pursue such cases.

2) Assignments

There are constraints on free disposability. For example, there can — at least in the common law provinces — be no assignment or grant of copyright in a work that is still just a gleam in its intending author's eye, any more than one can transfer non-existent land or goods.[8] Some copyrights also revert to their author's estate twenty-five years after death, whatever the assignment or grant may say.[9]

Moral rights, being personal to the author, cannot be assigned or licensed at all. They may, however, be waived or asserted by the author or her estate for the duration of the copyright. A waiver of moral rights may be oral or written, express or implied.[10]

a) Formalities

To be valid, an assignment of copyright or grant of an interest in copyright by licence must be in a writing that is signed by the copyright owner or her authorized agent.[11] The validity of the assignment or licence cannot later be contested by the assignor. Back-dating is permissible, although it may not create rights against non-parties.[12]

The following comments on the U.S. rule relating to writing apply equally to Canada:

> Common sense tells us that agreements should routinely be put in writing. This simple practice prevents misunderstandings by spelling out the terms of a deal in black and white, forces parties to clarify

---

8   Such a purported transfer may nevertheless be given some legal effect: see section B(3)(d), "Equitable Assignments and Licences," in this chapter. Other countries — and, perhaps, also Quebec (see below note 52) — may allow assignments or grants of future copyrights: for example, *Copyright, Designs and Patents Act*, 1988 (U.K.), c. 48 [*UK Act*], s. 91.

9   See section B(2), "Reversion," in chapter 4.

10 See section B, "Moral Rights," in chapter 6.

11 *Copyright Act*, R.S.C. 1985, c. C-42 [*C Act*; unless otherwise indicated, references to the Act are as amended], s. 13(4); these provisions apply to sound recordings, performances, and broadcasts; ss. 25, 26(6), & 81(2). An oral or informal grant may nevertheless have some effect. See section B(3)(d), "Equitable Assignments and Licences," in this chapter.

12 *Cheerio Toys & Games Ltd.* v. *Dubiner*, [1966] S.C.R. 206 [*Cheerio*]; *Star-Kist Foods Inc.* v. *Canada (Registrar of Trade Marks)* (1988), 20 C.P.R. (3d) 46 at 50 (Fed. C.A.).

their thinking and consider problems that could potentially arise, and encourages them to take their promises seriously because it's harder to backtrack on a written contract than on an oral one. Copyright law dovetails nicely with common sense by requiring that a transfer of copyright ownership be in writing. Section 204 [of the U.S. *Copyright Act*] ensures that the creator of a work will not give away his copyright inadvertently and forces a party who wants to use the copyrighted work to negotiate with the creator to determine precisely what rights are being transferred and at what price. . . . Most importantly, section 204 enhances predictability and certainty of copyright ownership . . . Rather than look to the courts every time they disagree as to whether a particular use of the work violates their mutual understanding, parties need only look to the writing that sets out their respective rights. [The writing] doesn't have to be Magna Charta; a one-line *pro forma* statement will do.[13]

So a document signed by **X**, saying "**X** hereby assigns all her worldwide copyright in work **Y** to **Z**," should work to achieve precisely what it says. Explicit language of this kind has even been said to be essential,[14] but this view seems too radical. An implied assignment can be as effective as an express one, if the implication is clearly discernible from some writing signed by the copyright holder or her agent.

Whether such an implication may properly be made depends on the standard legal principles relating to the interpretation of documents. The signer's intention to assign must be clearly inferable from her writing. So, a simple signed receipt for money received for "5 original card designs, inclusive of all copyrights," was found effective to assign the copyright in the designs, even though they needed to be identified orally. Similarly, the names and addresses of the parties need not be written out in full, if oral evidence clearly identifies who is involved.[15] A sale of all a firm's business assets and goodwill should also pass all its copyrights and other intellectual property. Thus, an engineering firm that sells all its manufacturing drawings to another firm impliedly also passes all its copyrights, if its discernible intent is to relinquish all its interest in its drawings to the buyer. Nevertheless, loose generalities, such as transferring all "property" in a physical

---

13 *Effects Associates Inc.* v. *Cohen*, 908 F.2d 555 at 557 (9th Cir. 1990) [*Effects*].

14 *Marquis*, above note 2.

15 *E.W. Savory Ltd.* v. *World of Golf Ltd.*, [1914] 2 Ch. 566 at 573–74; *IPC Magazines Ltd.* v. *MGN Ltd.*, [1998] F.S.R. 431 at 440 (Ch.) (assignor "News Team International Ltd." was sufficiently identified in the writing as just "News Team").

asset, should be avoided. Such language is ambiguous on whether associated intellectual property rights are also intended to pass.[16]

Stamping the back of a cheque with some statement such as "By endorsing this cheque, the payee hereby assigns copyright in the works for which this cheque is sent" should not usually be effective to assign copyright. The payee's signature may double as an endorsement and a transfer of copyright if the parties had earlier informally agreed to a transfer. The signature then gives effect to the prior agreement. Without such an agreement or some fresh benefit received by the payee, this strategy is just an underhand attempt to obtain something for nothing, since the payee may be unable to clear the cheque without an endorsement.[17]

i) Signature

What counts as a signature? This seemingly elementary point recently arose in a case where a rubber stamp carrying the transferor's name was impressed on an invoice that included a transfer of rights in an artistic work. The Federal Court rejected the stamp as a signature. The judge wanted evidence that the transferor customarily authenticated documents this way before she would give such a stamp effect.[18]

This view is too rigid. It does not square with the statutory and common law on signatures that should apply to the *Copyright Act*. On this theory, any mark that is used with the intent of authenticating the contents of a document operates as a valid signature, and any mode of representing or reproducing that mark in visible form amounts to a writing.[19] The case before the court involved a transaction between a French author-seller and U.S. buyers at a German trade fair. The author wrote the copyright transfer out in English on an invoice form. At the top left of the form was a stamp carrying her name and address. At the top right, the seller handwrote the buyers' names. Her stamp

---

16 *Massie & Renwick Ltd. v. Underwriters' Survey Bureau Ltd.,* [1940] S.C.R. 218; *Andritz Sprout-Bauer Australia Pty. Ltd. v. Rowland Engineering Sales Pty. Ltd.* (1993), 28 I.P.R. 29 at 39–40 (Austl. Fed. Ct.); compare *Webb & Knapp (Can.) Ltd. v. Edmonton (City)* (1970), 11 D.L.R. (3d) 544 (S.C.C.).

17 *Tasini v. New York Times Co.,* 972 F. Supp. 804 at 810–11 (S.D.N.Y. 1997), aff'd 52 U.S.P.Q.2d 1186 at 1188, n. 1 (2d Cir. 1999).

18 *Milliken & Co. v. Interface Flooring Systems (Canada) Inc.* (1997), [1998] 3 F.C. 103 (T.D.) (alternative holding) [*Milliken*]. The stamp also contained the name of the author's spouse, who apparently was interested in the business; but such added matter cannot invalidate an otherwise valid signature.

19 *Interpretation Act,* R.S.C. 1985, c. I-21 [*I Act*], s. 35(1): "'Writing', *or any term of like import, includes* words . . . represented or reproduced by any mode of representing or reproducing words in visible form."

appeared again at the bottom of the form alongside signatures hand-written by the buyers. Had the seller credibly testified that she did not usually sign by stamp and that she did not mean to do so here either, the court could have found that her stamping was, in fact, not a valid signature. But no such evidence of intention was offered. Nothing therefore should have displaced the ordinary inference that what looks like a signature should, in fact, operate as one.

The civil law approach to signatures, apparently applied in this case, is different: to be guaranteed validity, a signature should be both distinctive and habitually used.[20] Neither element is required at common law, which maintains a flexibility more attuned to modern conditions. People often do not sign in one way. I may agree with my bank to sign my name in one way alone, and the bank can reject cheques that are signed differently. Apart from cases like this, I may sign my name however I like. I may ink one or more of my initials onto some documents; on others, I may use my full name, my forename, or my printed stamp; on faxes and e-mails I may append different forms of my name automatically by computer, depending on whom I am writing to, and I may periodically change these practices for security or on a whim. All these variations should be effective as my signature. Thus, an assignment by e-mail, with the assignor's name inserted at the end of the message, should be as valid as an illiterate person's "X" on hard copy, if the sender's intention that this inscription operate as a signature is clear.

b) Partial Assignments

An assignment or licence need not grant the whole copyright. For example, **A**, the copyright owner of a musical work, can do all or any of the following:

- assign the right to reproduce the work in sheet music in Europe to **B** forever;
- assign the right to make a sound recording of the work in Europe and Australasia to **C** for ten years, while reserving the power, at **A**'s option, to terminate the assignment earlier and revert all rights to **A** if **C** breaks any obligation owed to **A**;
- grant an exclusive licence to reproduce a sheet music version on slides for the educational market in Quebec to **D** for fifty years.

---

20   M. Hancher, "The Law of Signatures," in R. Kevelson, ed., *Law and Aesthetics* (New York: P. Lang, 1992) c. 10, comparing the French and U.S. law on signatures. The comparison holds equally true between Quebec and Canadian common law.

In these examples, **B** and **C** are each partial assignees. They own their slice of the copyright for the stated period and can sue anyone who infringes it.[21] **D** is an exclusive partial licensee, who can also sue infringers but usually must join **A** in the litigation. **A** owns only those parts of the copyright he has not assigned. He no longer owns the parts assigned to **B** and **C** and cannot sue anyone who now infringes them. **A** still owns the rights that he licensed to **D** and can sue for infringement, although he must usually join **D** in the litigation.[22]

c) Assignment of Existing Rights of Action

If a copyright is infringed, only the owner of that right is entitled to sue the infringer. She cannot sell or give away the right to sue, on its own, to another person. The law makes such an assignment void, to prevent the stirring up of litigation. A stale claim might otherwise be sold to someone who had no real interest in it — for example, someone with a grudge who would use litigation as a way to pursue it. The start-up of businesses that buy, sell, and litigate cases that claimants may not themselves want to take on is also deterred. These policies are not violated where existing rights of action are assigned in association with the property to which they relate. The assignee or exclusive licensee can then recover from past infringers similar relief to what the transferor could have recovered.[23]

The parties' intention to pass such existing rights of action is best expressed by explicit language; but even general language, transferring "the right, title and interest in and to" a copyright, may show the assignor's intention to divest itself entirely of all her interests in the copyright in favour of the assignee.[24] To be valid, the assignment must be "associated" with the grant of copyright. This requirement suggests

---

21 *C Act*, above note 11, ss. 13(4), 13(5), & 36; *Jean-Claude Chehade Inc.* v. *Films Rachel Inc.*, [1995] A.Q. 1550 (Que. S.C.); *Husqvarna Forest & Garden Ltd.* v. *Bridon New Zealand Ltd.* (1997), 38 I.P.R. 513 at 516 (N.Z.H.C.).

22 Section B(3), "Licences," and section B(3)(b), "Right to Sue," in this chapter.

23 *C Act*, above note 11, s. 13(6), removing the cloud over copyright assignments left for patents by *Burns & Russell of Canada Ltd.* v. *Day & Campbell Ltd.* (1965), 31 Fox Pat. C. 36 at 53 (Ex. Ct.), and *Union Carbide Canada Ltd.* v. *Trans-Canadian Feeds Ltd.* (*No. 1*) (1967), 32 Fox Pat. C. 17 at 33–34 (Ex. Ct.) (transfer of existing causes of action may pass with assignment of a patent in Quebec, but in the common law provinces they offend the law of champerty and maintenance and are void).

24 *United Artists Corp.* v. *Pink Panther Beauty Corp* (1996), 67 C.P.R. (3d) 216 at 223 (Fed. T.D.), rev'd on other grounds (1998), 80 C.P.R. (3d) 247 (Fed. C.A.), leave to appeal granted (S.C.C., 1998), where such language in respect of a trade-mark assignment passed the right to continue a trade-mark opposition.

that the transfer should usually be made at the same time or in the same document as the grant of copyright. However, so long as the two transfers are related and not just afterthoughts, they should be treated as "associated." A later document may presumably confirm that an earlier one meant to pass existing rights of action where this intent was unclear from the earlier document.

A court may nevertheless still find that a particular transfer of rights of action, even though associated with a grant of copyright, is in fact meant unjustifiably to stir up litigation or to harass a particular defendant. The court may then still hold such a transfer to be void at common law.

d) New Rights Created by the 1997 Amendments

Copyrights and rights of remuneration in sound recordings, performances, and broadcasts may be assigned and licensed in the same way as copyright in traditional works.[25] But contracts with a clause assigning or exclusively licensing all copyrights or remuneration rights will not necessarily sweep up the new rights created by the 1997 Act. For example, music recording contracts commonly provide that the composer or performer assigns to the record company all her copyrights and other rights "whether or not now known, recognized or contemplated." The company might argue that this clause transfers to it such rights as the composer's and the performer's entitlements to share in the blank audio recording media levy.[26] The Act alleviates the injustice that may flow from such a broad interpretation. It provides that the assignment or grant of new rights under an agreement concluded before 25 April 1996 — the date Bill C-32 was first introduced into Parliament — is effective only if the agreement "specifically provides" for its assignment or grant.[27] This provision does not upset any promises that are specifically set out in an agreement. It seems prompted by two policies. First, grants should be read to favour the grantor, typically the author or performer, so she may share in the new benefits

---

25 *C Act*, above note 11, ss. 25, 26(6), & 81(2).

26 A written assignment made after the right was proclaimed into law may — at least in the common law provinces — be needed to perfect this title, since a right cannot legally be transferred before it exists. The earlier language may take effect in equity as a promise to transfer the right as it arises: *Canadian Performing Right Society Ltd.* v. *Famous Players Canadian Corp. Ltd.* (1927), 60 O.L.R. 280 at 289 (H.C.), aff'd (without reference to this point), *ibid.* 614 (C.A.), aff'd [1929] A.C. 456 (Ont. P.C.); *Campbell, Connelly & Co. Ltd.* v. *Noble*, [1963] 1 All E.R. 237 at 244 (Ch.). See section D(4)(f)(i), "Blank Audio Recording Media Levy," in chapter 9.

27 *An Act to Amend the Copyright Act*, S.C. 1997, c. 24 [*1997 Act*], s. 58.1.

that Parliament has introduced. Second, since copyright deals frequently occur on standard take-it-or-leave-it forms drawn up by grantees, general language should be interpreted strictly against their drafters. Clarity and comprehensibility are thereby encouraged, to the benefit of all concerned.

How do these principles apply to the blank audio recording media levy example? Such a levy was bruited about since the 1960s; so, a composer may conceivably have intended, as part of an overall recording deal made in the 1980s, to cede a possible right to share one day in such a levy. Nobody then knew whether such a right would ever be enacted or, if so, what its nature or worth would be; but people have bet on longer odds. The Act does not prevent parties from assigning mere hopes, but it does insist that the intention be spelled out "specifically" — that is, precisely, definitely, and explicitly. General words of grant ought not to trap the unwary into losing a valuable expectancy for a mess of potage. Nothing much short of language specifically granting "any future copyright or rights of remuneration for blank audio recording media" may work.[28]

The Act does not directly affect contracts concluded after 24 April 1996. The new rights are as disposable as other copyrights, and general granting language in post–24 April 1996 contracts, especially those made after the relevant new right was formally proclaimed into force, may not be interpreted to cover that right. Yet this conclusion should not be reached too hastily. The policies underlying the Act's provision on pre–25 April 1996 contracts — favouring grantors and encouraging transparency in contracts — may apply as strongly to all deals involving Canadian copyright.[29] Parliament may be unable constitutionally to tell judges how to interpret contracts, since this power lies within provincial jurisdiction over civil rights. But it may validly alert courts to its concern that grantors should not lose new federal benefits except by a clearly expressed promise.

---

28   Compare *Thompson v. Warner Bros. Pictures Ltd.,* [1929] 2 Ch. 308 at 330–31 (C.A.) on the U.K. equivalent of pre-1988 *C Act,* above note 11, s. 30(1)(b); also *Redwood Music Ltd. v. B. Feldman & Co.,* [1979] R.P.C. 385 at 395 (C.A.), aff'd (*sub nom. Chappell & Co. Ltd. v. Redwood Music Ltd.*) [1980] 1 All E.R. 817 (H.L.), on the U.K. equivalent of *C Act,* s. 60(2), holding that the "express" advance agreement to assign new rights conferred by the 1921 Act meant language "expressly referring to the substituted right identified as such."

29   See section B(1), "Interpretation," in this chapter.

3) Licences

An assignment changes ownership in the right from assignor to assignee. By contrast, a licence is just a consent, permission, or clearance (the terms are all interchangeable) to use intellectual property on the terms specified by the licensor, who remains the owner. A licence may be quite informal and even implied. Posting material, without any stated restrictions, on an electronic bulletin board may, for example, imply a licence to users to download and make a hard copy of it, at least for their private use. Licences are usually personal to the licensee unless transfer or sublicensing is clearly permitted or implied from the circumstances.[30]

Regrettably, people often speak loosely of "selling rights" without clarifying (or perhaps knowing) whether a licence or an assignment is meant. Documents referring to licensors and licensees can end up being construed as assignments, and *vice versa*: the labels the parties use are not conclusive.[31]

a) Exclusive, Sole, and Non-exclusive Licences

Licences can be exclusive, sole, or non-exclusive. An exclusive licence gives the licensee the power to exercise a right to the exclusion of all others including the licensor: it is as close to an assignment as a lease of land is to an outright conveyance of the fee simple. An exclusive licensee may grant an exclusive sublicence, and the latter sublicensee may presumably do likewise. Such exclusive licences and sublicences of copyright must be in writing.[32]

A sole licence means that the licensee is the only licensee appointed, but does not preclude the licensor from competing with the licensee. A non-exclusive licence implies that other licensees may be appointed to compete with one another and the licensor. The typical permission to download that is found or implied on the Internet likely falls into this last category.

An exclusive distributor is not a licensee unless it is authorized to do an act within the copyright owner's rights. For example, if he is also authorized to reproduce the protected material, even for limited

---

30   On a "no sublicensing" clause in a patent agreement, see *Eli Lilly & Co. v. Apotex Inc.* (1998), 80 C.P.R. (3d) 321 (S.C.C.). See also M.B. Eisen, "Copyright and the World Wide Web" (1996) 12 Can. Intell. Prop. Rev. 405.

31   *Messager v. British Broadcasting Co.*, [1928] 1 K.B. 660 (C.A.), aff'd (1928), [1929] A.C. 151 (H.L.) [*Messager*].

32   *C Act*, above note 11, ss. 13(4), 2(7), & 13(7).

purposes such as promotion, the distributor may be an exclusive licensee of the copyright to that extent. This status may enable him to sue infringers.[33]

Unfortunately, the terminology of exclusive, sole, and non-exclusive is not always used consistently. Parties can also create hybrid relationships. In any event, whenever a claimant sues for infringement, it must prove that the defendant had no licence or consent to do the acts complained of.[34]

The copyright holder may choose to license or not as it wishes. Its discretion may, no doubt, be limited by general laws like human rights codes that forbid discrimination on grounds of gender, religion, race, and the like. Restrictions included in a licence agreement, particularly those offered by a collecting society, may also be questioned by the authorities administering the *Competition Act*. Otherwise, a copyright holder's decision to license or not to license, or to refuse to license any particular applicant, cannot usually be questioned.[35] The *Copyright Act* has its own compulsory licensing schemes — for example, in relation to public performance of music or to cable retransmission — that are partly designed to offset any monopolistic powers wielded by copyright holders.

b) Right to Sue

At common law, all licences — from a simple oral copyright permission to quote extracts from a book, to a comprehensive written exclusive licence covering a complex technology — are treated alike in one respect. Being mere permissions, they are usually thought to convey no proprietary interest in the right and so give the licensee no power to sue for infringement.[36] This rule certainly applies to bare licensees of copyright. If **A** gives **B** permission to use **A**'s copyright photograph in

---

33   *Bouchet v. Kyriacopoulos* (1964), 45 C.P.R. 265 at 278 (Ex. Ct.), aff'd (*sub nom. Kyriacopoulos v. Bouchet*) (1966), 33 Fox Pat. C. 119 (S.C.C), finding (unusually) an implied right to this effect; compare *Avel Pty. Ltd. v. Multicoin Amusements Pty. Ltd.* (1990), 171 C.L.R. 88 at 103–4 (Austl. H.C.) [*Avel*].

34   *Avel, ibid.* at 94–95 and 119–20.

35   *Competition Act*, R.S.C. 1985, c. C-34, ss. 32 & 79(5) ("an act engaged in pursuant only to the exercise of any right or enjoyment of any interest derived under the *Copyright Act* . . . is not an anti-competitive act"); *Canada (Director of Investigation and Research) v. Tele-Direct (Publications) Inc.* (1997), 73 C.P.R. (3d) 1 (Comp. Trib.); *Canada (Director of Investigation & Research) v. Warner Music Group Inc.* (1997), 78 C.P.R. (3d) 335 (Comp. Trib.). Compare section B(14)(d), "Collecting Societies," in chapter 7.

36   *Domco Industries Ltd. v. Armstrong Cork Canada Ltd.*, [1982] 1 S.C.R. 907 [*Domco*]; *Oren v. Red Box Toy Factory Ltd.*, [1999] F.S.R. 785 at 795–800 (Pat. Ct.).

B's book, B cannot sue C if C copies the photograph from the book. If A sues C, B cannot be joined as a co-plaintiff because B owns no piece of the copyright and so has no legal interest that can be injured. C has wronged only A. Only A can get an injunction against C, and any money received by A from C for the infringement can be kept by her, unless she has earlier reached a different agreement with B.[37]

The *Copyright Act* has altered this position except where a bare licence is involved. If A grants B an exclusive licence in writing to copy a photograph, B can sue infringers, for an exclusive copyright licensee is now regarded as owning an interest in the copyright.[38] If C copies the photograph, B can sue C, whether C copied from B's book or elsewhere. B must usually join A in the litigation, as co-plaintiff if A agrees or as co-defendant if A does not agree.[39] Where A and B claim compensatory damages, C must presumably compensate each according to the respective harm he has caused them.[40] For non-compensatory relief — for example, statutory or punitive damages or an account of C's profits — A and B can agree on how to divide any award, and the court will respect their agreement. Otherwise, the court decides what division is appropriate.

The foregoing position applies equally to any exclusive sub-licence that is carved out of an exclusive licence. Suppose that in the previous example, B granted to B_1 an exclusive licence to reproduce the work in Territory 1, and to B_2 an exclusive license to reproduce the work in Territory 2. B_1 and B_2 each have an interest in the copyright, and each may sue for infringements occurring in their respective territory. Both A and B may have to join in their litigation. The rules applicable when B sues as an exclusive licensee apply equally to actions brought by B_1 and B_2.[41]

---

37 *Milliken*, above note 18.

38 *C Act*, above note 11, ss. 13(4), 13(7), 2.11, & 36; *Ashton-Potter Ltd. v. White Rose Nurseries Ltd.*, [1972] F.C. 689 (T.D.), rev'd on other grounds (*sub nom. White Rose Nurseries v. Ashton-Potter Ltd.*) [1972] F.C. 1442 (C.A.); D. Vaver, "The Exclusive Licence in Copyright" (1995) 9 I.P.J. 163 ["Exclusive Licence"].

39 A need not be joined in any interlocutory proceeding, in proceedings to stop goods at the border, or any time the court thinks his presence is unnecessary: *C Act, ibid.*, s. 36(2). The step of joining A in other cases clarifies that (1) B's interest derives from A; (2) C can raise against B defences that C has against A; and (3) C is protected against double jeopardy from A. If B does not join A, C may himself ask the court to make A a co-defendant, third party or *mis-en-cause* to protect C's position.

40 *Domco*, above note 36 (patents).

41 *C Act*, above note 11, ss. 2.11, 13(7), 13(4), & 36.

The Act clarifies that exclusive licensees and exclusive sublicensees can sue, but is silent on whether anyone else (other than the owner) may also sue. One possible claimant is the person who has an irrevocable, even non-exclusive, licence to reproduce a work, and who invests substantial time and money to make and distribute copies. Such a licensee may have enough of an interest in the copyright to have standing to sue infringers.[42]

The right to sue for infringement does not extend to agents or representatives who handle rights on behalf of an owner, nor usually to distributors.[43] The *1997 Act* does, however, allow sole Canadian book distributors the right to sue in respect of unauthorized imports and distribution of books.[44]

c) Duration and Estoppel

Licences may be given for free or for consideration. A gratuitous licence may be withdrawn at any time, even if it has a stated expiry date, although reasonable notice is usual. Inequitable revocations should also be preventable; for example, where the grantee has reasonably relied on the consent continuing.[45] Contractual licences may be withdrawn only if the contract expressly or impliedly allows, if the contract is avoided for some vitiating factor (e.g., misrepresentation, undue influence, unconscionability), or if the contract is discharged for a repudiation or serious breach.

Licences silent on duration usually last until the expiry of the right, presumably the last right, if more than one is licensed. The parties may, however, still be entitled to terminate on reasonable notice, depending on how the licence contract is construed. The ex-licensee must then respect the right on termination of the licence. Sometimes when a long-term licence covering confidential information expires, a licensee who has started up a new business on the faith of the licence may use the information after the licence has run its course; but this

---

42 "Exclusive Licence," above note 38 at 189ff; *Messager*, above note 31, [1928] MacG. Cop. Cas. 302 at 309–10 (C.A.).

43 *De Montigny v. Cousineau*, [1950] S.C.R. 297 at 306; *Bishop*, above note 2; *955105 Ontario Inc. v. Video 99* (1993), 48 C.P.R. (3d) 204 (Ont. Gen. Div.). The distributor may, however, sometimes also be a licensee: see section B(3)(a), "Exclusive, Sole, and Non-exclusive Licences," in this chapter.

44 See section A(10)(c), "Exclusive Book Distribution," in chapter 5.

45 *Dorling v. Honnor Marine Ltd.* (1963), [1964] Ch. 560 at 567–68, undisputed on appeal (1964), [1965] Ch. 1 at 13 (C.A.); *Computermate Products (Aust.) Pty. Ltd. v. Ozi-Soft Pty. Ltd.* (1988), 12 I.P.R. 487 (Austl. Fed. Ct.); compare *Katz v. Cytrynbaum* (1983), 2 D.L.R. (4th) 52 at 57 (B.C.C.A.).

use depends on what the contract says or implies, or the nature of the relationship between the parties.[46]

The mere granting of a licence does not imply that the right licensed exists or is valid. A licensor may, of course, expressly promise that the right does exist and is valid, but otherwise all that a licence means is that the licensor cannot, during the term of the licence, sue or threaten to sue the licensee for infringing the rights the licensor believes it has. In return, the licensee must abide the licence during its term despite the expiry, initial invalidity, or later invalidation of any intellectual property rights.[47] This rule of "licensee estoppel," drawn from feudal property law, is hardly self-evident when applied to copyright. In the United States, a patent licensee can stop paying royalties if the right is found invalid and can itself challenge the validity of the patent.[48] The most a Canadian copyright licensee can do is to contest validity if the licensor has expressly promised validity, if the licence expires, or if the licensee is sued for infringement.

d) Equitable Assignments and Licences

In the United States, an oral contract to assign or exclusively license copyright is ineffective as a legal assignment or exclusive licence, but it may imply a non-exclusive licence to use the work.[49] In Canada, too, some courts have interpreted the writing provisions literally: an unsigned or oral transfer is simply not "valid," with the result that an exclusive licensee can be dismissed from an infringement action simply because its deal was done orally.[50]

This conclusion is unsatisfactory. Elsewhere in the Commonwealth, courts have given effect to oral transactions in copyright. The starting point is that the *Copyright Act* was enacted in the context of a mature existing system of law, which includes principles of equity. These principles apply to supplement the literal provisions of the Act. For example, can it be true that a person who bought, paid for, and acted on a copyright gets nothing — except a right to a refund — simply

---

46   *Chicago Blower Corp.* v. *141209 Canada Ltd.* (1990), 30 C.P.R. (3d) 18 at 54–55 (Man. Q.B.); *Cadbury Schweppes Inc.* v. *FBI Foods Ltd.* (1996), 69 C.P.R. (3d) 22 (B.C.C.A.), rev'd on other grounds (1999), 167 D.L.R. (4th) 577 (S.C.C.).

47   For example, *Culzean Inventions Ltd.* v. *Midwestern Broom Co.* (1984), 82 C.P.R. (2d) 175 at 194 (Sask. Q.B.).

48   *Lear Inc.* v. *Adkins*, 395 U.S. 653 (1969).

49   *Effects*, above note 13.

50   *Jeffrey Rogers Knitwear Productions Ltd.* v. *R.D. International Style Collections Ltd.* (1986), 19 C.P.R. (3d) 217 (Fed. T.D.) [*Jeffrey*].

because the seller refused to sign a writing? Commonwealth law would say no.[51] Equitable principles have operated even further in trying to make sense of bargains that are not inherently unfair, but do not precisely comply with the formalities of the Act. For example, at least in the common law provinces, copyright in a non-existent work cannot in law be assigned, any more than one can transfer property in non-existent land or goods. Parties who agree to transfer such copyright are, however, treated in equity as promising to assign the future copyright once the work is created. At that point, the promisee becomes the equitable assignee and beneficial owner of the copyright, and the promisor is the equitable assignor with a bare legal title.[52] The assignee should therefore be able to have its interest perfected by a court order that either compels the assignor to put the assignment in writing or authorizes the registrar of the court to sign a writing binding the assignor.

An equitable title is, still, less than a legal one. For example, the legal owner may divest the equitable owner's interest by a transfer to a *bona fide* buyer without notice. The equitable owner can then sue the assignor only for restitution or breach of contract. And an equitable owner may obtain only interlocutory, not final, relief without joining the legal owner or producing a legal assignment.[53] The exclusion before

---

51   For example, *Western Front Ltd.* v. *Vestron*, [1987] F.S.R. 66 at 76–78 (Ch.); *Lakeview Computers PLC* v. *Steadman* (26 November 1999), (C.A.) [unreported] (U.K. writing provision applies only to copyright grants, not oral or implied agreements to grant); *Yaxley* v. *Gotts*, [1999] 3 W.L.R. 1217 at 1231 (C.A.) (under comparable U.K. legislation on land sales, the buyer under a partly performed contract that is void for lack of a signed writing can get a court order compelling the seller, as constructive trustee for the buyer, to perform the contract by transferring the interest). The buyer should get a refund anyway if the sale occurred in suspicious circumstances — for example, if the seller was tricked or hurried into a transaction that he or she would not have entered on reflection. Equity does not support sharp dealing.

52   *Performing Right Society Ltd.* v. *London Theatre of Varieties Ltd.* (1923), [1924] A.C. 1 at 13 (H.L.) [*London Theatre*]; *C Act*, above note 11, s. 89.

In Quebec, *Diffusion YFB Inc.* v. *Disques Gamma (Québec) Ltée* (12 May 1999), (Que. S.C.) [unreported] [*Diffusion YFB*], holds that the copyright transfer of a future work cedes the *legal* copyright as soon as the work is created. The common law is different, despite the Quebec court's contrary insistence. The principal U.K. authority relied on, *Ward Lock & Co. Ltd.* v. *Long*, [1906] Ch. 550, does not apply to the *Copyright Act*, 1911 (U.K.) and is inconsistent with equitable principles: *London Theatre*, [1922] 2 K.B. 433 at 448, 457–59 (C.A.), aff'd *ibid.* (H.L.). The U.K. position is now changed by legislation: *Copyright, Designs and Patents Act*, 1988 (U.K.), c. 48, s. 91, elaborating *Copyright Act*, 1956 (U.K.), s. 37. The Canadian *C Act*, above note 11, has not included such changes, even though Parliament has had ample opportunity to do so had it wished.

53   *London Theatre*, *ibid.* at 14 and 35.

trial of an oral exclusive licensee from even being a co-plaintiff in an infringement action[54] is inconsistent with this approach.

An oral assignment may be unhelpful to the assignee in other ways. A defendant who got copyright clearance from the legal copyright owner has successfully resisted a later claim of secondary infringement by a person to whom copyright had been merely orally assigned. A secondary infringer must have actual or constructive knowledge that he is infringing. He should not be affected by an oral assignment unless he actually knows of it, and perhaps not even then.[55] The same result should follow even where the defendant is alleged to be a primary infringer, again unless he knew of the oral transaction. It is hard enough that people can infringe copyright simply by relying on a deal with a person who did not say that he had already assigned his rights in writing. To turn innocent people into infringers where the copyright was earlier assigned orally would make copyright dealings intolerably hazardous.

4) Collective Societies

Collective societies sometimes run into enforcement difficulties because of the way in which their copyright inventories are held. For example, an Ontario-based society may take a written grant of copyright in a work or sound recording that has not yet been created, or in a performance or broadcast that has not yet taken place. No copyright technically exists at that time. It first comes into being only when the work or sound recording is made, or when the performance or broadcast occurs. The written document therefore operates as a promise to grant the interest when the copyright arises. At that time, the society becomes the equitable owner of the copyright. Without a further written grant from the assignor or the joining of the assignor in any legal proceeding, the society's equitable interest will be enough for it to obtain interlocutory relief against infringers, but not enough for it to be awarded compensatory or exemplary damages, an account of profits, or a final injunction.[56]

A collective society's title may be even flimsier. The society may be only an agent, authorized by the copyright owner to administer rights on the latter's behalf. This is the position of the Canadian Musical

---

54   *Jeffrey*, above note 50.

55   *Horton v. Tim Donut Ltd.* (1997), 75 C.P.R. (3d) 451 (Ont. Gen. Div.), aff'd (1997), 75 C.P.R. (3d) 467 (Ont. C.A.). Backdating a written assignment takes the matter no further. On secondary infringement, see section A(10), "Distributing and Importing Infringing Copies: Secondary Infringement" in chapter 5.

56   See section B(3)(d), "Equitable Assignments and Licences," in this chapter.

Reproduction Rights Agency Ltd. (CMRRA), which administers sound recording reproduction and synchronization rights on behalf of record producers. SOCAN also administers performing rights for some musical works (mainly United States compositions) as agent for the copyright owner. Infringement suits cannot be brought by a collective in respect of material for which the collective holds only agency rights. Such proceedings can be struck out. Only the copyright owner can sue in such a case, and the collective society cannot even be joined as a party.[57]

The Act does however set out specific instances where a collective society has standing to sue. Where, for example, the Copyright Board has fixed or approved a society's royalties, the society may sue for them in any competent court.[58] Similarly, SOCAN may recover as statutory damages up to ten times any royalties that are due, and the appropriate collective may also recover up to five times any blank audio recording media levy that is in default.[59] In all these cases, the Act specifically says the collective society may sue for these sums. It also says that these rights are "without prejudice to any other remedies" available to the society. This language does not in itself seem enough to entitle a collective society that is not an owner or exclusive licensee of copyright to avail itself of the standard infringement remedies as if it were such an owner or licensee.

5) Promises Made by Sellers on Supply of Copyright Goods

Sellers of goods usually promise that they have a right to sell the goods, and the buyer may use or sell (but not necessarily export)[60] the goods without interference from the seller or others. These promises of clear title and quiet possession often appear in any written contract the parties enter. Even if not so expressed, the promises will be implied in the contract of sale unless they are modified or excluded by the parties or by the circumstances of the transaction.[61]

The promises may be broken if the goods infringe copyright or moral rights at the time property in the goods passes to the buyer. One

---

57   *Bishop* v. *Stevens* (1987), 18 C.P.R. (3d) 257 at 263 (Fed. C.A.), aff'd above note 2.
58   *C Act*, above note 11, ss. 67.2(2), 70.4, & 70.65.
59   *C Act, ibid.*, ss. 38.1(4) & 88. See section D(4), "Statutory Damages," in chapter 9.
60   *Interstate Parcel Express Co. Pty. Ltd.* v. *Time-Life International (Nederlands) B.V.* (1977), 138 C.L.R. 534 (Austl. H.C.).
61   The *Sale of Goods Act*, R.S.O. 1990, c. S.1, ss. 13(a) & (b), is typical of the various provincial laws. See M.G. Bridge, *Sale of Goods* (Toronto: Butterworths, 1988) c. 10.

way to test whether this circumstance exists is to ask whether a right-holder could have obtained an order for an injunction or for delivery up of the goods against the seller, and whether such orders may now still be made against the buyer. If only monetary remedies are claimed or available against the buyer, presumably only the promise that the buyer will enjoy quiet possession of the goods is broken. The buyer need not wait until court proceedings are started before he acts. Competent legal advice that the goods infringe and that there is a serious risk of an injunction, delivery up, or substantial monetary remedy being awarded should be enough for the buyer to exercise his rights against the seller. The buyer may then return the goods, get a refund of the price paid with no deduction for depreciation, and claim damages for any foreseeable losses suffered from the breach of contract.[62]

The seller may, of course, choose to settle or satisfy the right-holder's claims. His right to resell is then automatically reinstated retro-spectively and he will no longer be breaking his promise. This event will not affect a buyer who has already rejected and claimed other remedies against the seller. Buyers who have not yet done so will, however, lose their right to reject, and any monetary claims they had against the seller may also diminish or disappear because of the new state of affairs.[63]

C. REGISTRATION AND EXPUNGEMENT

Copyrights and grants of copyright may be registered in the Copyright Office in Hull, Quebec, but they are effective even without registration. A copyright arises once a work or sound recording is made, or once a performance or broadcast signal occurs. The copyright remains in full force whether or not it is registered, since registration is optional, as it must be under the *Berne Convention*.[64] Written grants are also effective according to their terms, although registration may affect which of two or more grants of the same interest will prevail.[65] Most countries no

---

62   *Gencab of Canada Ltd.* v. *Murray-Jensen Manufacturing Ltd.* (1980), 29 O.R. (2d) 552 at 561 & 563ff (H.C.J.); *Microbeads A.G.* v. *Vinhurst Road Markings Ltd.*, [1975] 1 W.L.R. 218 at 225–26 (C.A.) (patents); *Rowland* v. *Divall*, [1923] 2 K.B. 500 (C.A.).

63   *Butterworth* v. *Kingsway Motors Ltd.*, [1954] 1 W.L.R. 1286 (Q.B.).

64   *Berne Convention for the Protection of Literary and Artistic Works* (Paris, 1971), 9 September 1886, 828 U.N.T.S. 221 [*Berne*], art. 5(2), requires copyright to be enjoyed and exercised without "any formality."

65   Section C(1), "Priorities," in this chapter.

longer keep copyright registries. Canada and the United States are among the last holdouts.

A major consequence of the optional nature of registration is that errors appearing on the Copyright Register or on any certificate of registration do not affect the right involved. A claimant may prove its actual title, whatever appears on the register, since the register and any certificates issued by the Copyright Office are only presumptive evidence. Clerical errors in any recorded document can be corrected by the Copyright Office. Other errors may be corrected by the Federal Court or, if serious enough, can lead to the registration being expunged. Expungement may result where, for example, a copyright has been abandoned or the item claimed to be a work is no "work" at all or lacks originality.[66] Expungement then tells the world, not just the parties to the litigation, that the item is unprotected.

Registration provides four advantages for registrants. First, register entries and the certificate of registration are evidence of the facts that appear in them. The burden of pleading and proving the contrary lies on challengers. Second, registration of an assignment or exclusive licence usually gives the registrant priority over unregistered grants. Third, registration prevents a defendant from claiming that his infringement was innocent and exposes him to monetary liability to the claimant.[67] Fourth, certificates may be helpful evidence in foreign countries, especially those without their own copyright registries.[68]

Whether these incidents warrant retention of the copyright registry is a question that has not been systematically explored in Canada. Countries that have scrapped their registries or that never had them seem to do well enough without them. A mandatory — not merely optional — worldwide system of registration might help to clarify the often obscure state of copyright ownership, especially for older works, but such a mandatory system is banned by *Berne*. Careful practitioners today check the register when advising on copyright deals, but this expense is often wasted because only a tiny proportion of Canadian

---

66   *C Act*, above note 11, ss. 61 (clerical errors) & 57(4) (correction by court); *Canadian Admiral Corp.* v. *Rediffusion Inc.*, [1954] Ex. C.R. 382 at 410. See section A(1), "Originality," in chapter 3. For a fuller discussion on clerical errors and the powers of the court, see D. Vaver, *Intellectual Property Law: Copyright, Patents, Trade-marks* (Toronto: Irwin Law, 1997) at 248–251.

67   Section D(2)(e), "Defendant's Innocence," in chapter 9.

68   For example, *Fasold v. Roberts* (1997), 38 I.P.R. 34 at 100, aff'd (*sub nom. Plimer* v. *Roberts*) (1997), 80 F.C.R. 303 (Austl. Fed. Ct.), where a U.S. certificate helped as proof of title to the Australian copyright in a book.

copyrights are ever registered. Moreover, the case law on priorities and on the effect of certificates does not reveal a system that is operating smoothly or even comprehensibly. Tinkering may overcome some defects, but the system, such as it is, seems to struggle on largely through inertia.

We shall first examine priority issues and then the consequences flowing from registration or non-registration of copyright and grants of copyright.

1) Priorities

Provincial law usually regulates what effect registration or non-registration of a property interest has when the same person deals twice or more with the same interest. The issue is more complicated for copyright, because the *Copyright Act* contains its own priority provisions. These provisions — a collage of early Canadian patent and U.S. copyright law, with some Commonwealth and local variants thrown in[69] — are rather primitive when compared, for example, with the more modern registration and priority schemes adopted by most provinces for dealings in property and secured interests.

Under the federal scheme, copyright assignments, exclusive licences, and exclusive sublicences — including mortgages and charges of copyright — usually take priority in order of registration. If the grants are unregistered, the later grant has priority if taken for valuable consideration without actual notice of the prior grant. Otherwise unregistered grants are subordinated to later registered grants, except perhaps where reliance on the registration is fraudulent. No time limits for registration are prescribed, so registrations made years after the event may upset prior deals and expectations.[70]

These consequences so little impressed the one federal court that had to consider them that it subordinated the whole federal scheme to the system of priorities prescribed by the law of Quebec, the law of the province where all the dealings occurred.[71] This approach is nonetheless doubtful. The *Copyright Act* lays down its own national registration and priority scheme for copyrights. Little room seems left for the different

---

69   "Exclusive Licence," above note 38 at 197–98.

70   *C Act*, above note 11, s. 57(2); *Colpitts v. Sherwood*, [1927] 3 D.L.R. 7 at 13 (Alta. C.A.) (patents). For the comparable provisions for patents and plant breeders' rights, see *Patent Act*, R.S.C. 1985, c. P-4, s. 5, and *Plant Breeders' Rights Act*, S.C. 1990, c. 20, s. 31(3).

71   *Poolman v. Eiffel Productions S.A.* (1991), 35 C.P.R. (3d) 384 at 392 (Fed. T.D.).

provincial schemes to operate.[72] An attractive intermediate solution is to require federal filing only for old-style security instruments that transfer ownership, while requiring modern personal property security instruments that do not effect such a transfer to be filed in the appropriate provincial registry.[73] Careful practitioners, who presently hope for the best by registering both provincially and federally security documents that include intellectual property, would be relieved.

2) Presumptions

Copyright claimants are helped by various evidentiary presumptions, which may differ depending on whether or not the copyright or grant is registered. Such presumptions are especially helpful where proof of title or even of the existence of copyright is difficult because, for example, the copyright is old or of foreign origin. Their effect is to shift to challengers the burden and cost of proving facts that differ from those created by the presumptions.

a) Unregistered Copyrights

A set of presumptions applies in civil copyright infringement proceedings if the defendant puts in issue the existence of copyright or the claimant's title. If the item involved is a work, it is presumed to be protected; its author is presumed to be the owner; the author is presumed to be whoever is so named on a work in the usual manner; the publisher is presumed to be the owner of an anonymous or pseudonymous work if his name appears on it in the usual manner; and a film's maker is presumed to be whoever is so named on it. All these presumptions prevail unless the contrary is proved.[74]

Parallel presumptions apply to performers, sound recording makers, and broadcasters. For example, if the item involved is a performance, it is presumed to be protected; the performer is presumed to be the owner; the performer is presumed to be whoever is so named in the usual manner; and the publisher or owner of the performance is presumed to be its copyright owner, if the performance is anonymous or pseudonymous and if his name is indicated on the item in the usual manner.[75]

---

72 R.J. Wood, "Federal Law and the New Provincial Personal Property Security Regime" (LL.M. thesis, University of Toronto, 1982) c. 6.

73 See *In Re Cybernetic Services Inc.* (29 September 1999), (U.S. Bankruptcy Appellate Panel, 9th Cir.) [unreported] (patents).

74 *C Act*, above note 11, ss. 34.1(1) & (2). Oddly, the presumptions do not apply to proceedings for moral right infringements.

75 *Ibid.*

These presumptions apply only in litigation. A publisher who does not own the copyright in an anonymous or pseudonymous work cannot keep for himself any money that he recovers in an infringement suit. The money must go to the true owner or must be disposed of according to any prior agreement between the publisher and owner.[76]

b) Registered Rights

The presumptions in the previous section are displaced if a copyright, assignment, exclusive licence, or exclusive sublicence is registered. A different set of presumptions then arises, based on the particulars that appear on the Copyright Register entry or on the certificate of registration. These presumptions apply in any situation, including civil and criminal proceedings, as evidence of anything noted in the certificate or a certified copy of the register entry.[77]

A certificate of registration is evidence that copyright in the work or item exists and that the person registered is its copyright owner. Since 1997, certificates of registration may also be issued for assignments, exclusive licences, and exclusive sublicences, and are evidence that the person registered is indeed the assignee, exclusive licensee, or sublicensee. The particulars noted on the register reflect those required in the application for registration. These details include the name and address of the copyright owner or grantee; what sort of work or subject matter (e.g., artistic work, performance, sound recording, broadcast) is involved and its title (if any); for a work, the date of first publication, the author's name, and (where relevant) the date of his or her death; for a performance, sound recording, or broadcast, the date of its first fixation or occurrence.[78]

Persons challenging the certificate or certified copy of the register entry must plead and prove their case on the usual balance of probabilities standard. A simple pleading that the claimant is not the copyright owner, despite a certificate of registration saying he is, will be struck out or disregarded in a motion for summary judgment. The pleading must go on to allege specific facts that, if proved, would contradict the certificate.[79] Once evidence is introduced in the proceedings, the pre-

---

76 *Hogg v. Toye & Co.*, [1935] Ch. 497 (C.A.).

77 *C Act*, above note 11, s. 53; *Circle Film Enterprises Inc. v. Canadian Broadcasting Corp.*, [1959] S.C.R. 602; *Silverson v. Neon Products Ltd.* (1978), 39 C.P.R. (2d) 234 at 238–39 (B.C.S.C.).

78 *C Act, ibid.*, ss. 55 & 56. The application for registration may be made by or for the author, copyright owner, assignee or grantee of an interest by licence, who must make a declaration that his status is accurately claimed.

79 *Samsonite Canada Inc. v. Costco Wholesale Corp.* (1995), 61 C.P.R. (3d) 298 (Fed. T.D.).

sumption created by the certificate or entry disappears and the question is simply whether the evidence is sufficient to discharge the challenger's onus of proof.

The consequences of registration are not, however, entirely predictable. Courts are supposed to treat certificates and register entries as evidence of the facts stated. But these "facts" are really no more than the applicant's assertions made in the application to register. They may be made years after the event, just before the applicant decides to sue someone for infringement. The Copyright Office does not check the assertions, nor is a copy of the work or item even deposited. Outside copyright, "evidence" like this is usually taken with a grain of salt, and this attitude sometimes carries over to copyright. While some courts treat every registration equally, others place little or no weight on last-minute registrations that have plainly been obtained as part of a litigation strategy.[80] Thus, in a criminal prosecution, certificates of registration issued before the offence occurred were accepted, but later certificates were rejected as not providing the necessary proof beyond reasonable doubt required for criminal proceedings.[81] Similarly, conflicting certificates obtained by both parties in anticipation of litigation prove little, except that tit-for-tat is a game not confined to children.[82]

FURTHER READINGS

EL SISSI, R.H., "Security Interests in Copyright" (1995) 10 I.P.J. 35

HAEMMERLI, A., "Insecurity Interests: Where Intellectual Property and Commercial Law Collide" (1996) 96 Col. L.R. 1645

HENDERSON, G.F., "Problems Involved in the Assignment of Patents and Patent Rights" (1966) 60 C.P.R. 237

WOOD, R.J., "Federal Law and the New Provincial Personal Property Security Regime" (LL.M. thesis, University of Toronto, 1982) c. 6

---

80 *Grignon* v. *Roussel* (1991), 38 C.P.R. (3d) 4 at 7–8 (Fed. T.D.).
81 *R.* v. *Laurier Office Mart Inc.* (1994), 58 C.P.R. (3d) 403 (Ont. Prov. Div.), aff'd (1995), 63 C.P.R. (3d) 229 (Ont. Gen. Div.).
82 *Dubois* v. *Systèmes de Gestion et d'Analyse de Données Média Canada Inc.* (1991), 41 C.P.R. (3d) 92 at 104–5 (Que. S.C.).

CHAPTER 9

ENFORCEMENT

Most intellectual property disputes settle without going to court. The incentives for settlement or informal dispute resolution are high because litigation can quickly become prohibitively expensive. Alternative dispute resolution through mediation or arbitration is becoming more common as governments seek ways of reducing the constant pressure on the courts. For those copyright or moral right infringement cases that go to court, claimants may, as from 1 October 1999, use the court's fast-track procedures to have the case dealt with "without delay and in a summary way" unless the court decides a slower-track procedure is more appropriate.[1] Quite apart from this special procedure, courts are also dealing more expeditiously with flimsy cases, by granting motions for summary judgment against parties who fail early on to demonstrate that they have any seriously arguable claim or defence. Thus, the pleadings and evidence may show that an accused's work is just too different from the claimant's to be infringing, or that a particular defendant could not possibly be an infringer. If there is no genuine issue fit for trial, the defendant may apply for summary judg-

---

1   *Copyright Act*, R.S.C. 1985, c. C-42 [*C Act*; unless otherwise indicated, references to the Act are as amended], ss. 34(4) to (7). Claimants can proceed under the less formal procedure relating to applications instead of actions, unless the court decides otherwise.

ment in its favour.[2] If litigation is pursued, trials are sometimes bifurcated: liability is tried first, and the question of remedy is litigated later
only if the claimant has succeeded on liability.[3]

Infringements attract the usual remedies. Those most commonly
sought are final and interlocutory injunctions, damages, accounts of
profits, and delivery up and seizure of infringing goods.[4] After considering where to sue and who can be sued, we shall examine the main
remedies for infringement of copyright and moral rights. A section on
limitation periods concludes this chapter.

A. COURT SELECTION

Litigation for infringement of copyright or moral rights may be
brought in either the provincial courts or the Trial Division of the Federal Court of Canada. Both have concurrent jurisdiction. The Federal
Court is sometimes preferred because its judges are more experienced
in this class of litigation, the case can often be more quickly heard and
appealed, awards of legal costs may be at a more generous level than in
some provincial courts, and the Federal Court's orders are enforceable
across Canada.

Only the Federal Court may cancel or amend an entry on the
Copyright Registry. However, it lacks jurisdiction over disputes involving only provincial law. Suppose a licensee is not paying royalties, or a
party to an agreement settling a copyright or moral rights dispute does
not observe its terms or commits a tort. Since the dispute does not
involve copyright or moral rights, but is merely over the commission of
a breach of contract or an ordinary civil wrong, the Federal Court cannot hear it. The Court can, however, decide tort claims arising from a
valid federal statute.[5] The Court may also decide contractual points
incidentally to an infringement action. Suppose a defendant disputes a
claimant's title or standing to sue for infringement. The Court has

---

2   *Possian v. Canadian Olympic Association* (1996), 74 C.P.R. (3d) 509 (Fed. T.D.)
    [*Possian*]; *Wall v. Brunell* (1997) 75 C.P.R. (3d) 429 (Fed. T.D.).

3   *Illva Saronno v. Privilegiata Fabrica Maraschino "Excelsior"* (1998), 84 C.P.R. (3d) 1
    (Fed. T.D.).

4   Claimants sometimes seek declarations and may also want their costs and pre- and
    post-judgment interest. These remedies are not discussed here.

5   *Sabol v. Haljan* (1982), 36 A.R. 109 (C.A.); *Possian*, above note 2; *Asbjorn Horgard
    A/S v. Gibbs/Nortac Industries Ltd.*, [1987] 3 F.C. 544 (C.A.) (statutory passing-off
    under s. 7(b) or (c) of the *Trade-marks Act*, R.S.C. 1985, c. T-13 [*T Act*]).

jurisdiction to interpret and decide on the legal meaning of any documents the parties rely on to prove or disprove these issues.[6] Similarly, if a defendant pleads that an alleged infringement is in fact permitted by its contract with the claimant, the Court must interpret the contract to determine the infringement issue.[7]

It is quite possible for there to be two sets of litigation over the same matter, one in a provincial court, the other in the Federal Court. Two infringement proceedings may even be started. For example, a threatened party may begin an action seeking a declaration of non-infringement from a provincial court, and the right-holder may respond by bringing its own infringement action in Federal Court. One or other court may then stay the case before it, if the issues and relief sought are essentially the same; otherwise, both cases may proceed.

B. WHOM TO SUE

The *Copyright Act* extends liability beyond direct infringers to those who "authorize" infringement.[8] Otherwise, the Act is silent on precisely who can be implicated. General common law principles of complicity and vicarious responsibility should apply. Those who directly participate in the infringement, therefore, are as liable as the main actor. Principals, partners, and employers may be jointly and severally liable for infringements committed by their agents, co-partners, and employees acting in the scope of their authority or employment.[9] Parent corporations should not automatically be liable for their subsidiaries' acts unless these acts are done as agents. Nor may directors, officers, and managers be liable for a corporation's wrongs, unless they formed the corporation to infringe, or directly ordered, authorized, or procured infringement. Not preventing an infringement within one's

---

6   *Bouchet v. Kyriacopoulos* (1964), 45 C.P.R. 265 at 273 (Ex. Ct.), aff'd *ibid.* 281n (S.C.C., 1966).

7   *Titan Linkabit Corp. v. S.E.E. See Electronic Engineering Inc.* (1993), 44 C.P.R. (3d) 469 (Fed. T.D.).

8   *C Act*, above note 1, s. 3(1); see section A(8), "Authorization," in chapter 5.

9   See, for example, *Boudreau v. Lin* (1997), 150 D.L.R. (4th) 324 at 335 (Ont. Gen. Div.) [*Boudreau*]: university liable for copyright infringement by professor's production of infringing course-pack.

power to control, or not fulfilling one's duties to the corporation, apparently does not in itself attract liability.[10]

Those who merely "contribute" to infringement may not themselves be infringers. Sellers of video-cassette recorders may not be responsible for the unlawful copying of tapes by buyers, unless the former hatch a common design with buyers to infringe, or to induce or persuade buyers to infringe.[11] On the other hand, providers of online bulletin board services could be liable for infringing material posted by subscribers. The possible hardship such a rule may entail, especially for non-profit operators, has led to the proposal that liability should exist only if the operator knew or should have known that posted material infringed copyright and had not acted reasonably to limit potential abuses.[12] Meanwhile, the Copyright Board decided in 1999 that an Internet service provider (ISP) that acts as a mere conduit is not liable, at least for infringing telecommunication or performing rights, in respect of musical works that are posted or transmitted using the ISP's facilities. The ISP could be liable if "as a result of business relationships or other factors" it acts "in concert with others in a different manner"; for example, if it "posts content, associates itself with others to offer content, creates embedded links or moderates a newsgroup," or "creates a cache for reasons other than improving system performance, modifies the contents of the cached material or interferes with any means of obtaining information as to the number of 'hits' or 'accesses' to the cached material." Whether

---

10 *C. Evans & Sons Ltd.* v. *Spritebrand Ltd.*, [1985] 2 All E.R. 415 (C.A.); *King* v. *Milpurrurru* (1996), 34 I.P.R. 11 at 35 (Austl. Fed. Ct.); compare *Mentmore Manufacturing Co.* v. *National Merchandise Manufacturing Co.* (1978), 40 C.P.R. (2d) 164 (Fed. C.A.) (patents). For the proportions in which directors, employees, and the freelancers they employ may be held liable, see *Ateliers Tango argentin Inc.* v. *Festival d'Espagne et d'Amérique latine Inc.*, [1997] R.J.Q. 3030 (S.C.).

11 *CBS Songs Ltd.* v. *Amstrad Consumer Electronics*, [1988] A.C. 1013 (H.L.) [*CBS Songs*]; *Crédit Lyonnais Nederland N.V.* v. *Export Credits Guarantee Dept.*, [1999] 2 W.L.R. 540 (H.L.).

12 Information Highway Advisory Council, *Final Report: Connection, Community, Content: The Challenge of the Information Highway* (Ottawa: The Council, 1995) at 120; *R.* v. *M.* (J.P.) (1996), 67 C.P.R. (3d) 152 (N.S.C.A.): computer bulletin board operator, knowingly making infringing copies of computer software available to selected users, found guilty of "distribut[ing]" them to the copyright owner's prejudice: *C Act*, above note 1, s. 42(1)(c). Compare J. Ginsburg, "Putting Cars on the 'Information Superhighway': Authors, Exploiters, and Copyright in Cyberspace" (1995) 95 Colum. L. Rev. 1466 at 1492ff; *Religious Technology Centre* v. *Netcom On-Line Communications Services Inc.*, 33 I.P.R. 132 (D. Cal. 1995).

these views of ISP liability will be accepted outside the field of musical performing rights remains to be seen.[13]

Defendants must therefore be selected with care. Strategies such as taking out newspaper ads warning off the trade, or sending letters or copies of threatening correspondence to retailers and wholesalers, should be avoided. If the right later proves invalid, the plaintiff may itself be sued for the wrong of injurious falsehood and may have to pay damages for business disruptions. At common law, the plaintiff is liable only if it knew its right was invalid or non-existent, or otherwise acted inexcusably. Knowledge or dishonesty need not be proved where a federal right such as copyright is shown to be invalid or non-existent, and the injured party relies on section 7(a) of the *Trade-marks Act*; this provision requires only proof of injury to business caused by a competitor's false or misleading statement.[14]

A claimant who finds a dealer handling infringing goods and wants to trace the source of supply is not powerless. The dealer itself may be innocent of secondary infringement, since it may not have known or suspected that the goods were infringing.[15] But the dealer may be mixed up with someone who probably is an infringer, and so must supply the copyright owner with full information about the supplier. The claimant can then decide whether or not to sue the source. He can bring discovery proceedings for this purpose alone against an otherwise innocent defendant. Even the Customs authorities can be com-

---

13   *Statement of Royalties to Be Collected for the Performance or the Communication by Telecommunication, in Canada, of Musical or Dramatico-Musical Works (Tariff 22), Phase I: Legal Issues,* Copyright Board Decision of 27 October 1999 [unreported] at 41. Compare *Godfrey* v. *Demon Internet Ltd.,* [1999] 4 All E.R. 342 (Q.B.D.), holding an ISP liable at common law every time a subscriber accesses a defamatory message, and unprotected by the *Defamation Act,* 1996 (U.K.) if it fails to remove the message once alerted to it.

14   *S. & S. Industries Inc.* v. *Rowell,* [1966] S.C.R. 419, on *T Act,* above note 5, s. 7(a), and the common law; compare *M & I Door Systems Ltd.* v. *Indoco Industrial Door Co.* (1989), 25 C.P.R. (3d) 477 (Fed. T.D.); *Safematic Inc.* v. *Sensodec Oy* (1988), 21 C.P.R. (3d) 12 (Fed. T.D.).

15   See section A(10), "Distributing and Importing Infringing Copies: Secondary Infringement," in chapter 5; section D(4)(e)(i), "Innocent Defendants," in this chapter.

pelled to provide the identity of infringing importers if they are the only practicable source of the information sought.[16]

C. INJUNCTIONS

1) Final Injunction

The *Copyright Act* grants copyright owners a number of "sole" rights. Infringement of such rights makes the injunction an appropriate remedy unless it is barred by statute[17] or by some equitable reason such as acquiescence, lack of clean hands, or unconscionability. Injunctions may be issued to prevent persistent defendants from infringing the claimant's entire present and future copyright inventory, even though the defendants have so far infringed only some of it.[18] They may be issued even against unknown defendants — for example, street vendors selling fake Rolex watches on the run.[19]

An injunction may be avoided if the defendant gives the court an unqualified undertaking to behave. A claimant must have some good reason for continuing to pursue an injunction; otherwise, he risks liability for the costs of the injunction proceeding incurred after the date the undertaking was offered. But a defendant who gives an undertaking while still trying to justify its action on untenable grounds or while denying the plaintiff's rights cannot complain if the claimant rejects the undertaking and asks for the unqualified injunction to which it is entitled.[20]

Although injunctions are discretionary, the Federal Court of Appeal once said that only the claimant's conduct can bar relief, and the fact that no loss is suffered is irrelevant. To refuse an injunction

---

16   *Glaxo Wellcome PLC v. M.N.R.* (1998), 82 C.P.R. (3d) 497 (Fed. C.A.), following *Norwich Pharmacal Co. v. Commissioners of Customs & Excise,* [1974] A.C. 133 (H.L.) (patents); *Titan Sports Inc. v. Mansion House (Toronto) Ltd.* (1989), 28 C.P.R. (3d) 199 at 207 (Fed. T.D.); *Société Romanaise de la Chaussure S.A. v. British Shoe Corp. Ltd.,* [1991] F.S.R. 1 (Ch.); *Michael O'Mara Books Ltd. v. Express Newspapers Plc.,* [1999] F.S.R. 49 (Ch.); *Microsoft Corp. v. Plato Technology Ltd.,* [1999] F.S.R. 834 at 846–47 (Ch.) (defendant need not reveal all its suppliers where it had innocently handled infringing copies bought from just one supplier).

17   For example, a building should not be halted in mid-construction, even if it infringes copyright: *C Act,* above note 1, s. 40(1).

18   *C Act, ibid.,* s. 39.1; *Microsoft Corp. v. Electro-Wide Ltd.,* [1997] F.S.R. 580 at 597 (Ch.) [*Microsoft*].

19   *Montres Rolex S.A. v. Balshin* (1992), [1993] 1 F.C. 236 (C.A.) (trade-mark).

20   *Banier v. News Group Newspapers Ltd.,* [1997] F.S.R. 812 at 816 (Ch.).

otherwise is "tantamount to the imposition of a compulsory licence . . . [in] the absence of legislative authority."[21] The court accordingly granted the federal government an injunction against an unauthorized abridgment that infringed its copyright.

The Court of Appeal's holding should not be read so as to fetter a court's equitable discretion. The range of material that comes under copyright and the range of activities that constitute infringements require courts to be especially careful in deciding whether an injunction can be justly and conveniently ordered. Suppose a machine is constructed from photocopies of confidential drawings wrongfully made by an employee of the copyright holder. Not only the making of the copies but also the making of the machine itself may infringe the copyright. Suppose, however, that the machine could have been lawfully reverse-engineered in two years without the use of the photocopies, and that the two years have long since passed. The copyright owner should get damages for the headstart the defendant wrongly gained, but no injunction.[22] Similarly in the United States, damages instead of an injunction were suggested in a case where video-recorder manufacturers were said to be abetting copyright infringement by home-tapers.[23] Damages instead of injunctions have also been encouraged as one way to minimize incursions on free speech.[24] This flexibility seems preferable to the restrictive approach suggested by the Federal Court of Appeal. An injunction may "presumptively" be appropriate for intellectual property infringements, but this is a rebuttable presumption.[25]

---

21   R. v. James Lorimer & Co., [1984] 1 F.C. 1065 at 1073 (C.A.).

22   Schauenburg Industries Ltd. v. Borowski (1979), 25 O.R. (2d) 737 (H.C.J.) [Schauenburg]. The example assumes that fewer than fifty-one machines had been legitimately made at the time from the drawings; otherwise, the unauthorized copying may breach confidence but not copyright: C Act, above note 1, s. 64.1; section B(7), "Industrial Design," in chapter 2. A comparable remedy may equally be provided for breach of confidence as for infringement of copyright: Cadbury Schweppes Inc. v. FBI Foods Ltd. (1999), 167 D.L.R. (4th) 577 (S.C.C.).

23   Universal City Studios v. Sony Corp., 659 F.2d 963 at 976 (9th Cir. 1981), rev'd 5 to 4 on liability (sub nom. Sony Corp. of America v. Universal City Studios Inc.), 464 U.S. 417 (1984), the dissenters agreeing with the lower court on remedy, at 499–500.

24   P.N. Leval, "Campbell v. Acuff-Rose: Justice Souter's Rescue of Fair Use" (1994) 13 Cardozo Arts & Ent. L.J. 19 at 23–26.

25   Dableh v. Ontario Hydro (1996), 68 C.P.R. (3d) 129 at 152 (Fed. C.A.). The court awarded a declaration instead of an injunction in CCH Canadian Ltd. v. Law Society of Upper Canada (9 November 1999), (Fed T.D.) [unreported], although the court's discretion to refuse the injunction was not disputed.

2) Interlocutory Injunction

Quickly seeking interlocutory relief is common in copyright cases. The result of the application is usually influential: many parties settle or are loath to go to trial (sometimes years later) for a final adjudication of their rights, especially if the court has indicated a tentative view on the parties' respective merits. Still, the order is intended to be temporary. It may be dissolved if the claimant is not diligent in bringing the case to trial.[26]

Copyright cases have often figured in settling the principles for interlocutory relief for the whole range of disputes throughout the Commonwealth. The original *Anton Piller* injunction — a pre-trial order allowing seizure of infringing material that a defendant might otherwise hide — involved breach of copyright and confidence.[27] True, *American Cyanamid Co.* v. *Ethicon Ltd.*,[28] the leading U.K. case to settle when interlocutory injunctions should be granted, involved a patent rather than a copyright, but the court plainly had copyright cases in mind when it laid down the principles to be applied. Concerned that interlocutory hearings were turning into full-scale trials on incomplete evidence, the British court instructed judges merely to satisfy themselves that there was a "serious question to be tried" or the applicant had a "real prospect of succeeding in [its] claim for a permanent injunction at the trial" before considering other factors relevant to the grant of this discretionary relief.[29] The Supreme Court of Canada endorsed this approach in *RJR–MacDonald Inc.* v. *Canada (A.G).*[30] It said that judges should not initially ask whether a *prima facie* case was made out but must deal with applications "on the basis of common sense and an extremely limited review of the case on the merits."[31]

The Supreme Court instanced two "rare" cases where the judge could review the merits more fully. The first was where the practical result of the interlocutory proceeding is to decide the case finally — for

26 *Ciba-Geigy Ltd.* v. *Novopharm Ltd.* (1997), 77 C.P.R. (3d) 428 (Fed. T.D.) (patent).
27 *Anton Piller KG* v. *Manufacturing Processes Ltd.,* [1976] Ch. 55 (C.A.), followed in *Nintendo of America Inc.* v. *Coinex Video Games Inc.* (1982), 69 C.P.R. (2d) 122 (Fed. C.A.); *C Act*, above note 1, s. 38(1)(b). On how this procedure may be abused, see *Pulse Microsystems Ltd.* v. *Safesoft Systems Inc.* (1996), 134 D.L.R.(4th) 701 (Man. C.A.), discharging order in a computer software case; *Nike Canada Ltd.* v. *Doe*, [1999] F.C.J. 1018 (T.D.).
28 [1975] R.P.C. 513 (H.L.).
29 *Ibid.* at 541.
30 [1994] 1 S.C.R. 311 (*Charter* challenge to legislation restricting tobacco advertising) [*RJR-MacDonald*].
31 *Ibid.* at 348.

example, where the right has to be exercised immediately or not at all, or where the hardship on one or other of the parties is so great that a full trial would be pointless. The strength or weakness of the case can then be given due weight. These features may be present in a case where a complainant lacks money and the defendant is a wealthy enterprise that can easily spin out an unmeritorious case until the complainant gives up or faces financial ruin. The scenario may be typical of disputes between, on the one hand, authors and performers and, on the other, the large enterprises that distribute their material. If the benefits held out to the creative community by the *Copyright Act* are to mean anything, disputes with distributors need to be resolved as quickly and cheaply as possible.

Snow v. *Eaton Centre Ltd.*[32] exemplifies this approach. There, an artist complained that his moral rights were being infringed by the defendant, which had bedecked the artist's sculpture with Christmas wreaths. The court dealt with the case promptly by issuing a mandatory interlocutory injunction requiring immediate removal of the wreaths. The evidence on affidavit and discovery sufficiently convinced the judge of the strength of the claimant's case and of the inexcusability of the defendant's behaviour. Christmas would have come and gone had the case proceeded to trial. By then, the wreaths would have come down anyway, but the damage would have all been done. Meanwhile, the costs would have mounted as the defendant sought to justify its behaviour. Had the case gone on, the artist may well have had to drop his claim simply because it had become moot and he could no longer afford the legal bills.

The second situation the Supreme Court identified as justifying a more thorough review of the merits is where a "simple question of law alone" appears.[33] A court presented with a claim or defence that is obviously hopeless in law can decide so immediately.

Another exceptional case may be where the parties jointly request the court to treat an interlocutory proceeding as a final hearing on a point of law or even on the merits of the whole case. The court may accede to the request if it sees no resulting harm to the integrity of the judicial system. The Supreme Court seems unwilling to countenance many exceptions to the *American Cyanamid* rule. An exception once urged for copyright, that proof of irreparable harm is unnecessary where an infringement is clear or blatant, is no longer good law.[34] The

---

32   (1982), 70 C.P.R. (2d) 105 (Ont. H.C.J.).
33   *RJR-MacDonald*, above note 30 at 339.
34   *Teklogix Inc.* v. *Zaino* (1997), 79 C.P.R. (3d) 1 at 16–17 (Ont. Gen. Div.).

best earliest time to test the merits of a case may be on a motion to strike a party's pleading for failing to state a legal cause of action or defence, or on a motion for summary judgment. The use of interlocutory injunction proceedings as surrogates for these procedures should be discouraged.

On the standard approach espoused by the Supreme Court, the claimant faces three consecutive hurdles:

- First, does the claimant have a seriously arguable — not frivolous or vexatious — case? The claimant should undertake to pay any damages the defendant sustains from the grant of an injunction if the defendant is ultimately found not liable. The presence of the undertaking, sometimes backed by a third party bond, is not a reason for the court to grant the injunction. Rather, without the undertaking, the court may refuse to consider the case at all.

    A defendant with a clear cast-iron defence should obviously not be enjoined. Usually, however, defences raise questions of fact or degree, so that a defendant may merely demonstrate that it, too, has a seriously arguable case. This will not likely detract from the seriously arguable character of the claimant's case.
- Second, would the claimant suffer an injury that cannot be adequately compensated in damages if the injunction were refused and the claimant eventually succeeded at trial? Canadian courts require clear, not speculative, evidence of irreparable harm. Sometimes money cannot compensate for the kind of loss suffered: for example, the claimant will go out of business or will suffer permanent loss of market or reputation. Other times, the defendant cannot pay any judgment the court may eventually award against it. Both cases are instances of irreparable harm.[35]
- Third, does the balance of convenience favour the grant of an injunction? The court must consider the various factors that point to one party suffering more harm than the other from the grant or refusal of an injunction. It may take into account any goodwill or contracts the parties may lose if the alleged infringement continues or is stopped, any delays in enforcing the claim, whether the defendant acted innocently or with full knowledge of the risk, and, if matters are evenly balanced, the strength of either party's case.[36] The court may also

---

35 *RJR-MacDonald*, above note 30 at 341; *Tamec Inc.* v. *2804166 Canada Inc.* (1995), 63 C.P.R. (3d) 309 at 311 (Fed. T.D.).

36 *Turbo Resources Ltd.* v. *Petro-Canada Inc.*, [1989] 2 F.C. 451 at 477–78 (C.A.) (trade-marks).

consider how its order would affect third parties — that is, the public interest. For example, an applicant may be unable to suppress the dissemination of information affecting public health and safety unless he shows no risk of public harm resulting from an injunction.[37]

Ultimately, the court should look at the overall equities without being too strictly straitjacketed by any set formula including, it seems, any imposed by *American Cyanamid* itself. Thus, the Supreme Court has refused to apply *American Cyanamid* to cases of non-commercial speech of such little social utility as defamation and hate-mongering. To ensure that free expression is adequately protected, interlocutory injunctions may be refused against the continuation of critical comment or even hate speech unless the claimant clearly satisfies the court that a wrong has in fact been committed.[38] This approach could apply to cases where an attempt to use copyright as an instrument of state or private censorship occurs.

The *American Cyanamid* approach may be avoided even in commercial disputes that do not raise free expression issues. Thus, in a dispute over alleged misappropriation of computer software where the claimant's assertions were only weakly supported by evidence, a British court thought *American Cyanamid* did not preclude taking into account the claimant's likely merits as an important factor. Courts should not try to resolve difficult issues of fact or law on interlocutory applications, but they should be able to assess the relative strengths of each party's case as it appears from any credible evidence then produced. This approach helps parties reach settlements and reduces litigation costs. The court summarized its views on interlocutory injunction as follows:

1. The grant of an interlocutory injunction is a matter of discretion and depends on all the facts of the case.

2. There are no fixed rules as to when an injunction should or should not be granted. The relief must be kept flexible.

3. Because of the practice adopted on the hearing of applications for interlocutory relief, the court should rarely attempt to resolve complex issues of disputed fact or law.

---

37   *Acohs Pty. Ltd.* v. *R.A. Bashford Consulting Pty. Ltd.* (1997), 37 I.P.R. 542, aff'd (*sub nom. Bialkower* v. *Acohs Pty. Ltd.*) (1998), 41 I.P.R. 33 (Austl. Fed. Ct.). See also section B(10), "Public Interest," in chapter 7.

38   *Canada (Human Rights Commission)* v. *Canadian Liberty Net* (1998), 157 D.L.R. (4th) 385 (S.C.C.).

4. Major factors the court can bear in mind are (a) the extent to which damages are likely to be an adequate remedy for each party and the ability of the other party to pay, (b) the balance of convenience, (c) the maintenance of the status quo, (d) any clear view the court may reach as to the relative strength of the parties' cases.[39]

Whether these views will ultimately prevail in Britain, or how they may affect Canadian courts, remains to be seen. So far, the standard three-step approach continues to be loyally applied in Canada before the Federal Court and, with minor variations, in the provincial courts.

There is no presumption for or against interlocutory injunctions in copyright cases or any particular class of them. However, the prospect held out by *American Cyanamid* and the *RJR–MacDonald* case that interlocutory hearings would become much quicker and cheaper has not fully materialized. Each party still tries to stack the balance of convenience in its favour with kilos of evidence, as if physical and legal weight were equations; and each now argues that some nuance in *American Cyanamid* or *RJR–MacDonald* and the reams of jurisprudence applying them favours it more than the other party. *American Cyanamid* is thus honoured more in letter than in spirit.

It is worth recalling that the *American Cyanamid* trial judge, after dealing with the threshold question, exercised his discretion, with the House of Lords' approval, in less than two paragraphs to dispose of the case in the applicant's favour:

> The defendants, as already stated, are not yet on the market and so have no business in these sutures which will be brought to a stop; no factory will be closed down; and no workpeople be thrown out of work. The plaintiffs, on the other hand, have a substantial and growing market; and . . . I see no reason why the defendants should be allowed . . . to jump the gun and establish themselves in the market before trial. If they were allowed to do so, it would not only disrupt the plaintiff's existing and future business, but might well mean that the plaintiffs, even if they succeeded at trial, as a commercial matter could not in practice ask for a permanent injunction.
>
> [O]nce doctors and patients have got used to the defendants' product on the market in the period prior to trial, it would be, as a commercial matter, hardly possible for the plaintiffs, even if successful, by the grant of an injunction at the trial to deprive the public of it.[40]

---

39 *Series 5 Software Ltd.* v. *Clarke,* [1996] F.S.R. 273 at 286 (Ch.).
40 [1975] R.P.C. 513 at 520 (Ch.), aff'd [1975] R.P.C. 513 at 542–43 (H.L.).

Judges today could do worse than emulate this brevity. They should avoid returning to the days when cases were tried and appealed twice: once on an interlocutory injunction application, and a second time at the final trial on the merits.

D. DAMAGES

1) General Principles

Damages for infringement track those for tort generally. The claimant should receive monetary compensation (general and aggravated damages) restoring it to the position in which it would have been had the infringement never occurred. The claimant's present economic position is compared with that hypothetical state; the difference — excluding reasonably avoidable and "remote" losses (i.e., those not flowing naturally and directly from the wrong) — is what the infringer owes.[41] But every case will have its own peculiarities. The object is to compensate this claimant — not some other claimant, who could have lost more or less from the same infringement — for the particular wrong and, if appropriate, to award punitive damages against egregiously bad infringers.[42]

Every infringement is a separate wrong. A person who, without authority, scans an unpublished photograph into her computer and posts it on her Web site may infringe the copyright owner's rights of reproduction, first distribution, and telecommunication.[43] The copyright owner should technically get compensation for each wrong. A sense of proportion must, however, be retained, and double or overlapping recovery should be avoided. Some complaints are trivial and deserve no award: overcompensation is as much a vice as undercompensation.

The 1997 Act has muddied this picture by introducing an alternative remedy of "statutory damages," supposedly to simplify assessment by letting judges award damages on a more rough-and-ready basis. The new remedy will be examined after a consideration of the remedies of compensatory and punitive damages.

---

41 *Colonial Fastener Co. Ltd.* v. *Lightning Fastener Co. Ltd.*, [1937] S.C.R. 36 at 41 [*Colonial*]; *General Tire & Rubber Co.* v. *Firestone Tyre & Rubber Co. Ltd.*, [1975] 2 All E.R. 173 (H.L.) [*General Tire*].
42 See section D(3), "Punitive Damages," in this chapter.
43 See sections A(1), "First Public Distribution," A(2), "Reproduction," and A(5), "Telecommunication," in chapter 5.

2) Compensatory Damages

The following guidelines may help to assess damages as compensation.

a) Lost Sales

If a right-holder's business is selling the protected product, it can obviously recover its lost net profit on sales the infringer took from it by selling competing products. The infringer cannot escape by proving it could have sold a non-infringing substitute. A publisher once sold a school anthology containing a major section of a novel without obtaining copyright clearance. It had to compensate both the author for lost royalties and a rival publisher, who owned the copyright, for the latter's profit on sales lost from the competition.[44] An infringer may also undercut prices because it does not have the claimant's start-up cost (e.g., research, development, and market creation). A claimant reducing prices to meet this competition can also recover for its lost margin and any general business decline — for example, if the infringer produces an inferior product that makes the market turn against the claimant's product as well.[45]

b) Reasonable Royalty

What if the copyright holder could never have made the infringer's sales — for example, they would have gone to other competitors, or the infringer created a new market? The copyright holder is then entitled to damages based on a reasonable licence fee on those sales. For right-holders in the licensing business — for example, copyright collecting societies — this amount is the actual royalty fee they would have charged the defendant for a licence. A video store that wrongly copies videotapes for rental has to pay as damages the licence fee the copyright owner charges comparable video stores that acquire lawful copies.[46] If the right-holder never licenses (e.g., a painter who sells only originals and turns away all attempts to persuade him to allow reproductions of his work to be made or sold), then a notional reasonable royalty fee may be set: what a willing licensor and licensee in the shoes of the particular parties would have negotiated under existing market

---

44 *Prise de Parole Inc.* v. *Guérin, Éditeur Ltée* (1995), 66 C.P.R. (3d) 257 (Fed. T.D.), aff'd (1996), 73 C.P.R. (3d) 557 (Fed. C.A.) [*Prise*].

45 *Lam Inc.* v. *Johns-Manville Corp.*, 718 F.2d 1056 (Fed. Cir. 1983); *Catnic Components Ltd.* v. *Hill & Smith Ltd.*, [1983] F.S.R. 512 at 528–30 (Pat. Ct.).

46 *Profekta International Inc.* v. *Lee* (1997), 75 C.P.R. (3d) 369 at 371–72 (Fed. C.A.) [*Profekta*].

conditions. The factors that real-life negotiators, acting reasonably with a view to reaching an agreement, would use in that line of business are then taken into account: for example, comparable fees for comparable licences anywhere, the infringer's savings and profits, and any admissions by either party of the figure it would be willing to accept as a royalty.[47] Damages can also be mixed and matched. For example, an infringer may make some sales the claimant would have made, and may also make some sales the claimant could never have made. The infringer should then pay the claimant's lost profits on the first set of sales and the equivalent of a reasonable royalty on the second set.

The onus is on the claimant to provide a reasonable basis for the court to act on. But the reasonable royalty formula is ultimately a device to prevent unjust enrichment: the infringer is treated like the car thief, who has to pay the owner a reasonable rental for the time the owner was deprived of her property, even if the owner had put the car in storage for the winter. Neither party can avoid a calculation on this basis by saying that, in the real world, he would never have entered into licence negotiations with the other or would have settled only for other-worldly rates.

The temptation to grant damages "at large," instead of actual or reasonable royalty damages, should be resisted, especially in cases where defendants have behaved badly. Such defendants can always have punitive damages or an account of profits awarded against them in addition to the royalty fee. Claimants who want still more can choose the new remedy of statutory damages.[48]

c) Intangible Losses

Infringements may sometimes cause right-holders intangible losses. For example, someone who puts up a building infringing an architect's plans may deprive the architect of the reputation that would have come her way from news of the building (placards on the site, etc.). Damages for copyright infringement may compensate for this lost credit.[49]

---

47   Similarly for patents: *Colonial*, above note 41; *General Tire*, above note 41, applied in *Profekta*, ibid.; *Georgia-Pacific Corp. v. U.S. Plywood-Champion Papers Inc.*, 318 F. Supp. 1116 (D.N.Y. 1970), modified 446 F.2d 295 (2d Cir. 1971); *Schauenburg*, above note 22 at 748.

48   Sections D(3), "Punitive Damages," and D(4), "Statutory Damages," in this chapter; D. Vaver, "Infringing Copyright in a Competitor's Advertising: Damages 'At Large' Can be Large Damages" (1984) 1 I.P.J. 186.

49   *Kaffka v. Mountain Side Developments Ltd.* (1982), 62 C.P.R. (2d) 157 at 163 (B.C.S.C.). This loss may also infringe moral rights or amount to passing-off, and should be similarly compensable.

Sometimes, too, damages can cover embarrassment and distress, as when a national newspaper publishes a private photograph without copyright clearance.[50]

d) Apportioning Damages

Damages may sometimes need to be apportioned. An infringer who takes one chapter from a ten-chapter book should pay damages only on the loss caused by taking that chapter. Exceptionally, this proportion may be like taking the whole book: a newspaper that publishes the juiciest chapter in a biography might so satiate the market that demand for the book on general release might be much less, even zero. More often, the loss would be less. One might start with the proportion of pages taken in relation to the whole book and then increase or lower this rate depending on the importance of the chapter, the cost to the infringer of substitutes, the infringer's profit on the enterprise, and the likely effect on the copyright owner's own sales or future licensing efforts. A similar exercise occurs where an account of profits is ordered.[51] The success of a film may be more due to its cast, staging, and promotion than to the play whose copyright it infringed. To award the injured playwright the whole of the film's net profit would be unjust. A court faced with this scenario awarded 20 percent of the profits, but recognized that a different percentage would be justified on different facts.[52] Damages should be similarly apportioned. A claimant should not avoid apportionment simply by switching remedies, for then a punitive element creeps into an award in cases where punitive damages would not directly be awardable.

On the other hand, an infringer sometimes deals with a copyright holder's work as if it were his own, taking as much as he likes. Other times, he will so interweave the right-holder's work with his own as to make their separation impossible. The full loss flowing from the infringement may then justifiably be awarded as damages.[53]

---

50 *Williams* v. *Settle*, [1960] 2 All E.R. 806 (C.A.).
51 See section E, "Account of Profits," in this chapter.
52 *Sheldon* v. *Metro Goldwyn Pictures Corp.*, 106 F.2d 45 (2d Cir. 1939), aff'd 309 U.S. 390 (1940). Accord: *Dubiner* v. *Cheerio Toys & Games Ltd.*, [1966] 2 Ex. C.R. 801 (trade-marks) [*Dubiner*]; *Beloit Canada Ltd.* v. *Valmet Oy* (1995), 61 C.P.R. (3d) 271 at 279 (Fed. C.A.) (patents) [*Beloit*].
53 *91439 Canada Ltée* v. *Editions JCL Inc.* (1994), 58 C.P.R. (3d) 38 at 44–45 (Fed. C.A.) [*JCL*]; *Stovin-Bradford* v. *Volpoint Properties Ltd.*, [1971] 1 Ch. 1007 at 1016 (C.A.).

e) Defendant's Innocence

Infringers are usually liable whether or not they knew they were infringing. Innocence avoids liability only in two situations. The first is where the defendant is sued as a secondary infringer — that is, for dealing with or distributing already infringing goods, or importing copyright goods without the Canadian copyright owner's consent. The second situation is where the defendant has distributed or imported books on an exclusive Canadian distributor's list. In these cases, the defendant is liable only on proof that he knew or should have known he was infringing.[54]

A primary infringer — whoever copies, performs, broadcasts, or does any other act reserved to the copyright owner — can sometimes reduce his liability where the relevant copyright was not registered at the Copyright Office at the time of infringement. The defendant who proves he was "not aware of and had no reasonable ground for suspecting that copyright subsisted" in the item will be liable only to an injunction[55] and, perhaps, the obligation to deliver up infringing stock for destruction. He will have no monetary liability (including liability for statutory damages), except for any order for costs the court may make.

This defence is worded and interpreted so narrowly that few defendants have raised it successfully. Purity of mind or intent counts for little; ignorance or mistake of law for even less. The user does not succeed by showing he did not think he was infringing, or that everybody else is doing likewise "so I thought it was all right" (the *Cosi Fan Tutte* defence).[56] He must show that he did not know and could not reasonably have suspected that the work had copyright. Asking for permission — or getting it from the wrong person — works against him, for why seek permission except if one already suspected there was copyright? And any initial innocence disappears for the future once the user is alerted to facts that should make him suspect the work had copyright.[57]

Courts have sometimes said that potential users ought to assume that anything arguably within the *Copyright Act* is probably protected, at least where the material is not so ancient that the right must surely have expired. This approach seems excessive if applied across the board. Copyright has expanded so quickly and so far from its tradi-

---

54   *C Act*, above note 1, ss. 27(2) & 27.1. See sections A(10), "Distributing and Importing Infringing Copies: Secondary Infringement," and A(10)(c), "Exclusive Book Distribution," in chapter 5.

55   *C Act*, *ibid.*, s. 39.

56   Section A(3), "Customary Practices," in chapter 7.

57   *De Montigny v. Cousineau*, [1950] S.C.R. 297 at 312.

tional arena that many would be surprised to learn what it does now cover. What a user may reasonably assume must depend on the subject matter and the experience of ordinary people in similar situations. For example, an advertising agency might reasonably assume that logos are subject to copyright because it regularly deals with them, but an ordinary householder might be surprised. However, if the logo had a copyright notice or symbol or an author's name clearly associated with it, even an ingenuous householder might suspect that some right like copyright existed in the work. The defence of innocence would then be unavailable, even if this particular defendant was not alerted by the marking.

Only the occasional Candide, cryptomnesiac, or employee following superior orders will likely succeed with this defence. People whose daily business involves handling copyright material — newspapers, publishers, advertising agencies, libraries — will hardly ever succeed with it. Nor will corporations of any substance. It is not enough to tender the office simpleton to say he knew nothing about copyright. Only evidence of pervasive and understandable ignorance among relevant management personnel about the copyright status of the material in question may suffice.[58]

3) Punitive Damages

The main object of damages is to compensate the victim, but it is not the only object. Punitive damages can be awarded, as for any civil wrong, against a deliberate infringer who has behaved in a particularly appalling manner. The award marks society's disapproval of egregious conduct, deters its repetition, and generally teaches the world that infringement does not pay. Prime candidates for punitive awards in copyright cases have included the video store that deliberately dubbed tapes for rental and the employee who disloyally photocopied his employer's confidential machine drawings to use in a competing business.[59] Deliberate conduct that does not warrant a punitive award may indirectly cause compensatory damages to be awarded rather more liberally than otherwise.

---

58 *Mansell* v. *Star Printing & Publishing Co.*, [1937] 4 D.L.R. 1 at 8 (P.C.); *Gribble* v. *Manitoba Free Press Co. Ltd.*, [1931] 3 W.W.R. 570 (Man. C.A.); *Global Upholstery Co. Ltd.* v. *Galaxy Office Furniture Ltd.* (1976), 29 C.P.R. (2d) 145 at 159–61 (Fed. T.D.); *Bulman Group Ltd.* v. *"One Write" Accounting Systems Ltd.* (1982), 62 C.P.R. (2d) 149 at 156 (Fed. T.D.); *Slumber-Magic Adjustable Bed Co.* v. *Sleep-King Adjustable Bed Co.* (1985), 3 C.P.R. (3d) 81 (B.C.S.C.).

59 *Profekta*, above note 46 at 372–73; *Schauenburg*, above note 22 at 747.

The trial judge's decision whether or not to make a punitive award will be given due respect by an appeal court, but appeal judges have modified trial awards that seemed to them too high or too low, or have imposed a punitive award where they think the trial judge wrongly failed to do so. A punitive award should, however, not be considered until the court has decided how much a defendant has to pay in compensation, whether damages or an account of profits. Only then may one know whether an additional award is needed to concentrate the defendant's mind on the fact of its bad behaviour.[60]

The usual range of punitive awards in Canada is between $5000 and $50,000, and copyright cases have attracted their fair share. The publishing company that did not bother to get copyright clearance for an anthology it published and which then, denying any infringement until just before trial, cavalierly continued to sell the book over the copyright owner's complaints, had a punitive damages award of $20,000 against it upheld on appeal.[61] Punitive damages may be awarded even where the defendant has made an overall loss from its wrong. The fact that the defendant may have profited beyond what it has to pay in damages can be a reason to make a punitive award and so teach the defendant that infringement does not pay.[62] But the Act provides the same lesson against even an innocent copyright infringer because a special provision allows the court to award the total of both the plaintiff's loss and any non-overlapping profits the defendant made.[63] Copyright policy seems designed to prevent all infringers, whether innocent or not, from profiting from their wrong. A punitive award is only one means of achieving that goal.

4) Statutory Damages

For reasons to do more with lobbying than logic, copyright holders have long had better statutory remedies than the owners of any other form of property, let alone intellectual property. Even the first English copyright law of 1710 included a "penny-a-sheet" rule, under which infringers had to pay damages of a halfpenny to the Crown and a halfpenny to the copyright owner for each infringing sheet found in their possession. The British *Copyright Act* of 1911, followed in 1921 by

---

60   *Imperial Oil Ltd v. Lubrizol Corp* (1996), 67 C.P.R. (3d) 1 (Fed. C.A.).
61   *Prise*, above note 44. The copyright owner and author got $10,000 each, on top of substantial compensatory damages.
62   *Profekta*, above note 46 at 373.
63   *C Act*, above note 1, s. 35. See section E, "Account of Profits," in this chapter.

Canada, continued this tradition by fictionally making infringing copies the property of the copyright owner, who could recover possession of them or obtain damages equivalent to their full market value if they were sold. Under this theory, the copyright owner of a drawing engraved without authority onto a gold medallion would become the owner of the medallion and would be entitled to its full price if the article were sold.[64] The United Kingdom repealed this law in 1988 because of criticism about its punitive effects. Canada followed suit in the *1997 Act*, but, in doing so, as of 1 October 1999, replaced one form of punitive relief with another, this time drawn from the United States: the remedy of "statutory damages."

What pressing problem the new remedy was supposed to cure is unclear. Presumably, the present remedies must have been thought insufficient to deter infringement or too difficult or costly to enforce, although supporting data for such arguments are conspicuously lacking. In any event, the wheel has come full circle, for the lineage of the U.S. remedy that Canada has copied, like the remedy it replaced, can be traced directly back to the eighteenth-century "penny-a-sheet" English rule.[65]

The new remedy is a substitute for compensatory damages and an account of profits, but not for punitive damages.[66] The court must, on the claimant's request, award statutory damages from between $500 to $20,000 for all infringements involved in a proceeding, subject only to certain exceptions to be discussed below. The actual amount is left to the court's discretion: whatever it thinks "just."[67] In the United States, the award cannot be made unless the relevant copyrights were registered when the infringements occurred, but registration is not a precondition in Canada.

Because statutory damages may be partly punitive — for example, $200 is the minimum price for innocently faxing a newspaper clipping to a friend — the preconditions for the award should be strictly proved. Ambiguities in the Act's language should be interpreted in a

---

64   *Infabrics Ltd.* v. *Jaytex Ltd.* (1981), [1982] A.C. 1 (H.L.) [*Infabrics*]; compare *JCL*, above note 53. See also section F, "Delivery and Seizure," in this chapter.

65   *Copyright Act*, 17 U.S.C. [*Copyright Act 1976*], § 504(c), as amended in 1999 to increase the bottom award to $750 and the top to $30,000; *Feltner* v. *Columbia Pictures Television Inc.*, 523 U.S. 340 (1998).

66   *C Act*, above note 1, ss. 38.1(1) & (7).

67   *C Act, ibid.*, s. 38.1(1). The trial court's assessment may be upset on appeal only where an error of law or an abuse of discretion has occurred.

way that minimizes potential unfairness to defendants.[68] Unfairness to the claimant — for example, because he could have got more had he sued for compensatory damages — is irrelevant. Statutory damages are for the claimant to choose from a long list of remedies. Each remedy has its advantages and disadvantages. A claimant cannot complain in hindsight that one remedy might have worked better for him than another. Any injustice is, in any event, minimized by the claimant's ability to elect statutory damages at any time before final judgment. A claimant who is dissatisfied with the monetary relief awarded after the court has heard evidence of what he lost and of what the defendant gained may, even at this late stage, presumably refuse the relief and opt instead for statutory damages, so long as final judgment has not yet been formally entered.

Calculating statutory damages has proved an inexact science in the United States, and Canada will not likely be any different. The process is much like fixing fines for criminal offences, except the money goes to the claimant instead of the state. The court must look at all relevant factors to decide on the right sum. The good or bad faith of the defendant, the parties' conduct before and during the proceedings, and the need to deter infringement of the copyright in question will all be examined.[69] Evidence of the claimant's actual loss and of the infringer's actual gains is regularly considered in the United States, and such material should also be relevant in Canada. The foolish infringer of modest means, who candidly admits his folly and promises not to repeat it, will likely face an award around the $500 end of the range for a relatively trivial infringement. The $20,000 end of the range is for deliberate infringers of more valuable rights, especially those deep-pocketed defendants who try to wear claimants down through obstruction.

Some details of the scheme now follow, particularly those relating to multiple defendants, multiple infringements, and multiple items in a single medium (e.g., a CD-ROM). Instances where the $20,000 ceiling can be exceeded and where the $500 may be lowered are noted. The different schemes applicable to non-payment of blank audio recording media levies and musical performance and telecommunication right royalties are then examined. Finally, exceptions to the scheme are noted.

---

68 Compare *Canusa Records Inc. v. Blue Crest Music Inc.* (1976), 30 C.P.R. (2d) 11 at 13 (Fed. C.A.), and *JCL*, above note 53 at 41–44, on the approach to s. 38 of the *C Act, ibid.*, before that section was repealed by *An Act to Amend the Copyright Act*, S.C. 1997, c. 24 [*1997 Act*].

69 *C Act, ibid.*, s. 38.1(5).

a) Multiple Defendants

Only one award may be made where two or more infringers are liable jointly and severally for the same infringement.[70] A claimant cannot multiply awards by suing each partner of an infringing firm or each officer of an infringing corporation, even though the partners and officers may also be jointly and severally liable for the infringement.

b) Multiple Infringements

Only one award may be made for "all infringements involved in the proceedings, with respect to any one work or other subject-matter."[71] The number of copyrights or infringements involved in the same proceeding seems irrelevant. This rule will likely cause difficulties. Suppose, for example, that a wholesale merchant sells, over the space of three months, one million T-shirts, each carrying the unauthorized image of Mickey Mouse in a different pose. Is the "one work" the Mickey Mouse character or each different copyright version of it? In a similar case in the United States, Mickey Mouse was considered to be only the one work, even though Mickey's pose differed on various shirts and different copyrights may technically have been violated.[72] In the case postulated, Disney could therefore get only a maximum $20,000 statutory damages in Canada against the merchant in the same proceedings, despite the large number of infringements.

Suppose, on the other hand, that three television stations broadcast the television series *This Hour Has Twenty-Two Minutes* without authority. Station 1 broadcasts six different episodes, one per week for six consecutive weeks. Station 2 broadcasts the same episode six times in a single day. Station 3 broadcasts the same six episodes as Station 1, but consecutively over three hours on the same night. The copyright holder brings three separate actions against the stations and elects statutory damages against each. Presumably, the three actions will be treated as three separate proceedings, not just one.[73] Against Station 1, the holder can get $120,000 maximum, since each of the six episodes is a different work. Against Station 2, the holder should get only $20,000 maximum, since

---

70   *C Act, ibid.*, s. 38.1(1).

71   *C Act, ibid.*, s. 38.1(1).

72   *Walt Disney Co. v. Powell*, 14 U.S.P.Q.2d 1160 (D.C. Cir. 1990); *Phillips v. Kidsoft L.L.C.*, 52 U.S.P.Q.2d 1102 at 1106–7 (D.C. Md. 1999).

73   If the three stations were owned by the same person, the copyright holder could bring one action, but the remainder of the analysis holds.

the number of times the same work is infringed is irrelevant. Against Station three, the holder should get $120,000 maximum, as for Station 1.[74]

Strategic behaviour by either claimant or infringer should not affect these results. For instance, Station 3 might plausibly argue that a three-hour *This Hour Has Twenty-Two Minutes* fest is really only one work; why should the station be worse off than if it had broadcast the same episode six times consecutively over three hours? The obvious counter is that the disparate result, however arbitrary, is what the Act dictates. The Act intends that what is in essence a single complaint should be brought and resolved expeditiously in one proceeding. Courts may have to be on guard against strategies intended to improve a copyright holder's chances of recovery, such as bringing six separate actions against Station 2 or transferring the relevant copyright to different affiliates during the broadcast day.

c) Multiple Items in a Single Medium

A work such as an encyclopedia on CD-ROM may have its own copyright as a compilation. The compilation may include hundreds of other works, performances, sound clips, and broadcast material, each with its own separate copyright requiring a licence for use in the CD-ROM. Someone who copies the CD-ROM without authority could be potentially liable for millions of dollars in statutory damages to the multiple copyright owners of the included material.

The Act cures this potential hardship by removing the $500 floor where more than one work or other subject matter is included in a single medium, if fixing even $500 per item would produce a sum "grossly out of proportion to the infringement."[75] In other words, the infringer should not have to pay much more for infringing one CD-ROM with multiple copyright owners than he would have had to pay if the compiler had owned all the copyrights. The figure the court will fix for each included item will be somewhat arbitrary, but the policy is to prefer rough justice over the expense involved in more precisely apportioning what fraction of the CD-ROM's value can be attributed to individual items.[76]

d) Increases

In the United States, deliberate infringement can lift the maximum award to US$150,000 (before 1999, US$100,000). This rule has not

---

74   *Twin Peaks Productions Inc. v. Publications International Ltd.*, 996 F.2d 1366 (2d Cir. 1993).

75   *C Act*, above note 1, s. 38.1(5).

76   See section D(2)(d), "Apportioning Damages," in this chapter.

been imported into Canada. Instead, the statutory ceiling of Can$20,000 remains constant, but the court retains jurisdiction to award additional punitive damages against those deliberate infringers for whom $20,000 is mere pin money.[77] The only ceiling is the good sense of the court, checked where appropriate by appeal courts.

e) Decreases

The statutory floor of $500 may be lowered in two situations: where the defendant is innocent or where multiple items are included in a single medium.

i) Innocent Defendants

Similarly to the United States, an award of as little as $200 may be made against a defendant who proves she was unaware and had no reasonable grounds to believe she had infringed copyright.[78] A defendant who does not turn up to court cannot expect this indulgence. A default judgment for the minimum $500 may be issued, unless the court has other evidence of the defendant's purity of mind. On the other hand, the simple employee who mindlessly follows orders may qualify for a reduced award, as may the small business run by newcomers who know nothing of copyright.

The claimant's conduct or other equitable reasons may preclude some claims. For example, a defendant may consent to an injunction without admitting any past infringement. If the claimant calls no evidence, no basis exists on which to award any, let alone statutory, damages.[79]

ii) Multiple Items in Single Medium

Where a single medium, such as a CD-ROM or other compilation, houses more than one work or other subject matter, an innocent defendant may be liable for less than $200 per item if that award would be "grossly out of proportion" to the infringement.[80] The same factors that make a $500 per item award grossly disproportionate against a non-innocent defendant also apply here.[81]

---

77   C Act, above note 1, s. 38.1(7).

78   C Act, ibid., s. 38.1(2). The test of innocence that avoids all monetary relief, including statutory damages, is much stricter: see section D(2)(e), "Defendant's Innocence," in this chapter.

79   D.C. Comics Inc. v. Mini Gift Shop, 15 U.S.P.Q.2d 1888 (2d Cir. 1990) (flea markets and gift shops selling unauthorized Batman clothing).

80   C Act, above note 1, s. 38.1(3).

81   Section D(4)(c), "Multiple Items in a Single Medium," in this chapter.

f) Debts Involving Music Royalties

Special provisions apply to the non-payment of blank audio recording media levies to the appropriate collecting society, and to the non-payment of royalties to SOCAN and the societies administering public performance and telecommunication rights for performers and record companies.

i) Blank Audio Recording Media Levy

Non-payment of this levy makes the defaulter liable for five times the unpaid sum.[82] There is no requirement that the creditor "elect" this remedy, although the society should indicate in its pleading that it intends to ask for a multiplied amount. The court can decide not to multiply the amount due at all, or it may apply whatever multiplier up to five it thinks just. The relevant factors it will take into account are much the same as those in the standard statutory damages scheme: the defendant's good or bad faith, the parties' conduct before and during the proceedings, and the need to deter non-payment.[83] The deliberate obstructer will face more unpleasant consequences than the defendant whose remittance got lost in the mail or who wrongly, but genuinely, disputes liability.

ii) Musical Performing and Telecommunication Rights

The simplicity of the blank audio recording media levy scheme is missing when one comes to deal with unpaid royalties for musical performing or telecommunication rights.[84] The potential for injustice here is also greater.

The creditor can elect statutory damages of three to ten times the royalties payable, instead of claiming the royalties as a debt or asking for compensatory or punitive damages or an account of profits. The actual multiplier between three and ten is left to the court's sense of justice in the light of the usual factors, including the defendant's good or bad faith, the parties' conduct before and during the proceedings, and the need to deter infringements of the copyright in question.[85]

Why the maximum multiplier should be ten, instead of the five that appears for the blank audio recording media levy, is unclear. Equally unclear is why, again unlike the position with the blank audio recording media levy, a minimum multiplier was needed at all and why

---

82 Section B(14)(c), "Blank Audio Recording Media Levy," in chapter 7.

83 *C Act*, above note 1, ss. 88(2) & (4).

84 Sections A(4), "Public Performance," and A(5), "Telecommunication," in chapter 5.

85 *C Act*, above note 1, ss. 38.1(4), (5), & (7).

it is as high as three. The result is that a debtor may apparently be liable for at least treble the unpaid royalties, however innocent and reasonable was her belief that she was not infringing copyright, and however dilatory the creditor was in pursuing its claim.[86] Yet it seems impossible to believe that Parliament meant treble royalties to be awarded to a creditor who sat back and watched the royalty bill steadily mount before making its claim, or against a debtor whose royalty remittance was lost in the mail or who genuinely disputed liability.

A provision that causes such unjust results must be strictly interpreted. A court might, for example, conclude that the creditor can elect multiple royalties only at the end of the hearing, after all the evidence is in and the debtor has had an opportunity to admit liability and to pay up in light of the evidence and the arguments presented. The right to elect would thus be lost if the debtor paid the sum owing, plus any due interest, any time before then.[87]

g) Exceptions

Statutory damages are not available against parallel importers, including those importing books on a Canadian exclusive distributor's list, if the item was initially made with the foreign copyright owner's consent.[88]

Such damages are also unavailable against non-profit educational institutions for not paying royalties or not observing conditions for off-air recording.[89] Non-profit educational institutions and LAMs with a licence from a reprographic collective are also exempt from statutory damages for copying material outside the collective's inventory. The offended copyright owner may recover from such institutions only a fee similar to that charged by the collective.[90] Similarly, a copyright owner who does not belong to a cable retransmission collective cannot claim more than the tariff fixed by the Copyright Board for retransmissions. Statutory damages seem unavailable.[91]

---

86 The innocence defence in the *C Act, ibid.*, s. 38.1(2), applies only to elections made under s. 38.1(1), the $500-to-$20,000 scheme. The societies' scheme appears in s. 38.1(4).

87 *C Act, ibid.*, s. 38(4), significantly does not say, as *ibid.*, s. 38.1(1), does, that the creditor's election may be made "at any time before final judgment." Since elections, once made, are irrevocable, the court may decide that only elections in court should count.

88 *C Act, ibid.*, s. 38.1(6)(c).

89 *C Act, ibid.*, ss. 38.1(6)(a), 76(2), & 76(3). See section B(13)(b)(v), "Off-Air Recording," in chapter 7.

90 *C Act, ibid.*, ss. 38.1(6)(b) & 38.2.

91 *C Act, ibid.*, ss. 76(1) & (3).

E. ACCOUNT OF PROFITS

An infringer sometimes profits more than the right-holder loses from an infringement. The latter may then find it convenient to elect to recover the infringer's net gain. This remedy, called an "account of profits," prevents unjust enrichment and deters infringement. This remedy has recently resurged in Canada because (1) it is available even where the claimant can prove no loss; (2) the infringer, instead of the right-holder, has to lay open its books of account and prove what charges against revenue are proper to produce a net profit figure;[92] and (3) the claimant can usually recover compound prejudgment interest at prime rate on those profits.[93] However, there are limitations.

- An account is typically an alternative to damages. In copyright, however, a plaintiff may have both, but double-counting must then be avoided. The plaintiff should not recover both its lost profit and the defendant's net gain on the same unit. Only such part of the profits "that were not taken into account in calculating the damages" are recoverable.[94] The plaintiff may even mix and match remedies. It may recover multiple accounts of profits against multiple infringers in respect of the same goods, or an account against one and damages against another.[95] An infringer's total liability on an account of profits is its net profit from its infringing business. So the maximum liability on a defendant who makes $100,000 from infringing six copyrights held by different owners is $100,000. If only one owner sues and if the profit derived from each copyright is roughly equal, the infringer's bill on an account should be only around $17,000, for "there is only one profits 'pot.'"[96]
- An infringer is liable for only such profits as the court thinks just.[97] The court may therefore deny an account in its discretion — for

---

92 C Act, ibid., s. 35(2), restates equity practice.

93 Reading & Bates Construction Co. v. Baker Energy Resources Corp. (1994), [1995] 1 F.C. 483 (C.A.). Generally, see C.L. Kirby, "Accounting of Profits: The Canadian Experience" (1993) 7 I.P.J. 263; M. Gronow, "Restitution for Breach of Confidence" (1996) 10 I.P.J. 219.

94 C Act, above note 1, s. 35(1).

95 Ray Plastics Ltd. v. Canadian Tire Corp. (1995), 62 C.P.R. (3d) 247 (Ont. Gen. Div.); Catnic Components Ltd. v. C. Evans & Co. (Builders Merchants) Ltd., [1983] F.S.R. 401 at 423 (Pat. Ct.).

96 Celanese International Corp. v. B.P. Chemicals Ltd., [1999] R.P.C. 203 (Pat. Ct.) [Celanese].

97 C Act, above note 1, s. 35(1).

example, if the infringer did not know it was infringing or made no profits, or if the claimant delayed long before suing or was less than candid in presenting its evidence at trial.[98]

- Only "such part of the profits that the infringer has made from the infringement" are recoverable.[99] The starting point is usually net after-tax profits.[100] Beyond that, determining what the infringer gained from the infringement can be controversial. The old story that no movie ever makes a profit — at least for any writer or actor foolish enough to contract for a percentage of the "net"[101] — is not confined to Hollywood and films. Sometimes sales profits have to be apportioned because the infringement was not the main reason for sales.[102] Other times, deductions are disputed. Thus, Canadian courts have often disallowed fixed overheads, but this decision has rightly been condemned elsewhere as punitive on infringers. Any overhead, fixed or variable, that assists the infringement should in principle be deductible.[103]

- What profits were caused by the infringement is a question of fact. Where the trial is bifurcated, the question of whether profits should be apportioned is best considered, with other questions of fact, on the remedy reference.[104] So, for example, a builder whose plans have been infringed by the unauthorized erection of a building cannot ask for the whole profit the infringer made on selling the building. The profit caused by the infringement may be only the increased value of the building that resulted from the use of that design.[105] But infringers cannot reduce or avoid liability by showing they could have achieved the same goal and still have harmed the claimant equally if they had taken a different, but non-infringing, course. Similarly,

---

98 For patent cases, see *Consolboard Inc.* v. *MacMillan Bloedel (Sask.) Ltd.*, [1981] 1 S.C.R. 504, aff'g (1978), 39 C.P.R. (2d) 191 at 220–22 (Fed. T.D.); *Globe-Union Inc.* v. *Varta Batteries Ltd.* (1981), 57 C.P.R. (2d) 254 at 257–58 (Fed. T.D.), aff'd on this point (*sub nom. Johnson Controls Inc.* v. *Varta Batteries Ltd.*) (1984), 80 C.P.R. (2d) 1 at 22 (Fed. C.A.).

99 *C Act*, above note 1, s. 35(1).

100 *Celanese*, above note 96. The court should provide in its order that any tax on the stripped profits that is recovered from Revenue Canada should be disclosed and paid to the claimant.

101 See P. O'Donnell and D. McDougal, *Fatal Subtraction: The Inside Story of Buchwald v. Paramount* (New York: Doubleday, 1992).

102 See section D(2)(d), "Apportioning Damages," in this chapter.

103 *Dart Industries Inc.* v. *Decor Corp. Pty. Ltd.* (1993), 179 C.L.R. 101 (Austl. H.C.), disapproving *Teledyne Industries Inc.* v. *Lido Industrial Products Ltd.* (1982), 68 C.P.R. (2d) 204 (Fed. T.D.).

104 *Lubrizol Corp.* v. *Imperial Oil Ltd.* (1997), 71 C.P.R. (3d) 26 (Fed. C.A.).

105 *Charles Church Developments plc* v. *Cronin*, [1990] F.S.R. 1 at 10 (Ch.).

claimants cannot improve their position by showing that the infringer would have made more profits had it run its business better.[106]

The problem with the remedy of account is less its theory than the cost of working it out. Experts may have to analyze infringers' books, and hearings can run into weeks as infringers demonstrate their unease at competitors' nosing around their confidential information. Nor is the court bound by the figures proffered by the parties. In a recent U.K. patent case, the court rejected both parties' view of what profits the infringer had made. The plaintiff had initially claimed £180 million, while the defendant countered with £4 million. The court awarded just over half a million pounds.[107] Over a century ago a British judge said of this remedy:

> [T]he difficulty of finding out how much profit is attributable to any one source is extremely great — so great that accounts in that form very seldom result in anything satisfactory to anybody. The litigation is enormous, the expense is great, and the time consumed is out of all proportion to the advantage ultimately attained; so much so that in partnership cases I confess I never knew an account in that form worked out with satisfaction to anybody. I believe in almost every case people get tired of it and get disgusted. Therefore, although the law is that a Patentee has a right to elect which course he will take, as a matter of business he would generally be inclined to take an inquiry as to damages, rather than launch upon an inquiry as to profits.[108]

The experience in Canadian patent cases is similar.[109] Simple copyright cases should not attract such strictures, but not all copyright cases are simple. Calculating what profits a film earned may be as labyrinthine an exercise as an accounting in the most tortuous patent case.

F. DELIVERY AND SEIZURE

Like any other holder of an intellectual property right, a copyright holder who obtains an injunction against infringement is usually entitled to an ancillary order requiring the infringer to deliver up any infringing goods in its possession. This removes temptation and makes

---

106   *Celanese*, above note 96.
107   *Ibid.*
108   *Siddell v. Vickers* (1892), 9 R.P.C. 152 at 163 (C.A.).
109   For example, *Beloit Canada Ltd. v. Valmet Oy* (1994), 55 C.P.R. (3d) 433 at 435 (Fed. T.D.), rev'd (1995), above note 52.

injunctive relief fully effective. The goods do not, however, belong to the right-holder. The order commonly allows infringers the option of destroying the goods on oath.[110] The court should make the least disruptive order that protects the claimant's rights. Where goods carry trademarks that infringe copyright, the appropriate order may be to have the offending labels delivered up and any infringing markings obliterated from goods left in the defendant's possession. Similarly, if only part of an item infringes copyright, no order to deliver up the whole item should be made if removing the part can make the item non-infringing.[111]

Two situations should be noted where a copyright or infringing goods may be ordered to be handed over to a claimant to keep as his own.

1) Copyright Created in Breach of Obligation

A constructive trust can be imposed on property to avoid unjust enrichment. Where, for example, a copyright is acquired by using information confidentially entrusted to the acquirer, the defendant may have to hand over the copyright and its gross proceeds to the claimant. Thus, a trust may be imposed in favour of the Crown on the copyright in the memoirs of a secret service agent, if his writings broke obligations of secrecy owed to the Crown. The copyright must, presumably, be transferred to the Crown on demand.[112] Similarly, if the customary law of an aboriginal clan requires that clan members cannot use communal knowledge to make artworks except with the clan's permission, the clan may become equitable owners of the copyright in any work that is so made by a member in breach of this fiduciary duty.[113]

Different issues arise in cases where a criminal exploits his crime by telling or writing an account of it for reward. Victims with a court judgment against the offender may, of course, enforce the judgment in the usual way on the proceeds. They may sometimes be assisted by provincial legislation such as that passed by Ontario in 1994,[114] which

---

110 *Dubiner*, above note 52.

111 Compare *Baxter Travenol Laboratories of Canada Ltd.* v. *Cutter (Can.) Ltd.* (1983), 68 C.P.R. (2d) 179 (Fed. C.A.) (patents).

112 *C Act*, above note 1, s. 89; *A.-G.* v. *Blake*, [1996] 3 W.L.R. 741 at 750 (Ch.), rev'd on other grounds, [1998] 2 W.L.R. 805 (C.A.); *LAC Minerals Ltd.* v. *International Corona Resources Ltd.*, [1989] 2 S.C.R. 574. See also section B(3)(d), "Equitable Assignments and Licences," in chapter 8, and section A(1)(c), "Joint Authors," in chapter 4.

113 *Bulun Bulun* v. *R. & T. Textiles Pty. Ltd.* (1998), 41 I.P.R. 513 at 527ff (Austl. Fed. Ct.).

114 *Victims' Right to Proceeds of Crime Act*, S.O. 1994, c. 39, inspired by "Son-of-Sam" laws enacted since 1977 in the United States.

seeks to make such proceeds more easily available to victims and their families. Common law claims to impress the copyright or the royalties with a constructive trust to prevent a criminal from benefiting from his wrong are, however, unlikely to succeed. Unless the crime was committed specifically to profit later from media exploitation, any copyright or other benefits derived from such exploitation come more from the offender's literary efforts than from the crime. Royalty payments made to an offender are not typically owed by the payer to the victim or his family, nor is the copyright in any work produced by an offender created in breach of any duty he similarly owes. Therefore, although the offender may appear to be "unjustly enriched," the victim or the victim's family will find it difficult directly to recover the benefits because they have not been correspondingly "unjustly deprived" by the offender's enrichment. In short, keeping the copyright or the royalties does not detain anything the offender owed to the victim or the family.[115]

2) Seizure of Infringing Copies

Before the 1997 Act, copies that infringed copyright were deemed to be the property of the copyright owner. The owner could have them delivered up as his own property and could keep them or their whole proceeds on any sale. On this theory, the unauthorized painting of an artistic work onto the side of a supertanker made the copyright owner of the artistic work the owner of the ship. If the ship was sold, its proceeds had to be handed over to the copyright owner![116]

This nonsensical result no longer holds. The copyright owner may still recover possession of all infringing copies and of any plates used or intended to be used for their production, and may also seize them before judgment "as if" the items were his property. But the defendant or anyone else with an interest in the items can apply to the court to have the items destroyed or to have some other appropriate order made. The court will consider all the circumstances, including the relative importance of the infringing items to their substrate and how far they are severable from, or a distinct part of, the substrate.[117] So, no

---

115 A. Young, "'Son of Sam' and His Legislative Offspring: The Constitutionality of Stripping Criminals of Their Literary Profits" (1988) 4 I.P.J. 25; R. Goff & G. Jones, *The Law of Restitution*, 5th ed. (London: Sweet & Maxwell, 1999) c. 38; *Rosenfeldt v. Olson* (1986), 25 D.L.R. (4th) 427 (B.C.C.A.).

116 *Infabrics*, above note 64; see section D(4), "Statutory Damages," in this chapter.

117 *C Act*, above note 1, s. 38.

court would today consider making a gift of the offending supertanker to the copyright owner. The tanker owner might be ordered to paint out the infringing work and to pay some damages, but little else. The damages would certainly not equal the market value of the tanker, as in theory they might have before 1997.[118]

G. REMEDIES FOR INFRINGEMENT OF MORAL RIGHTS

The remedies for moral right infringements are similar to, but less extensive than, those for copyright infringement. Section 34(2) of the *Copyright Act* states that the court "may grant" an author or his estate "all remedies by way of injunction, damages, accounts or delivery up and otherwise that are or may be conferred by law for the infringement of a right." The provision was first introduced in 1988 because of uncertainty about what remedies were available for violations of the delphic moral right provision then in force.[119]

1) Remedies Discretionary

The formula in section 34(2) of the Act mirrors section 34(1) on copyright infringements, except in one respect: section 34(1) states that the copyright owner is "subject to this Act, entitled" to the stated remedies, while section 34(2) states only that the court "may grant" the moral rights owner the specified remedies. The language of section 34(1) thus alerts the reader to the fact that the usual law of remedies is somehow modified for copyright. The sections following section 34 do indeed make various significant changes, from alleviating the plight of the innocent infringer to providing statutory damages and different methods of calculating monetary compensation. These provisions, however, apply explicitly only to copyright, not moral rights.[120]

By contrast, the language of section 34(2) dealing with moral rights — the court "may grant" the specified remedies — suggests that, for moral right infringements, the court has a discretion to decide on what

---

118 *Infabrics*, above note 64; *JCL*, above note 53.
119 D. Vaver, "Authors' Moral Rights in Canada" (1983) 14 I.I.C. 329 at 354–55 & 360.
120 See *C Act*, above note 1, ss. 34.1 to 36, & ss. 38 to 40.

remedies best fit the individual case and on their appropriate extent.[121] The court cannot apply any of the special copyright remedies directly, but may, presumably, apply their underlying policy by analogy.

This difference in approach between sections 34(1) and 34(2) is explicable historically. When moral rights were first introduced into the Act in 1931, the only explicit remedy made available was an injunction for breach of the integrity right. Whether any other remedy was available remained in doubt. Lawmakers were eventually pressed to clarify the situation of moral rights and to extend the standard copyright remedies to such rights.[122]

Section 34(2), as passed in 1988, partially responded to this pressure. It extended to moral rights virtually the full set of copyright remedies. Past experience, however, shed little light on the difficulties that might flow from introducing a rigid system that "entitled" a moral rights owner to all the usual copyright remedies. So, while section 34(2) made all legal and equitable remedies available, their application was left to the discretion of the courts. Judges were left to tailor the nature and extent of the remedies they awarded to avoid any injustice that might arise from the new, more comprehensive, and apparently more intensive moral rights regime.

We now look at how the remedies may work in practice in light of these considerations.

2) Injunction

Like any other claimant, a moral rights owner may seek a final or interlocutory injunction against a continuing infringement. So, for example, a continuing failure to attribute authorship could be rectified by the issue of a mandatory injunction against the offender. An injunction against infringement of works other than the one in suit may also be available, as for copyright.[123]

The best-known example of an interlocutory injunction is the mandatory order issued by an Ontario court in favour of Michael Snow in 1982 against the Eaton Centre in Toronto. The order required the centre's operators to remove wreaths and other Christmas decorations

---

121   Compare *Quebec (Curateur Public)* v. *Syndicat national des employés de l'hôpital St-Ferdinand*, [1996] 3 S.C.R. 211, 138 D.L.R. (4th) 577 at 614–15, on comparable language in the punitive damages provision of the *Charter of Human Rights and Freedoms*, R.S.Q., c. C-12, s. 49.

122   Most recently in 1985 by a parliamentary subcommittee.

123   *C Act*, above note 1, s. 39.1; *Microsoft*, above note 18.

they had put on Snow's Canada geese sculpture for the holiday season.[124] Not all claimants may, however, fare as well as Snow. A little-known author would likely fail to get interlocutory relief because of the difficulty of showing irreparable harm to his honour or reputation. Paradoxically, the same result may occur even if the author is well known. Architect Douglas Cardinal learned this lesson when he tried to prevent additions from being made to a church he had designed. Relief could easily have been refused by analogy with the comparable bar in copyright infringement cases, where no injunction is ever granted to stop a building in mid-construction.[125] Instead, the court stressed that Cardinal had taken no action against earlier alterations made to the church and to other buildings he had designed. Moreover, Cardinal's stature would not fall among those responsible for commissioning architects: "a sophisticated clientele who can readily understand the impact of the St. Mary's project on Mr. Cardinal's reputation."[126] The inference that only authors who have a prickly public persona and a fragile reputation among sophisticates need consider applying for interlocutory relief is unfortunate. Relief should be equally open to a reticent author if his reputation is hurt with any important sector of his market, including the general public.

3) Monetary Awards

Section 34(2) of the Act indicates that damages or an account of profits may be awarded for a moral right infringement. Damages compensate the claimant for his loss, while an account of profits strips the infringer of any gains it made that are attributable to the infringement. The gains are handed over to the claimant.

a) Damages
General, aggravated, and punitive damages — but not statutory damages — should be awarded in much the same way as for copyright infringement.[127] Certainly, if the infringer knew or should have known it was acting improperly, courts may readily decide to exercise their discretion in favour of compensating the claimant for the full amount of his loss, applying the usual rules of recovery in copyright and at

---

124 *Snow v. The Eaton Centre* (1982), 70 C.P.R. (2d) 105 (Ont. H.C.J.).
125 *C Act*, above note 1, s. 40(1).
126 *Cardinal v. Parish of the Immaculate Conception*, [1995] F.C.J. 1609 (T.D.).
127 Section D, "Damages," in this chapter.

common and civil law.[128] For example, damages for violating an artist's integrity right by defacing the work could include the cost of repair.

Damages for non-attribution may be big or small, depending on the case. They may be small for the architect whose name does not appear on plans submitted to a municipality for planning permission, if the municipality does not care whose name appears on plans.[129] Damages may be greater for the architect whose building is constructed anonymously, contrary to the usual practice of placing an advertisement containing his name on the site. The lost opportunity to promote his name and attract business may be substantial. Substantial damages could also be awarded against a professor who fails to attribute a student paper that is included in a university coursepack. Quite apart from the distress caused by the failure to have his work credited, the student might have referred in his résumé to this endorsement of his work, and so may have made himself more attractive on the job market. Some compensation can be awarded for the deprivation of this advantage.[130]

b) Account of Profits

A court may, in its discretion, award an infringer to account for and hand over the profits he made from a moral rights violation.[131] We may, however, expect such awards to be less frequently sought or granted than for other intellectual property infringements, for two reasons.

First, when theorizing about remedies, courts tend to assimilate copyright and other intellectual property infringements with thefts of property and say that, just as a thief must hand over the proceeds of his wrongful sale, so must the infringer hand over the profits of his wrongful exploitation of intellectual property. Moral rights are, however, personal rights, not property. Courts are disinclined to award an account of profits for infringements of personal rights — for example, defamation — although they do sometimes indirectly insinuate an offender's gains into their calculation of the claimant's damages.

---

128   See *Clairol International Corp.* v. *Thomas Supply & Equipment Co.*, [1968] 2 Ex. C.R. 552 at 577, on the comparable discretion in s. 22(2) of the *Trade-marks Act*, R.S.C. 1985, c. T-13. See also section G(3)(d), "Infringer's Knowledge or Innocence," in this chapter.

129   *Blair* v. *Osborne & Tomkins*, [1971] 2 Q.B. 78 (C.A.).

130   Compare *Goulet* v. *Marchand* (18 September 1985), (Que. S.C.) [unreported] with *Boudreau*, above note 9. See also *Ateliers Tango argentin Inc.* v. *Festival d'Espagne et d'Amérique latine Inc.*, [1997] R.J.Q. 3030 (S.C.), where $2000 was awarded to a photographer for violation of his attribution right.

131   Section E, "Account of Profits," in this chapter.

Second, many moral right infringements will not yield their infringer any gain. Suppose a vandal defaces an artist's painting and blanks out her signature. The offender has certainly harmed the artist and should compensate her for infringing her integrity and attribution rights. But the vandal does not usually gain economically from his act. One may, no doubt, envisage a case where two paintings are in competition for a prize and the vandal is the competing artist, who corners the prize the other would have received. Apart from such special cases, moral right infringements are more likely to recall Desdemona's plaint: "He that filches from me my good name / Robs me of that which not enriches him, / And makes me poor indeed."[132] Many moral right infringements impoverish the author without enriching the offender. No account of profits may be ordered where there is no profit to account for.

c) Damages and Account May Be Cumulative

Whether a claimant can seek both damages and an account of profits simultaneously from the same infringer is unclear. A special rule allows a copyright holder to do so.[133] This rule departs from the traditional position, under which damages and an account are alternative remedies: a claimant must elect between them and cannot have both. A court dealing with a moral right infringement may nonetheless be inclined to apply the copyright rule by analogy because the traditional rule is outmoded and illogical.[134] But since, as we have seen, an account will rarely be appropriate for a moral right infringement, the question whether cumulation is possible seems largely theoretical.

d) Infringer's Knowledge or Innocence

Punitive damages may also be awarded if the infringement was malicious or otherwise egregious. Such an award might be thought particularly appropriate in cases such as that against a university professor who deliberately plagiarized a student paper and used it without attribution for personal gain. Somewhat surprisingly, however, punitive damages were denied against either the professor or the university that had dealt only perfunctorily with the student's complaint.[135]

---

132   Shakespeare's *Othello*, Act II, scene iii.
133   *C Act*, above note 1, s. 35(1).
134   See D. Vaver, "Civil Liability for Taking or Using Trade Secrets in Canada" (1981) 8 Can. Bus. L.J. 253 at 297–300; *SOCAN v. 348803 Alberta Ltd.* (1997), 79 C.P.R. (3d) 449 (Fed. T.D.).
135   *Boudreau*, above note 9 at 336.

H. LIMITATION PERIODS

1) Civil Cases

The limitation period for bringing actions for copyright or moral right infringement is three years.[136] The three years starts running from when the claimant knew or could reasonably have been expected to know of the infringement. The period may be further postponed if the infringer acted secretly or deliberately concealed the wrong.[137] Suppose an infringing photograph is published in a newspaper on 1 September 1998. If the copyright holder learned of the infringement that day, his right to sue expires on midnight, 1 September 2001. If he first learned of the infringement on 1 October 1998, the cutoff date is still in 2001, but it could be anywhere between 1 September and 1 October, depending on when the claimant could reasonably have been expected to have learned of it. This is a question of fact. There is no cap on how far back the act occurred. Infringements happening twenty or more years ago may be sued on now if the claimant could not reasonably have found out about them earlier, or if they were fraudulently concealed.

If any infringements go back (say) six years before suit, the claimant will get compensation — damages or an account of profits — only for what the infringer did in the last three years. The infringer escapes for the earlier three years.[138] The limitation period is not, however, critical in two cases. First, delays within the period may affect the discretionary grant of equitable relief, such as injunctions and accounts of profits. Delay may, for example, cause enough injustice to a defendant to prompt a court to deny an injunction and even truncate the period for which the infringer must account for his profits. Second, time-

---

136   *C Act*, above note 1, s. 41.

137   *Underwriters' Survey Bureau Ltd.* v. *Massie & Renwick Ltd.*, [1940] S.C.R. 218; *M.(K.)* v. *(M.(H.)*, [1992] 3 S.C.R. 6 (fraudulent concealment prevents time from running).

138   *Black* v. *Imperial Book Co.* (1903), 5 O.L.R. 184 at 196, aff'd (1904), 8 O.L.R. 9 (C.A.), aff'd (1905), 35 S.C.R. 488; *Nicol* v. *Barranger*, [1917–1923] MacG. Cop. Cas. 219 at 228–29, rev'd on other grounds, *ibid.*, 230 (1921, C.A.) [*Nicol*]; *J.M. Voith GmbH* v. *Beloit Corp.* (1993), 47 C.P.R. (3d) 448 (Fed. T.D.) (patents); *Smith* v. *Clay* (1767), 3 Bro. C.C. 639 at 640, 29 E.R. 743 at 744. *Milliken & Co.* v. *Interface Flooring Systems (Canada) Inc.* (1996), 75 C.P.R. (3d) 481 at 489 (Fed. T.D.) [*Milliken*], suggesting all equitable claims are unaffected by the limitation statute, is wrong: D. Vaver, "Limitations in Intellectual Property: 'The Time is Out of Joint'" (1994) 73 Can. Bar Rev. 451 at 459–60 ["Limitations"].

barred infringements can be used to support a claim for a *quia timet* injunction against a threatened infringement.[139]

The usual common law and equitable principles that apply generally to limitation statutes also apply to *Copyright Act* limitations.[140] Once the limitation period has run, a defendant has a vested right freeing him of the claim. This right may, however, be waived by agreement or otherwise, and cannot be asserted by a defendant who fails to plead it properly and timeously.[141] A defendant cannot have a time-barred claim struck before filing a defence, since the court will not assume that the defendant will properly plead the limitation. Once the defendant does properly plead it, the limitation point may be argued and decided in advance of any trial. If the point is good, no trial is needed.

A limitation defence is not easily waived or barred. For example, claimants who negotiate with an infringer without first filing legal proceedings act at their own peril. The infringer need not say that a limitation period is looming. Of course, if the infringer does or says something that leads the claimant reasonably to believe the limitation defence will not be relied on, the infringer may be bound by his representation. But an offer of settlement or even an admission of liability may not in itself bar a defendant's right to plead a limitation defence.[142]

2) Criminal Cases

An indictment for criminal proceedings for copyright infringement may be laid at any time. The rule is different for summary proceedings. For moral rights infringements, summary proceedings must be brought within six months.[143] For copyright infringements, this six-month period was extended in 1997 to two years.[144] In both instances, the period starts running when the offence is committed. The civil rule, that

---

139 *Warner Brothers–Seven Arts Inc. v. CESM-TV Ltd.* (1971), 65 C.P.R. 215 (Ex. Ct.); *Milliken, ibid.*

140 Apart from immaterial changes made in 1988 and 1997, s. 41 is copied from s. 10 of the *Copyright Act* of 1911 (U.K.), itself patterned on the wording of s. 3 of the *Limitation Act* of 1623, 21 Jac. I, c. 16 (Eng.): see "Limitations," above note 138.

141 *C Act*, above note 1, s. 41(2); *Nicol*, above note 138; *Tolofson v. Jensen* (1994), 120 D.L.R. (4th) 289 at 319 & 322 (S.C.C.).

142 *Milliken*, above note 138; *Maracle v. Travellers Indemnity Co. of Canada* (1991), 80 D.L.R. (4th) 652 (S.C.C.) (insurance).

143 *C Act*, above note 1, s. 43; *Criminal Code*, R.S.C. 1985, c. C-46, s. 786(2). See section A, "General Features," in chapter 6.

144 *C Act, ibid.*, s. 42(5).

a limitation period may be postponed to the time when the claimant could reasonably have discovered the infringement, does not apply.[145]

FURTHER READINGS

BLACKMAN, S.H., "Alternative Dispute Resolution in Commercial Intellectual Property Disputes" (1998) 47 Amer. U. L. Rev. 1709

BROWN, R.S., "Civil Remedies for Intellectual Property Invasions: Themes and Variations" (1992) 55:2 L. & Contemp. Probs. 45

CAIRNS, D.J.A., The Remedies for Trademark Infringement (Toronto: Carswell, 1988)

HAYES, M.S., "Copyright Infringement on the Internet," in M. Racicot et al., The Cyberspace Is Not a "No Law Land": A Study of the Issues of Liability for Content Circulating on the Internet (February 1997), available at <http://strategis.ic.gc.ca>

KLIPPERT, G.B., Unjust Enrichment (Toronto: Butterworths, 1983)

MADDAUGH, P.D., & J.D. McCAMUS, The Law of Restitution (Aurora: Canada Law Book, 1990)

PATERSON, R.K., "Directors' Liability for Infringements — Of Drams and Delicts: White Horse Distillers Ltd. v. Gregson Associates Ltd." (1985) 1 I.P.J. 369

PURI, K., "Anton Piller Relief — Palatable in Europe?" (1995) 8 I.P.J. 347

SHARPE, R.J., Injunctions and Specific Performance, 2d ed. (Aurora: Canada Law Book, 1992)

VAVER, D., "Infringing Copyright in a Competitor's Advertising: Damages 'At Large' Can Be Large Damages" (1984) 1 I.P.J. 186

WADDAMS, S.J., The Law of Damages, 2d ed. (Aurora: Canada Law Book, 1991)

---

145   See section H(1), "Civil Cases," in this chapter. The omission in C Act, ibid., s. 43(5), of wording comparable to ibid., s. 41(1), is conclusive.

CHAPTER 10

CONCLUSION

Copyright law, as part of intellectual property law, seems ripe for wholesale reconsideration, both nationally and internationally. One might start with its fundamental premise: that the system of rights it establishes enhances the goals of desirable innovation, creativity, and the widest distribution of ideas, information, products, and technology in the most efficient and, generally, the best way. This premise is of course empirically unprovable, even if all agree on what "best way" means. It assumes that throwing a private property right around every activity with potential value in exchange and creating a market in such rights ultimately benefits not only the right-holders but also, in equal or at least reasonable measure, the communities of which they form part. It further assumes that this best of all possible worlds can exist only if the property/market model is the sole mechanism to achieve the stated goals, and that no other system — even one that includes the model as one component — could be devised that would benefit the community more.

In fact, intellectual property, in general, and copyright, in particular, already function within a mixed system of public- and private-sector policies that affect cultural and economic behaviour. These policies include tax incentives, government contracts, direct subsidies and charitable contributions to arts, regional development funding, honours and prizes, and social rewards for generally approved activities. The idea that intellectual property or copyright should dominate discourse, to the reduction or elimination of all else, is simply one ideology. It cannot be true of all times and places. It is not true of Canada today. Whether it should be is a different question.

Even if copyright, as part of intellectual property law, is accepted as the best method of stimulating high levels of innovation and social progress, the way it operates in Canada hardly achieves these goals or seems compatible with the aspirations of a modern liberal democracy. The law is not well drafted, is poorly integrated with other intellectual property laws, and cannot be understood except by specialized lawyers. The rhetoric of authors and creators may be employed, but the *Copyright Act* itself seems designed more by big business for big business. Smaller operations and the general public are left to the side as passive viewers — to be affected, but not themselves to affect anything.

Intellectual property rights can be fiendishly expensive to enforce. A few years ago a doyen of the intellectual property bar pointed with apparent pride to the fact that Canadian patent litigation was five to ten times cheaper than its U.S. counterparts. Still, bills in the hundreds of thousands of dollars were "reasonably common," although it was "very rare" for fees and disbursements to exceed $1 million.[1] Copyright litigation is usually less complicated and less expensive than patent litigation but, in practice, it is sufficiently complicated and expensive for mainly big business to be able to afford it. The aggrieved individual author or performer rarely has the means to sue, unless he is supported by an organization with a deep pocket or unless he finds a lawyer who is prepared to take the case for little or nothing.

Intellectual property litigation has been said to be "by and large . . . the most technical both in terms of the factual subject matter and the law itself," even when compared to tax, constitutional, and competition law cases.[2] Factual complexity may be largely unavoidable, although less "technical" law could reduce the range and hence the expense of factual inquiries. It is important, however, to understand what is meant by "technical" in this context. The laws are certainly hard to read and understand; but, even when explained, the results they produce hardly square with the way many ordinary, law-abiding citizens think and act. To tell these people, as copyright owners periodically do, that it is unlawful to record a television broadcast without first obtaining clearance from umpteen right-holders is to invite disbelieving stares. This is but one example of the lack of a comprehensible

---

1   G.F. Henderson/Consumer & Corporate Affairs Canada, *Intellectual Property: Litigation, Legislation & Education: A Study of the Canadian Intellectual Property and Litigation System* (Ottawa: Consumer & Corporate Affairs, 1991) at 17.

2   *Ibid.*

and coherent moral centre which makes much of intellectual property law so "technical" and unpersuasive.

We can now review some of these "technicalities."

A. DRAFTING STANDARDS

A degree of mystique and uncertainty in the part of intellectual property law regulated by the common law may be thought tolerable because of the much-vaunted benefits flowing from the common law's adaptability and capacity for growth. Mysticism and uncertainty should not, however, be a feature of laws passed by Parliament. Yet anyone reading the *Copyright Act* for the first time is struck by its complexity and tortuousness. This is not a "user-friendly" law, even for lawyers. The Act's British progenitor, passed in 1710, was, according to its preamble, "for the encouragement of learned men to compose and write useful books." Most such men and women would be stumped were they to try to read today's *Copyright Act*. Almost anything written, drawn, recorded, or published virtually anywhere in the world has, in some way, copyright in Canada: yet that simple thought takes pages and pages of labyrinthine provisions to express.

These internal deficiencies are magnified by inconsistencies among the *Copyright Act* and the intellectual property statutes. Inconsistency is undesirable intrinsically, as well as practically, for much technology crosses rights. A single piece of computer technology may involve patents, trade-marks, copyrights, integrated circuit topography rights, and industrial design rights — quite apart from common law rights. Purely technical issues relating to the creation or transfer of rights should not depend arbitrarily on what right is involved. Two examples will suffice: registration and limitation. All the intellectual property statutes have registries for recording title, yet the provisions for registration and expungement differ only because they were drafted at different times by different hands. These discrepancies encourage a search for subtle differences even where they do not and should not exist. Meanwhile, basic issues like priorities between competing transfers are either left completely to provincial law or (as for patents, copyrights, and plant breeders' rights) differ among themselves and leave relationships with provincial priority laws unsettled. This is not good enough for the amount of traffic the registries carry: about 100,000 new entries, 60 percent representing changes of title, are recorded every year. Entries on the copyright register represent about 10 percent of this total.

As for limitations, the time limits differ arbitrarily among rights. The basic drafting of the limitation provisions is not standard. And, even where two provisions do read the same in the English, the French version reads differently.[3]

The *Copyright Act*, like other intellectual property legislation, barely complies with the basic precept of the Rule of Law that laws must be written clearly and comprehensibly for those whose conduct is regulated and affected by them — businesses and the general public alike, not just lawyers or a small specialized clique of them. Unclear, inconsistent, and archaic laws impose deadweight costs on the economy, to say nothing of the frustration of those whose conduct they aim to guide.

The idea of a single technology code covering all intellectual property rights has often been floated. It is desirable if for no other reason than to standardize stock provisions such as acquisition and transfer of rights, remedies, administration, registries, limitations, and even application forms and procedures among rights.

B. SUBSTANCE OF THE LAW

The idea that copyright should protect, and so encourage, the whole gamut of creative endeavour sounds good in principle, but even before the impact of the digital revolution was felt, copyright policy had sunk into incoherence. The law is supposed to reward workers in the fields of art, literature, music, and drama, yet employers, repackagers, and distributors frequently make much more from the system than do the toilers in the field. It is supposed to stimulate the production of work that would not otherwise have been produced at all or as well, yet much routine material is protected: trivial correspondence, private diaries, simple logos (amply protected by trade-mark and passing-off laws), and even the doodlings of toddlers. It is supposed to encourage the dissemination of local culture. Yet, on the one hand, this goal is thwarted by international regulations like *Berne, NAFTA, TRIPs,* and the *WIPO* copyright treaties of 1996, which require foreign material to be as freely disseminated and fully protected as local material, while, on the other hand, much of the traditional culture of Canada's aboriginal peoples is left unprotected. It is supposed to protect products that are in fact cultural,

---

3   *Patent Act*, R.S.C. 1985, c. P-4, s. 55.01; *Industrial Design Act*, R.S.C. 1985, c. I-9, s. 18; D. Vaver, "Limitations in Intellectual Property: 'The Time Is Out of Joint'" (1994) 73 Can. Bar Rev. 451.

yet how computer programs (essentially electronic machine parts) or business and legal forms — classed alongside novels and poetry as original literary works — qualify as culture, except in some trivial sense, has never been explained and, indeed, is unexplainable.

Digital technologies have thrown copyright's anomalies into starker relief. More fundamentally, they have thrown into question whether copyright can or should exist in the digital world. After all, copyright is premised on the initial production of a tangible original work, which is then exploited either through mass marketing of copies, public performance, or broadcast. Unauthorized intrusions into this market are usually relatively quick and easy to detect and to close down through the use of civil or criminal sanctions. But as existing works are digitized, with or without authorization, or new works are made available solely in digital format, copyright becomes powerless to cope with the manipulation and movement of intangible electronic streams. Detection and enforcement become difficult, sometimes impossible, and rights that appear on the books are ignored in practice. Access to music, art, literature, and other material in digital form has given users the power to modify these works or data at will, replicate them almost infinitely, and transmit them anywhere in the world to others, who in turn have the same capabilities; and power, once given, will inevitably be used. In this world, every user is a potential re/author and re/distributor of material made available electronically to her. In this world, the only way in which an initial provider of a work or information can practically profit from its investment may be through reliance on shared ethical understandings, encryption technology, and good marketing (e.g., the provision of services like help lines and regular updates to which users wish to subscribe).

Whether or in what way copyright will ultimately cope in this new order is far from clear. Business and governments alike still seem committed to preserving copyright, and recent efforts have gone towards trying to strengthen the system, tightening copyright owners' control over electronic activity, adapting copyright rules to achieve that goal, and shrinking the scope of the public domain. Whether these efforts amount to overkill is a legitimate issue. The present criminal and civil sanctions seem draconian, especially in the context of a law that is often uncertain and ill-attuned to the daily habits of many people. The sanctions include criminal penalties of up to $1 million, fines and/or five years' jail, and statutory damages of up to $20,000, which do not have to correlate with the copyright holder's actual loss. Added to other available remedies, they impose liabilities on infringers more extensive than those for the meanest patent infringer, environmental polluter, or trespasser to land.[4] What makes copyright infringers more morally culpable than them?

C. SOCIAL CONTROL

If one feature stands out about intellectual property law, including copyright, it is how much the law affects the public, but how little the public affects it — indeed, how little the law lets the public affect it. Intellectual property law is a social construct that shuns social participation, let alone control. Few Jane and John Does turn up at legislative hearings when revision or amendment of the law is contemplated; they are certainly not present at the international meetings where global intellectual property standards are set. The registries of the Canadian Intellectual Property Office are open to the general public, but are rarely consulted by it. Trials involving intellectual property matters are by a judge alone, without a jury. The Acts justify themselves by how they benefit the public, but the justifications are long on assertion, short on proof. Beneath the veneer, one finds an infrastructure inhospitable to public entry.

The substance of the law is no more embracing. The tone is well set by the British judge who, admitting that the "public interest" could override a copyright, indicated how atrophied this "public" interest is: "[T]here is a world of difference between what is in the public interest and what is of interest to the public," he said, with no trace of embarrassment.[5] If intellectual property rights really do benefit the public, any member of the public should be able to oppose grants that may not operate in the public interest, or have those that are not so operating expunged. But that is impossible with copyrights, which conveniently appear automatically without further government involvement.

---

4   The scheme introduced by Bill C-32 was, before enactment, called "one of the most complex and some would say draconian remedial structures in the common law world": J. Berryman, "Copyright Remedies: An Ever Tightening Noose," in H.P. Knopf, ed., *Copyright Reform: The Package, the Policy and the Politics* (Toronto, Ont.: Insight, 1996). Alan Young has also questioned why the criminal law should apply to vindicate essentially private rights: "Catching Copyright Criminals: *R. v. Miles of Music Ltd.*" (1990) 5 I.P.J. 257 at 273.

5   *Lion Laboratories Ltd. v. Evans*, [1985] Q.B. 526 at 553 (C.A.).

D. FIRST NATIONS

In 1991 the Trade-marks Opposition Board allowed the registration of the mark NISKA for clothing, without even bothering to notify the Nisga'a people of British Columbia of the proceeding. After all, the Nisga'as' existence was said by the board to be known to "relatively few Canadians."[6] This example shows how one intellectual property law, that of trade-marks, can affect a particular social group without its knowledge until it is too late. Sometimes this result occurs through neglect; other times the policy is quite deliberate.

Consider how copyright law affects First Nations peoples. It certainly protects the work of contemporary Aboriginal artists, writers, and their publishers and distributors, just as it does the work of their non-Aboriginal counterparts.[7] Traditional First Nations work, however, is more vulnerable. What is to stop anyone from commercializing, with or without embellishment, traditional Aboriginal stories and artwork, even when this behaviour may be deeply offensive to the group that feels these stories and their art are integral to its culture, part of the glue that binds it together? First Nations peoples have valid concerns about how their stories and their art are being taken and commercialized, sometimes by their own peoples, more often by others. Sometimes the commercialization itself may be offensive, as when the story or the piece of art is treated as sacred by the group to which it belongs; other times, the commercialization, while not in itself offensive, distorts the original story or artwork.

Copyright and moral rights pass these issues by. The objections to protection under the current law are often insuperable. The author may be unidentifiable because he or she is long since dead, or the work may have been communally made. The work may have been oral and unfixed. There may be no one who can put forward a plausible claim to be the author or the copyright owner, in the sense of having derived title from an identifiable author or authors. Any possible term of copyright may also have expired.

Protecting traditional culture in some way raises controversy because it suggests that some areas of thought and expression are off limits except to one identified group: a type of censorship that is anathema

---

6 *Lortie v. Standard Knitting Ltd.* (1991), 35 C.P.R. (3d) 175 at 179 (T.M. Opp. Bd.).

7 See, for example, *Milpurrurru v. Indofurn Pty. Ltd.* (1994), 30 I.P.R. 209 (Austl. Fed. Ct.), and *Bulun Bulun v. R. & T. Textiles Pty. Ltd.* (1998), 41 I.P.R. 513 (Austl. Fed. Ct.), for sensitive attempts to reconcile copyright law with the customary law of an Australian aboriginal people.

to writers and artists. First Nations peoples may respond that the act of translation itself may be a form of cultural oppression that, intentionally or unintentionally, recreates traditional stories according to the translator's perspective. The reformed stories then may be treated as the authentic expression of the group's culture, even by the group itself. Differences like these are best settled through rules not designed in bureaucrats' offices, but coming out of discussions involving interested Aboriginal and non-Aboriginal leaders, writers, and artists.

The present situation has come about quite deliberately. The issue of bringing traditional culture ("folklore") under copyright was discussed during *Berne*'s 1967 revision process. An international consensus developed that favoured protection, and a working group was struck to look further into the matter. Immediately, the Canadian delegate was on guard, and he is recorded as saying that "he had been unable to speak earlier on the question of folklore. His country had a very considerable body of folklore, which it had always regarded as falling within the public domain. Canada was therefore opposed to any action likely to restrict the public use of folklore material. His Delegation was extremely unwilling to enter into a discussion as to who owned or was entitled to use such material. He hoped the new Working Group would bear his remarks in mind, since the matter was of great concern to his Delegation."[8] Given *Berne*'s rule of unanimity, this objection was enough for the provision on traditional culture to be watered down to an inoffensive non-binding scheme that has attracted few adherents. Needless to say, Canada is not one of them.

E. RETHINKING COPYRIGHT

For the meantime, the international community has accepted the notion that intellectual property in general, and copyright in particular, are integral to national and international economic welfare; and, at some level, that the utility of intellectual property is of little doubt. Few would deny that some stimulus and protection has to be offered in some sectors to encourage production of goods that are easily appropriable, where copying avoids the producer's initial investment and deprives the producer of the opportunity of recoupment and making a fair profit. The question is what stimulus and what protection should

---

8   *Records of the Intellectual Property Conference of Stockholm* (1967), vol. 2 (Geneva: World Intellectual Property Organization, 1971) at 877–78.

be offered. The policy instruments for deciding these questions are readily at hand.

Whenever governments want fundamentally to review what services they provide or ought to provide, they introduce a system of zero budgeting. Under it, every department of government is allocated a budget of $0. To get more, the department has to show why it needs it and how much it really needs to achieve its goals. There is no presumption that a department has an entitlement simply because it has always had one or had one the previous year. Each project and the level of support to be devoted to it have to be justified separately. The map created by the total number of successfully justified projects is then surveyed, checked off against policy criteria, and finally adjusted for anomalies. The product is not timeless: there are periodic short-term reviews, based on the presumption of the prior budget's accuracy; there are periodic comprehensive audits to ensure that policy objectives are being achieved; and there are periodic longer-term reviews, where a return to zero budgeting and no presumptions are the order of the day.

Both intellectual property in general and copyright in particular seem ripe for a zero budget review, domestically and internationally. The broad questions to be asked would be:

- What activities do we as societies desire to encourage?
- What degree of stimulus needs to be offered for the activities to occur?
- Who should benefit from the stimulus? The initial producer(s)? Later distributors? In what proportions and to what degree? And who deserves to be called a "producer" in the first place: he who first has and develops the idea, he who puts it into tangible form, he who reworks it, or the entity that pays for the production?

Along the way, some other equally fascinating questions will no doubt need answering, for example:

- Should society simply set up a market for ideas and allow entrants in that market to sell those ideas to the highest bidder? Should it be concerned about people who do not have the resources to enter the market?
- Should society be concerned about the unequal distribution of intellectual property, nationally and internationally, in the same way it may be concerned about the unequal distribution of traditional property? Or should intellectual property laws be devised that do not entrench and enhance existing distributions of power and wealth?
- Should society be concerned that intellectual property laws may play a part in causing people to invest too much time and money in inventive and creative activity, to the detriment of more modest but

as worthwhile improvements to existing technology? Or that the laws may contribute to new technology being introduced and exploited before its potential social impact can be fully and fairly assessed, because its promoters naturally want to reap the rewards of monopoly quickly? Or that intellectual property laws may need to be modified or supplemented to encourage activity in areas that society considers particularly necessary for its well-being or survival and which those laws are doing little or nothing to encourage?

In the heat of the battle between owners and users of intellectual property, such systemic questions are rarely asked. Not only should they be, but attempts should also be made to answer them, so laws can be devised which have a coherent moral centre that the public can comprehend and accept.[9]

FURTHER READINGS

ALFORD, W.P., "How Theory Does — and Does Not — Matter: American Approaches to Intellectual Property Law in East Asia" (1994) 13 U.C.L.A. Pac. Basin L.J. 8

BARLOW, J.P., "The Economy of Ideas: A Framework for Rethinking Patents and Copyright in the Digital Age (Everything You Wanted to Know about Intellectual Property Is Wrong)" (1994) 2:3 Wired 84. See <http://www.wired.com/wired/archive/2.03/economy.ideas.html>.

BENTLY, L., & S. MANIATIS, eds., *Intellectual Property and Ethics* (London: Sweet & Maxwell, 1998)

BETTIG, R.V., *Copyrighting Culture: The Political Economy of Intellectual Property* (Boulder: Westview Press, 1997)

BLAKENEY, M., "*Milpurrurru & Ors* v. *Indofurn & Ors*: Protecting Expressions of Aboriginal Folklore under Copyright Law" (1995) 2:1 Murdoch U. Electronic Jo. Law, <http://www.murdoch.edu.au/elaw>

---

9 Some paragraphs of this chapter were drawn from D. Vaver, "Some Agnostic Observations on Intellectual Property" (1991) 6 I.P.J. 125; "Rejuvenating Copyright" (1996) 75 Can. Bar Rev. 69; and "Rejuvenating Copyright, Digitally," in *Symposium of Digital Technology and Copyright* (Ottawa: Department of Justice, 1995) 1.

BOYLE, J., *Shamans, Software and Spleens: Law and the Construction of the Information Society* (Cambridge: Harvard University Press, 1996)

BOYLE, J., "A Politics of Intellectual Property: Environmentalism for the Net?" (1998), <http://www.wcl.american.edu/pub/faculty/boyle/ip.HTM>

BRASCOUPÉ, S., & K. ENDEMANN, *Intellectual Property and Aboriginal People: A Working Paper* (Ottawa: Ministry of Indian Affairs & Northern Affairs, 1999)

COOMBE, R.J., *The Cultural Life of Intellectual Properties: Authorship, Appropriation, and the Law* (Durham: Duke University Press, 1998)

CORNISH, W.R., "Authors at Law" (1995) 58 Mod. L. Rev. 1

DRAHOS, P., ed., *Intellectual Property* (Aldershot & Brookfield, USA: Ashgate & Dartmouth Publishing, 1999)

FAWCETT, J., & P. TORREMANS, *Intellectual Property and Private International Law* (Oxford: Clarendon Press, 1998)

FICSOR, M., "Indigenous Peoples and Local Communities: Exploration of Issues Related to Intellectual Property Protection of Expression of Traditional Culture" ('Expressions of Folklore,' Paper No. ATRIP/GVA/99/27, presented to the Annual Meeting of the International Association for the Advancement of Research in Intellectual Property (ATRIP), Geneva, 7–9 July 1999)

"For a Legal Protection of Folklore?" (1998) 32:4 Copyright Bulletin 5

GINSBURG, J.C., "Copyright, Common Law, and *Sui Generis* Protection of Databases in the United States and Abroad" 66 Cincinnati L. Rev. 151 (1997)

GOLDSMITH, J.L., *Against Cyberanarchy*, Occasional Paper No. 40 (Chicago: The Law School, The University of Chicago, 13 August 1999)

HENDERSON G.F./CONSUMER & CORPORATE AFFAIRS CANADA, *Intellectual Property: Litigation, Legislation and Education: A Study of the Canadian Intellectual Property and Litigation System* (Ottawa: Consumer & Corporate Affairs, 1991)

INFORMATION HIGHWAY ADVISORY COUNCIL, *Final Report of the Copyright Subcommittee: Copyright and the Information Highway* (Ottawa: The Council, 1995), <http://strategis.ic.gc.ca>

INFORMATION HIGHWAY ADVISORY COUNCIL, *Final Report: Connection, Community, Content: The Challenge of the Information Highway* (Ottawa: The Council, 1995), <http://info.ic.gc.ca>

Intellectual Property Rights: The Politics of Ownership (1991) 15 Cultural Survival Q. 1

LADDIE, H., "Copyright: Over-strength, Over-regulated, Over-rated?" [1996] 5 E.I.P.R. 253

MARTIN, B., *Information Liberation* (London: Freedom Press, 1998)

NAIR, K.R.G., & A. KUMAR, eds., *Intellectual Property Rights* (New Delhi: Allied Publishers, 1994)

PALMER, T.G., "Intellectual Property: A Non-Posnerian Law and Economics Approach" (1989) 12 Hamline L. Rev. 261 (1989)

PASK, A., "Cultural Appropriation and the Law: An Analysis of the Legal Regimes Concerning Culture" (1994) 8 I.P.J. 57

PURI, K., "Cultural Ownership and Intellectual Property Rights Post-*Mabo*: Putting Ideas into Action" (1995) 9 I.P.J. 293

Report of the Working Group on Intellectual Property Rights, Intellectual Property and the National Information Infrastructure (Washington, DC: Patent and Trademark Office, 1995) (Chair: U.S. Commissioner of Patents Bruce A. Lehman), <http://iitf.nist.gov/ipc/ipc-pub.html>

SAMUELSON, P., "Challenges for the World Intellectual Property Organization and the Trade-Related Aspects of Intellectual Property Rights Council in Regulating Intellectual Property Rights in the Information Age," in N. Imparato, ed., *Capital for Our Time* (Stanford, Cal.: Hoover Institution Press, 1998)

VAVER, D., "Copyright in Canada: The New Millennium" (1997) 12 I.P.J. 117

VAVER, D., "Copyright in Europe: The Good, the Bad and the Harmonised" (1999) 10 Aust. I.P.J. 185

WOODMANSEE, M., & P. JASZI, eds., *The Construction of Authorship: Textual Appropriation in Law and Literature* (Durham, NC: Duke University Press, 1994)

GLOSSARY

* Indicates cross-reference to another entry.

Account of profits: A discretionary remedy that requires an infringer to detail the net profits made from an *infringement and to pay the sum over to the claimant.

Assignment: The voluntary transfer of ownership of a right. The person transferring is the assignor, who transfers (assigns) to an assignee. Called "cession" in Quebec.

Berne Convention [Berne]: The *Convention for the Protection of Literary and Artistic Works* signed at Berne in 1886. The latest version of this *treaty is the *Paris Act* of 1971, of which Canada became a member as from 26 June 1998. Until then, Canada was bound only by the 1928 version of *Berne*. Canada's laws nevertheless substantially complied with the *Paris Act* earlier because of Canada's obligations under *NAFTA and later *TRIPs.

Bill C-32: The Copyright Amendment Bill of 1996, introduced into the Canadian House of Commons on 25 April 1996 and passed into law on 25 April 1997 as *An Act to Amend the Copyright Act*, S.C. 1997, c. 24. It strengthens *copyrights (particularly the rights of record companies, broadcasters, and performers), gives Canadian book distributors the right to stop unauthorized imports or distribution, and provides some exemptions for educational institutions, libraries, archives, museums, and the disabled.

Bootleg: *See* Piracy; Theft.

Breach of confidence: The wrong of disclosing or using information confided to or improperly taken from another for a purpose not authorized by the confider. *See* Trade secret.

Canada Gazette: The periodical in which regulations and notices of the federal government are officially published.

CIPO: Canadian Intellectual Property Office, located in Hull, Quebec. The umbrella government department under which the Copyright Office, Patent Office, Trade-marks Office, and the like operate.

Clearance: *See* Licence.

Common law: Judge-made law, used here to include rules of *equity.

Consent: *See* Licence.

Convention: *See* Treaty.

Copyright: The protection that literary, dramatic, musical, and artistic works receive internationally, typically for the author's life plus fifty years. In Canada, the term includes neighbouring rights. *See *Rome Convention.*

Copyright Board: A tribunal established under the *Copyright Act*, with authority mainly over rate approvals for cable retransmission, performing, broadcast, and blank audio recording media levy rights for music, and tariff disputes between collecting societies and users. Appeals go directly to the Federal Court of Appeal. The Board's recent decisions are found at <www.cb-cda.gc.ca/decisions-e.html>. The Web site is at <http://strategis.ic.gc.ca/sc_mrksv/cipo/welcome/welcom-e.html>.

De minimis: A shortened form of the Latin legal maxim *de minimis non curat lex*: the law does not concern itself with the trivial. For example, an act that is technically an *infringement can be called *de minimis* if it is thought to be outside the purpose of the law to catch it; the claim can then be dismissed with costs. This decision involves a value judgment that the complaint should either have been resolved without taking up the time of a court or is a minor irritant that, like the unintentional jostle in a crowded street, the complainant should have borne with equanimity.

Employee: An individual employed under a contract of service (*see* chapter 4) with an employer; distinguished from a *freelancer, who is not on an employer's payroll. Employers often *prima facie* own the *intellectual property rights in subject matter produced by employees on the job. This ownership may be true even where a *freelancer is working under contract (e.g., an industrial designer or *ICT creator), but a specific agreement is usually required where a *copyright is involved.

Equity, equitable rights: Terms used here in the technical sense of rules or rights historically derived from those recognized by courts of chancery to supplement *legal* rules or rights — those administered by the ordinary courts of the land. For example, a writing may be required for a valid *legal* *assignment of *copyright; but a court of chancery accepted that an oral *assignment can effectively transfer the right between the parties, although the right could disappear if the assignor resold to an innocent third party. Such an *assignment is called an equitable assignment; the rights that flow from it are equitable rights. See further chapter 8, section (B)(3)(d), "Equitable Assignments and Licences."

Equitable rights are not recognized in Quebec, although the *Code Civil* may, through other means, redress some of the injustices equity targets.

Estoppel: A legal bar, from medieval law French, meaning "stop." For example, assignors are *estopped* from challenging their assignee's title, and licensees are *estopped* from challenging their licensor's title: the assignor or licensee sued by the assignee or licensor for *infringement cannot defend by (is *estopped* from) showing that the right is invalid. Hence, the terms "assignor estoppel" and "licensee estoppel." Someone may be estopped without intending or knowing it. Thus, if A leads B to assume that a certain state of affairs exists, and it would be unfair to let A have a change of heart in the light of what has since happened, B's assumption is treated as true: that is, A is estopped from denying its validity.

EU: The abbreviation for the European Union and the states that belong to it. The way *intellectual property laws are harmonized within the EU frequently influences international *treaties and other international developments.

Ex parte: A term literally meaning "from one side"; an application is *ex parte* when it is made to a court or tribunal without notifying or serving anyone else with the proceedings. Because of the proceeding's one-sided nature, applicants owe the decision maker a high duty of good faith; in practice, this means they should reveal to the decision maker any objections that might result in a decision adverse to them.

Expunge: A term meaning to strike or delete; it is used in this book in relation to an entry on the *copyright or other *intellectual property (e.g., *ICT) register. The *CIPO can expunge entries in limited specified circumstances — for example, for a clerical error. More usually, the Federal Court exercises this power. Expungement invalidates the right as against the world, not merely the parties to the litigation. An entry may also be amended, corrected, or rectified, a lesser remedy than expungement, which changes, but does not delete, the entry.

Freelancer: An independent contractor or contracting company. An individual working as a freelancer is different from an *employee; the latter is under a contract of service with an employer. See section A(2)(a)(i), "Contract of Service," in chapter 4.

GATT: The acronym for *General Agreement on Tariffs and Trade* of 1947, a *treaty designed to eliminate discrimination in international trade relations. The latest of its periodic revisions is the 1994 *WTO Agreement.*

ICT right: Integrated Circuit Topography right, granted on registration under the federal *ICT Act* for ten years. The U.S. equivalent is a semiconductor chip right, also lasting for ten years.

Industrial design: Features of shape, pattern, or ornament applied to a finished article. Mass-produced designs for most useful articles can be protected only by registration under the *Industrial Design Act*; limited protection until the fifty-first copy is made can be had under *copyright.

Infringement: Violation or breach of a statutory *intellectual property right, allowing the right-holder to recover civil remedies against the infringer. Some infringements are also criminal offences — for example, certain deliberate *copyright infringements. "Substantial infringement" denotes the unauthorized taking of something less than or different from the protected subject matter — for example, taking a chapter from a *copyright book. What takings are or are not substantial is often controversial.

Injunction: A court order requiring someone to stop doing a specified act (negative injunction) or requiring the doing of a positive act (mandatory injunction). Injunctions can be granted pre-trial (interim or interlocutory injunctions) or after a full trial (final injunction). Disobedience can result in proceedings for contempt of court, leading to a fine or even imprisonment.

Intellectual property: A term that denotes *copyrights, *patents, *trade-marks, trade-names, *industrial designs, plant breeder rights, and *ICT rights, and sometimes rights arising from provincial law relating to, for example, *trade secrets, *misappropriation of personality, and *passing-off. Both "intellectual" and "property" may be misnomers: see chapter 1.

Interlocutory relief: Orders granted by a court before trial. An interlocutory injunction is granted to preserve the claimant's rights before trial; if the claimant then loses, it may have to compensate the defendant for losses caused by the *injunction.

Intra vires: See ultra vires.

Licence: Consent, permission, or clearance (all interchangeable terms) given by a right-holder (the licensor) to someone (the licensee) to exercise a right held by the licensor. The licence can be oral or written. An exclusive licence gives the licensee alone the right of exercise, to the exclusion of even the licensor (this licence usually has to be written). A sole licence is the same, except the licensor can compete with the licensee. A non-exclusive licence allows the licensor to appoint other licensees in the same area to exercise the right.

Limitation: Generally, a restriction placed on a right; specifically, a time-bar within which legal proceedings must be commenced, failing which a claimant can no longer sue.

Misappropriation: *See* Unfair competition.

Misappropriation of personality: The right to prevent commercial uses of one's name, voice, or image. It is roughly equivalent to the U.S. "right of publicity."

Moral rights: Authors' rights to have work properly attributed and not prejudicially modified or associated with other products; a poor, but commonly used, translation of the French *droits moraux* ("personal" or "intellectual" rights). The rights are as legally enforceable as any others; they have nothing to do with morals or morality. See chapter 6, "Authors' Moral Rights."

NAFTA: *North American Free Trade Agreement* of 1992, between Canada, Mexico, and the United States. Chapter 17 obliges the parties to maintain high levels of *intellectual property protection. Canada implemented this *treaty through the *North American Free Trade Agreement Implementation Act*, S.C. 1993, c. 44, mostly effective from 1 January 1994, which made substantial changes to all *intellectual property legislation.

National treatment: An obligation to extend the rights a state grants its own citizens, residents, and corporations to foreign citizens, residents, and corporations without discrimination. Most international *intellectual property *treaties oblige their adherents to extend national treatment to one another, but not necessarily to non-adherents. Thus, Canada as an adherent of the *Berne Convention* must extend to people from other *Berne* states exactly the same rights relating to authors' works as it extends to Canadians. The other states do the same for Canadians.

Neighbouring rights: *See Rome Convention.*

Originality: *Copyright's threshold requirement for protection: that a work not be copied and that it have some minimal creativity. For *industrial designs, some difference from prior designs or the adaptation of an old design to an article to which it has not previously been applied is also required; for *ICTs, the topography must not be commonplace among *ICT designers or manufacturers.

Parallel import: The importation, without the authorization of the owner of a Canadian *intellectual property right, of a product lawfully made abroad; it is sometimes pejoratively called "grey marketing." It is often (controversially) barred by Canadian law, but is challenged by global technology like the Internet.

Passing-off: The wrong of misrepresenting one's business, goods, or services as another's, to the latter's injury; for example, by a confusingly similar *trade-mark or trade-name.

Patent: A term used here to denote a patent for invention, an exclusive right granted to work new inventions. It is sometimes called "letters patent," from the Latin *litterae patentes* ("open letters"), meaning that the royal seal was placed at the bottom of the document, making the document a public record open for all to see. The *Patent Act* still defines "patent" as "letters patent for an invention," being one species of the genus of letters patent, which at various times covered franchises, land grants, honours, and company incorporations.

A patent lasts for twenty years from the date when the application for it is filed, but the actual monopoly period runs only from the date when the patent is granted, typically around two years later. The application is made public no later than eighteen months after the filing of the application. If a patent is granted, the patentee can get compensation from unauthorized users of the invention as from the date of making public. An *injunction and money remedies are available against unauthorized uses after the date of grant.

Permission: *See* Licence.

Piracy; pirated goods: Abusive terms, used by those who know no better or who have vested interests in a strong *intellectual property system, to describe the products of deliberate *infringement. These terms are sometimes used more loosely to describe any acts right-holders object to: for example, when British *copyright owners complained of U.S. copying of their books in the nineteenth century even though U.S. law permitted this activity. They are best reserved for the exploits of Captain Bluebeard, and are not otherwise used in this book.

Prima facie: Literally, "at first sight." A *prima facie* position is one that prevails unless contrary evidence is presented.

Priority: In *copyright, the better title to a proprietary interest when a right has been *assigned or *licensed more than once. So if **A** purports to *assign the same *copyright to **B** and then later to **C**, **C** will have priority if its title is better than **B**'s. This means **C** owns the *copyright and **B** can claim against **A** only for breach of contract. Registration of the *copyright by **B** or **C** may affect this result. See section C(1), "Priorities," in chapter 8.

Public domain: A term denoting that an item is not protected under *intellectual property laws and so is free for all to use. A work is most commonly said to be in the public domain when its *copyright has expired. Users may still be under some constraints. For example, they may not misrepresent the work (e.g., claim it is recent when it is old) or its authorship, or use it in *breach of confidence.

Quia timet **relief:**   Relief, typically an *injunction, sought where the commission of a wrong is anticipated. *Quia timet* literally means "because he or she fears"; so a *quia timet* *injunction is granted when a claimant reasonably fears it will be injured by the imminent commission of a wrong.

Registrant: The holder of a registered *copyright or interest in *copyright. A *copyright registrant is the person registered as the *copyright's owner.

Right of remuneration: The right of a *copyright-holder to receive a payment for a stated use. Performers, sound-recording makers, and broadcasters have rights of remuneration in respect of the public performance or telecommunication of their material.

A right of remuneration differs from other rights within *copyright. A *copyright holder can usually prevent the use by others of any right within *copyright for any reason or for no reason at all, just as a landowner may arbitrarily deny access to his property. Thus, a *copyright-holder can get an *injunction to prevent the translation of her work, however much money the user tenders for the right and however worthy the enterprise. On the other hand, the owner of a right of remuneration cannot prevent the use of his material by any user who tenders the prescribed fee. For example, the *copyright-holder of a published sound recording of a musical work cannot prevent a broadcaster who tenders the appropriate payment from airing any sound recording; the *Copyright Act* grants the right-holder only a right of remuneration in respect of this activity.

Right-holder: A term used to indicate anyone with a proprietary interest in a *copyright or other *intellectual property right: for example, an owner or exclusive *licensee.

Rome Convention [Rome]:   *Rome Convention for the Protection of Performers, Producers of Phonograms and Broadcasting Organisations* of 1961. This *treaty protects performers, record producers, and broadcasters through *droits voisins* ("neighbouring rights") similar to traditional *copyright. The *Act to Amend the Copyright Act* of 1997 implemented these rights in Canada and enabled Canada to adhere to *Rome* as of 4 June 1998. About fifty states presently adhere to this Convention, though the United States is notably absent. *Rome* may be partly eclipsed by the *WIPO Performances and Phonograms Treaty*.

Royalty: Money payable on the amount or duration of the authorized exercise of a right.

Theft: An abusive term used to describe an *intellectual property *infringement or, sometimes more loosely, any act to which a right-holder objects. An association of computer software manufacturers even calls itself the Canadian Alliance against Software Theft. But *intellectual property *infringement is not "theft" in Canada because, after the "taking," the right-holder is still left with the "property."[1] Still, right-holders have never let facts get in the way of a good pejorative. *See* Piracy.

Trade-mark: A mark distinguishing one trader's product or service from another's. Also spelled "trademark" (U.S.) and "trade mark" (other countries).

Trade secret: Commercial information that derives its value from the fact of its not being generally known and from the protection the law erects around it, mainly through contracts and the *breach of confidence action.

Treaty: An international agreement, also sometimes called a convention. Under Canadian law, Canada's signature on a treaty indicates its commitment to seek legislative approval of the treaty terms, usually by Parliament or other relevant legislatures passing appropriate implementing legislation. Once legislation is passed, Canada may indicate its ratification of the treaty — that is, it may notify the relevant international organization (e.g., *WIPO) that the treaty is now formally binding on Canada. Unless legislation is passed, the treaty does not form part of Canadian law. Canada's practice resembles that of most other common law countries, including the United States. The practice of civil law countries (e.g., France, Germany, Japan) sometimes differs, depending on the treaty. Some treaties there become part of the country's law without the need for further legislation.

---

1   R. v. *Stewart* (1988), 50 D.L.R. (4th) 1 (S.C.C.).

TRIPs: Acronym for *Agreement on Trade-Related Aspects of Intellectual Property Rights, Including Trade in Counterfeit Goods* (Annex 1C to the **WTO Agreement* of 1994). It was probably coined by survivors of the 1960s with redirected energies. Most countries of the world (major exceptions are presently China and Taiwan) are members, although even China seems set on a course that will see it become a member in 2000. Canada implemented this **treaty by the *World Trade Organization Implementation Act*, S.C. 1994, c. 57, effective as from 1 January 1996.

Ultra vires: Beyond lawful authority. A statute is *ultra vires,* and therefore invalid, if Canada's *Constitution Act* does not authorize the legislature that passed it to legislate on that matter. The opposite is *intra vires,* within lawful authority.

Unfair competition:

1. A general term describing a basket of harms — for example, *passing-off, injurious falsehood, interference with economic relations, conspiracy, *breach of confidence — that amount to torts against businesses harmed by them.
2. Sometimes used as a synonym for misappropriation, the wrong of unfairly taking or using business assets to the injury of their holder. It was used, for example, in the United States by Dow Jones to prevent the Chicago Board of Trade from adopting a futures trading contract based on the Dow Jones index.[2] The civil law of Quebec may recognize a similar wrong, but no Canadian common law province presently does; nor may the federal parliament constitutionally enact it.[3]
3. An abusive, legally insignificant term an enterprise may use to describe any practice by which another manages to undersell it.

Universal Copyright Convention [UCC]: Signed in 1952 and revised in 1971, this *treaty enabled the United States and other Pan-American countries that had *copyright registries and marking requirements to join with *Berne countries in an international treaty. Less demanding than *Berne, it allowed a marking like "© David Vaver 2000" to satisfy any formalities a state required as a prerequisite of *copyright. Canada adheres to the *UCC*'s 1952 version. The *UCC* is less important today because most states, including the United States, have since joined **Berne*, and **TRIPs* also mandates compliance with **Berne*'s higher obligations and "no-formalities" rules.

---

2   *Board of Trade of the City of Chicago v. Dow Jones & Co.*, 456 N.E.2d 84 (Ill. S.C. 1983).

3   *Macdonald v. Vapor Canada Ltd.* (1976), 66 D.L.R. (3d) 1 (S.C.C.).

Waiver: The giving up of a right. It may be done expressly or may be implied from the circumstances.

WIPO: World Intellectual Property Organization. This UN agency, headquartered in Geneva, administers most of the international *intellectual property *treaties (e.g., *Berne) and holds periodic intergovernmental conferences to revise them. It is a long-time promoter of the view that extensions of *intellectual property rights make the world a better place (at least for some).

WIPO Copyright Treaty: Signed on 20 December 1996 at Geneva by about fifty countries at the same time as the *WIPO Performances and Phonograms Treaty, this *treaty is a *Berne-plus Convention that seeks to bring *copyright into the digital age. Among other measures, states must prevent circumvention of encrypted information and the removal of digital tracking measures, although the implementation of these obligations in 1998 by the United States in its *Digital Millennium Copyright Act* indicates that some decryption and circumvention is legitimate (e.g., for research, police, or individual privacy reasons). Canada may soon bring its law in line with this treaty.

WIPO Performances and Phonograms Treaty: Signed at Geneva on 20 December 1996 by about fifty countries at the same time as the *WIPO Copyright Treaty*, this *treaty improves on the rights that record makers and performers have under the *Rome Convention. Thus, performers are granted *moral rights, and the same measures against decryption and circumvention of tracking devices are provided for records as the *WIPO Copyright Treaty provides for traditional "works." Canada may soon bring its law in line with this treaty.

WTO: World Trade Organization. The *WTO Agreement* of 1994, a successor of *GATT, contains in its *TRIPs Agreement extensive provisions binding on WTO members relating to *intellectual property rights. Breaches of this *treaty can lead to trade sanctions. Implemented by Canada, effective 1 January 1996, by the *World Trade Organization Agreement Implementation Act*, S.C. 1994, c. 57.

TABLE OF CASES

INDEX

Asterisked items also appear in the Glossary.

ABOUT THE AUTHOR

David Vaver, M.A. (Oxon.), B.A., LL.B. (Auck.), J.D. (Chicago), is the Reuters Professor of Intellectual Property and Information Technology Law in the University of Oxford, the Director of the Oxford Intellectual Property Research Centre at St Peter's College, Oxford, and a Professorial Fellow of St Peter's College. Before coming to Oxford in 1998, he taught intellectual property law for some twenty-seven years, variously at Osgoode Hall Law School of York University, the University of British Columbia, and the University of Auckland.

Professor Vaver was the founder of the *Intellectual Property Journal* and its Editor-in-Chief until 1998. He remains as a consultant editor. He also served as an adviser to the Department of Canadian Heritage on the reform of Canadian copyright law, including the 1997 amendments to the *Copyright Act*. Professor Vaver has researched and written extensively on national and international intellectual property law and policy, and his works are often cited by courts and legal writers. He is the author of *Intellectual Property Law: Copyright, Patents, Trade-marks* (1997) in Irwin Law's Essentials of Canadian Law series.

Professor Vaver's e-mail address is <david.vaver@st-peters.oxford. ac.uk>. The Oxford Intellectual Property Research Centre's Web site is at <www.oiprc.ox.ac.uk>.